ALSO BY SUSAN PAGE

The Matriarch: Barbara Bush and the Making of an American Dynasty

Madam Speaker: Nancy Pelosi and the Lessons of Power

THE
RULEBREAKER

THE LIFE AND TIMES OF

BARBARA WALTERS

SUSAN PAGE

SIMON & SCHUSTER

New York   London   Toronto   Sydney   New Delhi

1230 Avenue of the Americas
New York, NY 10020

First Simon & Schuster hardcover edition April 2024

SIMON & SCHUSTER and colophon are registered trademarks
of Simon & Schuster, LLC

Simon & Schuster: Celebrating 100 Years of Publishing in 2024

For information about special discounts for bulk purchases,
please contact Simon & Schuster Special Sales at 1-866-506-1949
or business@simonandschuster.com.

The Simon & Schuster Speakers Bureau can bring authors to your
live event. For more information or to book an event, contact the
Simon & Schuster Speakers Bureau at 1-866-248-3049 or visit our website
at www.simonspeakers.com.

Interior design by Joy O'Meara

Manufactured in the United States of America

1 3 5 7 9 10 8 6 4 2

Library of Congress Cataloging-in-Publication Data is available.

ISBN 978-1-9821-9792-6
ISBN 978-1-9821-9794-0 (ebook)

For Esther and Abe

CONTENTS

Introduction

MILLION-DOLLAR BABY

1976

She had been warned.

Barbara Walters had finally won the anchor's chair, the prize she had long sought and one that NBC News had refused to give her. ABC, then the third-ranking network with little to lose, offered her the job of co-anchoring the nightly news with Harry Reasoner and hosting four annual specials for the then-breathtaking salary of a million dollars a year. She was the first newswoman—the first newsperson, in fact—to get such an astronomical sum. She achieved that distinction by shrewdly playing each network against the other. But her price came with its own price. No one would ever let her forget it.

"Barbara Walters: Million-Dollar Baby?" *The Miami Herald* asked in a headline trumpeted across all six columns at the top of page 1. "A Million-Dollar Baby Handling 5-and-10 Cent News?" ridiculed a column in *The Washington Post*. Richard Salant, the president of CBS News, asked sarcastically, "Is Barbara a journalist or is she Cher?" Walter Cronkite said he had experienced "a first wave of nausea, the sickening sensation that perhaps we were all going under, that all of our efforts to hold network television news aloof from show business had failed."

Despite that queasy feeling, Cronkite demanded a big raise himself, to $900,000 a year, plus summers off, membership in private clubs, and a corporate plane to take him to and from Martha's Vineyard. "Walter complained about me getting $1 million," Barbara said. "But he soon was the great beneficiary. He didn't complain about making a lot more money a year, because I broke the mold, very loudly."

Loudly, and to the particular dismay of Harry Reasoner. He got a raise, too. But he didn't want to co-anchor the news with anyone. Especially with a woman.

"You're going to have a rough time," veteran broadcaster Howard K. Smith cautioned her beforehand. "Do you know that?"

"I'm beginning to think so," she replied. But she had no idea how bad it would be.

Smith was her predecessor on the show and a member in good standing of the old boys' club, part of the fabled team of CBS World War II correspondents known as the Murrow Boys. He had begun co-anchoring the evening news in 1969, paired first with Frank Reynolds and then with Reasoner. In 1975, to Reasoner's satisfaction, Smith had been sidelined to be a commentator. He knew better than anyone how unenthusiastic Reasoner was about having a partner on the air.

"Be strong and stand up to it, but he's not going to treat you well," Smith predicted.

Smith didn't do her many favors, either. On the Friday night before Barbara's debut the following Monday, Smith delivered an essay on the evening broadcast. He called Walters "network television's first female anchorman, a lady whose beauty sometimes disguises a talent rarely equaled in this craft." He noted that women were making inroads in other jobs in TV news as well. "Now on this report I will answer to a lady anchorman, Barbara," he said, referring to his continuing role as the show's occasional commentator. "Any bruise to the male ego is assuaged by the thought that if you've got to go, then being a male island in a sea of pretty women, well, what a way to go." The condescension came from the man who supposedly was in her corner.

Reasoner made no pretense that he was on her side.

He was fifty-three years old, with graying hair and an affable manner that masked his sharp edges. He had already described himself on the air as a chauvinist, proudly out of step with an age in which women were pushing for more parity in the workplace and more possibilities in their lives. He made comments about women and about feminism that would have cost him his job a half-century later. They raised eyebrows even then.

He opposed the Equal Rights Amendment. He endorsed a bride's vow to "obey" her husband, "observing" that women "who are submissive to a husband with a strong personality seem to be happier than those who are equal or dominant decision-making partners." He called the first issue of Gloria Steinem's *Ms.* magazine "pretty sad" and predicted it would soon fail, although he said "the girls" who were putting it out were "prettier than H. L. Mencken if not as good when it came to editing." He questioned whether the advent of the first female anchor would really be a "step forward."

When female flight attendants were battling sexist stereotypes and airline rules about their appearance, he said he preferred that they retain an ornamental role. "They should remain patches of color in the business of flying," he opined. "They should be there for a few years and then, like the clouds outside the windows, be replaced with soft and fluffy new ones."

There was nothing "soft and fluffy" about Barbara Walters, of course. She was now forty-seven years old (although she told everyone she was forty-five), twice divorced and a single mother of a child who would struggle with substance abuse. She was supporting her aging parents and special-needs sister. She was determined and ambitious, if cautious about aligning herself too closely with the emerging women's movement. And she had experience in dealing with resistant men. Near the beginning of her career, at NBC's *Today* show, host Frank McGee had issued an edict that she couldn't speak during on-air interviews with Washington newsmakers until he had asked the first three questions.

Now, in a commentary at the end of their first joint *ABC Evening News* show, Reasoner raised a spookily similar objection to how much airtime Barbara could claim. Even in the mid-1970s, when the Supreme Court had recognized abortion rights nationwide in *Roe v. Wade* and First Lady Betty Ford had endorsed the Equal Rights Amendment, some things apparently hadn't changed all that much.

They sat side by side at the anchor desk for a show more notable for Barbara's arrival than the news they reported that first night, starting with the resignation of Agriculture Secretary Earl Butz and including a satellite interview with Egyptian president Anwar Sadat. In a commentary at the close, Reasoner said he had a "little trouble" in thinking what to say to greet her that didn't sound sexist or patronizing or sycophantic. It was an odd beginning; how hard could it be for a noted wordsmith to say "Welcome"?

"The decision was to welcome you as I would any respected and competent colleague of any sex by noting that I've kept time on your stories and mine tonight," Reasoner finally told her. "You owe me four minutes."

Looking a bit perplexed, Barbara laughed. He didn't.

After those early shows, Victor Neufeld, then a junior producer, would walk Barbara back to her office from the studio, which was in a building across the street. "She never said a word to me, but I knew she was very anxious and upset," he told me, describing her as hurt and humiliated. "Her fists were clenched. She grabbed the script in her hands. She held on to the script, just walked looking down, not a word said. And I said, 'It was a good show.' She didn't answer me."

Reasoner's bullying unnerved her. So did the onslaught of commentary dissecting her speech patterns, her looks, her clothes, her credentials, her performance in ways no man had ever faced. On Capitol Hill, a powerful congressman weighed in, outraged. "It's ridiculous," said Democratic senator John Pastore of Rhode Island, an important figure in the broadcast business because he chaired the Commerce Committee's subcommittee on communications. "The networks come before my committee and shed crocodile tears and complain about their profits. Then they pay this little girl a million dollars. That's five times better than the president of the United States makes."

This little girl.

She was by then a woman who had spent a dozen years working her way up the ranks at NBC, where she had become co-host of the nation's top-rated morning show. Other critiques also took a demeaning tone, referring to her as "Barbie" and "baby." "Doll Barbie to Learn Her ABC's" was the headline on the front page of the New York *Daily News*.

One newspaper depicted her in a cartoon as a chorus girl, reading the news.

Everything she had achieved, and at considerable personal cost, seemed imperiled. "I would pick up the paper every day and read what a flop I was," she said. She thought about quitting. Instead, for nearly two years she waged what became a war of attrition against Reasoner, one that would damage both of their careers, at least for a time.

He eventually would retreat to a perch on the venerable CBS news program *60 Minutes*. He survived the disastrous pairing. Barbara transcended it. In the decades that followed, her career would span and define the golden age of television journalism in a way no one else, male or female, would ever exceed.

———

Barbara Jill Walters was a force from the time TV was exploding on the American scene in the 1960s to its waning preeminence in a new world of competition from streaming services and social media a half-century later. She was a groundbreaker for women. She expanded the big TV interview and then dominated the genre. By the end of her career, she had interviewed more of the famous and infamous, of presidents and movie stars and criminals and despots, than any journalist in history. With the media landscape changing, she would set a record no one was likely to ever break. Then, at sixty-seven, past the age many female broadcasters found themselves involuntarily retired, she pioneered a new form of talk TV called *The View*. The show would still be going strong a quarter-century later.

"She was so brilliant," Diane Sawyer, an erstwhile rival and a groundbreaking journalist herself, told me. "She had such a wonderful idea for creating a signature, just writing it across the sky."

None of it came easy. Barbara broke in not only before the #MeToo movement spotlighted sexual harassment but before *The Feminine Mystique* had been published and validated bigger ambitions for women. She had no role models, no mentors. Reasoner was just one of the colleagues who pulled for her to fail. Traditionalists like Cronkite viewed her with disdain, even as she was scooping them on historic interviews in the Mideast and elsewhere. Some rivals never saw her as a real journalist but as a "celebrity interviewer," one step from her father's vaudeville roots.

Yet she became an inspiration for many women and girls who followed, in journalism and other fields. A seventeen-year-old high school student in Nashville entered the local Miss Fire Prevention Contest and told the judges that her aspiration was to be a TV journalist. "I want to be like Barbara Walters," Oprah Winfrey told them. Growing up in Stamford, Connecticut, Jen Psaki would negotiate with her parents to stay up past her bedtime to watch Barbara on ABC's *20/20*. "You didn't feel like you were in a history class and you were bored," Psaki, who would become a White House press secretary for President Joe Biden and then pursue a TV career herself, told me. "You were being brought on a journey."

Young people with broadcast ambitions would come up to Barbara and say, "I want to be you." She had a stock response: "Then you have to take the whole package."

For her, the whole package included a dysfunctional childhood—a father she couldn't remember ever hugging as a girl; a distracted and disgruntled mother; a disabled sister she both loved and hated. It encompassed three failed marriages and a daughter who was estranged before reconciling. While she savored her success and all it brought her, contentment was forever elusive. Toward the end, she withdrew into bitterness.

She succeeded not because she was confident, but because she was not. She was a perfectionist and a second-guesser who could drive those around her crazy. (Her second husband, Lee Guber, jokingly told her that the inscription on her gravestone should reflect her constant indecision: "On the other hand, maybe I should have lived.") She was ferociously competitive—her rivalry with Diane Sawyer became a drama of epic dimensions—and she worked harder than anyone else.

"Given everything she's accomplished, what is it that keeps her at that level of intensity?" Diane asked in 1996. "What is it she fears will happen if she doesn't work this hard?"

A quarter-century later, after Barbara had passed away, I asked Diane if she had ever found the answer to those questions. "I'm not sure I ever cracked the code of what kept her getting up in the morning the way she did, and this sheer desire every day," she told me. "There was nothing more that she could do to make us honor her more than we did."

Barbara titled her 2008 memoir *Audition* because she had "always felt I was auditioning, either for a new job or to make sure that I could hold on to the one I had." The trepidation never went away, not entirely. "No matter how high my profile became, how many awards I received, or how much money I made, my fear was that it all could be taken away from me," she said late in life, when she could have simply relished all she had achieved. She never did.

Av Westin, a producer who worked with her at the start of her career and at its peak, described her restless drive to me in words that were cinematic. We talked in his West Side apartment one afternoon, not long before his death at age ninety-two. As we spoke, Barbara was in failing health just across Central Park, in her East Side apartment. They were almost precisely the same age, born weeks apart, though she wouldn't always admit that. In 2022, they would die months apart.

They had known one another for a lifetime, since he was the twenty-something director of the CBS morning show where she had landed her first job as a TV writer. Decades later, they worked together at the *ABC Evening News* and *20/20*.

Even when she was dominating the ratings and earning millions of dollars a year, she was never at peace, Av said. "I used to characterize her—describe it as Barbara waking up in the middle of the night . . . and in the reflected light from a streetlight, which came through the bathroom window, was Barbara's shadow," he told me, waving one hand in the air as if conjuring the image. "And she would say to the mirror, 'Tomorrow, they will find me out.'"

She would feel that knot of insecurity even at moments of triumph. Perhaps especially then. If she never stopped running, it was because her ambition and her fear were fueled from the start by her mercurial impresario father. He was both an inspirational figure and a cautionary tale.

His name was Lou Walters.

1

A GLASS EYE
AND A BRITISH ACCENT

1909

He was fifteen years old, just five feet four inches tall and slight, with an owlish mien and an energetic manner. He had a glass eye and a British accent. And he needed a job.

Louis Abraham Warmwater was born in Whitechapel, London, on January 26, 1894, the second child and first son of seven children. When his family emigrated to New York from London in 1909, he was unhappy about leaving the English city he loved. "It made me the most desperately lonely kid in the world," recalled Lou Walters, whose family, like many others, simplified their surname when they arrived on America's shores. "I wanted to go back." He was forced to make other adjustments, too. Before they left, he was playing when he fell on a broken milk bottle and a shard of glass pierced his right eye. He would wear a blue glass eye for the rest of his life.

After they arrived in New York, he didn't have the option of enrolling in school, though he would be an avid reader his entire life and was said to be a talented writer. As a schoolboy in London, he received a silver medal for an essay he had written; in some versions of the story, the award came from King Edward VII. But his family needed his paycheck, so he searched for work. That discouraging enterprise stretched for seven months, through the entire first winter in his new city. Each morning, he would walk nearly three miles to Times Square from their tenement on Rivington Street on the Lower East Side, he wrote in an unpublished memoir, "It's a Long Walk." There, a building at the corner of Broadway and 42nd Street posted want ads on its windows. He would race to the address of a listing that sounded promising only to find twenty or thirty boys lined up ahead of him; soon there would be another twenty or thirty lined up behind him.

When the bosses announced the position had been filled, he would rush to the site of the next prospective job, where there would be another forty boys ahead of him. "It was hopeless," he said. After months of fruitless effort, he spied this notice: "Office boy wanted. Independent Booking Offices. 1440 Broadway. Apply after 2:00 p.m."

He didn't know what a booking office did; he only cared that it was a job. At noon, he wandered over to the Knickerbocker Theatre building at the corner of Broadway and 38th Street and introduced himself to the desk clerk, who to his astonishment ushered him in to see the man in charge, Mr. Stermdorf. Had he worked anywhere before? No. Could he type? No. Hadn't he read that applicants weren't supposed to show up for another two hours?

Yes, he replied, but by then there would be an endless line.

Stermdorf sent him away with instructions to come back at two. When the teenager showed up five minutes early, the reception room was jammed and his heart fell. "Sorry, the job's been filled," the clerk told him. He was halfway down the stairs when he realized it wasn't yet 2 p.m.; how could the job be filled? As it turned out, the people who crowded the reception room were entertainers looking for work, and the office boy position was still open.

"Oh, you're Lou Walters, the one who came early," the clerk said. "Come in."

He was hired. Lou suggested it was because Stermdorf was British and appreciated his accent. His daughter would speculate it was because of the gumption he had demonstrated—and that she inherited—by showing up early that day. Whatever the reason, he had succeeded in landing a job, at a weekly salary variously reported at $4 or $6. It would launch him on his life's course. It would set a path as well for the career his daughter would pursue decades later, one also wrapped in the public's fascination with celebrities and their stories. Quite by accident, the Walters family had found its calling.

When one of the agency's owners, Johnny Quigley, left soon afterward to open a branch office in Boston, Lou Walters went with him. Walters's parents and younger siblings soon moved to Boston, too, although they wouldn't stay long before settling in New Jersey. By the time he was seventeen, not old enough to drink or to vote, Lou had worked his way up to the job of booker. The field was dominated by the competing United Booking Office, which had signed many of the biggest acts to exclusive, long-term contracts. That meant the Independent Booking Agency, a shoestring operation, had to scramble to line up the remaining singers, dancers, comedians, jugglers, magicians, musicians, and acrobats for smaller towns and vaudeville halls. Despite his youth, Walters turned out to be preternaturally skilled at spotting prospects, then persuading theater owners across New England and in Canada to hire them.

By the time he was twenty years old, he boasted, he was booking four hundred acts and earning a magnificent $30 each week. He was a small man and not particularly handsome. His wire-rimmed glasses made him look more like a bespectacled professor than a master of vaudeville. But he had a big personality and a zest for the business. He had street smarts and a sharply honed instinct for what the public would want to see.

He also was more than willing to take a gamble—for better and worse, the hallmark of the life that followed. He asked Quigley for a $20-a-week raise. "He put an extra five in my envelope," Lou recalled. "I returned it, and quit." He founded the Lou Walters Booking Agency instead, renting a second-floor office above Macy's drugstore, at the corner of Tremont and Stuart Streets. He had $75 in his pocket, just enough to pay the rent and turn on the lights.

By now the young man was a familiar figure in show business circles up and down the Northeast. His new agency represented rising stars and falling ones, everyone from accordionists to zitherists. He signed up Fred Allen when he was billing himself as Fred James, "the world's worst juggler." Allen would become a top comedian and pal of Jack Benny. Walters also discovered Jack Haley, then a comic, who would gain fame as the Tin Man in *The Wizard of Oz*. He represented a young Boston songwriter and pianist named Jimmy McHugh, who would write classic songs that would be recorded by Bing Crosby, Ella Fitzgerald, Peggy Lee, and Judy Garland.

It was the Roaring Twenties, and vaudeville was at its peak. The speakeasies operating in Boston—illegal during Prohibition, and typically run by racketeers and mobsters—were hungry to book entertainers. Lou was making more money than he had ever imagined, and he wasn't shy about spending it. "He wasn't one to say, 'Let's hold back and put it in the bank,'" said Ed Risman, who would be his business associate for a quarter-century. "If he had the money he spent it, or he gambled it." Lou's personal bookie set up permanent quarters in the small waiting room outside his office. By some estimates, Walters was earning $65,000 to $75,000 a year. Adjusted for inflation, that would be around $2 million in 2023 dollars.

In a way, Lou Walters was a "million-dollar baby" a generation before his daughter would famously gain that sobriquet.

2

ROOTS

Barbara insisted that religion played almost no role in her life.

"I had no religious education at all," she said without a hint of regret. Her father's younger brother, Harry, and his wife, Minna, were observant Jews, fasting on Yom Kippur and celebrating Passover, but Lou Walters called himself an atheist. Barbara's mother, Dena Walters, would light candles on Friday nights but the family didn't say the traditional Sabbath prayers, and Barbara couldn't remember either of her parents ever setting foot in a synagogue. When they died, she didn't follow the Jewish tradition of sitting shiva to mourn them. "So someone says, 'Are you Jewish?' I would say, 'Yes, I'm culturally Jewish,'" she said. "Does it govern my life in any way? No."

But being Jewish had defined and uprooted the life of her ancestors. Both sides of her family fled the Russian Empire to escape antisemitic pogroms that swept across what is now Ukraine and Poland and elsewhere in the late nineteenth century. The Jews who were targeted called it "Storms of the South." Another wave of attacks, even bloodier, followed in the early twentieth century.

Abraham Isaac Waremwasser, her paternal grandfather, was born in 1866 in Zgierz, near Lodz, now part of Poland. As a young man, he immigrated to London, an orphan without money, education, or prospects.

He was hired as an apprentice in a knitting mill owned by the Schwartz family, who had left Eastern Europe themselves years earlier.

Family legend then describes a fairy-tale romance, the stuff of a Hallmark special. On the holidays, the story goes, the elder Schwartzes would send their lovely daughter, Lillian, to the factories with baskets of food—geese and ducklings, bread and cakes—for the apprentices. On this occasion, she was said to be wearing a pale blue coat and a white ermine muff and hat. When she and Abraham spied one another, it was love at first sight. They would marry despite the reservations of her parents, proof of the power of the heart.

At least, that was the story told by one of their granddaughters, Shirley Budd, Barbara's favorite cousin. Barbara would relate it in an eye-rolling way that indicated she wasn't convinced it was true—a "fairy tale," she called it. Even on matters of family lore, she could be a skeptical journalist.

Abraham became a custom tailor in London, but he and Lillian were restless. The clothing trade in the East End was notorious for working conditions so malign that the word "sweatshops" had been coined to describe them. In 1899, Abraham made the long journey to San Francisco, followed in short order by Lillian and their three oldest children, including Lou, then five years old. They may have been among those drawn by stories of the fortunes to be won during the California Gold Rush.

They returned to London a few years later but there were no signs that they were any richer. During a strike in 1906, the family moved for a time to Belfast, then a major Irish port where a growing number of Jewish immigrants had headed. But neither seemed satisfied with that as their final destination. Abraham was interested in emigrating to Johannesburg, in South Africa, then part of the British Empire. But Lillian preferred America, and that was that.

"My father told me my grandmother wanted to come here, not there," said Lorraine Katz, another cousin of Barbara, "so that was the choice."

Abraham and his three sons—Louis, Harry, and Barnet—arrived in New York from Liverpool aboard the SS *Cedric* on August 28, 1909. Seven months later, Lillian and the four girls—Rose, Rebecca, Belle, and Florence—arrived on the SS *Columbia*. The family moved into an apartment on Rivington Street in lower Manhattan, a neighborhood of tenements crowded with new arrivals trying to get a toehold in an adopted land.

In England, Abraham's last name of "Waremwasser" had been Anglicized to "Warmwater." For a time after returning from San Francisco, they used "Abraham" and "Abrahams" as their last name. A year after arriving in the United States, the family changed its name for good to "Walters." Barbara's fame led the family to rediscover that linguistic evolution, which had been lost in time. In 2012, on the first season of a PBS series called *Finding Your Roots*, hosted by scholar Henry Louis Gates Jr., she was one of the celebrities whose genealogy was traced by experts and then dramatically revealed on air.

No surprises here: The DNA analysis conducted for the show found that Barbara's bloodlines were almost entirely Jewish: 91.2 percent a match with Middle Eastern Jewish and less than 9 percent with European non-Jewish. "There was some sneaking and creeping going on there," she joked of her non-Jewish heritage. Beforehand, she had predicted on the air that she would be "99.9 percent" Jewish, at the least.

———

Selig Seletsky, Barbara's maternal grandfather, was her first ancestor to arrive in the United States, in 1890, carrying a single piece of luggage and promptly changing his first name to Jacob. He had been born in 1870 in Benyakoni, then part of imperial Russia and now just inside the Belarus side of the border with Lithuania. Her maternal grandmother, Celia Sacovich (later spelled Sakowitz), was born in 1875 in the same general neighborhood—in Vilna, now called Vilnius and just inside the Lithuanian side of the border with Belarus.

When Celia was about eighteen years old, she immigrated to Boston's North End, where she met Jacob and then married him two years later. After working as a peddler, he took a job in a shoe store owned by an older brother. Jacob and Celia had seven children: daughters Dena and Lena, then sons Edward, Samuel, and Max, and finally twin boys, Daniel and Herman.

Two generations later, Barbara would show occasional flashes of each of her grandmothers, of Celia's bluntness and of Lillian's flair. Both were matriarchs of big broods, strong-minded women who had been willing to cross an ocean in search of better lives. Both watched their families rise from working-class to middle-class lives.

Maternal grandmother Celia "was short and stout with thick glasses, like my mother," Barbara said. "Everybody listened to her; she was evidently strong and tough. She spoke English with a heavy Yiddish accent, and the few Yiddish words I remember I learned from Grandma." Most of the words she recalled seemed to have a certain burn. *Nebbish*, for one, meaning sweet but pathetic. *Farbissener*, a sourpuss. And *mishegas*, meaning a chaotic time, or *meshuga*, meaning crazy.

Paternal grandmother Lillian, who died when Barbara was seven years old, remained British to the core, even after years of living in New York and Boston and then settling in New Jersey. Each afternoon, her husband would come home from his tailor shop for a traditional High Tea, served on English bone china. Abe would slip into a smoking jacket; Lilly would cut the crusts off watercress-and-cucumber sandwiches. On Sundays, kippers and eggs and onions were served for breakfast. In 1936, when they listened on the radio to King Edward VIII's speech giving up the throne for the woman he loved, they wept for the monarchy they had left.

If Celia was stout and loud, Lillian was refined and precise, with a taste for the finer things. The Walters home was filled with books. Throughout his life, Lou always seemed to have a book in his hand. When times were flush, he collected first editions. Several of his siblings would follow paths related to the arts, to music and painting. Lilly took a nap each day after lunch, slathering Pond's Dry Skin Cream on her face and putting cold cucumber slices on her eyes. She favored milk baths and used cut lemons to smooth her elbows.

On the morning she died, Lillian asked Shirley Budd to polish her nails. "A lady should never live like this. How could she die like this?" she demanded. Then she proclaimed herself a virgin. Shirley asked, "How could you be, Grandma? You have seven children."

"I know," Lilly replied. "But I never participated."

3

LOU AND DENA

1920

Lou Walters was twenty-five years old and riding high when a mutual friend introduced him to Dena Seletsky at a charity dance in Boston. At twenty-two, Dena was dark-haired and attractive, though chagrined by the thick eyeglasses she had to wear to see almost anything. She was working in a men's neckwear store. They were a striking couple. Dena was known for elegant airs and a caustic sense of humor. Lou had become a bit of a dandy, favoring imported white shirts with French cuffs and elaborate cuff links.

One year after the dance, on May 30, 1920, they were married in a rented banquet hall, Rabbi Abraham Rosen presiding. For their engagement, Lou had given Dena an extravagant diamond ring. On the night of their wedding, he slipped a mink stole over her shoulders.

"Both the bride and groom are very well known in the younger social set, the bride having been active in many charitable and social affairs carried on by organizations of which she is a member," the *Boston Post* wrote in a wedding announcement. The groom "conducts an amusement agency" and is, it reported, "one of the best known theatrical men in New England."

Not everyone in the bride's family approved. They asked Dena why she didn't marry someone in the shoe business. Her uncle owned a shoe store, after all, where Dena's father worked. Show business was an uncertain enterprise, her relatives cautioned.

Those concerns dismissed, the young couple spent their honeymoon in Atlantic City before settling in Roxbury, where Dena's family lived. They soon moved into a lavishly decorated mansion in Newton, a tonier Boston suburb. It became a family compound. When Dena's father died two years after they married, her widowed mother and five younger siblings moved in with them. When sister Lena married Sidney Alkon, he lived there, too. There was room to spare in the fourteen-room house and luxury cars in the driveway. At one point, Lou owned a Pierce-Arrow, a Packard, and two Cadillacs. The family's earlier disapproval of him dissipated with his largesse. Lou was a soft touch, "a hell of a guy," one of his brothers-in-law, Herman Seletsky, recalled. "If I wanted anything, I could get it from Lou—money or anything else."

But there was also sorrow. Lou and Dena's first child, Burton, born in 1922, died from pneumonia soon after his first birthday. In 1926, when their second child, Jacqueline, was born, it soon became apparent that something was amiss. She was a beautiful baby, and as a young woman was the spitting image of her mother. But she had developmental delays and a crippling stutter.

Barbara was born on September 25, 1929, just as the family's high times were coming to a catastrophic close. A month after her birth, the stock market crashed and plunged the nation into the worst depression in its history. Like millions of other investors, Lou had bought stocks and bonds on margin. His fortune was wiped out, and he owed gambling debts. Vaudeville faced new competition, too. The first movie talkie, *The Jazz Singer*, had opened two years earlier.

The furs and the fancy furnishings were sold to cover rent and food and debts. The family was forced to move from the mansion in Newton to a $75-a-month two-family house in Brookline. "My mother was sure things were going to get worse, and for a long time they did," Barbara said. They kept moving to cheaper and cheaper homes, a disheartening descent. At one point, the family lived next to a funeral home. At another, they rented an apartment where, with Lou's frequent absences as he sought to revive his fortunes, Dena had to stoke the furnace in the basement so often that she hurt her back.

Lou's downtown office was shuttered. "For a fast two years or so, I was strictly a bum," he said, facing derision even from former clients. "You're a has-been, Lou," a saloon owner told him. "You're washed up. All you know is from acrobats." During the 1930s, there were times "when I thought of selling vacuum cleaners," he said. Barbara later saw her father as the protagonist of a classic tragedy. "My father cast as the self-deceiving Willy Loman, the doomed, disillusioned character in *Death of a Salesman*," she mused.

———

Step by step, as the nation was struggling out of the deepest economic collapse in its history, Lou began his comeback, too.

He started booking acts for trade groups including the Massachusetts Shoe Manufacturing Association. (What was it about that generation of the family and the shoe business?) "Not very glamorous, but it helped pay the bills," Barbara remembered. With vaudeville fading, he scouted talent for nightclubs. His first show, at a Boston club called the Lido Venice, featured a female impersonator from New York and what he billed as "a Chorus of Lovely Debutantes"—in fact, young women he had recruited from local dancing schools. Lou recognized the public's prurient interest in notorious people; his daughter would do the same a generation later with interviews on TV of the victims and the perpetrators of celebrated crimes. He persuaded Evelyn Nesbit to appear onstage, despite a lack of apparent talent. She was famous for having had an affair with architect Stanford White that prompted her millionaire husband, Harry Thaw, to shoot him dead. With those credentials, she packed the house to hear her recite "The Persian Kitten."

Then the Lido was sold. Lou rented the cabaret on the fifteenth-floor penthouse of the Bradford Hotel, booking acts for a percentage of the take and free office space. The Cascades Roof, which had been losing money, began to turn a profit. But the hotel chain went out of business and closed. Next, he took a traveling show on the road, twenty-some performers jammed into four cars, touring as far north as Toronto and Nova Scotia in search of a paying audience. The first car featured a big sign that read, "Stop. Look. And Listen." But he was barely eking out a living, and he was gone from home for weeks at a time.

Finally, in 1937, he took over the lease of a building with its own colorful history. At one time a Greek Orthodox church, the building at 46 Winchester Street had been converted to a Chinese restaurant and then an Egyptian-themed nightclub called the Karnak. The structure was dilapidated, but the ceilings were high; Lou could envision trapeze artists swinging over the heads of the customers. For his new club, he first considered the Congo as a theme—lions and tigers painted on the walls and a chorus line of "native" dancing girls. Or perhaps something bohemian and artsy that echoed Greenwich Village. Then he saw *Gold Diggers in Paris*, a Warner Bros. movie released in the summer of 1938. The musical starred singer Rudy Vallee as the owner of a failing New York nightclub who takes his dancers to Paris after a French diplomat mistakes his Club Balle for the Academy Ballet of America. There, they win the grand prize at an international dance exposition. Walters's twist was to (purportedly) bring Parisian dancers to America. He adopted as the club's name the title of one of the film's songs, "Latin Quarter."

The song would become the theme of the Latin Quarter nightclubs, and with that of Barbara's childhood. At age eighty-two, standing on the street at the site of the old Latin Quarter in New York during a TV interview, she began to sing it, still word-perfect.

> *"So this is gay Paree! Come on along with me!*
> *We're stepping out to see the Latin Quarter.*
> *Put on your old beret; let's sing the Marseillaise*
> *And put our wine away like water."*

Lou had little capital and no margin for error. He had borrowed money from loan sharks and needed a fast turnaround; for a loan of $1,200, he would owe $2,000 in six months, or else. He paid a local artist $250, and the promise of $500 later, to paint murals on the wall of Parisian café scenes and portraits of what he called "girls with watching eyes"—that is, "black haired, slit-skirted, French prostitute looking." He bought used tables and chairs from the Salvation Army. He melted candles around the necks of empty wine bottles as table decorations to set the mood. He called an old friend, Boston police commissioner Joseph Timilty, who in turn called an old friend, Massachusetts governor James Michael Curley, to get a liquor license. Both Curley and Timilty were known for being corrupt.

"What if it fails?" Dena Walters fretted. "What then? With two young children to support?" On opening night, Lou pulled all the money he had from his pocket and counted it: sixty-three cents. He turned to a nearby waiter and handed him the change. "Here," he said. "Now I start from scratch."

His gamble paid off, this time. The club was a hit from the start. By one estimate, the Boston Latin Quarter would gross three quarters of a million dollars in its first season.

The secret to his success, Walters said, was going over the top in everything from the cut of the steaks (the biggest) to the costumes on the chorus girls (the skimpiest). "Just let me get my hands on enough velvet and chromium and I will build nightclubs like the world has never seen before, luxury like the Roman emperors never dreamed of," he said. "I will give them shows that will be lovely, but also breathtaking. I will have teams of apache dancers touring all over the world. And I will give all this, and an eight-course steak dinner, too, for a reasonable price." ("Apache," pronounced *ah-PAHSH*, was a dramatic style of modern dance associated with the streets of Paris.)

For the grand finale at each performance, the dancers would perform what was billed as a French can-can, prancing around the stage and high-kicking in unison as they flounced layers of petticoats. One by one, they would drop into a split, raising their skirts over their heads and flashing their ruffled panties.

4

NEVER YOUNG

1938

In her father's new Latin Quarter in Boston, and in his nightclubs that would follow, nine-year-old Barbara discovered her private niche.

She was a child who grew up early, seeing her parents in bright and sobering lights—sometimes a painful dynamic since she was, unmistakably, the product of both of them. She would be an innovator and a showman like her father, and, like him, she would never be entirely satisfied by her success. But she also learned a lesson she never forgot from her mother, the foreboding that today's good fortune could disappear tomorrow, a recipe for an insecurity that would gnaw at her for the rest of her life.

Barbara was small and wiry, with dark hair and a watchful manner. The forceful, take-charge adult she would become was nowhere in sight, not yet. Her family's affectionate nickname for her was "Skinnymalinkydink" because, she said, she was "all angles and bones, like a little dark spider." Her mother would pick her up from the Lawrence School, the neighborhood public school in suburban Brookline that she had attended since kindergarten, and take her and her older sister downtown.

Jackie had briefly attended Lawrence, too, assigned to a class of children with special needs, but she had to repeat first grade and never made it to second. Already isolated from the world, the club was almost the only place where Jackie could sit in the midst of life's hubbub and feel welcome.

In the nomenclature of the day, she was diagnosed as "mildly retarded." Years later, Barbara wondered if her sister might have been autistic. When they were children, Jackie was prettier and softer looking than the angular Barbara. But her extreme stutter made it all but impossible to understand what she was trying to say; when she began to speak, strangers would realize something was off. She was prone to tears and tantrums. She needed help even to comb her hair and get dressed in the morning. She would never marry, or hold a job, or live on her own.

While Jackie found solace in the noise and distraction backstage, Barbara preferred to climb into the lighting booth, where the spotlights would track the dancers and the musicians, the acrobats and the magicians onstage. From her perch, she could watch them practice, seeing them without being seen. She had a bird's-eye view of the glamour and the artifice. She could repeat the comedians' jokes and sing the Latin Quarter theme song, mimicking the high can-can kicks that went with it. She would remember sitting in George Burns's lap.

But she also saw them as they idled backstage, without the makeup or the bravado. Some were on their way up; some were on their way out. All that gave her a sense not only of their spark but also of their insecurities. It gave her an attitude toward headliners that was both unromantic—she would never be particularly cowed by someone's fame—and empathetic. "Behind these fantasy figures were real people," she said, with the same strains and sorrows of everyone else.

She also learned how to focus amid chaos, a useful skill years later when covering breaking news. Joy Behar, a co-host of *The View*, the talk show Barbara would create more than a half-century later, marveled at her ability to shut out the world around her. "When you see her on a plane, she has her glasses on," Behar said. "She sits by the window and just reads. And I remember people telling me, when her father owned the Latin Quarter, the comedians would come in and out. It must have been tumult all the time. And a couple of them told me they remember seeing the young Barbara in the corner, with her glasses, reading."

Barbara's visits to the club highlighted the dysfunctions of her family. Her mother was there in part because she wanted to keep tabs on her husband, who was prone to reckless impulses, from gambling to dalliances with women. "She'd sit in on discussions, and she wasn't afraid to tell Lou what she felt or how she felt," said Ed Risman, the club's manager. "She wasn't a little Jewish mother. She was a ballsy woman." Lou complained that she harped on every problem without comprehending the glorious possibilities. "She sees the seams but not the satin," he would say.

————

Young Barbara found herself uneasy and perplexed by the growing gulf between her parents. Years later, she analyzed it with some remove. "On paper, they seemed ideally suited for each other," she said. "Each was a member of what seems now to be a huge family—seven children. Each was a child of immigrant parents whose journey from persecution in the 'old country' could be the history of thousands of Jewish refugees transforming their lives in America."

But over time their relationship became toxic—"torturous," their daughter would call it—though they never divorced. He was absent; she was anxious. He was a dreamer; she was a skeptic. His infidelity was not exactly a rarity in his line of work; Dena installed one of her brothers, Eddie Selette, on the nightclub payroll to report on her husband's comings-and-goings.

Lou was said to have an extended and serious affair with one of his showgirls, something Barbara said she learned only years later. By then, reports of her own love life were the stuff of gossip columns. "If true, I certainly can't judge him too harshly," she said. "Let's face it, it would have made sense. Most people in show business were, and are, romantically involved with other people in show business. My father was surrounded by the most beautiful young women, and he was married to an ordinary, middle-aged woman."

That ordinary, middle-aged woman was less tolerant of her husband's indiscretions. Even when her daughter was a youngster, Dena would vent to her about Lou's absences, about his failings. Barbara wouldn't fully appreciate his gifts, his aspirations, until years later, until she was in her forties. Dena wasn't meant for life with Lou, their daughter concluded. "My mother should have married the way her friends did, a man who was a doctor, or who was in the dress business."

Or the shoe business, perhaps. Just as the Seletsky family had warned before their wedding.

The afternoons at his nightclub were sometimes the only time Barbara saw her father during the week. She resented his frequent absences. "I don't know whether it was animosity, but I think it was a little bit of anger," said Shirley Budd, Barbara's cousin. "Instead of being home when Barbara went to bed at nine o'clock, Lou was off [at] the club."

Even when he was around, he could seem absent. For a showman with a big presence in public, he had a hard time showing affection in private. "I can't remember my parents ever kissing in front of us, or hugging or even having a laugh," Barbara said, wondering if they would have stayed married in a later era. Nor was he given to expressions of fondness for his daughter. "I don't remember ever trying to hug him, even after he came home from a long trip," she said, a wistful admission.

She had some sweet childhood memories of outings with him, but they were rare: eating chicken chow mein in Boston's Chinatown, for one, and riding on the Swan Boats at the Boston Public Garden. (As an adult, she bought a watercolor by John Whorf titled *Swan Boat, Boston Public Gardens*, and hung it over her bed.) During summers, they would share a house with Aunt Lena's family in Hull, Massachusetts, which featured Nantasket Beach. On Sundays, if he was there, Lou would take them to watch the local baseball team play.

"To this day, thanks to him, I love baseball," she said later. "I am a Yankees fan now, but then I rooted for the Boston Red Sox. It all sounds very ordinary, doesn't it? Well, it was." But those halcyon days were the exception, she noted. "The summers were a welcome respite from the quieter, darker days of our winters."

———

If her father was distressingly distant for most of the year, her mother could be all too close.

Dena relied on her daughter for companionship and used her as a sounding board. She had few more suitable friends. She was close to her sister, but Lena lived several miles away, in Dorchester, and had two young sons of her own. Dena didn't drive. She didn't play cards or golf or tennis. Her days were dominated, and perhaps her maternal reserves exhausted, by the demands of caring for her disabled daughter; the family never managed to find a suitable school for Jackie.

With her father self-absorbed, her mother distracted, and her sister in need of constant care, Barbara fended for herself. Years later, one of Barbara's closest friends told me she would describe her childhood with resignation. "My mother really took care of my sister all the time and I was ignored," she told her. "I had to look after myself pretty much a lot of the time." Dena treated her like a peer with whom she could share her grievances. Most nights, she would cook dinner for the two girls while her husband was at the club or on the road. She would ask Barbara about her day. Then she would unload about her own.

Barbara grew up with "tension in the air," one of her closest friends, a psychotherapist, would say later. "It did not seem odd to me that I was her confidante," Barbara said of her mother, "but looking back now, I realize I was never young." When she was about to turn eighty years old, she described her upbringing to another celebrity interviewer, Larry King. "I ask you," she said to him. "Is this a childhood?"

"THE STRONGEST INFLUENCE IN MY LIFE"

Sisters.

Jackie was the source of love and empathy, embarrassment and guilt. Even, at times, hatred.

When Barbara wrote her memoir in 2008, she considered calling it *Sister*, though she settled on *Audition* as the title instead. Still, the first paragraph in the prologue is just that one word: "Sister." Jackie, she said, "was unwittingly the strongest influence in my life." Her sister's limitations often defined her own.

When Barbara would invite friends over or go out on a date, her mother would urge her to include her older sister, who had no friends of her own. The result was less to integrate Jackie than to isolate Barbara, not yet confident enough in her own skin to stand up for a sibling who was so different. It reinforced her sense of being an outsider herself. It was because of Jackie and the complications she posed, Barbara said, that she didn't host birthday parties or join the Girl Scouts.

She would always have mixed feelings about her. Jackie gave her "a compassion and an understanding of people" that she might never have had, she said, and she would name her only child after her. But Jackie's disability also embarrassed Barbara. Then she would feel guilty about being ashamed of her.

"I loved my sister," Barbara said late in life, years after Jackie had died in 1985 of ovarian cancer. "She was sweet and affectionate and she was, after all, my sister. But there were times I hated her, too. For being different. For making *me* feel different. For the restraints she put on my life. I didn't like that hatred, but there's no denying that I felt it." She wondered if people would be "horrified" by that admission, but she said those who had a disabled sibling would understand.

———

Barbara's earliest memory of her sister was a painful one. She was perhaps three; Jackie was six. After hearing her stutter, some boys in their Brookline neighborhood made fun of her and pulled at her skirt. Their ridicule was humiliating; the two girls ran into their house in tears. A few years later, when the girls were taking tap dance lessons, their mother dressed them in identical costumes for a local talent show. But Jackie panicked onstage, forgetting her steps, staring in desperation at Barbara. Someone in the audience began to boo.

Almost as piercing for Barbara was this memory: One of the happiest times of her childhood was a brief stretch when Jackie was away, enrolled in a boarding school in Pennsylvania for children with special needs. The family had just moved to Miami Beach from Boston. "This meant I had my parents all to myself," Barbara said, thrilled with the focus on her. Her mother's mood brightened, too.

But Jackie was desperately unhappy. She came home six months later, never to be sent away again.

Backstage at her father's nightclubs, the chorus girls would fuss over Jackie. Some of the stars would, too, Frank Sinatra among them. Broadway legend Carol Channing, the daughter of a leader in the Christian Science church, had grown up in a household that had welcomed people with developmental disabilities. She invited Jackie to her shows and would call and visit her, forging a friendship that was genuine.

Singer Johnnie Ray, a pioneer in rock-and-roll, called her "Jackie darling" and sent her birthday cards and autographed pictures when he was on tour. His own childhood may have made him especially sensitive to her isolation. He was a budding musician when he lost hearing in his left ear at age thirteen in a Boy Scout accident, an injury that went unrecognized for a time and prompted him to withdraw from others.

That experience gave him a stronger need to connect with other people, he said, and contributed to his trademark emotional displays onstage. His biggest hits were "Cry" and "The Little White Cloud That Cried"; he became known as "The Prince of Wails" and "The Million Dollar Teardrop."

Jackie had a crush on him, and in her innocence believed he felt the same way about her. Her diary was laced with his name. "Johnnie is working in Chicago. Hope he calls me," she wrote. And again, "Johnnie is in Dallas. Someday I will marry him."

At age seven or eight, Barbara began complaining about constant stomach pains—not because she had them, but because it meant her mother would leave Jackie with Dotey, an elderly woman and the only babysitter she trusted, and take Barbara to a round of doctors. After the examinations and the tests, for a treat, they would stop at a restaurant and she could order a plate of spaghetti. "Bliss," Barbara recalled, both for her favorite meal and for the time alone with her mother.

A diagnosis of her phantom pains naturally proved elusive; the best prescription would have been the attention she yearned to get. No one seemed to suspect she was faking her complaints. "Finally one bewildered doctor said I should have my appendix taken out," she recalled.

This was, it would seem, an extreme remedy. But Barbara embraced it. "It seemed the only choice," she said. "So I did, happily. More attention."

She spent almost a week in the hospital. Each day, her mother would take the streetcar from Brookline to Boston, then walk ten blocks to see her. One night, when Barbara heard someone entering her room, she feigned sleep until the visitor, presumably a nurse, had left. "I finally opened my eyes and saw at the foot of my bed my favorite doll," she recalled. "My mother, worried that I would feel alone, had taken the streetcar at night to visit me one more time."

The memory stayed with her. "It makes me so sad for her," she said.

As an adult, Barbara related her experience in a matter-of-fact tone, as if it were just another childhood anecdote. But it was more than that. Children often fake stomachaches for some psychological need—because they want more attention, as she did, or because they're anxious about going to school. But it's rare for that to lead all the way to a risky and unnecessary surgery. If her pretenses had persisted, it might have suggested a mental illness psychiatrists diagnose as factitious disorder. The effort to gain emotional support, sometimes deliberate and sometimes unconscious, is often associated with childhood trauma. Even short of that, the episode is shocking, most of all because of what it revealed about her family. How is it possible that neither her mother nor her father nor any of her doctors recognized what was at the heart of a little girl's mysterious pain?

Barbara seemed to suffer no long-term repercussions from the loss of her appendix, and she apparently never carried out a similar untruth about her health again. Instead, she would find other, more acceptable ways to command the attention of her family and the world.

———

She was a solitary child and a diligent student. "A very serious pupil," Mildred Gillis, her fifth-grade teacher at the Lawrence School, would say years later. Miss Gillis was usually "stingy" with As, she said, but she gave them to Barbara. The child was "delightful" and a "good writer." But she didn't seem to have any playmates, Miss Gillis recalled. "I don't remember Barbara as being social. School was a place of business for her."

Not by choice.

"I desperately wanted playmates, to have friends over to my house, to belong instead of always feeling like an outsider," Barbara said. She didn't boast about her father's glamorous profession; she was chagrined about it. While some in Brookline admired the glitz, others didn't consider a nightclub that featured nearly nude showgirls and risqué comics as entirely respectable. "To other people, to have a father who owned a nightclub: Hey, wasn't that great?" she said. "But I wanted him to come home every night, and not just Friday nights. I wanted him not to sleep until 2:00 in the afternoon. I guess I wanted my father to be a dentist."

She wanted to be just like the others in her class. Not to stand out. To fit in.

"When I was about seven years old, the school put on a little performance for adoring parents," she remembered. "It featured a robin redbreast as the lead and a chorus of little brown-costumed chirpers. I was assigned the leading role of the robin. But here's the thing: I didn't want to be the star. I wanted to be in the chorus, to be like all the other kids." Her mother, a skilled seamstress, made her a robin costume with a red belly and wings. When Barbara tried it on, she burst into tears. She explained why to her bewildered mother.

The next day, Dena went to school with her and talked to the teacher. At the performance, Barbara was, happily, a chirper in the chorus. Just like nearly everyone else.

———

Later, of course, Barbara would decide she didn't want to be a chirper in the chorus.

As a girl, she would get glimpses of a more traditional life when they visited her uncle, Harry Walters, a leading citizen in the seaside town of Asbury Park, New Jersey, about an hour from Manhattan. Uncle Harry and Aunt Minna had a happy marriage, three healthy daughters, and a successful dry-goods store. Harry was the patriarch of the Walters clan. "He was handsome, easygoing, sweet, and, I guess, predictable," Barbara said. "His older brother, Lou, my father, was adventurous, a gambler, an artist in his way, and definitely not a family man."

At times, she envied her three cousins. She was the one who didn't have "the most normal" childhood or the happiest one.

And yet.

"[W]hen we grew up forgive me for saying this—my life was so much more interesting than theirs," she said of her cousins from Asbury

Park. "Not necessarily better, but much more interesting. And for better or worse, I came to value 'interesting' far more than 'normal.'" She would choose interesting over normal, ambition over three marriages, an interview with a big newsmaker over a planned holiday with her daughter. She would choose power and prominence and fortune, the chance to be the robin redbreast at center stage rather than a chirper in the chorus.

For better or worse, she would decide to take the shiny paper over the plain, as she once put it, any day of the week. Just like her father.

6

THE FIFTH-GRADER
AND THE BOOTLEGGER

1939

Palm Island is a peculiarly Floridian invention, a narrow strip of land created by dredging and reachable by a causeway that connects the cities of Miami and Miami Beach. In the 1930s, with only a handful of houses on the site, it was famous mostly for the presence of Earl Carroll's Palm Island Club, favored by big spenders and a fast crowd until the state outlawed slot machines in 1937.

Without profits from the casino, the club went bankrupt, but Lou Walters, as usual, had a vision of the possibilities. The Latin Quarter in Boston was going gangbusters. Now he saw the prospects of opening another one here. The big white building was a Hollywood version of what a nightclub should look like, with wide steps leading up to a marble entrance, seating inside for some six hundred customers, dormitories on the premises for the dancers. "I was in love with the big, beautiful Palm Island Club," he wrote in his unpublished memoir. There was more, he added. "I was in love with the adjoining 15-room mansion."

He signed a ten-year lease with a Baltimore mortgage company for the club, at $7,500 a year, and leased the mansion across the street for another $2,500. Uprooted from Miss Gillis's fifth-grade class in Brookline, Massachusetts, Barbara moved with some reluctance from the family's apartment there to the sprawling house on the bay. It was painted pistachio green—"just like the ice cream," she said—and situated on five acres of hibiscus, bougainvillea, and palm trees. They moved into the house in November 1939.

A month later, a man named William Dwyer showed up at the front door, accompanied by his bodyguard or his chauffeur or, possibly, his partner in a more personal regard. Dwyer was the previous owner of the Palm Island Club; band leader Earl Carroll had been his front man, producing a show called the "Vanities Revue." Dwyer had defaulted on the club's mortgage, but he had continued to rent the house across the street. His lease had run out a year earlier, but he said he had an understanding that the owner wouldn't rent it to someone else without letting him know.

Here he was, ready to move back in for the winter. "Mr. Dwyer is here," announced Mrs. Speiler, a middle-aged housekeeper who also apparently came with the house.

Legally, Dwyer had no claim to the mansion, that was clear. But in the world of clubs and casinos, of gamblers and mobsters, "Big Bill" Dwyer was not a man to be casually dismissed. During Prohibition, he had been known as "king of the bootleggers." He spent thirteen months in the Atlanta federal penitentiary in the 1920s—"a little vacation," he called it—after being convicted of trying to bribe members of the Coast Guard to overlook his rumrunning operation. The jail time didn't quell his ambitions. Once released, he bought an expansion National Hockey League franchise and introduced professional ice hockey to New York City; later, he bought a National Football League team and moved it to Brooklyn. He renamed it the Dodgers. But he had encountered a spot of trouble seven months before he showed up at the Walters's front door. He had been convicted of tax evasion after a ten-minute trial in Brooklyn Federal Court and ordered to pay the government an astonishing $3,715,907 in back taxes and penalties.

Legal problems aside, Dwyer was still president of the nearby Tropical

Park Race Track, and he remained a formidable figure around town. Lou understood exactly who was standing on his doorstep, surrounded by a pile of suitcases.

"They say your life passes in front of you in a flash when you are drowning, that a drowning man clutches at straws," he said of that first encounter with Dwyer. Lou knew he had a signed-and-sealed lease for the nightclub and the house. But he was less certain about the extralegal repercussions for sending on his way a man known locally as "The Fixer." "You took care of Bill, Bill took care of you," he noted. The reverse might also be true: You crossed Bill, and perhaps he would take care of you in an entirely different way.

Fortuitously, only three of the mansion's seven bedrooms were currently occupied by the Walters family, leaving spare rooms for Mr. Dwyer and his odd entourage. They would stay for five months, until spring, when the winter season ended and they would head back to his home in Queens.

With that began one of the closest and surely the strangest of Barbara's childhood friendships. It was an early example of her comfort with men who had complicated backstories, even criminal ones.

"He took a shine to me," she said as though that explained everything. She took a shine to him, too. She remembered him as a kind-faced man with round rimless glasses and combed-back hair. He was fifty-six years old; she was nine. Perhaps he took the place of the doting father she yearned to have. On the weekends, he would take her to his racetrack. She was too young to go inside, but they would park where she could see the horses run. Her father would slip her a few dollars, which she would give to Dwyer to place bets on her behalf.

"Magically I always won," she recalled. That first winter in Miami Beach was "one of the happier times of my young life."

Her only other friend at the time was Phyllis Fine, a girl of a more suitable age who was in her class at school. Her father was in show business as well, and he was also a gambler. Born Louis Feinberg, his stage name was Larry Fine, one of the renowned Three Stooges. (He was the one with the circle of bushy hair around a dramatically receding hairline.) They were living in a Miami Beach hotel, where Barbara would occasionally sleep over. But the remoteness of Palm Island, and the need to have an adult drive them back and forth, made getting together difficult.

The isolation was hard on Dena, who had never learned to drive. She finally took lessons and practiced by driving Barbara to and from appointments with her orthodontist in Miami. The parking lot outside his office meant she didn't have to parallel park, a daunting challenge. But she was never a confident driver, and as the streets became more congested, she stopped trying. It was a life skill Barbara would never acquire, either.

Big Bill Dwyer was in Florida without his wife and five children, who presumably had stayed at their home in New York. Later, Barbara would wonder if Dwyer was gay, not a question that occurred to her at the time. "In those days the only reference to 'gay' I'd ever heard was in the Latin Quarter's theme song, 'So This is Gay Paree,'" she said. "But in retrospect it seems somewhat logical." For one thing, despite the surplus of bedrooms in the mansion, he and his bodyguard/chauffeur shared the same one.

———

The new Latin Quarter opened on Palm Island on December 23, 1940, just in time for Christmas. It was an instant smash.

The $6 minimum promised what Lou billed as "delicious food" and "startling shows," presumably a reference to the scant attire of the showgirls. At first, he couldn't afford top entertainers; instead, he booked novelty acts. An ad in the *Miami Daily News* depicted a pair of dramatic Apache dancers, purportedly from the streets of Paris, both smoking thin cigarettes, the man in a beret. Their act included a choreographed brawl between the man and several women that ended, twice a night, when a woman shot him for two-timing her.

The club's second winter season opened three weeks after the attack on Pearl Harbor on December 7, 1941. The surprise Japanese assault on the Pacific fleet prompted the United States to enter World War II, but the show went on anyway. It did reflect some wartime realities. In one routine, titled "Blackouts in Rhythm," the showgirls dressed as lightning bugs.

By then, the success of the club meant Walters could book some of the biggest names in show business, from Jimmy Durante and Sophie Tucker to Joe E. Lewis and Martha Raye. Dean Martin and Jerry Lewis, then a comic duo before each pursued individual movie careers, took the stage. So did exotic dancer Sally Rand and her white feather fans. In 1947, actress Jane Russell would command $15,000 a week. Comedian Milton Berle became such a regular that Barbara could mimic his opening gag decades later.

"He would walk up to the standing microphone, touch it, then jump back as if in shock and say, 'I've just been goosed by Westinghouse,'" she said. It always got a laugh. She could also re-create on demand the patter of a Spanish ventriloquist known as Señor Wences, who would later gain fame with forty-eight appearances on *The Ed Sullivan Show*. He would make a fist, color his closed finger with lipstick to form a mouth, create two "eyes" with black chalk, and drape a floppy orange wig across the top. With that, the falsetto-voiced "Johnny" would mercilessly tease Señor Wences, whose real name was Wenceslao Moreno Centeno.

There were also the showgirls, of course, balancing towering head-dresses as they strode and posed onstage. Tiny sequined pasties covered their nipples, a nod to the laws barring nudity, and their G-strings were constructed of feathers and fur. One showgirl carried an actual black kitten in a fur-lined muff over her private parts.

"This place puts on perhaps the most elaborate show in the Miami area," read the most unusual of reviews, a memo written in 1944 by the FBI Miami field office and sent to FBI director J. Edgar Hoover. "Due to this fact, it attracts . . . the hoodlum and gangster element." The regular visitors included eccentric business magnate Howard Hughes and Joseph P. Kennedy, father of John F. Kennedy; his chauffeur would drive him from the family's summer compound in Palm Beach. The most notorious resident of Palm Island visited occasionally, too.

Al Capone had bought a ten-thousand-square-foot home with a hundred-foot dock in 1928 from Clarence Busch, a prominent local real estate investor. More than a decade later, after a stint in Alcatraz, he and his bodyguards drove to Florida, arriving on Palm Island in March 1940, a few months after the Walters family had moved in down the street. Increasingly frail and suffering from dementia, Capone was a shadow of the fearsome criminal nicknamed Scarface. He would sit at the Latin Quarter, sip a club soda, and pull a crisp twenty-dollar bill from his pocket to pay. "He never interfered with anyone and believe me, no one wanted to interfere with him," Lou recalled.

Barbara would ride her bike past Capone's house, hoping to catch a glimpse of him, though she never did. She spent her days reading books and playing with her elaborate dollhouse. She would walk to the docks to wave at the tourists on the sightseeing boats. Until she was sent to bed at 10 p.m. on weekends, she was allowed to watch the evening shows at the Latin Quarter, tucked into her favorite spot in the lighting booth.

In 1972, when Barbara was beginning to attract attention as a correspondent on the *Today* show, she was interviewed by Sonya Hamlin, host of a Boston program called *People Games*. "Free-associate," Hamlin said. "Give me one word for your childhood."

"Lonely," Barbara replied.

ANOTHER OPENING, ANOTHER SHOW

1941

Barbara was ready to enter the eighth grade when her father announced they were moving out of the pistachio-green house on Palm Island.

The Latin Quarter was doing so well that Lou and his show had been featured in *The Saturday Evening Post*. "A spectacular and magnificent night club venture," *The Miami Herald* proclaimed. "One of the outstanding clubs in the country," the *Miami Daily News* agreed. He took his "Midnight in Paris" revue to Nassau for a benefit for the British Red Cross sponsored by the Duke and Duchess of Windsor. A photo from that night shows Lou and Dena chatting with the Duchess, all of them in evening clothes.

Lou was eager to expand to other cities. On the first day of 1941, the morning after raucous New Year's Eve celebrations had rung in the new year, he was sitting alone in the Palm Island club. Irving Zussman, a PR man from New York, called with an offer too good to resist.

"How'd you like to run a nightclub on Broadway?" he asked. "In

Times Square. The best location in the world. And you won't have to put up a cent."

Elias Moses (E. M.) Loew, an Austrian émigré who had amassed a fortune in movie theaters and real estate, wanted to get into the nightclub business. The two men already knew one another. Back in the day, Lou had booked vaudeville acts into some of Loew's theaters. Now, Loew had found a prime location for a club with a ten-year lease. He would provide the capital; Lou would stage the show in exchange for a salary, some equity, and his name on the marquee—an offer, Loew's widow would explain, "to boost Lou's ego and make him work harder."

Lou was thrilled to be heading back to New York, the town he had left as a teenager, fueled by nothing more than hustle and hope. To Times Square, the neighborhood where he had searched so desperately for his first job three decades earlier.

The vacant building on a triangular-shaped lot at Broadway and 48th Street had a cautionary history. A string of nightclubs already had failed on the site: the Cotton Club, George White's Gay White Way, the Palais Royal. But when Lou's Latin Quarter opened on April 22, 1942, five months after the United States entered World War II, it was packed with an audience drawn by his classic prescription: steaks, showgirls, and a touch of Paris for anyone who could afford the $2 minimum. He titled the first show "Folies des Femmes." The Broadway correspondent for United Press called it "as lavish a show as a night club has brought to town in well over a year."

———

In New York, the Walters family moved to the Buckingham, a residential hotel with an arch of stained glass over double doors at the entrance. At the corner of 57th Street and Sixth Avenue, it was in the middle of the city, across the street from Carnegie Hall and a block from the Automat. Barbara enrolled at Fieldston, a private school with a leafy high school campus in Riverdale, in the Bronx. Affiliated with the Ethical Culture Society, the school gained renown over the years for its prestigious alumni, from physicist J. Robert Oppenheimer to composer Stephen Sondheim to power broker Robert Moses. Notorious lawyer Roy Cohn attended for a year, too.

Barbara was miserable, especially at first. "It was coed and full of cliques," she said. When she arrived, she realized with horror that her shoes, bought in Florida, were a mistake—white open-toed "Cuban heels" rather than the requisite black-and-white saddle shoes—and that she wasn't wearing the right socks with them. Every single thing about her seemed wrong, she worried. Her clothes made her look like a hick and her unusual speech pattern, what she tried to explain away as just a Boston accent, made her sound affected. In the beginning, she would take her lunch tray and walk slowly around the cafeteria, hoping that one of the popular girls would invite her to sit down.

She made mostly As and Bs in her academic classes, though she confessed to flunking home economics and gym. She would never be particularly good at or interested in cooking or sports; she would never be an early choice when teams were picked. The only recognition she recalled winning during those days was at sleepaway camp that summer in the Poconos. She was voted "most improved athlete," a compliment with a backhand.

Her social life got better through the year, but she never felt fully at ease. "I never really made the A group," she recalled. Years later, she spied the class beauty whose cascade of blond hair had helped make her the object of desire for upperclassmen. By then, the woman's youthful good looks had faded, Barbara noted with a bit of spite, while she had become the famous co-host of *Today*. "Okay, so I'm bragging," she wrote in her memoir, "but after all those years of pushing so hard, I'm entitled."

The Latin Quarter in Times Square, which opened in 1942, was a hit, a glamorous respite for soldiers and tourists as World War II raged. Within months, Lou had moved the family from the Buckingham to a penthouse on Central Park West.

Their home was fancier, but their family dynamic was no more stable.

Barbara came home from school one day to find her mother in tears. "Daddy has left us," Dena told her. The breach sounded more serious than their usual squabbles. "You go talk to him," Dena instructed her fourteen-year-old daughter. "Tell him to come back." She told Barbara to take Jackie with her, a play for sympathy.

The two girls went to the Latin Quarter, not yet open for that night's business. "I remember very clearly sitting with my father at his table in that darkened, empty nightclub, crying and begging him not to leave us," Barbara recalled. Jackie was crying, too, though she didn't understand what was happening, only that something was wrong.

"My father didn't say anything during my plea. He kissed Jackie and me and simply said he had to go back to work. I didn't know what to do. I definitely didn't know what to tell my mother. So I took Jackie to a movie with a stage show playing nearby. I dreaded returning home, and we sat in the theater for hours. But when we did go home, my mother was smiling. She told me my father had changed his mind and decided not to leave."

Barbara had rescued her family, and not for the last time.

———

Lou Walters, never really satisfied, wanted to expand his ambitions.

A year after the Latin Quarter opened in New York, he ventured into Broadway musicals, producing the *Ziegfeld Follies of 1943* in association with the Schuberts at the Winter Garden Theatre. The show, a revival of Flo Ziegfeld's celebrated series from 1907 to 1931, starred comedian Milton Berle. The reviews were mixed but the wartime audiences loved the extravaganza; the show would run for 523 performances and was still going strong years later on tour. An ad for the show at the Oklahoma Semi-Centennial Exposition in 1957 billed stars Mickey Rooney and Dorothy Lamour, along with "30 OF THE MOST BEAUTIFUL GIRLS IN THE WORLD." A local newspaper enthused, "Walters is bringing 360 different costumes of the kind that has earned him volumes of praise for daring, originality and elegance."

But Walters's other Broadway shows were flops, and expensive ones. *Artists and Models* was an updated vaudeville revue from the 1920s that featured a young comedian named Jackie Gleason. "Walters has conceived some cute notions," a reviewer wrote in *Billboard*, then added sarcastically, "which is possibly the chief ailment." It opened on November 5, 1943, and closed three weeks later. Three months after that, he revived and produced another show, *Take a Bow*, starring Chico Marx, the oldest of the Marx Brothers and a self-taught pianist. The show folded even faster, after fourteen performances.

In September 1944, Lou launched another Latin Quarter, this time in Detroit. Comic and singer Martha Raye was one of the headliners—at a premium $17,000 for two weeks—but the club was troubled from the start; $7,500 in receipts went missing in its opening days. "When Lou was out of town, the waiters robbed him blind," a local columnist later wrote. A year after the grand opening, with fewer patrons in the club and no profits in sight, Lou and partner E. M. Loew sold it to a Detroit syndicate.

Lou would even lose his original Latin Quarter nightclub in a gin rummy game, a longtime friend named Ben (Ford) Abrams told author Jerry Oppenheimer. Caught in an all-night losing streak at the Friars Club in New York, Lou called a business acquaintance in Boston and landed a quick line of credit, using the Boston Latin Quarter as collateral. By dawn, he was broke and the club was gone. Just what happened to the Boston club isn't clear. Years later, *The Boston Globe* reported that Walters had sold the club in 1943 for $350,000 to Michael (Mickey) Redstone, a notable local figure of his own. Redstone, a high school dropout, had established first a trucking business and then a family entertainment empire that would become ViacomCBS.

Regulars at the Friars Club talked for years about another epic streak, the day Lou lost $30,000 in cash to showman Mike Todd in a gin rummy game. Broadway columnist Dorothy Kilgallen rated Walters and Todd as the "keenest gin rummy players" in town. One of them was, anyway.

———

Lou decided he would focus on the New York nightclub and new enterprises in Florida. He signed leases to open a gambling casino at the Colonial Inn, just north of Miami, and to take over a club called the Dunes in Palm Beach County.

With that, they moved back to Florida. "I was furious," Barbara said. "I had finally made friends. I had a life." Looking back, she said those years reminded her of the show tune "Another Op'nin', Another Show," from the Cole Porter musical *Kiss Me, Kate*, that would open on Broadway a few years later.

> *Another job that you hope, at last,*
> *Will make your future forget your past,*
> *Another pain where the ulcers grow,*
> *Another op'nin' of another show.*

"For me," she said, "another audition."

She would attend four schools in five years. In each of them, "she had to start cold," her mother recalled. "She'd come home at night and cry." What Barbara remembers is "being always on the outside." That she had to audition, again and again.

Barbara enrolled at Miami Beach Junior High for the ninth grade, then at Miami Beach Senior High for the tenth grade. She knew some classmates from elementary school in Florida, and the academic and social pressures were lower than at Fieldston. She pledged one of the sororities that ruled the students' social life—not the most exclusive one, Kappa Pi, but the second-ranking one, Lambda Pi. She went on dates and to dances.

But Lou was struggling, again. Being able to open a casino at the Dunes depended on defeating a resistant county sheriff who opposed the proposal to legalize gambling. At a time of gas rationing during wartime, it was hard to convince people to drive from Miami to the Colonial Inn in Hallandale, on the outskirts of the city.

Dena nagged her husband and confided in her teenage daughter. "She was always afraid that something would happen to the club or that my father would lose too heavily at cards, and they'd wind up broke again," Barbara said. After all, it had happened before. "This fear was communicated to me from an early age. I became consumed with the same worry. What would we do when the money ran out?" Not if. When.

She described her family this way: "My father, a gambler and a dreamer. My mother, a realist whom my father considered a pessimist. Me? I was a worrier whom both parents considered to be too serious for a very young girl."

The Florida clubs were failing. To Barbara's dismay, they were moving again, back to New York.

———

Fieldston authorities had informed Barbara that she wouldn't be welcomed back to the school. They complained that her attendance had been too irregular, she said. The morning after shows opened at the Latin Quarter, her parents would let her sleep in and skip her classes. She and her mother and sister would have been up all night, first at the club and then at Lindy's, the deli where the comedians and other showbiz folks would hang out after the club closed.

It was 1945, and World War II had finally ended. Americans were ready to celebrate. The Latin Quarter grossed $10 million in its first decade and was visited by more than five million people, ranking second only to Radio City Music Hall as a New York City destination for tourists. The biggest stars played there. "I knew Lou Walters before he could speak Latin and didn't have a quarter," Milton Berle would joke at the beginning of his routine.

Lou had more than a quarter in his pocket now. He was flush again. They moved into a penthouse at 91 Central Park West, an apartment that was said to have once been occupied by the Hearst family. (In 2019, the four-bedroom penthouse sold for an eye-popping $17.5 million.) Huge terraces encircled it on all four sides. The living room had elaborately carved wood panels; the library was filled with the first editions Lou Walters collected; the music room featured a piano that was rarely played. The kitchen had a butler's pantry. For a time, the family also had a butler, albeit one who turned out to be an alcoholic, stashing his empty bottles in a secondary kitchen off the playroom that was rarely used.

Dena decorated the library with red-leather couches and the living room with yellow-and-lavender brocade upholstery. Overstuffed pillows with tassels were scattered around. "The whole thing looked like a huge Easter egg," Barbara said.

Her father took his family to the openings of the biggest shows on Broadway—to *Oklahoma!* and *Carousel* and *Annie Get Your Gun* and

South Pacific. They spent the summers at rambling resort hotels on Long Island and upstate in the Adirondacks and in Connecticut. She enrolled at Birch Wathen, another exclusive private school, this time on the West Side.

By now, she had an easier time making new friends, and she was getting good grades. She was teased about her father's occupation in the *Birch Peel*, a student parody of the school newspaper, *Birch Bark*. An article described her as "the present owner of that successful club, 'The Arabian One Third,'" a wordplay on "Latin Quarter."

In the yearbook, though, she still has the look of someone who was not quite sure she belonged. A photo of the staff for the *Birch Leaves*, the school's literary magazine, shows four smiling students clustered around the faculty adviser while Barbara stands apart, an uncertain expression on her face.

During these years, it is hard to see signs of the formidable figure Barbara would become. She showed little interest in world affairs. She wasn't elected "most likely to succeed." The biggest academic award she received was when she was chosen "Miss French Club" during the tenth grade at the Miami Beach Senior High. She seemed to have no idea what career she might pursue, or even that she would necessarily pursue any career. When she graduated from Birch Wathen in 1947, young ladies of her ilk generally weren't encouraged to have any ambitions beyond landing a presentable husband and rearing well-behaved children.

It would be a decade before a crisis in her family would ignite her ambition and define her way.

———

With no particular direction in mind, Barbara did the same thing as most of her high school classmates at graduation. She went to college.

She applied to three of them, all women-only at the time and none of them far from home. Wellesley, in Massachusetts and one of the Seven Sister schools, was the most prestigious. Pembroke College in Rhode Island was her safety school. Sarah Lawrence was in Bronxville, just north of the city in Westchester County. It was relatively new, founded in 1926, with a progressive curriculum that particularly appealed to artsy and intellectual types. The biggest draw for Barbara was that her best friend was applying there.

The application form for Sarah Lawrence included essay questions, which Barbara answered with something less than honesty. She would later describe it as full of "barefaced lies," deceptions for which she offered no defense. They reflected more of a flair for PR hype that might be used to promote a nightclub than the thoughts of a high school senior, serious about her future, much less of a journalist's commitment to the truth. If TV interviewer Barbara Walters had uncovered such fabrications by a subject, she might well have cross-examined him or her about them, and what they revealed. What insecurities did they reflect? What fears that the truth would not be good enough to be accepted?

"What has meant the most to you in your education outside of school?" one question asked. Barbara's family was Jewish by heritage but not observant in practice, and she had never attended religious training of any sort. Still, she replied, "Sunday school, which helped me appreciate the force of God and enabled me to increase my faith and understanding in His power."

What experience had she had in the arts? She wrote that she was "particularly fond of dramatics"—that was true—and that she had gained "so much valuable technical experience" by working in a summer stock company in Connecticut. That wasn't true. She seemed to be appropriating for herself the experiences of a friend at Fieldston, Enid Kraeler Reiman, who had told her about the summer she spent working as a gofer at the Greenwich Playhouse in Connecticut.

When a teacher at Birch Wathen had assigned students to write an autobiographical essay, Barbara cautioned a friend, Joan Gilbert, later Joan Gilbert Peyser, about the perils of revealing too much. "Barbara, even at the young age of sixteen, saw the value of secrecy," Peyser, who became a prominent musicologist, said years later. "She was astute enough to know that indiscriminate self-revelation is not a skillful way to go through life."

No one would ever accuse Barbara Walters of indiscriminate self-revelation. Even then, she had secrets and scars.

In her photo in the high school yearbook, she is unsmiling. The quotation under her picture is appropriate enough, from a seventeenth-century English poet, Francis Quarles: "The glory of a firm, capacious mind." But at the senior assembly, which featured the reading of favorite poems, Barbara chose a melancholy verse by Wilfrid Wilson Gibson, "The Stone," about a woman's devastation over the accidental death of her lover. A fictional short story she wrote for the literary magazine, *Birch Leaves*, depicted a dystopian world of icy loneliness, without warmth or shelter. It was titled "Beyond."

By the time Barbara graduated from high school, Pembroke, her safety school, had rejected her application. Wellesley had put her on the waiting list. But Sarah Lawrence accepted her, the applicant who had touted her deep religious faith and experience in summer stock theater.

Sarah Lawrence it would be.

8

THE OSTRICH

1947

At the age of eighteen, Barbara believed she had found her calling.

As a freshman at Sarah Lawrence, she performed a scene from Lillian Hellman's *The Children's Hour* with another student at a school workshop. "Both of the actresses did competent jobs, and Peggy Eppenstein's frightened crying was especially real," the campus reviewer wrote. A year later, Barbara landed a leading role in the school production of Sean O'Casey's *Juno and the Paycock*, playing the anguished Mary Boyle for the three-night run.

Then she won the biggest part of all, the title role in George Bernard Shaw's *Candida*. She played the wife of a preacher whose marriage was threatened by her love affair with a young poet. To the frustration of the director, though, she turned out to be visibly uncomfortable with having any physical contact with the men onstage, a significant problem given that her character was intimate with two of them. Even so, she would recall in her memoir receiving "if not a standing ovation, at least healthy applause at my curtain call."

She had caught the acting bug, an infection she would diagnose in many of the performers she would interview in decades to follow. "I remember the thrill of hearing applause and the joy of getting laughs," she said. She met with the college dean, Esther Raushenbush, to discuss whether she should drop out of school and pursue a career on the stage. To Barbara's surprise, Raushenbush wasn't perturbed; she encouraged her to consider it. Perhaps the dean had met with previous students in the thrall of new enthusiasms, fleeting or otherwise, and understood the limits of dissuasion.

Whether Barbara had theatrical talent isn't entirely clear, though her early forays don't sound especially encouraging. But she did have theatrical connections. Lou Walters knew every producer and agent in town. As a child, she had been at times chagrined about her father's role in showbiz; now it proved valuable. He made some introductions, and one of the agents he contacted arranged for an audition for a part in a Broadway production of Tennessee Williams's *Summer and Smoke*. Few actors with such a slender repertoire could have commanded such consideration.

First, she was thrilled. Then she was panicked.

As the audition approached, she became terrified over the possibility—indeed, the likelihood—of being rejected. Endless cattle calls and repeated rebuffs were part of the routine for most would-be actors, but she wasn't sure she was prepared to weather that. She had discovered she loved being in the spotlight but getting there might carry a price she wasn't willing or able to pay. "It was just like being back in high school with the same fear I had of being turned down by a sorority or by the popular girls who didn't want me in their group," she said. Decades after Miami Beach Senior High's most prestigious sorority didn't tap her for membership, she could remember the sting. What would it be like when the Broadway director of *Summer and Smoke* sent her packing? And the next director? And the next?

"I had the pull because of my father's prominence in show business, but I didn't have the push," she said. She never showed up for the audition, and she headed back to school. It's possible Dean Raushenbush was not surprised.

If she couldn't perform in plays, Barbara decided that perhaps she could write about them. She volunteered to be the dramatics editor and the theater and movie critic for the school newspaper, *The Campus*. She took over one column called "Reviewer's Corner" and another called "Aisle Seat." She enrolled in a course called "Theater" all four years, and at the end she managed to graduate with a liberal arts degree despite having never taken a class in science or math.

———

At Sarah Lawrence, for the first time in her life, Barbara found herself free from the limitations that her father's lifestyle and her sister's disability had placed on her.

She gained a tightknit group of girlfriends and an expansive circle of men to date, many of them future doctors and lawyers and businessmen attending nearby schools. She was admired around campus for an expensive wardrobe of silk blouses, cashmere sweaters, and plaid skirts bought at Saks Fifth Avenue and the Country Club department at Lord & Taylor. For her junior year, she was elected president of her dorm, a building with the easy-to-mock name of Titsworth. (On campus, they simply referred to it as "Sworth.") That position made her responsible for enforcing the rules, and it gave her a seat on the Student Council.

In a typical class at Sarah Lawrence, modeled on the British system of student-faculty tutorials, a small group of students would sit around a table with a professor. "What we did was talk," she recalled. "I learned to ask questions and to listen. I learned never to be afraid of speaking up." It was ideal training for a future TV interviewer. Sometimes the college president, Harold Taylor, and his wife, Grace, would invite students and teachers to their off-campus house to discuss the issues of the day. During her senior year, she was part of the college debate team that defeated three men from Yale after arguing the affirmative side of this question: "Resolved: That Traditional Education is Superior to Progressive Education."

"Cudos to Victors" was the triumphant headline over the photo on the front page of *The Campus*, the misspelling of the word "kudos" not diminishing the school spirit it conveyed. The cutline identified her by her college nickname, "Bobbie." ("Bobbie" would be a short-lived moniker.)

Down the road, she would interview the biggest newsmakers of her generation. But in college, there were few signs she was engaged by the national and international debates brewing around her. Over the onset of the Cold War with the Soviet Union. Or the early protests of the civil rights movement that would lead to sit-ins at lunch counters and the *Brown v. Board of Education* Supreme Court decision. Or Senator Joseph McCarthy's explosive claims of communist infiltration of the State Department and Hollywood and academia.

In contrast, some of her classmates were paying attention to developments beyond campus. Barbara's election as president of her dorm made the front page of the student newspaper. But the lead story in that edition of *The Campus* covered a forum discussing whether the United States and Russia could coexist peacefully. (The optimistic headline: "Peace Is Possible, Conclude Speakers.") Another front-page story reported on a campus visit by a Textile Workers Union of America leader focused on the future of the labor movement. A third chronicled a visit to the college by five women from Germany who were trying to build democratic organizations.

At her graduation, on May 30, 1951, the speaker was Henry Steele Commager, the historian and intellectual who was helping define modern American liberalism.

But Barbara called herself "a bystander." Politics had never been a part of her home life. Her father's focus was on entertainment, welcoming customers of all persuasions. "I don't remember having a single conversation about the Rosenberg case, Roy Cohn, or Senator McCarthy with my mother or father," she said. In her senior yearbook at Sarah Lawrence, in 1951, her picture is solemn and the accompanying quote, drawn from *A Midsummer Night's Dream*, is open to interpretation: "Merry and tragical! That is, hot ice and wondrous strange snow. How shall we find the concord of this discord?"

Beside each senior's photo was a small cartoon—the line drawing of a comic lion, for one, and of a leaping dancer for another. Bobbie Walters was depicted as an ostrich with its head in the sand.

THE SPEEDWRITING
SECRETARIAL SCHOOL

1951

Fresh out of Sarah Lawrence, Barbara wasn't looking for a career. She had written for the school paper, but she wasn't yet set on journalism as a profession. "All my friends seemed to know exactly what they were going to do after graduation," she said. One was going to work in an art gallery; another planned to be a social worker; others were headed to graduate school or to Europe. "That left me. What was I going to do with my life? My problem was that there was nothing that I really wanted to do, and nothing that I thought I was particularly good at."

She did want to have some fun before settling into what just about every Sarah Lawrence classmate assumed was her destiny: marriage.

What she would get as well as fun were lessons in sexual discrimination and harassment in the workplace, a reality then so pervasive that no one found it particularly notable. She would have to figure out how to handle the overtures and the affronts —sometimes to exploit them, sometimes to ignore them, only rarely to protest them head-on—then and for the rest of her life, even after she was established as a star.

In a crash course at the Speedwriting Secretarial School on 42nd Street, she learned how to type and take notes, skills more valuable for employment than her liberal arts degree. But neither of those credentials won her that first job, at an advertising agency. Her boss told her he was hiring her because he liked her legs. "I did have good legs, and I needed the job," she said later, unfazed. The small agency placed mail-order ads to sell vials of perfume advertised as "Big and Inexpensive." She and two friends who also managed to get hired there as secretaries dubbed the firm "Small and Cheap."

She described her boss as a "pink-faced man with blond hair," a would-be suitor who gave her a dog named Raul to show his affection. When he became "overly amorous"—the boss, not the dog—she decided it was time to leave.

A friend, Rhoda Rosenthal, was working at WNBT, the NBC affiliate in New York. She told her there was an opening in the station's publicity department, and Barbara applied. It was a natural fit. She may have been unsure about what, if any, career she wanted, but public relations and entertainment were the family business. Her father's name helped. As Lou Walters's daughter, she already knew the columnists the station was trying to cultivate. She met first with Ted Cott, an NBC vice president and the station's general manager, and then with Phil Dean, the director of publicity, promotion, and advertising. Dean had exactly one underling. That was the job she was hired to fill in 1952.

She wrote press releases, schmoozed columnists, covered for Dean when he returned to the office sloshed after long lunches at Toots Shor's restaurant, and had an affair with their boss. Ted Cott had made a name as a wunderkind in the world of radio. Now he was well into his thirties and in the middle of a divorce. "Ted was at least ten years older than I, balding and short, with a little bit of a belly," Barbara recalled, a description no more romantic than the one she gave her first amorous employer. She added, casually, "Even with the belly, he was the first man I slept with." It wasn't passion that prompted her to lose her virginity, she said. "I just thought it was time."

As Barbara surely knew, the relationship also offered benefits. Cott had been a protégé of TV and radio pioneer David Sarnoff, and he knew nearly everyone in the media world. When he entertained in his penthouse apartment in Greenwich Village, she would sometimes act as hostess. That was where she met PR agent Tex McCrary and TV and radio personality Eloise McElhone; both would later give her jobs. At the station, Cott assigned Barbara to work on a daily, fifteen-minute children's show called *Ask the Camera*. The director of the show was the definition of a young man in a hurry. Roone Arledge had a hard-charging personality and a distinctive shock of red hair.

"Can you imagine having Roone as the director of your local program?" Barbara asked to scattered laughter a half-century later, speaking at his funeral mass. The director of *Ask the Camera* had become a TV legend. The media elite, from Rupert Murdoch and Walter Cronkite to Michael Eisner and Peter Jennings, crowded the pews at St. Bartholomew's Episcopal Church in New York. "But there he was. Our studio was way uptown and he used to drive up every day in a convertible with the top down, even in winter," she said. "How could I ever forget that red hair and how could I ever forget that name 'Roone,' especially since I didn't pronounce my 'R's' too well."

That line got a laugh, too.

The premise of *Ask the Camera* was that children would send in questions and host Sandy Becker would show some appropriate video to illustrate the answer. But the reality of *Ask the Camera* was often backwards, Barbara acknowledged. If they had footage, say, of a pelican, "we would make sure that somebody wrote a letter about the pelican even if I had to call my mother and say, 'Mom, are you interested in how big a pelican is?'"

She would pull the clip, draft the voice-over, and help edit the film. Hunched over a Moviola machine with a film editor, she began to figure out the fundamentals of what made a good story, among them an engaging beginning and a powerful ending. "I learned how to edit this footage down to the second, and it got to the point where I could do it without a stopwatch," she boasted in 2000. "And I can still do it to this day."

Walter Winchell and Earl Wilson mentioned in their gossip columns that Lou's daughter had landed a new job, and *TV Guide* ran the first profile of her. "Young Producer" was the headline in the May 15, 1953, issue. "She may be the youngest in the field," the story said, calling her one of the "bright, young people in responsible jobs" in television. The article was illustrated by three photos of her, including one holding hands with her famous father at the Latin Quarter. When she retired, she still had a copy of that edition of the magazine.

Eventually, predictably, her workplace romance created complications. Ted kept proposing, but she wasn't interested in marrying him. She wanted to date other men. He began to stalk her, waiting outside her parents' apartment building on Central Park West for her to come home from evenings out. One night he emerged from the shadows and challenged her current boyfriend, Joe Leff, to a fistfight. They briefly came to blows. The dispute apparently cooled any ardor Joe might have been feeling; he dropped her. She dropped Ted, which in that day meant leaving her job, too. "Ted had become so obsessive and controlling that I had no choice but to quit," she said. For a woman in the 1950s, that was just the way things worked.

She managed to get another job in the business, thanks to the connections she had made through Ted. WPIX, a local New York station, hired her to produce a daily half-hour show hosted by Eloise McElhone that featured cooking lessons, fashion tips, exercise demonstrations, pet advice, and a segment called "Answer Your Male." In it, Eloise would offer relationship advice for problems submitted by viewers. But it didn't always work like that. When there weren't enough queries from the lovelorn, Barbara would draft them herself. French ballerina Colette Marchand and actress Jinx Falkenburg, a talk show host with her husband, Tex McCrary, were among the celebrity guests. Liberace once played a tiny toy piano on the air.

Barbara even filled in briefly as the on-the-air host when Eloise went to Europe on vacation. "Barbara Walters, daughter of Latin Quarter owner Lou Walters, takes over the Eloise McElhone program on WPIX, which she has been producing, while Eloise is vacationing in Europe, effective next Monday afternoon at 2:30," the TV and radio column in the *Daily News* reported in April 1954.

A few months later, the show took a break for the summer. Barbara went to Europe with Anita Coleman, the friend from Sarah Lawrence who had been a fellow secretary at the "Small and Cheap" advertising agency. They had flings with Italian men and then visited Paris, where Anita's boyfriend, Warren Manshel, was working. Manshel was the chief administrative officer of Le Congrès pour la Liberté de la Culture, an anticommunist group that turned out to be backed by the CIA; he would later be identified as working as a CIA analyst during that time. He became an investment banker in New York, founded *The Public Interest* and *Foreign Policy* magazines, and served as U.S. ambassador to Denmark under Jimmy Carter.

Warren proposed to Anita while she was visiting, and in September her parents flew over for their wedding on the isle of Capri. The local mayor performed the ceremony.

By then, Barbara had picked up a letter at the American Express office in Rome from WPIX informing her that *The Eloise McElhone Show* had been canceled. She wasn't dismayed; she was delighted by the chance to keep traveling. She went to the south of France to see friends and then to Paris, where she moved into an inexpensive hotel on the Left Bank. She got a job modeling for the House of Carven, located on the Champs-Élysées and known for its designs for petite women. At five feet five inches, she wasn't tall enough to model for the classic French designers, but she was the perfect size for Mademoiselle Marie-Louise Carven's line.

Her picture from a photo shoot on a Paris street showed a slender young woman in a stylish suit with a graceful collar, a matching chapeau on her head. She was wearing long leather gloves and carrying a small white pot with a plant. Her dark hair was cut in a short bob with bangs— "Audrey Hepburn hair," she called it—and her expression was cool and a bit aloof.

Her European adventure ended after another letter arrived, this one from her father, who had been financing her travels. "It's time for you to come home," he told her. She met him in London, where he was producing a performance of a Latin Quarter revue. Soon after he left, she sailed on the SS *United States* and headed back to Florida to visit her parents and Jackie.

———

Those days in Paris would be the most carefree time of her life. She didn't yet feel the weight of responsibility to support her parents and sister. She didn't feel the fierce need to succeed, whatever the cost to her personal life.

"I was free, free, free!" she said. As a lively young American woman in Paris, she called herself "a popular novelty" with friends and admirers. She would never forget a moment of perfect contentment one day when she sat amid the blooms at a local flower market. Years later, she bought a small work by American Impressionist Childe Hassam of that same Paris market; the painting, *Flower Girls (Peonies)*, would hang in her Fifth Avenue apartment until the day she died, a reminder of a simpler time.

When she was seventy years old, ABC was planning an around-the-world special to mark the Millennium, a broadcast that would stretch for twenty-four hours from December 31, 1999, to January 1, 2000. Peter Jennings would anchor from a makeshift newsroom at Times Square as correspondents reported in at midnight from cities around the globe. "Okay, Barbara, you get your choice," Phyllis McGrady, her former producer who was now a network vice president, told her. McGrady related the poignant conversation to me. "Where do you want to go?"

"Paris," Barbara replied. "My happiest times were in Paris." By now she was beginning to slow down a bit. "I just always feel young when I'm there."

THE MOST FORGETTABLE HUSBAND; THE MOST NOTORIOUS FRIEND

1955

When Barbara returned to Miami Beach from Paris in the winter of 1955, she met two men who would figure in her life. "I remained stead-fastly loyal to one of them in the face of enormous criticism," she said decades later. "The other I married." In retrospect, her connection with the kinetic Roy Cohn is easier to understand than her marriage to the stolid Robert Katz.

Lou Walters introduced his daughter to Cohn, a regular at his night-clubs. The ambitious young lawyer was five feet eight inches tall and trim, a natty dresser with a fighter's face. They would share the longest friend-ship Barbara ever had with a man, longer than her three marriages com-bined, and the most controversial relationship of her life.

Roy Marcus Cohn, then twenty-eight, had already gained a measure of notoriety. He was a Justice Department prosecutor in the celebrated trial of Julius and Ethel Rosenberg for espionage; they were executed in 1953. He had been in the spotlight as the chief counsel for Wisconsin senator Joseph McCarthy during the Army-McCarthy hearings in 1954; the televised Senate inquiry helped lead to the red-baiting senator's eventual censure. Barbara was twenty-five, staying with her parents and sister at the fashionable new Fontainebleau Hotel in Miami Beach after her six-month sojourn in Europe. "I have a daughter who's a great admirer of yours," Lou told Roy. "She'd like to meet you."

Precisely how she responded to the introduction is the subject of subtle dispute, though both Barbara and Roy agreed she wasn't entirely friendly. He quoted her as correcting her father: "I said I would like to meet him. I didn't say I admired him." But she would deny even that limited cordiality, recalling more of a rebuke of her father: "I *am* your daughter, but I *never* said I wanted to meet him."

(Some accounts have said Barbara and Roy dated while she was a student at Sarah Lawrence College, but both said they met in Florida in 1955.)

Undeterred by her tone, Roy called her the next day. Later, in New York, he took her to a Bronx County Democratic dinner for their first date. On their way home, she told him she was engaged to someone else, to Bob Katz. They wouldn't see one another again for three years.

From that scratchy beginning followed a romance that didn't last and a friendship that did. There was an undeniable spark of some sort between Roy, a closeted gay man, and Barbara, a connoisseur of complicated men. He would later compare her to Richard Nixon, high praise in his worldview. ("Two of a kind," he said. "Both have a crisp factuality, a no-glamour approach.") She said he looked "like a lizard" and called his role in the McCarthy hearings "despicable," but she also described him as good company. That was high praise in her worldview. She had always been able to compartmentalize her attraction to men who also had a dark side or a deep flaw.

Both Barbara and Roy were sharp and quick and loved to dish. Both appreciated fortune and fame. And both could be transactional. "I think she was his beard," helping him shield his sexual orientation, said Jessica Stedman Guff, a producer who worked for Barbara at ABC for years. "He was gossipy and smart, super-smart, and he fed her tidbits that she could use on the *Today* show. And she performed a service for him, so making him more acceptable in society."

They were closer in private than she acknowledged in public. Her ties to the most toxic lawyer in America—one who defended mobsters and beat federal charges of his own of conspiracy, bribery, and fraud—appalled the establishment in New York and Washington and became one more reason some journalists didn't accept her as entirely one of their own. "How could you possibly have had Roy Cohn for a friend?" Walter Cronkite once demanded disapprovingly.

She did little to defend Roy to him, but she also didn't break things off with her old friend. There were reasons for that, ones she didn't choose to share with Walter Cronkite.

―――――

Robert Henry Katz, then in his mid-thirties, worked for his father, Ira, a manufacturer of children's hats and caps. It was an unexciting business but a stable one. In a way, Barbara was following the course that her mother had so often expressed regret for having rejected herself. He was an eligible bachelor, and she was a young woman at loose ends. They moved in the same social circles. Getting married seemed to be the natural thing to do.

To her friends, Barbara nicknamed her fiancé "Katz Hats," an affectionate moniker but with a mocking tone. She described Bob as dark and handsome, well-mannered and a good dancer. He had graduated from the prestigious Wharton School of Finance and Commerce at the University of Pennsylvania and served in the Navy during World War II. But she also said to friends that he was boring and phlegmatic and passionless. Whatever else he might be, Roy Cohn was never boring.

She called off what she referred to as their "rather dreary engagement," prompting no protest from Katz, a passivity that somehow made him more appealing. "I could understand perfectly why I didn't want to marry him . . . but how could he not want to marry me?" she wondered. "What was wrong with me?" She changed her mind again. The wedding was back on.

"Mr. Katz, Bride Go to Europe," the *Miami Herald* headline on the story on their wedding read, her photo identified as "Mrs. Katz."

Down the road, Barbara would become the most unconventional of women, but at this point she married for the most conventional of reasons. "Young women like me graduated from college, got their first jobs, then left to get married," she said, calling it "the fifties you-must-get-married mentality." What else could she possibly do? Two days before the ceremony, she had second thoughts again. She went to her mother; her mother sent her to her father; her father said that her concerns would surely be fleeting, and that in any case, they had surfaced too late. Rooms for the ceremony and the reception had been booked at the Plaza Hotel, he noted, and the caterer and the orchestra were lined up. Matchboxes had been printed with their names and the date: June 20, 1955.

It was six months after their first date in Florida.

More than a hundred people attended the black-tie affair in the Plaza's Terrace Room, a grand space with Gilded Age opulence and crystal chandeliers that replicated those in the Palace of Versailles. *The Miami Herald* described her elegant dress, one Barbara bragged she had bought on sale at Bergdorf Goodman. "The wedding gown was a white sheath of Italian satin brocade with a silk mousseline-de-sole overdress," it said. "A long veil of illusion [a soft tulle fabric] was attached to a crown of lilies of the valley and pearl clusters." But in the accompanying photo of the bride, in full wedding regalia, Barbara looks more sardonic than aglow. The "long veil of illusion" proved to be an apt choice.

Lou Walters, ever the impresario, lined up pop star Johnnie Ray to perform at the reception; comedian Milton Berle was among the guests. Jackie was her sister's maid of honor and Ira Katz the best man for his son. The bridal couple spent their wedding night across Fifth Avenue at the Hotel Pierre, then left on a three-week honeymoon in Europe. "During many of these days, Bob was busy buying straw and ribbons for the next season's crop of children's hats," Barbara said of the trip. Not that she minded; even then she was just as happy to go sightseeing without him, surely a warning flag for their married life ahead. Engraved matchboxes wouldn't be enough to save it.

———

Bored with the life of a stay-at-home wife, Barbara began to work as a writer on *The Morning Show*, CBS's year-old effort to challenge NBC's *Today* show. It was more a way to get out of the house than it was the deliberate launch of her storied career. Her looks, not her skills, were crucial in landing the job. "I hired Barbara mostly because she had a darling ass, which I never got near," producer Charlie Andrews said in a 1988 interview with author Jerry Oppenheimer. "I was looking for a guest-getter. Barbara came up for an interview and she was obviously a sharp, aggressive, ambitious girl—and really stunning in those days."

One of the show's first hosts had been a thirty-something Cronkite; he chatted on the air about the news with a lion puppet named Charlemagne. By the time Barbara arrived, Cronkite had left and Dick Van Dyke, an aspiring actor and comedian, was one of the co-hosts; he would become an acclaimed performer on TV and in film. The job opening Barbara filled was created when Estelle Parsons moved to *Today*, the dominant morning show. Parsons, then working as a TV writer and weather girl, would later become an award-winning actor, too.

Most of the show's staffers were journalists, but her calling card—a background in show business—provoked detractors, as it would throughout her career. The journalists in the room "were either put off by the show biz bullshit or enchanted by it—and refused to admit that—or maybe a combination of both," recalled producer Robert (Shad) Northshield, a veteran of the *Chicago Sun-Times*.

With an eye to attracting female viewers, she frequently choreographed fashion shows. The producers used a rotating set of models willing to show up at the studio before dawn. One would be on the air while another was ready to come on the set next and a third was quickly changing outfits backstage.

"She came to me one day very upset," Av Westin, then the director of *The Morning Show*, told me. One of the models had canceled from a segment on swimwear. Barbara was upset and worried about the impact of the snafu on her job. "She came to me with hopes of salvaging what could be a total disaster," he said.

"What can I do?" she asked him.

"I said, 'Why don't you do it?'" he recalled.

Through necessity rather than design, Barbara appeared on network television for the first time modeling a gold-lamé swimsuit. A publicity still shows her and four other young women lying on the hard floor in the corner of an unadorned office in a line, each propped up on her elbow, their legs stretched out and artfully arranged. She was sporting a one-piece suit with decorative trim along the top and ruching down the front. With her short dark hair and broad smile, she fit right in. "I don't look half bad," she said later.

On *The Morning Show*, she also was sent out for the first time to do reporting on a breaking news story. In 1956, the Italian luxury liner *Andrea Doria* had sunk off Nantucket after colliding with the Swedish ship *Stockholm*, one of the worst maritime disasters in American history. A total of fifty-one people died; many of the passengers and crew members who had been rescued were arriving at the pier aboard the *Île de France*. "At that point, we probably were sending everybody including the elevator operator" out to try to line up interviews with the survivors, Av Westin told me.

For Barbara, it was her first lesson in the delicate process of convincing people in the midst of chaos and tragedy to tell their story to the world on television. She would need both doggedness and a display of empathy. "What a horrible experience you've been through," she said to one victim after another. "You must be feeling terrible. But could you come into our studio tomorrow morning at 7:00 a.m. to tell us about it?" To her surprise, some of them did.

"We scooped everybody," producer Jim Fleming said, crediting Barbara. "Anything you gave her to do she delivered. You could say get Herbert Hoover and she would."

Though CBS was dominating prime time—the most popular shows in 1955 were *I Love Lucy*, *The Ed Sullivan Show*, and *The $64,000 Question*, all airing on the network—those in charge still hadn't figured out morning TV. The show floundered and then folded, even after being renamed *Good Morning!* and installing a new host, Will Rogers Jr., son of the famous humorist, to replace Dick Van Dyke. Fleming briefly hired Barbara as a researcher on a proposed CBS show called *The Day That.* . . . The pilots for the series were "The Day That FDR Died" and

"The Day That a Plane Crashed into the Empire State Building." (A B-25 bomber, lost in a dense fog, flew into the seventy-ninth floor of what was then the world's tallest building and killed fourteen people.) But neither documentary made it on the air, and a few months later she was out of a job again.

The show ended. So did her marriage.

———

After three years of halfhearted efforts to stay together, the couple agreed to get a quickie divorce in Alabama, a state that required no official waiting period. Barbara traveled to Hamilton, a remote town of a few thousand people along the Buttahatchee River. She was required to swear that she was a legal resident of Alabama, where she hadn't lived a day in her life. On May 21, 1958, Circuit Court Judge Bob Moore Jr. signed the papers ending the marriage.

On the final decree, Barbara Walters Katz is listed simply as a resident of Alabama, the lines to name the city and county left empty. Neither she nor Robert H. Katz filled out the other parts of the official form with information including their date and place of birth, race, and "usual occupation." She sued for the divorce, citing legal grounds of "cruelty," a justification often given in states that didn't yet permit no-fault divorces.

In their separation agreement, Katz agreed to pay a single lump sum of $1,600 to his ex-wife as well as weekly alimony of $115 unless and until she remarried. He ended up remarrying himself in 1960, to Rita Kupsick, who coincidentally had attended the Fieldston School at the same time Barbara did. The Katzes' marriage would last for the rest of their lives. When he died in 2005, at age eighty-five, his family's paid death notice didn't mention his first wife.

Perhaps he and Barbara shared the same instinct—to erase the memory of the marriage as a youthful mistake.

"She never talked about it," Bill Geddie, her longtime producer, told me. "When you said, 'How many times were you married?' she always said 'two.' I said, 'But what about . . .' She would reply, 'No, that doesn't count.'" (Her denial of the incontrovertible truth was reminiscent of her grandmother's insistence on her deathbed that she was a virgin, despite having given birth to seven children.) For years, Barbara succeeded in making her first husband effectively disappear, no small trick after a society wedding held at the Plaza and reported in newspapers in New York and Miami. When she married entertainment executive Merv Adelson in 1986, the wire services called it her second marriage, after Lee Guber, not her third. A fan paperback titled *Barbara Walters: TV's SuperLady*, published in 1976, was promoted as "revealing" her wedding to Katz. "She regards him as a taboo subject," the book reported.

Later, in a lavish spread in *Newsweek*, Barbara acknowledged that she had been married, briefly and "sadly," to a businessman whose name she declined to disclose. "The marriage was annulled after eleven months," the newsmagazine reported. That wasn't accurate. The marriage lasted three years, from 1955 to 1958, and ended in divorce.

She would recognize her unhappiness more than a decade later when she saw *Diary of a Mad Housewife*, a movie released in 1970 during the awakening of the women's movement about an educated woman trapped in a loveless marriage. Barbara herself found keeping house stultifying, even after her husband agreed to move from his Greenwich Village apartment to her preferred neighborhood on the Upper East Side. She saw a psychiatrist to discuss her frustrations; she decided the therapist, "a young man with a placid face," had nothing helpful to offer.

Apparently, though, there were no hard feelings. A quarter-century after her quick trip to Alabama, Barbara was entering a building in New York to go to a dinner party when a man who looked vaguely familiar was leaving. He said hello; she said hello. That was all. "My God," she exclaimed to her escort. "That was my first husband!"

CATASTROPHE

1957

Lou Walters would make a fortune, lose a fortune, gain it back and then gamble it away. At the moment when things were at their best, he seemed to feel an irresistible impulse to risk it all. His family said the loss of his right eye as a boy meant he somehow couldn't quite track what was going on during those marathon gin rummy games, although that hardly explains the compulsion that made him play, and bet. No success slaked his thirst for more, a trait he would pass on to his daughter. He had already been dubbed "the modern Ziegfeld" by the gossip columnists in New York. But he bristled at the budget constraints set by his business partner, and he longed to launch a string of even more spectacular clubs that would be all his own.

The cost of that ambition would prove to be catastrophic.

His wife and younger daughter had painful memories of Lou's propensity to press his luck, financially and otherwise. But while risk terrified Dena, Lou craved it. He reassured her, "Don't worry. I'm opening another nightclub that will be even more successful." The New York Latin Quarter was now grossing $5 million a year. Lou thought his name and his showmanship could translate to big profits at his own club.

His vaulting vision had long clashed with E. M. Loew's desire to score the largest possible profit. "I knew the blood had been bad between them for years," Barbara said later. "Loew continued to challenge every penny my father spent on costumes, on scenery, on talent, until my father couldn't stand it anymore. So he walked away from the gold mine he had founded and sold his share in the Latin Quarter to the partner he had long detested."

After fifteen years, their partnership was over, although as with many divorces it took months to negotiate the details. "Lou Walters and E. M. Loew huddling all week over the final settlement of the divorce," Lee Mortimer reported in his *New York Daily Mirror* column in January 1958. In the end, Loew got the Latin Quarter and Walters got $500,000. He signed away rights to use his name to advertise a competing club for three years, a provision he would rue. Another associate, Cass Franklin, gained control of Lou Walters Enterprises, which was in the lucrative business of booking trade shows; Franklin also took over the representation of an odd lot of performers, including big band singer Betty George and Turkish belly dancer Nejla Ates.

The final spectacular that Walters mounted at the club, called "Latin Quarter Follies," had his characteristic panache as well as a flashback to his vaudeville roots. Onstage were acts including singer Gillian Grey, comedian Jack Durant, mime George Manson, a dancing duo known as the Szonys, and a pop group called the Debonairs. The show also featured the Morlidor Trio, a European acrobatic act. Two showgirls pulled a rag doll from an oversized toy chest—the doll was a white man wearing blackface and a clownlike costume—and then moved him into contortionist positions as the band played. In time, the "golliwog" rag doll and the use of blackface would be recognized and decried as racist caricatures.

"No swan song," Mortimer wrote in "New York Confidential." "The fabulous Lou Walters produced his greatest show and then bowed out of the world-famed Latin Quarter which he built 15 years ago." The syndicated columnist called the nightclub a monument to Lou and "a

Mecca for merrymakers, the last of the landmarks that made Broadway an international synonym for brightness and beauty and carefree happiness."

After the final curtain came down on the midnight show, the cast and crew threw Lou a surprise party with gifts, speeches, and tears.

Lou plowed all his profits into his new venture, with the initial Café de Paris set to open in Miami Beach. (The club's first reservation had a private resonance: a fundraising dinner for the Hope School for Retarded Children, which would later provide a place for daughter Jackie.) As the decorator, he hired Rube Bedenhorn, who had designed the original Latin Quarter in Boston. Lou had innovations in mind himself. "Lou's new ideas include a water curtain encircling the stage, a transparent plastic stage hiding the orchestra, remote applications without mike cords, live foundations and other splendiferous novelties in the historic Walters' fashion," Mortimer reported, "but he's sticking to one old stand-by for which no new improvements have been invented: Gals!"

Nearly nude showgirls were part of the draw in a Lou Walters production, cast not as tawdry exhibitionism but as art, as a sort of European-style sophistication. When the Café de Paris opened in Miami Beach in December 1957, cabaret singer Danielle Lamar was the star attraction. She brought "songs, routines and Dior gowns straight from Paris," columnist Leonard Lyons gushed, with a "show-topper" that came with a story: She had found her striking yellow toreador pants in a shop on the Riviera where Pablo Picasso happened to be browsing; they ended up sharing lunch and he autographed the pants for her.

Not even Picasso-endorsed toreador pants turned out to be enough, though. The country headed into a recession in August that year, and an uncharacteristically cold winter in Florida dampened the flight of snowbirds there in search of warmth and a good time. The Café de Paris had closed its doors and filed for bankruptcy by spring, six months after it opened.

That setback didn't discourage Walters from moving his wife and older daughter to the Hotel Navarro and trying again in New York with another Café de Paris.

By now, Barbara was twenty-eight years old and aimless. She had followed the get-married script of her friends, but that relationship had ended in a whimper and a quickie divorce. The CBS documentary series she had been hired for as a researcher had been canceled without an episode making it on the air. She stayed with a high school friend at the family's apartment on the Upper East Side as she tried to figure out what to do with the rest of her life.

Lou, as always, expressed confidence that any problems were passing ones. An economic downturn could be a good thing for the nightclub business, he insisted. "Back in Boston in '32, people were selling apples on the street. The week Roosevelt closed the banks was the biggest week I ever had at the old Cascade Roof," he said. "When things are tough people are likely to go out at night. They need a first-class escape, and I'm going to give it to them."

But it was not 1932 anymore. Now people could get a first-class escape sitting in their living rooms. The singers and comics and acrobats who had drawn crowds to the Cascade Roof were being booked by *The Ed Sullivan Show* on CBS. Outside of Las Vegas, the era of the big nightclubs was fading. Lou recognized the existential threat from TV. In 1957, Johnnie Ray had a contract to perform at the Latin Quarter, but Lou raised such a ruckus about his appearances on television that the singing sensation switched to the Waldorf instead. There was this irony: The burgeoning TV industry would help usher Lou into financial ruin, then make his daughter rich and famous.

The new Café de Paris was constructed in the old Arcadia Ballroom on Broadway, near 53rd Street. The nightclub was bigger than any New York had ever seen, featuring six stages and the capacity to seat 1,200 people. It was five blocks north of Lou Walters's Latin Quarter.

But he encountered problems at every turn, some of them from rival club owners. He suspected Loew was fomenting trouble behind the scenes, encouraging the union reps and the restaurant suppliers and the city inspectors to make things hard for him. Loew even won a temporary injunction in New York State Supreme Court to block Lou from putting his own name on the marquee. (As Loew's lawyers argued, the contract Walters had signed with Loew prevented him from using his name to promote a competing New York nightclub for three years.)

In a wink to his most loyal patrons, Walters instead put up in lights the name of one of the showgirls most identified with him, one who had been willing to walk the stage wearing nothing but a G-string. "Chickie James Presents Café de Paris," the marquee read.

The feud with his former business partner and other complications pushed back the planned opening of the new club for two weeks, from May 6 to May 20. Then it was delayed a few days more. The liquor license wasn't approved until hours before the bar began to sell drinks. Finally, on May 22, the Café de Paris opened in New York. It featured Walters's classic over-the-top touches. The color scheme was shocking pink and golden white. A swimming tank shaped like a giant goblet featured an all-but-naked "mermaid" swimming in it—actually, stripteaser Sherry Britton.

On opening night, Barbara sat at a table with her mother and sister, just like the old days at the Latin Quarter. "Lou Walters' new Café de Paris is one of the handsomest night clubs ever opened in N.Y., and Betty Hutton gave it a memorable premiere," Earl Wilson wrote. Hutton, who had starred a few years earlier in the hit movie *Annie Get Your Gun*, "sings, dances and mugs winningly."

The review by Dorothy Kilgallen was more mixed and more prescient. Hutton "is as cute and pretty as anything on Broadway, with a flawless figure and as much vitality as she had when she was 17," Kilgallen wrote in her column. But Hutton's comedy bit bombed, with jokes about figures from the vaudeville stage "that nobody under 60 in the audience could possibly identify with"—a warning that showbiz was moving past Lou's era.

"Welcome to Lou Walters' rent party," Hutton greeted the packed house at the launch, a joke that hit close to home. Word was that Walters had signed a lease with the highest rent of any club in New York, $125,000 a year. He was paying a premium for his star performer, too, at $22,500 a week. He counted $70,000 in revenue that first week, but that was still $10,000 short of expenses.

Even so, after her nine-day run he begged Hutton to sign up for another two weeks. She refused. "I'm really in a fix," he worried. "Who do I get of her stature? There's no one available at a minute's notice." The last-minute replacement, eccentric rock-and-roller Jerry Lee Lewis, proved to be no draw, and unreliable; he didn't show up after the first night.

The club was floundering. In what could have been a metaphor, the oversized goblet cracked and shattered, sending the mermaid to the hospital and drenching customers seated nearby.

Lou frantically tried to raise enough funds to keep the Café de Paris afloat. His skeptical relatives in New Jersey, the ones he had helped support as a teenager after their family immigrated from London, turned him down. "Look, Lou, we'll loan you money for yourself, but we're not giving you any more money for your nightclub," one of his younger brothers told him. Lou managed to borrow from the club's maître d' and the waiters and the busboys and the cigarette girls.

By then, Barbara had started a job at a public relations firm; she had saved a grand total of $3,000. She gave Lou all of it. She would always do whatever it took to rescue her father, even from disasters of his own making. There was a sobering lesson here from her mother, too: Fame and fortune could be fleeting, and one wrong move could destroy the work of a lifetime.

12

"A HALO OF FEAR"

1958

When Dena Walters found her husband ashen-faced and unconscious in their hotel bed, his bottle of sleeping pills emptied, she didn't call an ambulance.

She called their daughter.

Barbara had just gotten divorced and moved temporarily to the family apartment of her friend Marilyn Landsberger. The two young women were having breakfast that Saturday morning when Dena phoned.

"I can't wake your father up," her mother said, her voice frantic. "He just won't wake up!"

Barbara ran to the street and hailed a cab for the Hotel Navarro on Central Park South, a mile away, where her parents were staying. When she got there, she tried to shake her unconscious father awake—"Daddy! Daddy!" she shouted—as her mother and sister watched. Jackie, who as always was living with her parents, didn't fully understand what was happening but she knew it was a crisis. Lou didn't respond. Barbara was the one who called for an ambulance. After the paramedics arrived and loaded her father on a stretcher, she was the one who rode with him to Mount Sinai Hospital.

"Daddy, Daddy, Daddy," she repeated, sitting next to him in the back, stroking his face. *Please, God*, she prayed, a practice she wasn't sure she believed in and almost never exercised. *Don't let him die.*

She and her father had never been given to heartfelt conversations. He had been a distant figure, his praise and his embrace rare. By the time she came home from school, he would usually be at the nightclubs he ran; when she left the next morning, he would still be asleep. She spent more time with her disgruntled mother, listening to a litany of his faults. At the elite private schools she attended, she worried he was less respectable than the fathers who worked as doctors or lawyers or on Wall Street.

He had been a mercurial breadwinner, making a fortune that meant they sometimes lived in the most fabulous penthouses, but always with the risk that he might gamble it all away. That was precisely what he had done this time. Now everyone's money was gone, the nightclub was headed toward bankruptcy, and his reputation as the grandest impresario in the city was in jeopardy.

Throughout her life, Barbara had felt a roiling mix of emotions toward her father—anger, resentment, annoyance, embarrassment. But there was love, too, and pride. Lou Walters was a man of charm and guile and an irrepressible belief in himself and in his success. "A sorcerer of magic and fantasy," she eventually concluded. She yearned for his approval and worried she didn't have it. She didn't have to invest all her savings to save a business she suspected was doomed. She didn't have to race home to help him out of his latest misfortune. But she did.

She quickly pieced together what had happened.

The night before, when headliner Jerry Lee Lewis hadn't shown up, Lou had left the club earlier than usual. In his hotel bathroom, he swallowed an overdose of the sleeping pills he had been taking for years, handfuls of them, then lay down to die. There was no doubt that it was intentional; the sheer quantity of pills he had swallowed made that clear. At the hospital that morning, after his stomach was pumped and his life saved, he was put in a room on the ground floor, a precaution for suicidal patients who might be tempted to jump out the window on a higher floor.

Dena had stayed behind at the hotel for fear of traumatizing Jackie.

Now they arrived at the hospital, too, and hovered. After he was conscious, Lou didn't say a word to any of them about the suicide attempt that had brought them all here. "Not then," Barbara said, "not ever."

She understood in an instant that everything was about to change for her. She didn't have a husband or a paycheck. But now she needed to be the adult in the family again, just as she had been when she stitched her parents' disintegrating marriage together again at the age of fourteen. She was in charge now—responsible for her suicidal father, her anxious mother, her disabled sister, and her own survival. Whatever the uncertainties ahead, she would have to provide the financial and emotional ballast to keep them all afloat, now and for the rest of their lives.

"Everything I had always dreaded might happen *had* happened," she would recall a half-century later. "There was no time to cry and I was too busy to feel sorry for myself."

The drive, the energy, the empathetic core that helped her connect with people in crisis had all been ignited by a fear for her security and her family's well-being. She would always feel that calamity lurked just around the corner, and that it was up to her to prevent it.

"I think a halo of fear affected Barbara and affects her today," Lou would say years later.

Barbara had been trying to figure out what to do with her life. Life had just figured that out for her.

———

No one had to warn the daughter of Lou Walters about the perils of bad press.

At the hospital, once her father's stomach had been pumped, she recognized the risks to his reputation and his future prospects if word got out he had tried to take his own life. On this, when it came to imperatives about telling the truth, she would have a show business perspective, not a journalistic one. Sometimes bad news required a shiny finish.

She and her mother confided in almost no one about the suicide attempt, then or decades later. Barbara was determined to get out her own version of what had happened, a version that could take hold before anybody heard something different. It wouldn't be the last time she did whatever it took—shaving the truth, cashing in chits, accepting favors from questionable characters—to protect her father and her family.

She decided to call Walter Winchell, the most influential gossip columnist of the day. They had met occasionally at the Latin Quarter. She told him that her hardworking, softhearted father was exhausted and had suffered a mild heart attack. Winchell could have the story as an exclusive. The first mention in Winchell's column said simply that Walters had been hospitalized "after several setbacks (and worry)" and mentioned that he had been offered a new gig with a Vegas hotel, a bit of gilding Barbara presumably had concocted. But by the next day, Winchell had learned the hard truth; he tucked a thirty-three-word item in the middle of his column. "Café de Paris chief Lou Walters took an overdose (over 100 pills) to stop the agony of all those Bad Breaks," he wrote. "His worried wife (shaking him for an 8 a.m. appointment) saved him."

Everyone in New York's entertainment world read Winchell's column like a Bible; they all would have seen the news. But Barbara managed to neutralize even his influential voice. In the same issue of the *New York Mirror* in which Winchell reported the overdose, Broadway columnist Lee Mortimer a few pages later said Walters was "suffering from exhaustion and a heart attack." A few days after that, Hy Gardner wrote in his "Night Letter" column that Walters was "bedded at Mt. Sinai following what his medics describe as exhaustion and a mild heart attack." The "medics" quoted might well have been Barbara herself. Her cover story, not Winchell's reporting, would become the accepted version of the truth, just as she had hoped. Two decades later, the *New York Times* obituary for Lou reported flatly that in 1958 he had "suffered a heart attack and went to Florida to recover."

"Seems like everyone is pulling for the game little fellow lying on his back at Mount Sinai Hospital, suffering from exhaustion and a heart attack," Mortimer wrote in his "New York Confidential" column. "Lou Walters' sad plight has all Broadway sympathizing with him—and rooting," Dorothy Kilgallen said. Gardner rallied support, too. "The fight to keep the Café de Paris open and sparkling during courageous host Lou

Walters' recuperation from a heart attack is everybody's fight in show business and Broadway," he wrote.

But there wasn't enough time or star power to save the Café de Paris. On June 20, soon after Lou had been discharged from the hospital, the club filed for bankruptcy. Its liabilities were listed at a crushing $500,000, the same amount he had gotten for selling his share of the Latin Quarter a year earlier. Creditors and vendors showed up to demand payment, to seize the furniture, to claim the costumes. Barbara stopped by the club to ask for a single memento, her father's typewriter.

His indefatigable ambitions had been extinguished, at least for a while. Hers had been ignited, forever.

For the first time in her life, perhaps an acknowledgment of her new responsibilities, she decided to live on her own. She rented an apartment in a building owned by friends of her parents, at 69th Street and Second Avenue. The neighborhood wasn't yet particularly fashionable and the view was dismal, overlooking the backs of other buildings. But it was cheap and it was rent-controlled, and it was hers.

Her parents could no longer afford to stay in the Hotel Navarro. They headed back to Miami Beach, to the house they had kept on North Bay Road. In lieu of counseling or even conversation about all that had happened, they took to playing endless games of gin rummy, even as everything seemed to be closing in around them. A year later, the Latin Quarter in Miami Beach, the jewel Lou had launched that led to his New York enterprises, burned to the ground.

Another year would pass before Lou would come to terms with the darkness that had enveloped him. But the debts he left in his wake wouldn't wait. Now they were Barbara's problem.

Enter Louis Chesler.

He was a big, bluff man, a Canadian with Ukrainian roots and mobster ties, and a friend of Lou. Chesler grew up poor, but he had a knack for making money, not all of it by meticulously legal means. He made a fortune developing land in Florida and helped establish casino gambling in the Bahamas, an industry notorious for its ties to organized crime. He became chairman of the board of Seven Arts Productions Ltd., a major film production and distribution company that allegedly was used to launder money for the mob. Legendary New York prosecutor Robert Morgenthau described him as "just another bagman for Lansky." That would be Meyer Lansky, also known as "the Mob's Accountant."

Chesler's profitable enterprises and shady associates drew the attention first of the Royal Canadian Mounted Police and then of the FBI, which amassed hundreds of pages of files on him from the 1950s to the 1980s. In 1959, an informant told the FBI that Chesler was an "anonymous donor" who gave $25,000 to the Baltimore Colts for winning the National Football League's championship over the New York Giants the previous December. (Presumably it was no coincidence that Chesler was said to have won $230,000 in a bet on the legendary game, decided in a sudden death overtime.) In 1964, in a message from FBI headquarters, the Miami and New York field offices were instructed to review information about Chesler's "connections to gamblers and hoodlums" to determine whether he had violated federal gambling statutes. In 1967, FBI files described him as the "notorious gambler Lou Chesler" who was "believed to be fronting for hoodlum Meyer Lansky." In 1981, Chesler was reported being seen with "large amounts of currency," believed to be money "made from large dope deals."

He owned the building in Miami Beach that Lou had rented for the original Café de Paris. He was also a regular at the club, known as a great craps player and as a participant in the marathon gin rummy games Lou hosted.

Barbara's upbringing had made her comfortable with powerful men— she was the same person who had tried to espy Al Capone on her bike and dated Roy Cohn—and willing to suspend the judgments of their character held by law enforcement. As for Chesler, she described him as a "saint" who rescued her, albeit a saint she allowed herself to acknowledge had "a rather dubious reputation."

Later, the two of them would offer competing explanations about exactly what happened during their 1958 encounter, but in both versions of the story she was desperate for help. "I became obsessed with finding the money to pay off as many of my father's debts as I could," she said. "I didn't know where I was going to find this money." There seemed to be no point in reaching out to her father's family; they had refused his appeal for a loan to try to keep the doors of the Café de Paris open in New York. "We were suddenly bereft," she said.

In Barbara's account, Chesler called her out of the blue to ask how Lou was doing in the hospital. She said he was in "bad shape," although she didn't mention the suicide attempt. She assured him the family would be all right. He asked if her father had debts. When she said he did, Chesler made "an amazing offer."

"With no more questions asked, he lent me $20,000, a very substantial amount of money at that time, or any time for that matter," and told her that she didn't need to pay him back, she recalled decades later. "I was grateful beyond words and I certainly didn't refuse the loan—my pride was no stronger than my need." But she insisted on repaying it, and she did, "little bit by little bit over the years."

Chesler's version of what happened, in an account that seems more credible on its face, casts Barbara less as the unwitting beneficiary of manna from heaven and more as the architect of her fate. He remembered the amount involved as $15,000.

He told a mutual friend, Irving Zussman, that Barbara called him and asked for an emergency loan to cover some of her father's debts, presumably for gambling. He didn't mind; he admired her for it. "This girl can have anything she wants from me," he said. In his world, $15,000 or $20,000 was small change. He confirmed that, over time, she paid it back. "Bit by bit every week she made payments until she cleaned up the debt."

Four years later, when she finally began earning what she called "pretty good money" as a writer on *Today*, about $500 a week, she was still sending regular payments to Chesler. She declined his offer to forgive the loan, and she never told her father what she had done for fear of humiliating him.

———

Barbara wouldn't publicly acknowledge her father's suicide attempt for a half-century, not until after her father and then her sister and finally her mother had passed away. Friends and colleagues who had been close to her for decades told me they had never heard a word about it until she recounted it in her autobiography, published in 2008.

One of those was Bob Iger, whose career at ABC spanned her own. He had been a production assistant on the *ABC Evening News* when Barbara arrived there in 1976; by the time she retired in 2014, he was CEO of the Disney Company, which owned the network. After he read her book, he confided his own story to her. His father had struggled with severe manic depression.

He and Barbara discussed how their childhood experiences had affected their lives. "Talk about hardening one's skin," he told me. "I think the Barbara that we witnessed, with all of her resilience, and toughness, and competitiveness, was very much a product of that upbringing."

Looking back at her life, she had wondered if her father's financial and emotional fall was the essential element in her rise. She called it "the big question."

"If my parents had not descended into financial ruin, would I have had the success I have had?" she asked. After some back-and-forth, she concluded with Lou-style bravado that the answer was "definitely yes!" Her career was her destiny, she insisted. Of course, it's true that the ingredients of her success were already there—her smarts and her stamina, her curiosity and her comfort with the prominent and the powerful. She reveled in her work, in the money and the fame. She loved the competitive chase for the biggest interviews and the acclaim for the groundbreaking broadcasts they created.

But decades of success can sometimes cast a gloss over the reality of the past. There were times Barbara let herself drift back to the day that changed her forever. Four decades after her father attempted suicide, she confided, "I still remember the ambulance." At that time, she hadn't yet demonstrated the drive, the focus, the initiative that would enable her to triumph in a way no woman and few men had succeeded before. Those characteristics didn't emerge in full until the desperate phone call from her mother that spring morning in 1958.

13

SUNRISE

1958

Earning a paycheck had never been much of an imperative for Barbara before. But now she needed more than the $115-a-week in alimony she was getting from Bob Katz. She couldn't find the sort of job she wanted back in television, so she took the job she could get, in public relations.

She went to work for Tex McCrary, Inc.

John Reagan "Tex" McCrary Jr. was a prominent PR man and newspaper columnist with a sideline in Republican politics. He pioneered the radio talk show format in shows called *Tex and Jinx* and *Hi Jinx*, co-hosted with his wife, actress Jinx Falkenburg. Their offices were in the storied Hudson Theatre on 44th Street, just off Times Square. A narrow wooden door behind the box office, discovered in a 2017 renovation, still bears their name in peeling gold letters: "National Broadcasting Company/Tex and Jinx Productions." They were also known for broadcasting from Peacock Alley, the colonnade in the Waldorf-Astoria, interviewing celebrities as they checked in or out of the ritzy hotel.

In 1952, Tex McCrary staged a rally in Madison Square Garden that helped convince a skeptical General Dwight D. Eisenhower there was a groundswell of public support for him to run for president; Ike would run and win two terms in the White House. At the opening of the American National Exhibition at Moscow's Sokolniki Park in 1959, McCrary's firm produced one of the most famous PR coups of all times on behalf of its client, All-State Properties, Inc., a builder of upscale tract homes. When Vice President Richard Nixon was giving Soviet leader Nikita Khrushchev a tour of a "typical" American home at the exhibition, a McCrary staffer managed to maneuver the two men into the sparkling all-electric kitchen for what became a lively exchange on the merits of capitalism. Dubbed the "Kitchen Debate," their impromptu conversation would air on all three American TV networks and in the Soviet Union. It was a triumph of product placement.

The McCrary staffer who orchestrated that moment was William Safire, the head of the firm's Radio and Television Department and, later, Barbara's boss. He would become a speechwriter in the Nixon White House and a columnist for *The New York Times*. But now, despite the impressive name, the Radio and Television Department's staff consisted, in its entirety, of Safire, his secretary, and Barbara. Her job was to draft press releases and pitch clients for TV and radio hits, regardless of their camera-readiness. McCrary gave her a mimeographed tract called "Couch Questions" on how to pre-interview guests for his radio show, guidance that she would adapt as her own style for the remainder of her career. McCrary offered the sensible advice that, to get clients comfortable with being interviewed, Barbara start with easy questions and then move to tougher ones. He suggested that she ask something offbeat to prompt a revealing response. One of his examples: "If you could be any character in history, who would you choose to be?"

"I didn't have the foggiest notion about her father's problems," about the personal situation that made her desperate for a job, Safire said years later, after Barbara was a famous broadcaster and he was a Pulitzer Prize–winning columnist. "She didn't make a point of it. I hired her strictly on merit. It struck me she would be a perfect woman to pitch guests to radio and television producers. She wasn't making much more than a secretary. But people would kill for those jobs. They were glamorous jobs, and frankly fast-track jobs."

Fearful of failure, Barbara became a workaholic, on that job and those that followed, eating lunch at her desk and almost never missing a day of work. She pitched a one-armed golfer to TV bookers. She got a client, the Lionel Trains Company, regular placement on the *Today* show; the host, forty-five-year-old Dave Garroway, happened to be a model train aficionado. For a Christmas show, he demonstrated the delights of an elaborate train setup Lionel Trains had erected on the set. Then he took it home. In those days before payola got a bad name, Barbara made sure to keep a continuing supply of Lionel locomotives and cabooses on track to Garroway.

She grew to hate the PR job, her "Dark Ages," she would later call it. Hired at $60 a week, she also concluded she was underpaid. When she summoned up the courage to ask for a raise, though, Safire replied with an unapologetic lecture on the sexist realities of the day. "Barbara, there are a great many young women in this big city who would give their eye teeth for this kind of job and that's why, because there's an enormous supply of labor for this job, we are able to get somebody for this low," he told her. "So supply exceeds demand, which is why the salary is so low, and that's why you're not getting a raise." He said she should be "grateful" for what she had.

By now, Barbara had turned thirty. Many of her girlfriends from high school and college were not only married but had started families. She was still scrimping to pay back the loan she had taken from Louis Chesler to cover her father's debts. She didn't have the movie-star looks of the few women who were landing roles on the air, and women were rarely considered for the broadcast jobs behind the scenes.

"There still seemed to be nothing for me in television, so I took myself to a top employment agency, deciding it was about time to start a new career," she said. The firm immediately offered her a job working for it, screening and hiring secretaries to send out to prospective jobs. It is hard to imagine an occupation more distant from the one she wanted. "They gave me a couple of days to decide," she said, "and I was on the verge of saying yes."

Then *Redbook* called. The women's magazine, full of advice for homemakers and known for its literary fiction, was looking for someone to promote its articles. The editors thought of her because of her PR experience at Tex McCrary's firm. They offered her a raise. It was hardly her dream job—she reported being bored and unhappy there—but at least it kept her in the media mix and out of the world of secretarial employment. She took it.

Within a few months, however, something closer to her dream job did open up. The *Today* show needed a researcher and writer. The gig was temporary, with a thirteen-week contract and a paycheck of about $300 a week. For once, her gender was an asset, not a liability. The job was to produce a daily, five-minute segment aimed at female viewers, sponsored by S&H Green Stamps, an early shopping rewards program. The show was hosted by Anita Colby, an actress and socialite nicknamed "The Face" who had been a supermodel and a force in Hollywood and New York. "She had class and looks and was of a certain age," Barbara said, "something that was much admired in those days before television wanted everyone to be young, young, young." She accepted the job on the spot.

In her retelling, the show's producer had called her with the offer in a bit of serendipity, or perhaps divine intervention. "Then, one absolutely wonderful day, I got a call from the new producer of the *Today* show, Fred Freed, saying he needed a writer," she said. "It wouldn't be a long-term job, he told me, it was for a limited time on a limited segment, but if I wanted to try it, it was mine. Did I want to try it? Is the pope Catholic?"

But others who were there described the job offer as the result of her relentless efforts and skillful use of her connections. She had kept in touch with Freed, one of her bosses when she had worked as a writer and gofer for a short-lived morning show at CBS. When he took the job at *Today*, then in the midst of turmoil as Garroway sank into mental illness and paranoia, she checked in with Freed again. At her request, Lester Cooper, a mutual friend from CBS, put in a good word for her. So did Paul Cunningham, a reporter at *Today*. When she was working for McCrary, she had turned a chance encounter with Cunningham at the Miami airport into a networking opportunity. He needed someone to ferry some film to the NBC offices in New York. It was footage of an interview he had done with a young Cuban revolutionary named Fidel Castro. She had volunteered to help.

Freed's wife, Judy, weighed in, too. "I had good judgment and he trusted me," she recalled decades later. "He gave me a rundown about Barbara. She obviously had the credentials and the background. Fred didn't feel *Today* was a serious journalistic show, so she seemed right for that sort of thing; and I was always eager for him to hire women. I said she sounds great, terrific. As long as Barbara didn't make life ridiculous for him, I just don't think he cared that much."

There was the rub, the double bind: *"As long as Barbara didn't make life ridiculous for him."*

That is, as long as she wasn't one of those pushy broads, although surely being pushy was a prerequisite for getting the job, especially for a broad. Sexism in the workplace was a given, at the time rarely questioned even by those who were victims of it. Betty Friedan's landmark *The Feminine Mystique* wouldn't be published for another two years; the women's liberation movement wouldn't begin to gain traction until later in the decade. Barbara had the job skills needed, but Freed assigned an associate producer, Craig Fisher, to take her to lunch and make sure she wasn't one of those women who would make trouble. Fisher came back recommending she be hired, though he also reported, "Barbara was obviously very verbal—and very intense."

She was also very ambitious, a trait she was still masking in her memoir a half-century later, even after all the success that her ambition had delivered. She still seemed worried the drive that would be considered admirable in a man would be seen as unseemly in a woman. The kind of woman who might make life ridiculous for her boss, some might say. Instead, she described getting her toehold in the business, and then getting on the air, as something that happened to her, however happily. Not something she had indefatigably engineered, against the odds.

———

Barbara began an early-morning routine that she would continue in various roles for the next fifteen years.

When she was hired, the plan was to tape the five-minute segment that aired on the *Today* show the previous evening. But on the day Barbara's first taped program was to air, on April 12, 1961, major news broke. The Soviet Union launched cosmonaut Yuri Gagarin into orbit, an unsettling victory for the Cold War adversary in the space race. The taped segments were scrapped. From then on, Garroway declared, the entire show would be done live.

She would take a cab from her apartment, then on 79th Street, to the NBC studio, arriving at 4:30 a.m. to get ready for the daily segment. The topics were fashion, beauty trends, and how-to advice—how to tie a scarf, how to entertain at home, how to prepare for the holidays. When the program ended that day, she would book the guests and draft the on-air patter for the next morning.

Anita Colby, the segment's host, was beautiful and poised, with a silky demeanor. She was just the sort of woman Barbara envied and resented, then and always. They were the sort who had made her feel clumsy and unwelcome when she was the newcomer at Fieldston and Birch Wathen. In her view, they were confident and fashionable and oblivious to the hurdles she had to face.

"Anita was very much a lady and a nice one, too, but she was limited as a performer," Barbara said dismissively. "She had done little television, and all this was extremely difficult for her. Her life was dinner parties and supper clubs. We could never do a cooking or food feature, for example, because Anita could barely find her way into her own kitchen." (The aside is ironic given the limited time Barbara spent in a kitchen herself. She favored bologna sandwiches for dinner until she was in a position to employ a cook.) Decades later, she would have the same reaction to rival Diane Sawyer at ABC.

But Anita, like Diane, was more than a pretty face. She was the first American supermodel, commanding an unheard-of $100 an hour. She was an actress, albeit a mediocre one, and an entrepreneur. She filed a patent for a chair that could convert into a bed. She wrote a beauty book, bought and sold the Women's News Service, and syndicated a newspaper column called "Anita Says." She was an influencer before there was social media. Movie mogul David O. Selznick hired her as his studio's "feminine director," a role that landed her on the cover of *Time* magazine in 1945. "'The Face' has a brain to match," the headline read.

She understood Barbara better than Barbara understood herself. She knew something about ambitious women operating in a man's world, although the sheer force of Barbara's drive took even her aback. Anita was forty-six years old when they met—"of a certain age," as Barbara had said. Barbara was fifteen years younger.

"Had I been the same age as Barbara, I'm not sure I would have been too happy about her because I think she would have killed me," Anita said with a laugh. It was a joke with a germ of truth. "She had a bit of pushiness and aggressiveness. I was not as forward as she."

She realized Barbara didn't want to stay behind the scenes; she wanted to be in front of the camera. "She didn't make any bones about it," Anita recalled. "She told me, 'I'd love to do this someday.'" Her description of her assistant sounds reminiscent of the 1950 movie *All About Eve*, about a calculating Hollywood protégée who pushes aside her mentor. "I could see, when I was on the air, the way she'd stand off to the side and mouth the words she'd written for me," Anita said. "She was pining to be in my spot."

When Anita offered to put in a good word for her with their bosses and to take her to her diction teacher, Barbara was elated. "Oh, yes. Oh, God. I want it so badly," Barbara told her. "I do. I do!"

The session with the voice coach didn't go well; her inability to pronounce "r's" would become the stuff of a classic *Saturday Night Live* lampoon. But Anita gave Barbara the chance to occasionally be seen on the air, if not heard. Her first appearance on *Today* was just a glimpse when she was covering a fashion-week show while Anita narrated the story from the studio. For a story about Revlon opening a salon in midtown Manhattan, Barbara was the willing mannequin, her body wrapped in a sheet, her face smeared with goop, her feet dangling into a little pond while she got a pedicure on the air.

That fall, after sponsoring the segment for another thirteen weeks, S&H Green Stamps decided not to renew the series. Anita was out. She expressed few regrets; the early-morning schedule hadn't been a good fit with her life as a socialite on the party circuit with her celebrity friends.

"Anita may have been fine with being fired, but I was distraught," Barbara would recall. "I thought the ax was going to fall on me, too. No

Clark Gable was going to whisk me away to El Morocco. For me it would be back to the employment agency. But just before the ax fell, lightning struck and my life changed, never to be the same again." The only woman on the eight-person writing team for *Today* was leaving to get married. Since the tradition was that one woman, and only one, could be on the writing team at a time, that created an opening for her.

Lightning may have struck, but once again she had been manipulating the weather. From the start, she knew the S&H Green Stamps segment wasn't going to last forever. She had been cultivating relationships with the producers, the directors, the camera operators, the floor managers, the writers.

"I never saw anybody who covered so much territory," Anita said. "If she couldn't get in through the door, she'd come through the window."

By the time Anita was shown the exit in 1961, Barbara was thoroughly ensconced in the office. Her identity would be so wrapped up in her years at *Today*—first as a writer and then as an on-air interviewer and finally as co-host—that she would title that chapter of her memoir "Becoming Barbara Walters."

A GODFATHER OF THE MAFIA SORT

1960

Barbara Walters and Roy Cohn were dating.

"Happy, Happy: Was that Lou Walters' daughter Barbara with fight impresario Roy Cohn at Sherm's Stork?" Walter Winchell's column clucked in August 1960. (Translation: Sherman Billingsley owned and operated the Stork Club; Cohn headed a syndicate that had staged a heavyweight rematch between Ingemar Johansson and Floyd Patterson at the Polo Grounds.) Six months later, Lee Mortimer's "New York Confidential" said suggestively, "The Roy M. Cohn dates with Barbara Walters, Lou's daughter, are beginning to take on that look."

A stack of psychiatric treatises and pop-psychology books have been written on the subject of fathers and daughters, including when the father is an absent or distant figure. But it isn't hard to see that Barbara was drawn to men who resembled Lou Walters, in his charm and his faults. She fell for men who had a certain swagger, who broke the rules. Men like Roy Cohn.

He commanded the best tables in the hottest night spots, at the Stork Club, El Morocco, the Diamond Horseshoe, the Copacabana, and of course the Latin Quarter. He was outrageous and amusing. She was smitten. He was "the first person she became extremely passionate about," said Joan Gilbert Peyser, a high school friend from Birch Wathen, though Barbara never publicly described her feelings with that intensity. "I know she wanted to marry Cohn. At least, I remember her telling me she did."

He made no secret that there were times when he wanted to marry her. Near the end of Cohn's life, *Washington Post* reporter Lois Romano asked him if he had any great loves. "Barbara Walters," he replied without missing a beat. "Barbara Walters. Oh, boy, did we ever discuss getting married. . . . We discussed it before her marriage, after marriage, during her marriage." But he added, wistfully, "You know how those things are."

One friend said Roy and Barbara were engaged for a time, something Barbara would dispute. The wife of Hearst columnist George Sokolsky, with whom Cohn was as close as a father, said Roy gave Barbara a ring sometime between her first and second marriages. "We were out together and Barbara showed me the engagement ring," Dorothy Sokolsky said. "Roy was sitting right there." Broadway columnists hinted at their engagement. "No Pain, but Plenty of Fun," Mortimer wrote. "Roy M. Cohn back with Barbara Walters, Lou's daughter, at the Stork, but refusing to confirm that he'll do the same as his law partner, Dick Schilling, for whom he's tossing a bachelor party."

Later, Roy delayed the purchase of an elegant four-story townhouse on East 68th Street that would become the base of his personal and professional life until Barbara could tour the property and approve it. He suggested that, after they married, her parents and sister could live in their own apartment on the building's top floor. It was the closest she came to accepting one of his marriage proposals, she said. "For one moment I thought maybe. But 'maybe' never became 'yes.'"

Besides other complications, Roy's domineering mother, Dora Marcus Cohn, didn't think Barbara, or any other woman, was good enough for her son. She dismissed her as "that girl." One evening, when Barbara knew she would see Dora at a friend's wedding, she slipped Roy's engagement ring off her finger and put it on a chain around her neck, Sokolsky said. Barbara and his mother "never got along," Roy said. "My mother always wanted me to get married, as long as I didn't get married to anybody."

For decades, though, Barbara and Roy were at least confidants, if not more. He teasingly inscribed a copy of his book, *A Fool for a Client*, to her: "For Chickie—Who I always knew would accomplish Joe McCarthy's dream of restoring me to daytime television." When Barbara's mother visited New York, Roy escorted them to lunch at Windows on the World, the posh restaurant on the top floor of the World Trade Center's North Tower.

Roy and Barbara and another friend, Yvonne O'Brian, became a regular threesome for long, gossipy lunches at the East Side's most fashionable restaurants. Yvonne was married to Jack O'Brian of Hearst, one of the first TV columnists. At a lunch at "21," the two women once took from Roy a pair of his cuff links they admired, in the shape of leopards jumping, and discovered they were the right size for their fingers. They wore them out of the restaurant as rings and never gave them back. One of Yvonne's daughters still has hers.

Barbara said she and Roy were never intimate, their physical contact limited to "a peck on the cheek." He never told her he was gay; she never made it clear when she realized he was. It was a time homosexuality carried serious cultural and legal stigmas; until 1962, same-sex activity was a crime in all fifty states. On his deathbed, he was still denying rumors that he was dying of HIV/AIDS and threatened to sue anyone who said he was. Then muckraking columnist Jack Anderson revealed that Roy was part of an AIDS trial at the National Institutes of Health. When he died, the NIH listed a virus linked to AIDS as a secondary cause of death. A square for him in the Memorial AIDS Quilt labels him "Bully. Coward. Victim."

In retrospect, Barbara said, he might have portrayed her as his romantic partner "because I was his claim to heterosexuality." By then, at least, she understood what he had hidden for so long.

———

In the fall of 1960, Barbara got yet another panicky call from her mother.

Her father finally seemed to be recovering from his attempted suicide and the collapse of the Café de Paris two years earlier. He had landed a contract to stage shows at the Tropicana Hotel in Las Vegas, and he and Dena and Jackie had moved there. Now Dena was on the phone, telling Barbara that her father had to cancel a planned trip to New York. "He can't, or he'll be arrested," she said in the desperate voice her daughter knew too well. He was still dealing with the Internal Revenue Service over his failure to pay taxes for his nightclub, now defunct, and he had missed the latest court date in New York. For that, a warrant had been issued for his arrest.

Roy happened to call that night, she said, and he insisted they get together to talk about it. A week later, the warrant against her father was dropped in a process that was surely extralegal.

Roy Cohn was a master fixer.

"He had strong connections and friendships with most of the major judges in New York," Barbara said. His father, Albert Cohn, had been a judge. "Over the years, for one reason or another, Roy had done a lot of favors for various judges and politicians." He never told her how he had made her father's legal problem evaporate, but she assumed that he asked someone powerful for a favor and got it. "Roy was like a godfather," Barbara said—a godfather of the Mafia sort, not of the religious variety. "You do a favor for me, I do a favor for you."

For nearly a half-century, Barbara told almost no one what he had done for her, not even when friends expressed mystification about her relationship with such a controversial figure, a man who, among other things, was charged three times with professional misconduct and later became a mentor to Donald Trump. For Barbara, unsavory allegations and even Mob ties weren't necessarily disqualifying; protecting her family came first. Like her emergency loan from gangster Louis Chesler to repay her father's debts, a powerful man with a shady reputation once again had provided a safety net when she needed one.

"I knew all his faults, but I could never forget what he had done for my father," she said of Roy. And for her. The day would come when she would return the favor.

15

BECOMING BARBARA WALTERS

1962

For the six months since she had been hired by the *Today* show as a writer, Barbara had been angling to make her way on-air, not that she was willing to admit it.

"[I]t never occurred to me that I would ever have a regular on-air role myself," she wrote in her memoir. "All I wanted was to do whatever I was asked to do so I wouldn't be replaced by some other female writer. I just wanted to keep my job." Those were her words. But her actions, and the observations of nearly everyone she worked with, described someone who was being propelled not by some happy accident but by her own ambition. "Barbara was nagging to be on the air," recalled Jane Murphy Schulberg, then a production assistant on the show. "She was just badgering everyone half to death."

The odds were stacked against her. Her voice wasn't mellifluous; her easy-to-mock lisp had resisted the corrective efforts of voice coaches. Her manner could be intense, in contrast to the light touch of the most successful morning hosts, the sort viewers found easy to listen to as they had their first cup of coffee of the day.

"You don't have the right looks" to be on the air, Don Hewitt said flatly while congratulating her on getting the writing job. The CBS producer had met her when both worked on the network's morning show; he later gained fame for creating *60 Minutes*. "And besides, you don't pronounce your r's right. Forget about ever being in front of the cameras." What Hewitt failed to realize, not until years later, was just how determined she was, looks and lisp aside.

She began to pitch occasional story ideas that could give her experience and exposure. One of the first was a feature about bicycling in Central Park. A few weeks later, she convinced producer Shad Northshield to send her to the Paris fashion shows. When she returned, her narration on the set was her real introduction to the *Today* audience, on August 29, 1961. Newscaster Frank Blair opened the segment.

"We forced our staff writer Barbara Walters to go to Paris to cover the fashion openings," he said with a smile. "Today's the day that pictures of these clothes are released to the public, and we wanted to have them first. Barbara, would you tell me was this a very trying experience for you?"

"Oh, Frank, it was awful," she replied coyly. Her dark hair was cropped fashionably short, with bangs. "First of all, every day I had to go look at fashion shows. And then I had to have lunch at Maxim's and drink champagne. And then I had to smell all the perfumes at Dior. I mean, it was so trying that I took absolutely the last plane, the very last plane that I could to get back here today."

When Blair asked if she had bought anything on the trip, she pulled out a twisted metal ring and stroked it against her cheek as the camera framed a tight shot of her face. She seemed completely at ease.

Less than a year later, she got her biggest early break: a plum assignment to cover First Lady Jacqueline Kennedy's goodwill tour to South Asia.

The beautiful and youthful first lady, such a contrast to Mamie Eisenhower and Bess Truman, had already become an international sensation. *Life* magazine called her "arguably the most famous woman in the world." She was one of television's first political celebrities, her every move a headline.

Indian prime minister Jawaharlal Nehru and his daughter, Indira

Gandhi, greeted Jackie's arrival at the Delhi airport aboard a chartered Air India flight from Rome. Pakistani president Ayub Khan hosted a formal dinner for her at the presidential residence in Karachi. Every outfit Jackie wore and every stop she made, from the Taj Mahal to the Khyber Pass, was catnip for photographers, the pictures published around the world.

Sander Vanocur, NBC's White House correspondent, was covering the trip to produce a one-hour special that would air a week after the first lady's return, and foreign correspondent Welles Hangen, then based in New Delhi, was filing stories for the evening news. But Northshield and host John Chancellor wanted more coverage for their morning show, especially for the female viewers who had become thoroughly enchanted by the nation's fashionable first lady.

"It's a terrific story!" Northshield said as he raised the idea with his staff. "Can you imagine Jackie climbing up on an elephant!" (Indeed, she and her sister, Lee Radziwill, would climb up on an elaborately decorated elephant during their visit to Jaipur, perching gingerly in a small carriage on his back for a short procession.)

Barbara argued that the story needed a woman's touch. "A woman's story, reported by a woman," she said. Then she added, boldly, "Why not send me?"

She made a promise to clinch the deal, a promise she wouldn't be able to deliver. She told Northshield she had helpful connections that would get her time with Mrs. Kennedy, who was being pursued by more senior journalists. Barbara had been a student at Sarah Lawrence when Lee Radziwill had enrolled there, she noted, and she had met Letitia Baldrige before she became the social secretary in the Kennedy White House. "I know I can swing this," she assured him. She enlisted a mutual friend to send Baldrige a letter asking for favored treatment. "I will keep an eye out," Baldrige replied.

Forty-five reporters were credentialed by the White House to travel with the first lady for the two-week trip. Seven of them were women. Six of those worked for newspapers and wire services. Then there was Barbara, the only female television reporter on the trip, and the greenest of them all.

Marie Ridder, on assignment for *The Washington Star*, was just five years older than Barbara, but she was much more experienced. Her grandfather, B. W. Fleisher, had been the publisher of *The Japan Advertiser*, which he had built into the most influential English-language daily newspaper in the Far East. When the rise of war fever before World War II cost him his Japanese copyboys, he enlisted his teenage granddaughter to work in the newsroom. She had been in the business ever since. On a stop in Pakistan during this trip, the hotel space was taken up by the traveling officials and the reporters found themselves staying in tents, albeit elegant ones. "Not camping," Marie noted. She and Barbara and Joan Braden of *The Saturday Evening Post* were assigned to be roommates.

Six decades later, at age ninety-seven, Marie Ridder told me she remembered both the younger woman's determination and her insecurity. On her first big assignment, Barbara seemed intimidated by everything and everyone. She fretted about how she looked and whether she was doing a good job. The standard rough-and-tumble of the traveling press corps seemed to overwhelm her. "These guys—she was slight then, and young and terrified; they terrified her. And she said to me, 'How come you're not terrified of them?'"

On the trip, Barbara agonized over everything, including her hair. She brought a wig with her; oddly, she boasted about it in an NBC press release issued before she left. "By having a brunette wig identical to my natural hair, I'm prepared to look my best for the fanciest occasion at a moment's notice," she was quoted as saying, adding, "Even Mrs. Kennedy is taking a wig." In Marie's view, a wig was a questionable call, given the steamy climes they were visiting, not to mention the unlikelihood that the cub reporter would be included in the fanciest occasions of the trip.

Barbara kept hitting roadblocks. She fumed when Sandy Vanocur declined to share the TV correspondent's spot in the press pool, the small group of reporters who saw events up close. "Would it have killed him to let me once be the broadcast pool reporter?" Barbara griped. She filed radio reports but complained to other journalists on the trip that she wasn't getting time on the *Today* show. "I've been on this trip and never got anything on the air," she told the *Time* correspondent, who described her as depressed and frustrated.

At one stop, Joan Braden casually borrowed money from Barbara to buy some bracelets, at a time Barbara didn't have money to spare. After a childhood of booms and busts, money was a lifelong source of anxiety, even after she had banked millions. She would tell an associate years later that Joan never paid her back. A doyenne of the Washington establishment, she was another target of Barbara's envy—another of those beautiful women who seemed to have things easier than she did. She described Joan as "very slim and rather wrinkled from too much sun." To be fair, some other female reporters, including Marie, had their own grievances with the blithe, charming Joan. "The hard-bitten male reporters fell all over one another offering to carry her bags, her typewriter, her anything," Barbara said. "Nobody offered to schlep any of my bags."

She did seem to have a lot of bags to schlep. In the NBC press release before the trip, she worried about how she would be able to manage "her typewriter, tape recorder and extra tape, wigbox, brief case, pocketbook and overnight bag" when she trundled on and off the plane at each stop.

Worst of all, Joan landed the trip's only interview with Jackie, on the flight back to the United States. That had been Barbara's priority and the promise she had made to her boss.

Throughout the trip, an increasingly desperate Barbara begged and pleaded with Letitia Baldrige for even a few minutes of Jackie's time. It didn't work. The closest she came to an exchange with the first lady occurred when the press corps had gathered to watch Jackie visit a monument in Pakistan. "Mrs. Kennedy, there's a bobby pin falling out of your hair," Barbara said. Jackie smiled and replied in her distinctive, breathy voice, "Thank you." Years later, Barbara called that, sarcastically, "my exclusive interview."

She did get two notable interviews for the *Today* show during the trip.

The first was with Indira Gandhi, the Indian prime minister's daughter who four years later would become prime minister herself. Before she left New York, Barbara sent her a letter requesting an interview. Her connection with Marie Ridder helped, too. When they were on the ground, Marie, who had met Gandhi on a previous trip, agreed to put in a good word for her. When Barbara got the interview, Marie said, she fussed endlessly over arranging her wig for the session. Gandhi took Barbara on a tour of the prime minister's residence, a huge mansion but one without enough closets, she complained—a lament Barbara said she shared about her three-room apartment back home.

In Pakistan, she sat down with President Khan, who had seized power in a coup d'état four years earlier. He would be the first head of state she would ever interview—the first of many, as it turned out. "My first with a head of state," she said years later, "and I can't remember a thing about it."

But for the "get" that mattered most, a chastened Barbara had to settle for interviewing the reporter who had landed the prize. When they arrived back in the United States, she sat down with Joan Braden on the *Today* set in New York to talk about Joan's conversation with the first lady. "An Exclusive Chat with JACKIE KENNEDY," *The Saturday Evening Post* trumpeted. Just the sort of interview that would define Barbara down the road.

The reviews her bosses gave Barbara for her first big foreign foray were mixed.

Northshield said Barbara had done "a beautiful job," but not everyone at the show agreed. "She hadn't really done this kind of thing," one of them told Robert Metz for his 1977 book, *The Today Show.* He and *Today*'s veteran film editor sat down with her to critique the footage she had shot. "When she got back, Tom Galvin and I told her how bad it was and explained what she should have done. We went into some detail, and she listened to us. She didn't like it one damn bit at first, but she did listen to us."

She rarely made the same mistake twice. At least not on the job.

———

In her personal life, she would never seem to find firm footing. Barbara once said she was "attracted to men who are smart and powerful," adding that she wasn't sure why. "I think it's because I'd always hoped there would be a strong, successful man to take care of me so I wouldn't have to take care of myself."

Consider the character known in New York society as Philippe of the Waldorf.

Lou had first introduced his daughter to Claudius Charles Philippe, an impresario of catering and events at the Waldorf-Astoria hotel, when they were planning her first wedding, in 1955. (For that event, Lou settled instead on the Plaza Hotel, considering it a classier venue.) Three years later, Barbara met Philippe again, when she had taken a job at Tex McCrary's PR firm. By then, her first marriage had crashed. So had her father's fortunes.

That fall, Philippe had troubles of his own. A federal grand jury indicted him on four counts of income tax evasion, accusing him of evading payment of $88,706 in taxes from 1952 through 1955. He was accused of concealing the receipt of "cash, currency or kickbacks" from caterers who supplied the hotel with food and beverages. Prosecutors said he had amassed $300,000, none of it reported as income. Each charge carried a penalty of up to five years imprisonment and a $10,000 fine.

"Waldorf Officer Indicted on Taxes," the *New York Times* headline said. Next to it was a remarkably buoyant column about the defendant titled "Arbiter of Good Food." The photo of Philippe was captioned "How to orchestrate a meal."

He was an institution among the socialites and business tycoons and charity planners inclined to rent the Waldorf's ballrooms. Journalist Edward R. Murrow visited Philippe's country home to interview him for CBS's *Person to Person*. *The New Yorker* published a profile of him, almost an ode. "He is a man of unflagging energy, tact, ruthlessness, charm, know-how, school spirit, and heroic working habits," it said.

In court, Philippe protested his innocence, if only for a while. He managed to get a consulting job with one hotel company and then a contract to manage two other hotels. Along the way, his new employer hired McCrary's PR firm, and Barbara was assigned to the account. She was charmed.

"I guess his indictment didn't bother me too much," she said. "Claude Philippe and I had a delightful lunch," followed by a torrid, two-year affair.

The parallels between her lover and her father were hard to miss. Philippe was eighteen years older than she was, closer in age to her father than to herself. Both men were born in London to parents who had immigrated from elsewhere—Philippe's father from France, Walters's parents from the Russian Empire—before moving to New York. By their late teens, both had achieved remarkable success based on charisma and hustle. Both were natty dressers, favoring bespoke suits and French cuffs. Neither was particularly handsome, not in the traditional way, but they shared a certain intensity. Even their round, horn-rimmed glasses were similar.

Both liked to live on the edge, in business and in life; neither was faithful to their wives. Both got in trouble with the law over tax evasion, though neither went to prison, thanks in part to the help of powerful friends. Philippe eventually pleaded guilty in U.S. District Court to evading $24,472 in income taxes and was fined $10,000.

During his romance with Barbara, Philippe was still married to his second wife, a French actress named Mony Dalmès, who lived in Paris. Barbara didn't care about that inconvenient detail, she said, but that may be one reason the affair had a clandestine air. Barbara never told her parents about it, not after her favorite cousin, Shirley Budd, insisted on referring to Philippe as "the headwaiter," denigrating his position as head of catering at one of New York's fanciest hotels. Philippe's assistant recalled him using a code for Barbara's name when he put their engagements in his appointment book. "Seven o'clock LQ," he would write—the "LQ" for "Latin Quarter."

They spent weekends at Watch Hill Farm, his country home near the Hudson River Valley town of Peekskill, about an hour north of the city. "Magical," she called them, with gourmet meals, fine wines, and fabulous sex. "Philippe, older and more experienced than the men I had known, was a great lover, tender and passionate," she wrote in her memoir. "I grew up sexually." She said she fell in love, perhaps for the first time, but he dragged his heels about getting a divorce. Their passion cooled.

Soon after that, she did marry again; Philippe did, too. But not to one another.

———

Barbara called the *Today* Girls "tea pourers," not an appellation that reflected much regard. They were supposed to read the weather report, engage in perky chitchat with the men on the air, and look pretty. "TV's equivalent of a geisha," one writer put it. Actually, many of them had excelled in one field or another: actresses Betsy Palmer and Estelle Parsons, singers Florence Henderson and Helen O'Connell, former Miss America Lee Ann Meriwether.

When Barbara was hired as a staff writer, the *Today* Girl was Beryl Pfizer. She had climbed from the show's writing ranks herself and had a wary insight into the ambitions of the new staffer hired to write for her. "The one writing job on the *Today* show and the one on-air job on the *Today* show had everybody in town fighting," Pfizer recalled. "Barbara knew about all those beauty queens who had worked on the show and she didn't think she could make it as a beauty queen. She saw me and she said, 'Okay, a writer can make it.' And so she decided that she was going to lay heavy on being a writer and make it on the show that way."

Almost nothing fazed Barbara. She went to the office of director Otto Preminger for a pre-interview the day before he was scheduled to be on the show to promote his movie *Advise and Consent*. Soon after she got back to NBC, Preminger, so fearsome a figure that he was known as "Otto the Ogre," was on the phone. "Put your hand on your leg," he told her. "Higher, higher," he demanded. "No. Higher."

Then she realized she had lost her garter, then standard female equipment to hold up hosiery. "That's why I'm calling," he said. "It dropped off here." She didn't take offense at his suggestive tone. He returned the errant garter to her in an envelope attached to a bouquet of a dozen roses.

Northshield expanded her assignments to include not only light features for the *Today* Girls but also some more serious stories, many of them with a female focus. She reported on the rise of political conservatism at several women's colleges. She profiled the nuns at a Catholic convent. She visited a reform school for young women in Michigan and a training program for policewomen in New York.

And she spent two days training to be and working as a Playboy bunny, recorded on a hidden camera as she served drinks wearing the club's signature scanty costume. For the rest of her life, she would be proud she had been pretty enough to pass for a bunny, feminists' objections to the role aside. The final posting on her @BarbaraJWalters Twitter account, on September 28, 2017, was a retweet of a video clip showing her on the job in the Playboy Club.

"A Night in the Life of a Playboy Bunny," the segment was titled. It was not the exposé about the exploitation and objectification of the "bunnies" that Gloria Steinem would write a few months later for *Show* magazine after working undercover in a Playboy club herself. Instead, Barbara's story had the air of a lark as she exclaimed when her "bunny trainer" tightened the corset that would narrow her waist and boost her boobs. She peered over her shoulder as the fluffy bunny tail was attached to her derriere. The segment showed her chewing on her pen as she "studied" the thirty-five-page bunny manual detailing the arrangement of the serving tray and the garnishes for various drinks.

"I can still do the 'bunny dip,'" she said years later, the maneuver to deliver drinks to the table without leaning over and unintentionally exposing her breasts. She described it this way: "Keeping your legs together, slightly bend your knees and shift a bit to the right while leaning slightly backward. The squared-off position protected your cleavage but it was murder on the thighs."

"You make a very cute bunny," Hugh Downs told her on the *Today* set when the segment ended. He declared that, despite the furor raised by the sexual innuendo of the Playboy brand, the clubs were "almost depressingly moral" and allowed "no hanky-panky whatever."

To which Barbara replied with a suggestive smile, "Hope springs eternal."

Eventually, in addition to her writing duties, she was doing a story every week or two, and on consequential topics. In 1963, after John F. Kennedy was assassinated in Dallas, she got her first on-the-air assignment covering a breaking news event. She stood just outside the U.S. Capitol for hours to cover the arrival of the horse-drawn caisson carrying JFK's coffin from the White House, then reported on the long lines of dignitaries and citizens arriving to pay their last respects.

"These are the honor guards who have been guarding the casket of President Kennedy," she said into the camera at the end of the day, poised and somber. "If I feel or seem a bit choked up, it is because I have just left the last guard."

But she had to try and try again, and again, before she finally got a job that officially put her in front of the cameras, not behind the scenes.

Host Dave Garroway had been pushed off the show in 1961; Beryl Pfizer was let go soon afterward. She was replaced by Robbin Bain, a winner of the popular New York beauty contest sponsored by Rheingold beer; she was succeeded by actress Louise King. Then a new producer, Al Morgan, wanted to hire a fresh *Today* Girl. He said he wanted to cast the show "almost as if it were a soap opera," with the *Today* Girl representing "the female interest: quick, bright, good-looking." Barbara applied for the job, but Morgan hired Pat Fontaine, a former weather girl from St. Louis. Fontaine lasted a year and a half. She turned out to have a drinking problem. "[T]here were mornings when she'd arrive at the studio in no shape to go on the air," Barbara recalled. When she left, Barbara applied again.

Instead, in 1964, Morgan hired actress Maureen O'Sullivan. But Maureen feuded with Hugh Downs and struggled with the improvisational demands of live television; she later disclosed that she had been abusing prescription drugs. In the middle of the 1964 Democratic National Convention in Atlantic City, before her thirteen-week contract was up, she was abruptly fired. Columnist Jack O'Brian, describing O'Sullivan's tenure on the show, said she had "decided in leisure and repented in haste."

The *Today* show then courted actress Betty White for the job.

"They asked me if I would be interested in doing the morning, the *Today* show, being the gal on the show," White, who was living in California, recalled decades later. "And they said, again, it would mean living there and I couldn't do that. I explained all that. That was one of those getting-up-at-four-o'clock-in-the-morning-and-going-to-the-studio and it was a way of life and terribly interesting and a great idea. But I said, 'I don't think so.'" She refused even after NBC offered to put her up at the posh St. Regis Hotel in New York every week and pay for her flights back to California every weekend.

"The poor network, poor NBC," White went on, "was stuck with a gal named Barbara Walters, and they somehow managed to muddle through."

———

After all the other alternatives seemed to be exhausted, Barbara's qualities finally were appreciated. She didn't have a drinking problem, wasn't abusing prescription drugs, understood how things worked on a live TV set, got along with Hugh Downs, and was already getting up at four each morning. She wanted the job, and she would work cheap. Union scale of $750 a week represented an "unbelievable-to-me salary," she said. That mattered since the show still had to pay off Maureen O'Sullivan's much more generous contract for another year and a half. Barbara didn't expect to be put up at the St. Regis or to be flown cross-country, at least not yet.

"Why not take someone who's grown up with television?" Downs suggested when the producers began to search for a successor to the ill-cast Maureen O'Sullivan. Such as? "Such as Barbara Walters," he said. He recognized her talent and her drive, and he didn't look down on her show business background. He had his own unconventional rise in journalism, working as the announcer for Jack Paar on *The Tonight Show* and as the host of the game show *Concentration* before signing on with *Today*. "I always tried to promote Barbara because I figured that some of the glory would spill over on me," he said later.

Not everyone was enthusiastic. Morgan worried that her lisp would grate on viewers. Some thought her manner was too aggressive to wear well on morning TV and "too Jewish" to appeal to middle America. But Morgan didn't have an alternative, and Barbara was once again knocking at the door. "Well, like the ingenue in a corny movie, there I was: the patient and long overlooked understudy," she said. "Hugh was all for trying me out. By this time I was a known and trusted colleague. Plus I was no threat. And I could certainly perform adequately, if not spectacularly."

Morgan finally agreed she could be on the air two or three days a week, while movie critic Judith Crist and art historian Aline Saarinen would appear on the other days. "The three of us were his insurance against disaster," Barbara said, "much like the story of the advertising producer who hired triplets for a Johnson & Johnson diaper cream commercial to ensure that at least one of the babies wouldn't have diaper rash on the day of filming."

One more thing, a change significant beyond the semantics: Barbara would be known as a *Today* reporter, not as the *Today* Girl. If the title hadn't been changed, she would have been the thirty-second *Today* Girl. "A frivolous and sexist idea, one whose time had gone," Downs said.

She had finally prevailed, then and later, by working harder than anybody else. By paying attention. By learning her job and the jobs of everybody around her, which gave her skills she could use and authority she could build. By cultivating relationships. By understanding public relations in a way other journalists found undignified. By simply ignoring the sexist limits of the day. By showing up. "I started in my new role in October 1964 with no big fanfare, no publicity, and no official announcement," she said.

Well, maybe a little fanfare. Jack O'Brian, the columnist who had promoted her father's various endeavors for years, treated her start as major entertainment news in the *New York Journal-American*. NBC may not have been ready to make a PR pitch, but Lou Walters's daughter was.

"Dawn Greets Barbara, a Girl of *Today*," the headline over the story read. "A very attractive, shapely, well-groomed, coiffed and fashionably frocked feminine member of NBC's dawn patrol," O'Brian said in describing her, adding that she had "no wish to become a 'personality.'

"She wants to remain as she is," he said. "The prettiest reporter in television."

THE RUNAWAY BRIDE

1962

Barbara had no shortage of suitors throughout her life, among them big names in entertainment, government, and business. "I have been married more than once," she said, looking back, as though there were so many she couldn't keep count, "and I never wanted to get married when I did." For a person who rarely expressed regret, her failure to sustain any of her three marriages or any other romantic relationship became a source of sadness and envy.

She was "always questioning herself," said ABC colleague Diane Sawyer, who had an enduring marriage to director and producer Mike Nichols. "The sweetness with which she talked about my meeting Mike Nichols in my forties and finding of happiness you never dreamed you could have—she was wistful about that," she told me. "There is still a yearning there."

Barbara met Lee Guber on a blind date in 1962, just as she was about to cover Jackie Kennedy's trip to India and Pakistan, her big break on the *Today* show. Her best friend, Joyce Ashley, had arranged for them to meet. "He's nice, but you'll never marry him," Joyce predicted, setting expectations low for their dinner at the Friars Club. He had just moved to New York from Philadelphia. He was a jazz aficionado and a gourmet cook, an avid tennis and squash player, a ruggedly handsome man with dark hair and blue eyes. He was forty-one years old; she was thirty-two. He was considered a player and a catch.

His occupation: theatrical producer.

"Oh no. Not another one!" Barbara said later, in feigned horror. "After my experiences with my father, I had sworn to myself that I would never get involved with anyone in show business."

Growing up, Lee had carried bags for the occasional vaudevillian staying at the succession of small hotels his parents owned in downtown Philadelphia. After earning a bachelor's degree from Temple University and serving in the Army during World War II, he bought the Senator Hotel in the downtown Center City neighborhood. Its club, the Rendezvous, gained renown for hosting such jazz legends as Sarah Vaughan, Dizzy Gillespie, Billie Holiday, and Ella Fitzgerald.

In 1955, he and two partners launched the Valley Forge Music Fair in Devon, an instant success with a production of *Guys and Dolls*, then of *South Pacific*. They expanded their tent theater operation along the East Coast, eventually including the Westbury Music Fair on Long Island, the Painters Mill Music Fair in suburban Baltimore, and the Shady Grove Music Theater outside Washington, D.C. "I managed to convince myself that Lee wasn't the same kind of showman as my father," Barbara said, that he was a realist, not a dreamer. "That's what I decided he was—a businessman."

She was the one who pursued him, his friends said. She defied Joyce's prediction that Lee would never be a match for her. "I knew right away this was a man I could marry," she said. He said, "I knew right away that the trap was being set for me." They were engaged a year after they met.

————

The other man in her life was headed for trouble, again.

After a long recuperation from his attempted suicide, Lou Walters landed contracts to stage shows first at the Deauville Hotel in Miami

Beach, then at the Tropicana Hotel in Las Vegas. He began importing performers to Las Vegas from the Folies Bergère in Paris. "It wasn't Broadway, but it wasn't a low floor in a hospital, either," Barbara said dryly. Four years later, with the show established, the Tropicana let him go. By then, he was sixty-seven years old, but he lacked both the savings and the sentiment to retire.

He managed to get a job back in Miami Beach at the high-rise Carillon Hotel, staging what he labeled the "Oui, Oui Paree" show at an aptly named venue, the Café Le Can-Can. "ALL NEW! SAUCY! PERT!" an ad in *The Miami Herald* declared, laced with exclamation points as it promoted a "Spectacular Parisienne Revue Produced and Staged by LOU WALTERS." His name appeared in type as big as that of the featured entertainers, the "fabulous Barry Sisters" and Lynda Gloria of the Folies Bergère. "Delicious Food!" the ad promised. "A Cast of 50! Great Stars! Gorgeous Can-Can Dancers!"

In other words, a classic Lou Walters production.

The reviews were glowing, just like in the old days. "In the lavish costuming and production tradition of Lou Walters, of Latin Quarter fame," George Bourke wrote in *The Miami Herald* when the show opened just before Christmas in 1963. It had a healthy run of ten months, then was reprised for final holiday performances in late 1964. The evening's entertainments "have been compared with the best ever turned out by the veteran producer," the columnist said.

Barbara's buoyant father had rebounded. Her mother and sister had not. When the family moved back to Miami, they bought a house so far outside the city that Dena and Jackie, neither of whom drove, felt isolated and trapped, dependent on TV for entertainment and company. A "cheerless" home, Barbara said. She didn't step in to fix their complaints, then felt guilty that she hadn't. She began to dread her mother's frequent phone calls, full of grievance.

But Lou was already dreaming big again, no lessons learned from the Café de Paris fiasco five years earlier. The success of "Oui, Oui Paree" wasn't enough. His new plan: an aquacade. It was, essentially, the splashy extravaganza he had long staged in nightclubs, but on water. It would feature scantily clad women, flamboyant costumes, fireworks—a Latin

Quarter revue in an oversized pool, surrounded by an amphitheater. Billy Rose's Aquacade had been a hit at the New York World's Fair, he noted, never mind that it had been launched in 1939, a quarter-century in the past. "A show is a show," he assured his daughter. "You give the people something spectacular and they'll come."

All he needed, as always, was money.

Over a family dinner with Barbara and Lee in Florida during the summer of 1963, Lou Walters urged his daughter to invest in his new project. At the time, she had amassed a grand total of $5,000, a stock-pile she had rebuilt after giving all her savings to her father the last time he needed a bailout. She was making $500 a week at NBC; the salary bump with her new on-air role a year later would increase that, but initially only to $750. She turned to her fiancé for his advice. Lee asked Lou a question: "What would you do if you had only five thousand dollars to your name?" Lou declared, "I'd invest it in the aquacade." That was good enough for Lee. He told Barbara, "Give your father the money." Despite her doubts and their history, she had never been willing or able to deny her father.

The Aqua Wonderland Revue featured trick water skiers and high-diving clowns in the water while singers and dancers performed on an eighty-foot-long floating stage. Walters had leased Miami's new Marine Stadium for fourteen weeks, projecting net revenue of a half-million dollars and promising the city 25 percent of the profits. The amphitheater could hold 6,500 people, and the operation needed to sell an average of 3,000 tickets per performance to break even. But the biggest audience the show ever commanded was a fraction of that, just 700 people. The aquacade opened in mid-June and closed, abruptly, in mid-July. By then, Lou quietly had sold his interest for $5,000 to a New Zealand promoter named Bruce McCrea, who would file for bankruptcy a month later.

Barbara's investment? Gone.

No surprise that her father was willing to gamble his daughter's life savings, as he had when she invested in the Café de Paris in New York. No surprise, either, when another of his grand schemes flopped, once again taking with it every penny she had saved. Yet once again, Barbara didn't abandon him. She made one more attempt to rescue her father and his pride. She called Sonja Loew, someone she loathed—a "noisy and proprietary" woman who drank too much, she said. By now, Sonja was divorced from E. M. Loew, Lou's old business partner, but Barbara knew Sonja still had sway.

"I don't usually do this, Sonja," Barbara said. "But my father is very sick, he had a heart attack, and it would be such a wonderful thing if Mr. Loew would call him and say, 'Come on, Lou, come back to the Latin Quarter.'"

Barbara had the gift of persuasion. Loew offered Lou a contract as general manager of the club. He would never know that his daughter's intervention had prompted it. He immediately leaked the offer to columnist Herb Kelly. "Loew made me a flattering proposition when he was in Miami recently," Lou told Kelly, adding he had made "certain stipulations" about coming back to the club, as though he had a world of options. Then he agreed, telling Leonard Harris of the New York *World-Telegram and the Sun*, "When Loew said let's start over, I said okay."

Heading back to New York, the family rented a two-bedroom apartment at Eighth Avenue and 50th Street, a long way from their former penthouse on Central Park West. But the nightclub business was waning, and the Latin Quarter would face a strike by its dwindling lineup of showgirls. Lou's failure to pay taxes when he had his own club was catching up with him. Roy Cohn had dispensed with the arrest warrant issued when Lou had failed to show up for a court date, but he still owed $100,000 to the Internal Revenue Service and $8,300 to the State of New York. On December 3, 1966, he filed for personal bankruptcy, listing liabilities totaling $164,000 and assets of household goods and personal effects of just $400.

He was seventy years old, and he was broke. Again.

———

The aquacade fiasco didn't change Barbara's view of her father; she had a lifetime of watching his grand ambitions fail. But her fiancé's willingness to risk her nest egg raised questions about her rosy conclusion that he was a pragmatic businessman, not another risk-taking showman. "What I refused to acknowledge was that my father and Lee were more alike than they were different," she said. "Both of them lived for the next show." She grew increasingly uneasy about their engagement. Soon after their trip to Miami, she broke it off.

Three months later, they suddenly reconciled. A few days after President Kennedy's assassination that November, Barbara answered the doorbell at her apartment, a towel wrapped around her wet hair. Lee was standing there. "Life is too short," he said. "Let's get married right now."

"Yes," she replied. "Let's get married." For all her concerns about Lee being like her father, Barbara had inherited Lou Walters's impulsive streak when it came to her marriages. Marriage Number Two began as impetuously as Marriage Number One.

Barbara didn't see it that way, at least not in the moment. The national trauma after JFK's shooting made their differences seem petty and human connections precious. "We wanted to cling together stormily for two years," Barbara said later. "Neither of us really wanted to get married." But there wouldn't be time for them to have second thoughts, not until after the wedding was over.

Their turnaround was the lead item in Jack O'Brian's "On the Air" column in the *Journal-American*. "Pretty, perky, popular Barbara Walters called off the calling-off of her marriage to tent show tycoon Lee Gruber," the Hearst columnist wrote, a misspelling of Lee's last name that would recur elsewhere through the years. It was surely unintentional but still a sting to his ego.

Barbara had gotten one last-minute appeal to rethink things. The night before the wedding, Roy Cohn called and begged her to marry him instead. He had asked her before. "There I was at Chez Vito's, talking to her on the telephone for an hour," he said. "She said she couldn't marry me, because she and Guber had already given a [thank-you] present to the judge."

Two weeks after the assassination, on December 8, 1963, Lee and Barbara were married in the Fifth Avenue apartment of her high school friend Marilyn Landsberger Herskovitz. The wedding was so hurriedly arranged that there were few guests. Only her father flew up from Florida to attend; Dena and Jackie didn't make it. *The New York Times* notice gave Guber top billing and described his new wife as a writer and reporter for the National Broadcasting Company.

The wedding had gotten off to a fast start. The marriage didn't.

The weather was predictably cold and gray during their December honeymoon at a borrowed house in East Hampton. "I felt trapped and restless," Barbara recalled. "I remember when Lee produced our marriage license and told me he had to mail it to state officials for everything to be legal, I had an immediate urge to grab it, tear it up, and tell him to forget the whole thing." They continued to live in separate apartments for months, finally settling in a six-room, rent-controlled apartment on West 57th Street, across from Carnegie Hall.

"The hardest part was moving in together," she said. "It was so definite. And marriage is terribly tough." They didn't combine their bank accounts—more unusual for a married couple in that day than later. There was friction, too, over her desire to have a baby, and as soon as possible. She could hear her biological clock ticking; she was thirty-four years old when they wed. In keeping with the expectations of the time, she may have felt that a woman's life couldn't be counted as complete without children. Perhaps she hoped having a child would be an opportunity for her to give someone the comfort and unconditional love she had never really felt herself—and to get it back. But while having a child was an urgent priority for her, it wasn't for Lee, who had a son and daughter from his first marriage.

She was devastated when she suffered a miscarriage during the first months of their marriage. The couple consulted doctors. Following their advice, she began to track her menstrual periods and monitor her temperature to schedule sex at optimum times—not always an aphrodisiac in a marriage that had other strains. In vitro fertilization and surrogate mothers weren't yet options.

She suffered a second miscarriage and six months later, a third. "You're ecstatic at the high point, then you all but fall apart when you drop to the low," she would recall. She never slowed her work schedule, then worried that the stress and the travel had contributed to the miscarriages. But she wondered if it might be a good thing that she never carried a child to term. "I think of my sister," she said, who was developmentally disabled. "Was her condition hereditary? Was nature sparing a child of mine the fate that befell Jackie?"

Barbara's determination to be a mother never waned. Eventually, she would get her wish, if not in the way she had planned.

17

THE "PUSHY COOKIE"

1964

When the red light of the television camera blinked on, the newest reporter on the *Today* show instantly seemed more confident, more composed, even more extroverted.

Off the air Barbara could be frantic and uncertain, wracked with second thoughts over even small decisions. But on the air, she was at ease. "Exhilarated," she said. She felt that way from the start of her long career until its end. Decades later, when fellow panelists on *The View* worried that an aging Barbara was beginning to miss a step, a peril on live TV, they would watch her snap back when the cameras began to roll. "I'm very bold on camera," she said. "I'm not bold off camera." After all, her father's life had been a demonstration of the importance of putting on an appealing show for the audience, regardless of problems backstage or at home. In that way, she was made for the public, not the private.

In the beginning, in 1964, she shared airtime on *Today* with two better-known women, movie critic Judith Crist and art historian Aline Saarinen. In contrast, Barbara didn't debut with a prominent name or any particular credentials. "I'm a Lord-Knows-What," she told *TV Guide* after three months on the job. She conducted celebrity interviews and narrated fashion shows and sat at the curved desk to chat with host Hugh Downs, newsreader Frank Blair, and announcer and sportscaster Jack Lescoulie.

Her female colleagues, the renowned movie critic and the erudite art historian, could hardly be expected to sell dog food. It was Barbara who did live commercials for one of the show's sponsors, extolling the virtues of Alpo as a dog eagerly lapped it up. The canine enthusiasm at the key moment was guaranteed by keeping them hungry beforehand. That first week, a famished dog on a leash dragged her across the studio floor in pursuit of the bowl of the gelatinous food, prompting howls of laughter from her and everyone else in the studio and, presumably, from those watching at home.

At age thirty-five, she had finally found her place, a space that bridged journalism and entertainment and promotion. Traditionalists viewed the combination with consternation. She ignored their doubts as she redefined their industry. She saw herself as a journalist, albeit of a new and evolving sort. In some ways, she would make herself a leader in the news business by changing what, exactly, that could include.

There was, of course, the question about the way she sounded, the most fundamental of characteristics for someone in broadcasting. Some said she had a speech impediment; from her days as a schoolgirl, she would insist it was "bastard Boston." She already had visited one voice coach, courtesy of Anita Colby, the host of those early segments sponsored by S&H Green Stamps that Barbara had been hired to script. Now that she was going to be on the air regularly, *Today*'s producer, Al Morgan, dispatched her to what he called "remedial speech school," designed to correct what he called a "lateral lisp—the W's came out sounding like S's or V's." He complained she sounded like actor Boris Karloff, who had starred as Frankenstein's monster in the 1931 horror movie.

For three months, she was drilled in exercises in enunciation—*right, raisins, rrrich*—with marbles in her mouth. But the sessions left her feeling self-conscious and sounding stilted. Even some viewers wrote to ask why she was talking in such a peculiar way. She gave up on the expert and for a time tried to avoid sentences with too many "r's" in them, not the most realistic of long-term solutions.

A handful of pioneering women were working in TV news before Barbara arrived on the scene. Pauline Frederick began covering the United Nations for NBC in 1953, a beat she would hold for two decades. Lisa Howard, a stringer for Mutual Radio Network who was the first American reporter to interview Soviet premier Nikita Khrushchev, was hired by ABC as its first female correspondent in 1961. Marlene Sanders of ABC became the first woman to anchor an evening news broadcast when she filled in for an ailing colleague in 1964.

But Barbara rarely acknowledged the women who went before her, as though that might somehow diminish her own achievements. She saw them more as competitors than as potential allies; that was how some of them viewed her, too. She forged a handful of lifelong friendships in high school and college and on the East Side but rarely in the workplace, where there was often no place for any woman, much less more than one.

In her memoir, she didn't mention Lisa Howard or Marlene Sanders. She dismissed Pauline Frederick in two sentences, as a "trailblazer" but one who was "rather stern and unglamorous and got very little media attention." She disparaged Nancy Dickerson, who worked for CBS and then NBC as a Washington correspondent. She described Nancy as "a stylish figure" and someone President Lyndon Johnson "was particularly fond of," a sly allusion to their reported liaison. "She shot herself in the foot" by being high-handed and difficult, Barbara said—a common complaint leveled at women in the business, including Barbara. "So that left me, a new face on the air, and the object of curiosity."

Nancy blamed her fall on Barbara's rise. "Once Barbara Walters started co-hosting the *Today* show in 1964 it became less crucial for Mom to do pieces on the show," CBS anchor John Dickerson wrote in his book about his mother, *On Her Trail: My Mother, Nancy Dickerson, TV News' First Woman Star.* "Viewers were getting their dose of femininity from Walters." When Nancy's contract came up for renewal in 1970, her career in the balance, she wrote a list of the possible jobs she might want and the obstacles to getting them. Number One on the list: "Limited opportunities." Number Two: "Effect of Barbara Walters."

After writing the memoir, John Dickerson told me he had been struck by the "level of cruelty" that women like Nancy Dickerson and Barbara Walters had to endure. "The executives in the business are brutal," he said, "and the audiences are really mean, too," attacking women correspondents for their appearance and their competence. That "psychological weight" was particularly stunning "when I think about the fact that women like Walters and Mom had no allies."

For a time that summer, Nancy guest-hosted the *Today* show from Washington. Fifty-six viewers wrote in favorable letters about her, which she kept as potential ammunition for employment. Barbara would accuse her of orchestrating a letter-writing campaign in hopes of replacing her. Six years later, when Barbara got the job as co-anchor of ABC's evening news program, Nancy was scornful. Barbara didn't have the credentials as a reporter that she did. "They chose a personality rather than a newsperson," she said. She would snipe at her rival's news credentials and her speech anomaly. "[I]f you didn't watch her mouth it's hard to tell what she's saying," she said.

But perhaps Barbara's hard-earned edges, her lack of cool elegance, were a factor in her success. In a *New York Times* article published in 1965, headlined "Nylons in the Newsroom," feminist Gloria Steinem wrote about the long-standing refusal of the TV networks to put women on the air in positions of authority. "We figured that women didn't want to watch other women, except on very girl-type subjects," a network executive helpfully explained.

Barbara was different. As the least girly woman on television—especially when compared, say, to the glamorous Nancy Dickerson—Barbara could get away with doing more than "very girl-type subjects." Women viewers "identify with me because I'm not beautiful or remote," she said. She was more relentless than decorous. The producers had to coach her to speak more slowly and smile more often. She didn't flinch at selling dog food.

"They don't want me to be a glamour puss and that's fine," she said. "It means I won't have to quit or have face lifts after forty."

While not a classic beauty, she was attractive, meticulously groomed, and elegantly dressed. She claimed to be five feet five inches tall, though that may have been an aspirational height. She somehow seemed bigger and more formidable on TV; people she met were often surprised at how petite she was. Asked what she disliked most about her appearance, she replied, "How much time do you have?" But she had always been proud of her legs, one reason she favored shorter skirts. She had hazel green eyes and a direct gaze. Her hair was short and dark, though it got steadily lighter the more prominent and the older she became.

Steinem wrote the article two years after Betty Friedan's *The Feminine Mystique* had sparked a movement, as things were beginning to change for professional women in the workplace. Barbara became Exhibit A. "The woman now receiving more network exposure than any other is Barbara Walters," Steinem wrote. "The shift from the old 'Today Girl'—who was usually a coffee-server and amiable lightweight—to Barbara Walters—is the television industry's change of attitude in microcosm."

But Barbara didn't call herself a feminist, and she didn't closely align herself with female colleagues at NBC or ABC when they began to push for systemic change against sexual discrimination. She also didn't credit the emerging movement for her early breakthroughs in the business. "I think probably at this stage it would have happened with or without the women's movement," she said when she was named co-host of *Today*, although she added it might have "put a little fear into corporation executives" that they could face protests if women weren't treated fairly.

"Barbara Walters for Women's Lib, but Not Violently" was the headline on a newspaper interview with her in 1972, the perfect encapsulation of her approach. The article had other reminders of its era. The male author noted she looked "ravishing in a blushpink midi which clings to her figure—one any starlet would be proud to call her own." He called her "a credit, as they say, to her sex."

Barbara was determined to win the game, not change its rules. The path she ended up clearing for the women who followed her was, first and foremost, one that she was cutting for herself. She was focused like a laser on her own career. At least at the moment, another woman's gain could well be her loss.

"I think that a little of a woman goes a long way on television," Barbara said soon after she had landed the on-air job at *Today*, repeating the conventional wisdom that TV's male executives gave when they declined to expand opportunities for women. "For one thing our voices are different and can easily become tiresome. And, in the kind of things I do on 'Today,' I always think it is interesting to get the men on the show to participate and make some comment—particularly when dealing with things like fashion. I remember one feature we did on pants for women—they all had some scorching things to say."

After a year and a half on the air, one TV columnist wrote that she was "slimmer, better coiffed and clothed" than she had been at the start, that she had lengthened her hair and lightened it. "Within months of joining 'Today,' she was as fashionably chic as any female clawing her way up the Nielsen ratings," he wrote approvingly.

————

Barbara was gaining notice, and not by accident. She had watched her father have his name in lights one week only to be shown the door the next. She didn't want that to happen to her.

In 1964, she hired a manager, Ray Katz, to negotiate her contract and a PR firm owned by Arthur Jacobs and John Springer to get her name in the newspapers. Most TV journalists of the day, typically trained at newspapers and wire services, considered such tactics unseemly. But she understood from the start how to generate publicity and why it mattered. She was not only the daughter of Lou Walters but also a veteran of Tex McCrary's PR firm.

It was "a more clearcut indication that she looked on herself as a personality as opposed to a journalist," said Bill Monroe, who was the Washington bureau chief of NBC News when she broke on the scene. He was the epitome of the media's old guard, later moderating NBC's *Meet the Press* and then editing the *Washington Journalism Review.* He found her pitch for publicity "odd" and "different," and not in a good way. "I didn't know other journalists who did that, and this set her apart a little bit in my mind as somebody who had something else on her agenda beyond strict journalism. This was a show biz kind of thing."

That sort of critique may help explain why Barbara was less than candid about her PR campaign. She never tempered her ambition, but she regularly tried to shield its intensity from public view. She waged a campaign to deny she was waging a campaign to promote her image. "She refused to hire a press agent when given this more important exposure on *Today*," Jack O'Brian wrote in the *Journal-American*, a preemptive and inaccurate statement by a columnist with whom she was friendly. "She was advised to by some friends but dismissed all such advice, feeling she will do far better for herself without the transparent attention such pressurized praise begets."

In her biography, Barbara doesn't mention the publicists she hired for that crucial first year on the air, portraying the profiles and features that suddenly began appearing as serendipity. "There I was, if not the toast of the town, at least a good bite," she said. She noted that the network was so delighted with the attention that they moved her to an office with a window and assigned her a secretary.

"Guess Star: Can you identify this personality?" teased the Sunday magazine of the New York *Daily News*, then the largest-circulation paper in the country. "This young lady's assignments range far and wide for an NBC morning show," the item began, describing her as "green-eyed brunette." "Today's mystery miss began her TV career on graduation from Sarah Lawrence College in Bronxville, N.Y."

The answer appeared on page 20, below the crossword puzzle. Next to a coquettish headshot, the headline read: "TODAY'S GUESS STAR, Barbara Walters ('Today')."

During 1965, her first full year on the air, she was featured in friendly profiles in the Boston *Record* and the Boston *Herald-Advertiser*, in the *New York Post* and the *New York Herald Tribune*, in the *Newark Evening News* and the *Baltimore Sun*. Her close-up was on the cover of *TV Magazine*. She made a guest appearance on *The Tonight Show* with Johnny Carson. In short order, *The Ladies' Home Journal* was asking her to write a monthly column and *Vogue* wanted to know her "twenty-five beauty secrets."

The biggest splash was in *Life* magazine, the leading periodical of the day and proof that she had arrived. "Barbara Walters of 'Today' Show Looks Sharp—and Is Early to Rise, Wealthy and Wise," the headline declared. The main photo showed her in a little black dress and four strands of pearls, inexplicably perched on top of a table, her legs folded beneath her. "Planning the next day's show, Barbara Walters strikes a girlish pose atop a table, as *Today* host Hugh Downs and the show's staff listen carefully to what she has to say," the caption read, as though she were in charge.

That was a step too far. The affable Hugh Downs, the actual host of the *Today* show, had welcomed Barbara, in contrast to some male colleagues who would follow. As a game show host and onetime *Tonight Show* sidekick, he lacked the pretensions of journalism's would-be gatekeepers. He had suffered their condescension as well. But this was too much even for him. The bosses at NBC told Barbara to turn off her personal publicity machine, and she complied, firing her PR firm soon after the *Life* article was published in February 1966.

But the mission had been accomplished. Her career had been launched. An Associated Press profile that ran in newspapers from Miami to Milwaukee bubbled that her face "is becoming as familiar to the viewers as the pattern of their breakfast coffee cups."

———

One of her first interviews on the *Today* show was with Lee Radziwill, Jackie Kennedy's sister and then the wife of Prince Stanisław Radziwiłł of Poland. Before the show, Lee Radziwill professed no memory of Barbara from the brief time both were students at Sarah Lawrence, or from the trip to India and Pakistan with Jackie that Barbara had covered. Barbara asked what she should call her on the air; she recounted Radziwill's disdainful response: "Just call me Princess."

After that unpromising start, Barbara began an apprenticeship in the art of the interview that would make her as famous as the people she was interviewing. A decade later, Lee Radziwill knew who she was, singling her out for praise while she derided TV talk show hosts generally as glib, uninformed, and "literally offensive."

"The one exception is Barbara Walters, who is absolutely great," Radziwill would declare. By then, she was an ex-princess who was trying, briefly and unsuccessfully, to launch her own career doing TV interviews.

By Barbara's count, she often did two to four interviews a program, five days a week, for the next thirteen years on the *Today* show. She honed her ability to ask a hard question in a soft way and to make news, and her increasingly prominent profile made it easier for her to snare big names. She interviewed actors Peter Ustinov and Fred Astaire and Ingrid Bergman. She sat down with Judy Garland and Rose Kennedy. Her interview with author Truman Capote became an invaluable resource for actor Philip Seymour Hoffman when he was preparing for the lead role in the movie *Capote*. He watched the recording dozens of times to pick up Capote's speech and mannerisms; he would win the Academy Award for best actor for his performance.

She had the first, surprisingly pensive interview with Grace Kelly after she had married Prince Rainier III of Monaco and become Princess Grace. "Are you happy?" Barbara asked her on the air. "I've had many happy moments in my life," the princess replied tentatively, as if she wasn't quite sure. "I have a certain peace of mind." Once the cameras were off, she began to cry. Barbara chatted with Luci Baines Johnson about life with her father in the White House and covered Lynda Bird Johnson's wedding. She sat down with Tricia Nixon in the Rose Garden; the conversation went so well that President Nixon then agreed to an interview with her himself. He sent her a handwritten letter after he watched a replay of NBC's coverage of Tricia's wedding. "I want to tell you again how much I enjoyed and appreciated your very thoughtful and gracious commentary during the program," he wrote. "I hope your listening audience continues to grow!" He did his part to help, convincing a reluctant Prince Philip to agree to an interview with her, too.

During that interview, she asked, "Might Queen Elizabeth ever abdicate and turn the throne over to Prince Charles?" He replied flippantly, "Who can tell? Anything might happen."

The story made global headlines—"Queen left in lurch" the *Montreal Gazette* reported—and Buckingham Palace had to issue a clarification that, no, Queen Elizabeth II wasn't thinking about abdicating the throne for her son. "Philip Again: Palace Denies American TV Suggestion of

Queen's Abdication," the *Liverpool Daily Post* said at the top of its front page. In fact, she would reign for another fifty-three years, until her death in 2022.

The kerfuffle caused no hard feelings between Barbara and the prince. She wrote him a letter saying she was sorry if he or the royal family had been embarrassed by his "reasonable and moderate answer to a reasonable question." He wrote back telling her not to worry, blaming other journalists for misrepresenting his comments. The prince also sent a friendly note to Nixon. "I found Miss Walters particularly charming and intelligent," he said in a handwritten letter, written during a stop in Greenland.

One of those who watched Barbara each morning was Dean Rusk, secretary of state under Presidents John F. Kennedy and Lyndon Johnson. For eight years, Rusk was at the center of power while the Vietnam War expanded and American culture was convulsed by protests over the war and civil rights. He and Barbara had met at a cocktail party in Washington in the summer of 1967. Hugh was on vacation and she was filling in as host of the show. "We were deep in conversation and I'm sure anyone seeing us talk would think we were deep in conversation about some world problem," she said. Not so. The secretary of state was telling her he liked her hair longer.

A week later, Rusk wrote her a fan letter.

"As a regular viewer of the Today Show, my spirit moves me to write you a little note to say how much I admire and appreciate the job you are doing," he said, calling her hosting of the show in August "splendid." "If NBC Vice Presidents ever begin to bother you, show them this letter and others like it and tell them to leave you alone. Cordially yours, Dean Rusk." She framed the letter and hung it on the wall of her seventh-floor office.

When he left the State Department as the Nixon administration was taking office in 1969, Rusk was pursued by the biggest names in Washington journalism for an exit interview. He gave the first one to her, a prize. By then, he was a controversial figure, dogged by protesters and reviled for his role in escalating the Vietnam War. The stakes of the interview were high for his reputation, and for hers.

They met for lunch at the Hay-Adams Hotel, just off Lafayette Square, then went upstairs for an interview that lasted four hours. They could see the White House and the Washington Monument through the windows of the suite. "During a break, when we came to the end of the first reel of tape, we were sitting there smoking our cigarettes and Barbara turned to a colleague from NBC who was with her and said, 'We're not coming through with tough, hard-hitting reporter's questions,'" Rusk recalled. "'We gotta do something about that in the remaining twenty minutes.' So the first question after the break she asked me how I and my associates in government 'could have been so stupid' about the buildup of the Vietnam War."

Rusk's recollection was a bit faulty. She had asked that particular question in a subsequent interview, in 1971, not during their initial encounter in 1969. However, in the 1969 interview, she had also pressed him on Vietnam, noting that "close friends and colleagues" had turned against his support of the war, and that the public had as well. He didn't take offense. He laughed at her determination to look tough—a spontaneous reaction that wasn't shown on air—and then he answered her. "I'm not sure what the historians will eventually say on that point," he replied.

When the interview was over and the cameras were off, he thanked her for "not asking one frivolous or naive question." She said she had been determined not to ask "any dumb feminine questions."

The reporters who covered Washington were annoyed that Rusk gave his first interview since leaving government to her, a morning-show reporter based in New York whose bread-and-butter was conversations with celebrities shilling their latest movies. His decision helped give her an imprimatur as a serious journalist, and it was a blockbuster. The *Today* show ran a five-part series about it. "Rusk Denies Opposing De-Escalation" was the headline over the *Washington Post* story, which mentioned Barbara in the second paragraph. LBJ's office in Austin called to request a transcript.

Even all that attention left her a bit disgruntled. "I can't believe that if a man had been able to get this exclusive interview with Dean Rusk that it would have been shown only on a morning show," she grumbled. "I'm sure it would have been replayed on prime time in the evening." The news Rusk made did appear on the *NBC Nightly News*, but in a report by co-anchor David Brinkley that used clips from her interview.

The interview with Rusk not only changed other people's perception

of her. It boosted her opinion of herself. "I always knew I was hardworking, but I really never thought of myself as having a talent," she said soon
afterward. "It's only been recently that I began to realize I have a talent—
one of bringing people out."

That said, she would never feel entirely secure.

"It's as if she has to keep going, because if she ever slows down it will
all disappear, and with it her identity, her sense of her own worth," a *Life*
writer observed a few years later, in a 1972 profile. The headline on the
magazine cover asked, "What Is Barbara Walters Trying to Prove?"

That worry pricked her in the moments after that pivotal first interview with Rusk. He had just left the State Department after eight years in
the cabinet's top-ranking job, fourth in line to the presidency, the longest
tenure of any secretary of state except FDR's Cordell Hull. She went
downstairs with him to the entrance of the hotel, the White House in
sight across the square.

She had a limousine waiting to take her to the airport. He was hailing
a cab. The official cars and the bodyguards he had long been accustomed
to were nowhere to be seen. She offered to give him a lift; he declined.
Once you're on the outside, she thought then, "Boy, the power is over."

She saw the repercussions of losing the job that put you at the center
of events, that made you a person who would have a limousine waiting.
It gave her a chill.

"IT'S A GIRL!"

1968

If Roy Cohn couldn't be Barbara Walters's husband, he would be her guardian angel.

In 1968, Lee Guber and Barbara participated in the oddest of private adoptions, an arrangement facilitated by Roy. A wealthy couple had adopted a baby girl a few years earlier and now wanted to adopt a baby boy—specifically, a tall, blond, fair-skinned boy whose birth parents had no known hereditary diseases. The couple's lawyers were investigating the backgrounds and interviewing mothers-to-be. They had chosen a pregnant, nineteen-year-old woman who had decided to put her baby up for adoption. But the gender was nonnegotiable.

If the newborn was a boy, they would take him. If the newborn was a girl, would Barbara and Lee be interested in adopting her? Of course, they said. On the morning of June 14, 1968, soon after Barbara got off the air of the *Today* show, Lee called. "It's a girl!" he told her. "She's ours!"

Carol Kramer, a reporter with the *Chicago Tribune*, happened to be interviewing Barbara in her office at the time. "Congratulate me, I just became a mother," she told her, "bubbling with joy" and fielding celebratory phone calls. With a new baby, she acknowledged she would have to agree to "fewer speaking engagements and lunch appointments," but insisted it wouldn't have any impact on her hard-won role on *Today*. "After all, it's not a nine-to-five job," she said of her TV responsibilities. "It's a five-to-nine job."

Four days later, the expectant couple flew to pick up the newborn at the hospital. They paid the lawyer's fee and the birth mother's medical expenses. Barbara's cousin, Lorraine Katz, who owned a children's store in Asbury Park, New Jersey, sent a layette of bibs, undershirts, onesies, and towels. A friend loaned them a bassinet. The set designer for *Today* made oversized pastel butterflies to soften the look of the dark brown, faux leather walls in the library-turned-nursery at their apartment.

Barbara already had decided to name their daughter Jacqueline Dena Guber—Jacqueline after her sister, who would never have children herself, Dena after her mother. (For years, Barbara would call her sister "Jackie" and her daughter "Jacqueline," to distinguish them.) She named her after the two women with whom she had the most complicated relationships of love and guilt, of obligation and resentment—a sister whose disability had constrained Barbara's childhood, and a mother who had confided in her young daughter the grievances of her life.

In some ways, Barbara had raised herself, her father often absent and her mother preoccupied. It was a model she seemed comfortable following now as a parent. Others would provide the constant attention a baby demands. She and Lee employed a full-time baby nurse for the first year, then another for the second year. When Jacqueline was three, they hired a live-in French nanny, Thérèse de la Chapelle, and a live-out Jamaican housekeeper, Icodel Tomlinson. Icodel and the woman known to everyone as Zelle, short for "mademoiselle," would stay on the job for more than thirty years, long after Jacqueline had grown up and left.

"Jackie was never with an unfamiliar babysitter," Barbara would boast, as though that was enough. "Between the two of them, especially since Zelle was always there, I could travel anywhere in the world and know that Jackie would be all right, no matter what the circumstances."

Barbara didn't miss a step at work. She didn't take maternity leave. "I took her home on a Friday, and I went to the office on Monday," she said.

She didn't mention her daughter on the air for months. It never occurred to her to bring her to the studio. "It would be like bringing in a puppy that wasn't housebroken," she said. But Barbara was not a completely absentee mother in those early years. On the nurse's day off, she would hurry home when *Today* went off the air at 9 a.m. to spend the day with Jacqueline. During the summer, they would rent a vacation house on Long Island, and Barbara's parents and sister would visit from Florida. She kept a baby book, recording when her daughter first smiled (at one month) and began to crawl (at eight months).

As Jacqueline's first birthday approached, Barbara told a reporter during an interview that she had limited her traveling to devote time to the baby. That said, those limits didn't seem particularly limiting. That interview promoted a speech Barbara was delivering in St. Louis in April. She would spend the first week of June in Germany with *Today* and the first week of July in Wales to cover the investiture of Prince Charles.

"We spent every weekend I was home together," she said, a commitment with a hedge: *every weekend I was home.* Lee would grumble that his wife declared her devotion to their child while not actually spending much time with her. He called her a "surrogate mother." After her daughter had grown up, Barbara argued that children would inevitably leave, while a career would be forever—the reverse of the standard perception of what in life endures. "I have often said that if you don't work and you stay home with your child, there comes that day when the child is fifteen or sixteen and says, 'So long, Mommy,'" she said. "And you say: 'For this? For this brat who's walked out on me?'"

While relinquishing even a bit of her professional ambition was never on the table, Barbara did anguish over whether she was doing the right thing. Unlike male anchors, she was judged by others, and judged herself, by a different standard. No one worried about how much time Hugh Downs spent at home with his two children. She had yearned for a child, and she doted on Jacqueline. But the reality of rearing a daughter, the imperative for a parent to be present, was something she never seemed to understand or accept, not even after her own lonely childhood—or perhaps as a result of it.

Jacqueline could not have missed that hard lesson. It was one thing for a string of husbands to know that their wife's career would always be her top priority, no matter what. It was another for a child to understand that of her mother. "Sure, she'll say to me she wishes I didn't have a job; there are times when the job interferes," Barbara said when Jacqueline was eleven years old. Then she waved the worry away. "But I think children say that to mothers just when they [want to] go shopping."

When Jacqueline wasn't admitted to the elite Dalton School, her famous mother pulled strings. "Getting a child into private school in New York is notoriously horrendous, so I was very happy that I had good contacts at the Dalton School," Barbara said. For Jackie's seventh birthday, in 1975, Barbara sent Winnie-the-Pooh invitations to the children in her class, inviting them to Old-Fashioned Mr. Jennings Ice Cream Parlor on the ninth floor at Bonwit Teller, followed by a visit to the Alex & Walter Gym. "Come in leotard or play-clothes," it said.

But as her daughter got a little older, Barbara would be perplexed and disappointed that she didn't share her passions for the city, for society and fashion, for whatever news was breaking and whatever newsmaker was breaking it. Jackie preferred the outdoors to the indoors; she preferred camping to a Central Park view. She wasn't much for books; she would never graduate from college. When a paparazzo snapped them walking down a New York City street as adults, Barbara was wearing a coat with a sumptuous fur collar and lining; Jacqueline, a head taller, was in jeans and a black cap with flaps against the cold. "If Barbara is couture," Jane Pauley once said, "Jackie is fleece."

A MELODY PLAYED
IN A PENNY ARCADE

1969

The Women's News Service used Barbara Walters and Lee Guber as a case study in a 1969 story about the perils of marriages in which the wife is more famous than the husband. It quoted a psychotherapist as saying the husbands were likely to feel "envious, insecure, and bitter." Lee said the fact that they were in different businesses was helpful. "As a result, while sharing things, we have a life of our own," he said. "I don't counsel her and she doesn't counsel me."

A photo with the story showed Barbara beaming into the camera as she held their toddler aloft. Lee is gazing at them. The caption, which misidentified Jacqueline as a boy, read: "Lee Guber, wife Barbara Walters and son . . . the delicate balance."

A delicate balance, indeed.

Not even their schedules meshed. Lee was a night owl by nature, eager to go to Broadway plays and then hang out at Sardi's or Lindy's with the theater crowd until well past midnight. Barbara was an early bird by necessity, her two alarm clocks going off at 4:30 a.m. so she could arrive at the NBC studio an hour later. During weekends, Lee needed to visit his musical productions; that was when she wanted to catch up on her sleep. They tried compromises that left neither satisfied. Sometimes she would go with him to an evening show, then leave at intermission. During the first days of their marriage, Lee would get up with her during the week and they would have breakfast together, then he would watch *Today*. That didn't last. "After a few weeks," she said, "he would check to see what time my spot would be on the air and stayed in bed until then." Even that routine grew thin; soon he was just sleeping in.

Over time, the two saw one another less and less often. "Our schedules began to resemble that of my mother and father when he owned the Latin Quarter and she saw him perhaps one night a week," Barbara said. There was another unwelcome parallel to her father. Lee wasn't satisfied with his successful enterprise of staging musicals in the suburbs. Like Lou Walters, he wanted to produce on Broadway. Nothing could have alarmed her more.

Lee's first Broadway show after they were married was *Catch Me If You Can*, which opened in March 1965 to lukewarm reviews; it closed in less than three months. Two years later, he staged a musical adaptation of *The Man Who Came to Dinner*, renamed *Sherry!* It opened in March and closed in May. (She had taped the commentary for a faux newsreel to use in the production, but he ended up cutting it from the show.) The third and final production while they were together was a dark play, *Inquest*, a sympathetic portrayal of Ethel and Julius Rosenberg. It lasted onstage for all of twenty-eight days.

"Lee's involvement in the theater was driving me further and further away from him," Barbara said. "It wasn't entirely his fault. It was the culmination of all the years with my father's grandiose schemes—the Broadway flops, the failed nightclubs, the aquacade that never got off the ground. I couldn't bear to pretend to be upbeat time and again while Lee read another bad review. I'd lived through enough openings and sad closings for a lifetime."

Her father's latest plight was pressing that unhappy comparison. When the Latin Quarter finally closed in 1969, Lou and Dena and Jackie moved back to Miami Beach, able to afford the rent only for a one-bedroom apartment. Jackie slept on a pull-out couch in the living room. Once when Barbara came to visit, her parents got into a fight so ferocious that her father walked out and didn't come back until the next morning. She was terrified that he had once again attempted suicide.

It was too much for Barbara to ignore. She used her savings to buy her parents a two-bedroom condominium in what she called a "good" but not "great" building, located in a "nice enough" neighborhood and two blocks from a supermarket. "In retrospect, I probably could have afforded 'great,' and I should have bought them a condominium in a better building in Miami Beach," she said later, still feeling guilty. "But I was still so afraid of the vagaries of television that I didn't have the nerve to risk more money."

Lee's resemblance to her father, his optimism and his flair, was what attracted her to him in the first place. But it was also his resemblance to her father, the recklessness and the risk-taking, that undermined her relationship with him once they were together. He echoed Lou's confidence that his next enterprise was sure to be a hit. "We're going over budget, but I just have a feeling that word of mouth will be so great, we'll get it back," Lee assured a reporter before his summertime production of *Annie Get Your Gun* opened at Jones Beach Marine Theater. They were words Lou could have used about the Café de Paris or the aquacade. "I think we'll get a tremendous ride if we do it well. People will say something's happening out there."

But they didn't get "a tremendous ride" that time, or even a small one. "It looks to me like we're going to lose a lot of money," he acknowledged at the end of the summer. "We were dealing with a very fickle lady called the weather."

His career was on a slide. Her career was on the rise.

He wanted more of her support, more of her time and attention. Instead, she increased her workload by adding a daily syndicated show in 1971 called *Not for Women Only*, an afternoon gig on top of her morning TV duties. "There are not many husbands who would tolerate Barbara's absolute career- and ego-centeredness as long as Lee did," said film critic

Judith Crist, Barbara's colleague on *Today*. "Their marriage lasted much longer than one would have imagined."

The chance for a big story trumped a promise to spend time with her family. She was always traveling, Lee complained. "I don't want a wife one day a month," he told his brother-in-law.

Lee told friends he was lonely; he was reported to have a mistress. Barbara told friends she was unhappy; she began to draft goodbye letters to him, then tear them up. Finally, they decided to separate. She was about to leave to cover President Richard Nixon's groundbreaking trip to China in February 1972. Over a tearful dinner, they agreed he would move out of their apartment while she was away.

They had been married for nine years. Jacqueline was three years old.

In their final weeks together, they were still maintaining the ruse of a happy marriage when Sally Quinn of *The Washington Post* profiled a day in the life of Barbara Walters. Lee arrived at the apartment at 9 p.m. that night, "quiet and low key." Sally told me she didn't realize then that the marriage was in crisis. She asked him: What was it like being married to Barbara Walters? "It's a melody played in a penny arcade," he replied, a line lifted from "It's Only a Paper Moon." The musical reference to the jazz classic seemed playful, but the full lyrics had a sad context that went unnoted then.

> *Without your love, it's a melody played in a penny arcade.*
> *It's a Barnum and Bailey world, just as phony as it can be.*
> *But it wouldn't be make-believe, if you believed in me.*

In June, their separation was still a secret. Barbara included Lee among "the 10 most fascinating men I've known this year," a list that presaged the *10 Most Fascinating People* TV specials she would launch two decades later. This list started with Chinese premier Chou En-Lai and included Henry Kissinger, David Niven, Leopold Stokowski, and Joe Garagiola, her genial partner on the *Today* show. Her husband was the man she found "most" fascinating, she wrote in the kicker of the story, and was the one "who, thank goodness, returns the compliment."

A month later, their breakup made the gossip columns. "We had problems we couldn't solve," she told Earl Wilson in the *New York Post*, things that were "too painful" to discuss. "A lot is happening for her and a lot is happening for me," Guber was quoted as saying. "We both have to look after ourselves." The veteran columnist wasn't surprised. "The Barbara Walters-Lee Guber bustup had been rumored for years and always denied," he noted a few days later. In an aside that may have signaled skepticism, he added: "They say that there's nobody else involved." New York *Daily News* columnist Suzy made their separation the top item on a roundup of celebrity gossip. "Barbara, Lee Split," the column's headline in *The Miami Herald* read. "Divorce Ahead?"

Barbara called it the best of times in her professional life, doing "interesting, provocative interviews" and watching her reputation grow. "But all the while, my marriage was falling apart," she said, making it also the worst of times. That was a tradeoff she was willing to take, then and later. It was a choice she would make even with the man she would call the love of her life.

20

McGEE'S LAW

1971

When Hugh Downs retired from the *Today* show in 1971 at the age of fifty, the only people who seemed to think Barbara Walters would be a good choice to succeed him were the two of them. "I recommended to NBC that they hand over the program to Barbara," he said. "I think the public was ready for it. But the industry wasn't quite ready for it yet." That included the man in charge, NBC News president Reuven Frank. "I have the strong feeling that audiences are less prepared to accept news from a woman's voice than from a man's," he said.

Barbara thought she had earned the title of co-host, but she also understood the times. She had taken to heart hard lessons in realism from her father's failed aspirations. "It never occurred to me that they would make me hostess," she said, even in a 1973 interview using a feminine version of "host." "It was the decision of the network that the best image of the show might be a man. Maybe they felt that it's easier to listen to a man for two hours."

Reuven Frank wanted to install as host an established journalist who would take the show in a more serious direction. He settled on Frank

McGee, who had been a co-anchor of the *NBC Nightly News*. The Louisiana-born McGee was no fan of Barbara Walters, or of female colleagues in general. "He was not at ease with professionally equal women," Reuven Frank said. Barbara was blunter. "The idea that he had to work with a woman appalled him," she said.

McGee added daily interviews with Washington newsmakers to the show. But he bristled when Barbara, sitting by his side on the set, would cut in with her own questions. He viewed her as shallow and uninformed, as not a real journalist. When producer Stuart Schulberg dismissed his complaints, McGee demanded a meeting with Julian Goodman, the president of NBC, and included Barbara to make sure she heard the message. At the meeting, McGee argued that her participation undercut the importance of his interviews. She should stick with what he called the "girlie" interviews.

At that, she erupted. After seven years of sitting at the *Today* table, she wasn't ready to go back to the days of being relegated to fashion shows and happy talk. "There are days when I come in to the studio and have to do a feature on dolls and an interview with a lady who bakes her own bread—to the exclusion of serious material," she said soon after McGee had taken over. "On those days I could scream."

She was no longer a newcomer to hard news. She had done substantive interviews with presidents and prime ministers as well as softer fare with actresses and authors. When McGee arrived, she was leaving for Iran to cover the 2,500th anniversary of the Persian monarchy, a spectacular event hosted by the Shah at Persepolis, the ancient desert capital of Persia, and attended by some seventy heads of state and government.

After she returned to New York, resolving the conflict with her new colleague would fall in the lap of Richard Wald, a vice president of NBC News who succeeded Reuven Frank as president. "One of my first jobs . . . was to sit down with Barbara and Frank [McGee] and iron it out," Wald told me. Their perspectives could hardly have been more different. "She thought of Frank as an equal whom she wanted to approve of her. And he thought of her as an underling whom he didn't approve of."

When Wald told him Barbara would be covering President Richard Nixon's historic trip to China, he snapped, "China's not far enough."

Wald helped negotiate new rules: McGee would ask the first three questions without interruption during remote interviews from Washington. Only then was Barbara allowed to speak. If a newsmaker came into the New York studio, McGee would decide whether she could participate at all. The agreement was kept quiet. Barbara put the best sheen on it, portraying it as her choice, not his edict. She told a reporter she was allowing the men to ask their questions first because she was trying "not to be too authoritative, or people will say I'm aggressive."

By the time Wald and I sat down to talk, a half-century had passed since he had arbitrated that battle. He didn't try to defend the arrangement they negotiated. He agreed it would be laughable if it weren't so offensive by any modern measure, so sexist and insulting. But that was just the way things were then. He knew it. So did a triumphant Frank McGee. So did a fuming Barbara Walters.

Even so, Wald and Barbara became good friends and professional allies. He immediately liked her more than he did the stiff-spined McGee, a sourpuss to his colleagues. When Wald was new to NBC, he made a point of going around to introduce himself. "Mr. McGee, my name is Wald," he said. McGee replied with a sneer, "Another one." Wald was never sure what, exactly, he meant by that.

When Wald introduced himself to Barbara, she replied, "Hello, nice to meet you. What are you doing here?" Wald replied, "Well, I'm trying to learn how this place works." She said, "Call me the minute you know."

"I thought that was a pretty good answer," he said. "She's a very, very smart woman and that was apparent from the moment I met her."

They became so close that when she wanted to see *Deep Throat*, a pornographic movie that had gained mainstream attention when it was released in 1972, she demanded that he escort her.

"Everybody's talking about it," she told him. "I want to see it. I can't go by myself." They agreed they would go the next day, after *Today* was off the air, to the 12:30 p.m. showing at the World Theatre. Wald's wife was less than pleased. "I go home that night and I explained to my wife, 'I'm going to take Barbara Walters to a porn show.' And she said, 'You will not.' I said, 'Yes, I am,' and we had a big fight about it."

For the movie, Barbara donned a disguise: oversized hat, dark glasses, and, for some reason, gloves. "I don't want anybody to know who I am," she explained. She also brought food in her purse for them to share, given the lunchtime hour. When they arrived, the theater was packed. The only seats available together were in the middle of the center section, forcing them to climb over a long row of other patrons.

Wald described the scene to me in an interview at the Century Club, one of those private New York enclaves so old-school that cell phones and audio recorders could be deployed only in the waiting room. By then he was ninety-two years old, tall and bent and long retired, but every detail of the episode seemed fresh in his mind, and more hilarious than ever. As Wald's voice rose louder and we dissolved into laughter over the memory of the infamous pornographic movie, a respectable sort sitting in an upholstered chair across the room began to peer at us over his *Financial Times* broadsheet with clear disdain and perhaps a little alarm. That reaction presumably would have been even more common at the time.

"We start walking our way through and people are shouting as we're going through, 'Take off your hat, lady!' and Barbara is not taking her hat off when we finally sit down," he recalled. "The man behind us, as we are sitting down, says, 'Oh, Jesus Christ, take off your hat, lady.' She won't take her hat off. She reaches down into her bag. Pulls out all different kinds of candy and she said, 'We're going to eat candy and watch the movie' in a loud, Barbara Walters voice. I said, 'Missus, will you kindly shut up?' And the guy behind me says, 'Yeah, tell her to shut up.'"

By now the movie was under way. The plot, such as it was, involved a woman looking for advice on achieving an orgasm. A psychiatrist discovered that her clitoris was located in her throat, and she developed a particular technique for oral sex, dubbed "deep throat." As a provocative poster for the movie asked, "How far does a girl have to go to untangle her tingle?"

Barbara began to offer her own running commentary. She may have been insistent about keeping on her big hat as a disguise, but she made no effort to disguise her distinctive voice.

"She says sarcastically to me, 'What a wonderful dialogue,' in a loud Barbara Walters voice," Wald recalled. He tried to point out that the woman's eloquence might have been hurt by her sexual engagement. "'So what?' I said. 'It's hard for her to speak at the moment,' and Barbara says she could find a way. Well, twenty-five minutes later, the movie is fairly repetitious; has no deep plot. Barbara says, 'Okay, we've done it.' She stands up and starts to walk out, over me. I said, 'Well, at least give me a moment to get up.'" They both began climbing over the long row of moviegoers still watching the screen, or trying to.

"As we're walking out, she turns to the assembled," Wald recounted. "She said, 'Don't tell me how it comes out.'" At that point, he said, "I realize that she was not exactly a serious person all the time."

———

Facing the implacable hurdle that was McGee, Barbara devised a way to work around him. Their arrangement set rules for interviews from the New York studio. But nothing stopped her from arranging interviews outside the studio and asking the first question herself, along with all those that followed. "If I just came into the studio every morning, I would never be chosen as the interviewer instead of another man," she said. "I have to get my own interviews. I'm not whining or bitter, feel no competition with the other men—that would ruin the show. But there are certain things I have to do to maintain my position."

It was a crucial decision, one on which the rest of her career would turn. In a way, she would have McGee to thank. "[T]hat's when I got the reputation of being ambitious and aggressive in pursuit of interviews," she said with no regret. "The 'pushy cookie.'"

She began sending handwritten letters to newsmakers she wanted to interview, especially those who had rarely done interviews and who might be game to talk someplace other than the *Today* studio. She sat down with elusive auto executive Henry Ford II in Dearborn, Michigan. Presidential daughter Tricia Nixon in Monticello, Virginia. Renowned conductor Leopold Stokowski in his New York apartment. Cornelia Wallace, the wife of presidential candidate George Wallace, at a campaign office in Alabama.

And H. R. Haldeman, Nixon's top staffer, at his West Wing office.

The White House press corps couldn't believe how and why she had gotten what was believed to be Haldeman's first TV interview. A skeptical *New York Times* reporter called her to find out. "She said that she had first suggested the interview to Mr. Haldeman in September and convinced him at a Washington meeting in December to make his first television appearance," the story said. "She said that this was not a case of the White House seeking television time to attack its critics."

She interviewed Haldeman for more than an hour. The *Today* show would stretch the news across three days. (Four months later, the White House "plumbers" would break into Democratic offices in the Watergate Office Building, eventually forcing Nixon to resign from office and sending Haldeman to jail for conspiracy, obstruction of justice, and perjury.)

"What things, what kinds of criticism, upset the President?" she asked near the end of their session. He leveled the harshest of charges against those who had criticized the White House's eight-point peace plan for Vietnam, in effect accusing them of treason. "After the whole activity is on the record and is known," he said, "the only conclusion you can draw is that the critics now are consciously aiding and abetting the enemy of the United States." Those critics included South Dakota senator George McGovern, who would win the Democratic nomination to challenge Nixon's reelection that November.

"Nixon's Aide Says Peace-Plan Foes Help the Enemy" was the headline on the *New York Times* story, which led the front page. His comments "set off a fusillade of counterfire from high-ranking Democrats," the top of the *Washington Post* story said. Diplomatic correspondent Don Oberdorfer called Haldeman's comments "the strongest yet by an administration official in reply to critics of the peace proposals unveiled Jan. 25 by Mr. Nixon." Both stories credited Barbara by name. His comments sparked such a firestorm that White House press secretary Ron Ziegler tried to distance the president from them, telling reporters Haldeman was expressing "his own personal point of view."

Afterward, Haldeman sent her a friendly note. "Thank you for making me a household word," he wrote. Of course, he was helping to do the same for her.

One of Barbara's strengths was emerging: her comfort with powerful men and her ability to forge a connection with them. If anything, a dark side made men more interesting, more appealing to her. That applied to her view of Nixon, too. She had interviewed him at the White House a year earlier, her first formal interview with a president. She had met him while filming an interview with his daughter Tricia in 1969. She found Nixon "charming" and at the end of her career called him the sexiest president she had met, an assessment that was not widely shared in the press corps, or elsewhere.

On the *Today* show set, turmoil was brewing.

McGee had left his wife of three decades to live with a much younger production assistant, Mamye Smith, who was Black. Barbara found the romance astonishing, belittling Mamye as "fun, giggly, inefficient, and not even particularly pretty."

Wald took a kinder view, telling me that McGee had found the love of his life and acted on it, despite the risk that disclosure of the extramarital and interracial affair could have ended his career. That was a quandary Barbara would face down the road as well, when she would make a different decision for herself.

McGee's romance was an open secret, but it never made the gossip columns. "[E]veryone in journalism knew it, but . . . no one would print it," said Sally Quinn, who was then making a short-lived stint as co-anchor of the *CBS Morning News*. In a phone conversation at the time with Barbara, she pointed out that the courtesy of discretion wouldn't have been extended to either of them. They were often the topic of anonymous barbed items about their behavior on and off the set, some of them accurate and some not.

"A blatant example of sexism in news reporting," Sally complained. Barbara laughed with resignation. "That's just the way things are," she told her.

There had been rumors on the set that McGee was ill, though no one understood precisely what was wrong or how serious his condition was. His skin was pale and his silver hair seemed to be falling out; he began to insist on using a private makeup room, out of the view of the others. Wald could see that McGee was in excruciating pain as he took his seat on the set, aided by a solicitous Mamye Smith. But McGee flatly denied he was sick. Both the TV audience and the NBC brass were clueless about how dire his situation was.

Barbara was rarely clueless. Lee Stevens of the William Morris Agency, who had succeeded Ray Katz as her agent when Katz had moved to the West Coast, negotiated a three-year contract that she signed in September 1973. In it, Stevens won a significant raise for her and slipped in a new provision that the other side seemed to barely notice: If Frank McGee were to leave the show for any reason, voluntarily or involuntarily, she would have the title of co-host with whoever succeeded him.

Seven months later, McGee died of pneumonia, a consequence of an agonizing, secret battle against bone cancer that he had been waging for four years. He had managed to stay on the job until six days before his death. From a hospital bed, he assured the show's producer he would be back by the end of the week. He was fifty-two years old.

Mamye was by his side when he died. She told *Jet* magazine that their plans to be married had been stalled because McGee's wife wouldn't agree to a divorce. The estranged wife would preside over his funeral, and soon afterward, Mamye was fired from the show, though she was later hired elsewhere at NBC. She filed a complaint charging NBC with racial discrimination; the Office of Equal Employment Opportunity eventually dismissed it. None of that made the mainstream press.

"Frank *dead*?" Barbara said. "I couldn't believe it. We all thought he was sick, but we had no idea how ill he'd been." The day he died, in April 1974, she was in California. She flew back to New York and appeared on the show the next day. "Our own Frank McGee will not be with us this morning or any other morning," Walters said with an empty black chair to her left. Later, she privately noted the irony of the hundreds of condolences she received from viewers, "a testament to the seemingly pleasant—and totally false—relationship I'd had with Frank."

NBC announced that the network would search for a new *Today* host. Lee Stevens called the executives. "You mean co-host," he reminded them. Three days after McGee's funeral, the network released a statement that made it sound as though the groundbreaking promotion had been their idea, not an obligation that executives hadn't taken seriously when they had signed her new contract. "I wasn't billed as a co-host until it was over—literally—McGee's dead body," Barbara said. At more than one dinner party over the years, she would note the best thing that had happened for her career was McGee's sudden demise.

"Barbara Walters will be cohost of the NBC Television Network's Today program from now on," read the statement from Donald Meaney, vice president of television news programming. "This is the first time the program has had a cohost and Today is now the only network news or public affairs program to have a female cohost." (Sally Quinn already had appeared on the *CBS Morning News* for a turbulent six months, but in the news role as co-anchor, not the broader purview of co-host.)

The announcement wasn't accompanied by a bigger office or a salary hike or more say over the program, Barbara said. Even so, she said, "cohost" was "a very satisfying title."

Meaney was close to Barbara Walters and a booster of her career, but in an interview years later he described her as "often difficult" and "determined [to be] an anchorperson." She wasn't afraid to raise her voice and push, he said. "She was willing to do whatever was necessary."

Those were qualities that could make her hard to take—she cautioned female colleagues that ambitious women were routinely labeled "bitches"—but they were also qualities she presumably needed to do things no woman had ever done before. After her breakthrough, every morning television news program would have a female co-host. By 2006, both main anchors on one network morning show would be women—Diane Sawyer and Robin Roberts on ABC's *Good Morning America*. In 2018, Savannah Guthrie and Hoda Kotb became the first pair of women to anchor the *Today* show, Barbara's old stomping ground.

Barbara's new standing meant she had some control over who her cohost would be, and how they would work together. She and her bosses wanted a man who wouldn't make her look old in comparison—she was forty-five years old at the time—and someone who would complement rather than clash with her forceful persona.

The list of prospects included journalists at NBC, among them Tom Brokaw, Tom Snyder, and Garrick Utley. It included some who were working elsewhere, including Dick Cavett and Bill Moyers. Harry Reasoner of ABC was considered. It was "one of the most coveted on-the-air positions in all television," Les Brown wrote in *The New York Times*. Moyers removed himself from consideration because the job involved reading commercials on the air. Brokaw also found the idea of doing ads "repulsive"; besides, he didn't want to leave the White House beat during the Watergate scandal. Snyder was seen as a big personality who might clash with the forceful co-host.

In July, Wald announced that Jim Hartz had been chosen for the job. He was then working four floors above the *Today* studio as an anchor on the evening news shows at NBC's New York affiliate, WNBC. "Jim doesn't mind sharing the stage with me, and he isn't offended when I try to help him," Barbara said when he was named. In other words, he wasn't Frank McGee. Now she would be free to pose the first question, and more.

WHEN LOVE IS NOT ENOUGH

1973

Their first date was in the Senate Dining Room.

Edward William Brooke III, a liberal Republican, was the first African American elected to the U.S. Senate since Reconstruction. Barbara had met him in passing at a New York restaurant in 1973, introduced by mutual friends. She was taken by what she called his "big, wicked smile." She was still technically married to Lee Guber though they were separated; he had moved out of their apartment a year earlier. Brooke, who had just been elected to a second term as senator from Massachusetts, was more than technically married. He had celebrated his twenty-fifth anniversary with Remigia Ferrari-Scacco, whom he had met in Italy during World War II and was the mother of his two daughters. Their marriage had its strains, but she had been an important political asset for him with the state's Italian American voters.

A few months later, he ran into Barbara again in the least romantic of places, on a panel in Washington discussing President Nixon and China policy. He asked her to join him for lunch in the Senate Dining Room, another innocent venue but a meal marked by what she called "excessive" flirting.

It began the most serious affair of Barbara's life. Serious, and secretive. He was not only a married man but also a Black man. At the time, interracial relationships were still considered scandalous by some; the Supreme Court had legalized interracial marriages nationwide just six years earlier.

She called him Brooke, never Ed. They would meet in his apartment at the Watergate complex in Washington and at the home of some close friends in suburban Virginia. They were surreptitiously photographed sitting side by side on a banquette at a romantic Georgetown restaurant called Los Gitanos, intent in conversation, eyes locked. (After she had rebuked the restaurant's roving photographer when he asked if they would like a picture taken, he slipped out of view and took one anyway.) Both vacationed on Martha's Vineyard, arriving about the same time but not staying in the same place. He owned a house in Oak Bluffs; she rented a house nearby, and he would visit two or three times a week. In Washington and New York, they would deliberately accept invitations to the same parties; they would leave at the same time and he would ask, loudly, whether he could take her home.

"I was excited, fascinated, intrigued, and infatuated," she said, calling him "the most attractive, sexiest, funniest, charming, and impossible man." He wasn't particularly solicitous of her; perhaps that was part of his appeal. While he was ten years older than she was, he told her more than once that she was the oldest woman he had ever been attracted to—presumably other than his wife, who was a year older than he was. He could be distant and controlling; he would make plans with Barbara and then abruptly cancel them with little explanation and no apology.

Why did she keep seeing him? "The simple answer was that he excited me," she said. "Forbidden fruit and all that."

By the fall of 1975, after nearly two years together, their relationship had deepened. He had introduced her to his mother. ("God knows what she thought of me," Barbara said.) He spent Thanksgiving in New York with her rather than going home to Massachusetts. By now, rumors about the affair had begun to surface.

In September, White House photographer David Hume Kennerly was being grilled by Barbara in an appearance on the *Today* show about whether he was out of favor with President Gerald Ford and if he was dating the president's daughter, Susan, questions he didn't appreciate. "Well, Barbara, I put those stories in the same category as those about you and Senator Ed Brooke," Kennerly replied with a deliberate needle. "They are rumor and gossip."

Meanwhile, in *The Washington Post*, society columnist Maxine Cheshire began chronicling sightings of them together around town. "They have been luncheon partners at such places as the Senate Dining Room and LeBagatelle," she wrote in one of her syndicated "VIP" columns, published in Brooke's hometown *Boston Globe*. After Barbara dismissed the idea of an "alleged romance" as "ridiculous," Cheshire followed up. "Still denying any 'romance,' NBC's Barbara Walters and Massachusetts Sen. Edward Brooke were seen holding hands and attracting a lot of attention recently at a party Senator Jacob Javits and his wife gave in New York for Iranian Princess Ashraf, sister of the shah," she wrote.

The situation was becoming untenable, Barbara told Brooke. His marriage "had long ago run its course," she said, "but politicians didn't get divorced in those days."

Then he did the unexpected: He asked his wife for a divorce. But she did more than refuse. She hired detectives, Barbara said, and identified her as the other woman. *The National Enquirer* began to investigate, too, circulating photos of Barbara on Saint Martin, the Caribbean island where Brooke owned a vacation home. Had anyone seen her on the island? With him?

She began to worry about the consequences of their relationship becoming public. Pete Peterson, a good friend who was an investment banker and member of Nixon's cabinet, called to say he had heard about the affair and the story was likely to burst into the open soon. It would all but ruin her career, he cautioned her; NBC might not stand by her. She got a warning from someone even closer to her, someone she had long trusted to look after her best interests. "Roy Cohn told me it would ruin our careers," she told a colleague.

In thrall or not, that was a chance she wasn't willing to take. Two years earlier, she had watched Frank McGee leave his wife and risk his job as host of the *Today* show by having an affair with a Black woman on the staff. NBC executive Richard Wald saw it as an act of love but she found

McGee's decision inexplicable. Now she was established as the co-host of the *Today* show. Within months, she would sign a million-dollar contract with ABC.

The revelation that she was having an extramarital affair, and with a Black man, might have upended all that. Her reputation was "solid and aboveboard," she said then; her divorce from Lee had been "quiet and dignified." Barbara and Brooke agreed to walk away from one another. He finally got divorced in 1978—a messy split that contributed to his defeat in a bid for a third term in the Senate—and in short order married a much younger woman.

Brooke would never publicly acknowledge his relationship with Barbara, not even in his 332-page autobiography, published in 2007. After wavering over whether to include it in hers, she confirmed it for the first time in her memoir a year later. The chapter is titled "Special Men in My Life," and it begins with him.

22

CAREFUL WHAT YOU WISH FOR

1976

She wanted more.

Not only more money, though that was part of it. More credibility, more authority, more respect. After thirteen years at *Today*, she had risen from "the girl writer" to the co-host of the nation's most popular morning show. She made The Gallup Poll's list of the nation's top ten "most admired women" in the survey taken in 1976, just behind Mamie Eisenhower. Now Barbara wanted to be named anchor of the evening news, then the pinnacle for broadcast journalists. That was the position TV icons like Walter Cronkite and John Chancellor held, making them the faces of their networks. They didn't have to set two alarm clocks to wake up before dawn five days a week. They weren't expected to do dog food commercials.

"As the anchor, you are the automatic head," she said. "You are the one who does inaugurations. You are the one who does space flights. If the president goes on a trip, there's just no question of who is going to cover it." Besides, doing both the *Today* show and *Not for Women Only* five days a week "was killing me," she said. "I did 'Not for Women Only' because I wanted to prove that I could do my own show, that I didn't have to have a partner. It seems rather pathetic that I had to go out and prove that. A man wouldn't have had to."

By 1976, the women's movement was gaining momentum. Betty Friedan, author of the landmark *Feminine Mystique*, had helped found the National Organization for Women a decade earlier. President Richard Nixon in 1972 signed Title IX, banning sex-based discrimination in schools that received federal funding.

On the other hand, years would pass before the first woman was named to the Supreme Court or allowed to become an astronaut. While the Federal Communications Commission in 1971 began requiring local stations to file affirmative action plans for women as a condition for license renewal, no woman had ever been named anchor of a network's evening news show.

To Barbara's frustration, negotiations for a new contract with NBC were going nowhere despite the millions of dollars in advertising revenue she was pulling in for the network. She wanted "to move into a different level in her career," her agent said. Anchoring the evening news and hosting prime-time specials, say, for a million dollars a year. That was more than any other anchor had ever been paid; even Cronkite was making only about $400,000 a year.

The executives who had taken charge of NBC found Barbara Walters difficult to manage—one griped she had gotten "too big for her britches"—and they were offended by her demands for more money and power. (In his memoir, an exasperated Roone Arledge would liken hammering out her contracts to negotiating the Treaty of Ghent.) "They hated her," said her old ally Richard Wald, now installed as the president of NBC News. The company's top brass insisted on running the negotiations, not the news division's chiefs. "I did the wrong thing; I did not fight," Wald told me a half-century later. "But at the time, I was fighting seven other fires of a similar nature."

NBC was in upheaval. A few months earlier, RCA, which owned it, had ousted chairman and CEO Robert Sarnoff; the repercussions rippled through the rest of the company. The network was also deadlocked in negotiations with the National Association of Broadcast Employees and

Barbara Walters, left, and her older sister, Jackie. *(Family photo)*

Barbara, growing up in Brookline, Massachusetts. *(Family photo)*

Barbara, at left, with father Lou Walters, sister Jackie Walters, and mother Dena Walters.
(Family photo)

Barbara at Birch Wathen, the private
New York school where she received
her high school diploma in 1947.
(Photo from The Birch Wathen Lenox School archives)

Barbara in the yearbook at Sarah Lawrence College, where she graduated in 1951.

(Courtesy Sarah Lawrence College Archives)

Lou Walters at the Latin Quarter, circa 1950.

(Photo by Keystone Features/Hutton Archive/Getty Images)

The Latin Quarter dancers, featured in a CBS program, *Tonight on Broadway*, in 1949. *(CBS via Getty Images)*

Lou and Dena Walters meet the Duchess of Windsor, left, at a 1941 benefit show in Nassau for the British Red Cross. It featured performers from the Latin Quarter in Miami. *(Boston Globe, April 3, 1941)*

DUCHESS OF WINDSOR WITH BOSTON COUPLE—Lou Walters, Boston and Miami Beach night club impresario, took his entire show from the Latin Quarter at Miami Beach to Nassau last week to entertain in a benefit show for the British Red Cross, sponsored by the Duke and Duchess of Windsor. The expense of transporting and housing the show was underwritten by Mr. Walter as his contribution. Shown at the Colonial Hotel are left to right, the Duchess of Windsor, Lou Walters and Mrs. Lou Walters.

In 2006, New York mayor Michael Bloomberg, Barbara by his side, dedicates in honor of Lou Walters the stretch of West 48th Street at Broadway where the Latin Quarter stood.
(Michael Albans/NY Daily News Archive via Getty Images)

Barbara married her first husband, businessman Robert Katz, in 1955, at New York's Plaza Hotel.
(Miami Herald, June 21, 1955)

MRS. ROBERT KATZ
. . . *former Miss Walters*

Barbara and her second husband, Lee Guber, at their New York apartment in 1966.
(Rowland Scherman/Archive Photos/Getty Images)

Barbara married her third husband, Hollywood producer Merv Adelson, in Beverly Hills in 1986. *(AP Images/Peter Borsari)*

Barbara carries her two-year-old daughter, Jacqueline Guber, along Central Park South in 1970. *(Douglas Kirkland/Corbis via Getty Images)*

Barbara and her daughter, Jacqueline. *(Family photo)*

Barbara and her daughter, Jacqueline Guber Danforth, in 2008.

(Donna Svennevik/© ABC/Getty Images)

BELOW: Barbara and economist Alan Greenspan, circa 1977, when the two were dating. He later became chair of the Federal Reserve Board.

(Images Press/IMAGES/Getty Images)

Barbara and lawyer Roy Cohn attend a party at the Ritz-Carlton Hotel in Washington, D.C., in 1983.

(Guy DeLort/WWD/Penske Media via Getty Images)

Barbara and Virginia senator John Warner at a 1994 Friars Club dinner in New York honoring her. The two had previously been an item.

(Ron Galella, Ltd./Ron Galella Collection via Getty Images)

As a junior writer for CBS's *The Morning Show,* Barbara filled in at the last minute for a missing swimsuit model in 1956, her first appearance on the air. She is second from left. *(CBS via Getty Images)*

In 1965, Barbara, at right, reports on the Courrèges fashion collection from the rooftop of a Paris department store, La Samaritaine, for NBC's *Today* show.

(Jacques Haillot/Apis/Sygma via Getty Images)

Behind the scenes at NBC's *Today* show in 1966. *(Rowland Scherman/Archive Photos/Getty Images)*

Barbara extolls the virtues of a dishwasher on *Today* in 1966. Her on-air duties included commercials for Alpo and other products; host Hugh Downs is at right. *(Rowland Scherman/Archive Photos/Getty Images)*

Barbara and Hugh Downs on the *Today* set in 1966. *(Rowland Scherman/Archive Photos/Getty Images)*

Barbara, to the left of President Richard Nixon, was one of three female journalists credentialed to cover his breakthrough trip to China in 1972. Diane
Sawyer, then an assistant to the White House press secretary, stands in the
second row, third from right. *(White House Photo Office; Richard Nixon Presidential Library
and Museum)*

Barbara became the first female co-host of a network morning show. Here, she walks with assistant Mary Hornickle in April 1976 past a publicity photograph of herself in NBC's hallway. *(Bettmann/Getty Images)*

Harry Reasoner and Barbara at their opening show as co-anchors of the *ABC Evening News*, in October 1976. She was the first woman to be named co-anchor of an evening news program. *(AP Images)*

Barbara sits between Cindy Adams, left, and Liz Smith, columnists who chronicled her life and boosted her career. They are at a party in 2007 at the Four Seasons in New York. *(Patrick McMullan via Getty Images)*

Oprah Winfrey credited Barbara with providing a role model for her early broadcasting career. When Barbara died in 2022, Oprah posted this photo on social media.

(Virginia Sherwood/© ABC/Getty Images)

Publicity photo in 1990 of ABC's top anchors, dubbed "The Magnificent Seven." From left, Peter Jennings, Diane Sawyer, Ted Koppel, David Brinkley, Barbara Walters, Hugh Downs, and Sam Donaldson.

(ABC/Courtesy: Everett Collection)

Publicity photo in 2011 of ABC's top anchors. Barbara, seated at center, ignored instructions to wear black or navy. Diane Sawyer stands between Barbara and George Stephanopoulos; Katie Couric is to Barbara's left. *(ABC/Ida Mae Astute)*

Technicians, which represented its technical employees, thousands of them. The union called a nationwide strike when its contract ran out on March 31, 1976; those employees wouldn't return to work until almost two months later.

The negotiations for Barbara's next contract didn't seem to be a priority. She was making $700,000 a year. (That translates to more than $3.7 million in 2023 dollars.) She wanted that to increase by $100,000 in each subsequent year, and in a five-year contract, not a three-year one. "Over my dead body," NBC's chief negotiator, Al Rush, declared. "Three years. That's it." She wanted more say over the interviews she would do. And if there was going to be a new producer or co-host, she wanted a voice about who got hired. The network rejected those demands, too, arguing they represented an unprecedented and inappropriate usurpation of authority for a news show.

She had one more problem: Wald, her long-ago escort to *Deep Throat* and often her staunch defender, didn't think she would be particularly good as an evening anchor. He respected her as an indefatigable worker, an outstanding interviewer, a journalist with an instinctive sense of the audience. But he thought that reading a teleprompter of news somebody else had reported spotlighted not her strengths but her weaknesses. She didn't have the reassuring command and resonant tenor of the most successful anchors—all of them men, of course. "The prevailing thought was that delivering the news about politics, wars, and natural disasters would not be taken seriously if done by a woman," she said. A generation later, female broadcasters would still be struggling against that stereotype.

Wald told her he didn't think the anchor chair would be a good fit. "She gave me hell about that," he told me. Their friendship would survive, but so would her wound. "I liked, trusted, and respected him and thought he liked, trusted, and respected me," she wrote in her memoir. "But he obviously didn't."

The daughter of Lou Walters was about to make the biggest gamble of her career.

———

Lou Weiss, who with Lee Stevens at the William Morris Agency represented her, arranged a Saturday morning game of tennis with his Westchester neighbor Frederick Pierce, the president of ABC Television. "You know, Fred, Barbara Walters is looking for some additional challenges," Weiss told him. "She's not too thrilled with staying on the Today show." Before the two men parted that morning, the outlines of a deal had been sketched. "I don't know who won the game," Barbara quipped later, "but I do know that I was part of the score."

ABC was willing to make the leap, in part because the network had little to lose. Roone Arledge was making a name for ABC Sports and Fred Silverman had been lured from CBS to head the entertainment division, which was boasting hits including *Happy Days* and *Laverne and Shirley*. *Good Morning America* was beginning to gain ground on the *Today* show. But the news programs were a different story. They were running a distant third, the target of derision. "The joke used to be if you wanted to end the Vietnam War, put it on ABC and like all their programs, it would end quickly," Barbara said. She called ABC "the schlock news network."

ABC's executives were struggling to figure out how to boost their ratings. In 1975, the nightly news on CBS had a 28 percent audience share and NBC had a 26 percent share; ABC trailed at 20 percent. William Sheehan, the president of ABC News, shook up the show's staff, unveiled a graphics display device called Vidifont, and added a new economics correspondent. He also "conceded" to a TV columnist that "a female anchorwoman is not outside the realm of possibility."

Fred Pierce, Sheehan's boss, instantly saw the possibilities that would go with hiring Barbara, "a star personality with a lot of journalist credentials." Her departure would presumably create problems for the rival *Today* show, too. Not to mention the bragging rights ABC would get for being the first network to name a woman as a co-anchor of the evening news.

On the Monday morning after the tennis game, Pierce called Sheehan, and the two men met that day. Sheehan saw the possibilities, too. He already had been pushing the news division to devote more coverage to celebrities, pop culture, social trends—the sort of lifestyle topics that had always been in Barbara's wheelhouse. "People are interested in many things that are not intrinsically important," Sheehan had written in an internal memo that was quickly leaked, raising howls of protest from the industry's more traditional voices. He had underscored for emphasis his bottom line: "*I want more stories dealing with the pop people. The fashionable people. The new fads. Bright ideas. Changing mores and moralities.*"

Her million-dollar price tag seemed feasible because only half of it would be paid by the news division, the other half by the entertainment side for four hour-long specials she would host each year. "In truth it was a bargain for ABC," Barbara insisted. One more thing: She had regretted not claiming an ownership stake in *Not for Women Only*. In 1969, she formed her own production company, Barwall Productions, something more familiar in the entertainment world than in journalism. She would retain a stake in her ABC specials and, later, in *The View*, a source of income and power in her dealings with the network. "If you're going to work this hard, you want skin in the game," she advised some of her friends. "You want equity." That was surely a lesson learned from her father's spectacular successes and setbacks.

Pierce briefed chairman of the board Leonard Goldenson and ABC president Elton Rule. They signed on, too. Within a day or two, all the voices that mattered at ABC were on board. All but one: Harry Reasoner.

Harry had the credentials of the classic anchor. He had been a reporter for *The Minneapolis Times*, then joined CBS News in New York and became one of the original correspondents on *60 Minutes*. In 1970, he moved to ABC to co-anchor the evening news with Howard K. Smith. Harry had the deep voice and mane of graying hair the job was thought to demand; he was wry and adroit. But he also had a reputation for being lazy and a lunchtime drinker. "To tell you the truth, I don't exactly like working," he once acknowledged. That said, he had claimed the solo anchor chair once Smith left in 1975, and he had no interest in sharing it again. "He didn't want to be paired with anybody, whether it was a man, a woman, or a talking duck," the show's producer, Robert Siegenthaler, said.

But especially not with a woman. And especially not with Barbara Walters.

At the end of the month, Barbara was in Los Angeles for the Academy Awards; ABC had just taken over broadcast rights from NBC. (*One Flew Over the Cuckoo's Nest* swept the major categories that year.) Her agent, Lee Stevens, arranged a secret meeting for her in a private dining room at ABC's Century City complex. In a sign of their seriousness and their respect, the network's corporate heavyweights showed up: Goldenson and Rule and Pierce and Sheehan. The contrast could not have been starker with the lack of attention that the distracted NBC executives were showing her. NBC president Herbert Schlosser "never once took the time to meet with me," she complained.

The ABC executives put on a full-court press, expressing none of the reservations NBC had about her ambitions. They were looking to expand the half-hour evening news to forty-five minutes or a full hour, they told her, which would give the program the space to include some of the longer interviews she favored. Once a month, she would moderate ABC's Sunday morning interview show, *Issues and Answers*, a stodgy program but one that the old guard respected. She would host four specials a year and be featured in the network's coverage of election night and other big news events.

She was flattered by the attention and the offer, especially as NBC dithered, but she wasn't persuaded, not yet. NBC executives heard about the talks and scrambled, belatedly, to keep her. They offered to match the money and to sign a five-year contract, but they still wouldn't give her the anchor's job she wanted.

There was turmoil in her personal life, too. After a four-year separation from second husband Lee Guber, their divorce had just become final, on March 22, 1976. "Barbara Walters Sheds Mate No. 2" was the headline in the *Los Angeles Times*. One gossip columnist said "the television prima donna summarily dismissed him from their 13-year marriage." More quietly, her two-year affair with Senator Edward Brooke had ended, too.

Barbara had a casual romance with John Diebold, a pioneering business executive, and a more serious one with Alan Greenspan. Then the chairman of the Council of Economic Advisers for President Ford, the forty-nine-year-old bespectacled Greenspan had introduced himself by asking her to dance at a party in 1975 hosted by Vice President Nelson

Rockefeller. The very social New York media celebrity and the professorial Washington economist were an unlikely pair. "I escorted Barbara to lots of parties where I met people I otherwise would never have encountered," recalled Greenspan, who began a nineteen-year tenure as chair of the Federal Reserve in 1987. "I usually thought the food was good but the conversation dull. They probably thought the same of me."

At the time, she was also seeing Alan "Ace" Greenberg, an executive at The Bear Stearns Companies, Inc., who would become chairman and CEO of the investment bank. That led to some confusion at her apartment when one Alan or the other would call and leave a message with her housekeeper. Barbara would ask if "Alan" had spoken almost in a whisper (that would be Greenspan) or in a louder, jovial way (that would be Greenberg).

It was Greenspan who provided some reassurance she sought. After making back-of-the-envelope calculations, he told her that ABC could afford to pay the money they were promising.

Still, with the financial upheavals of her childhood never forgotten, she agonized over the decision, torn between the appeal of being a groundbreaker and the fear of being a flop. Was she repeating the mistakes of her father, risking a comfortable success for the draw of claiming even more? Then news of the negotiations leaked, tagging her with a label she would never lose, and one at odds with her desire to command more respect: million-dollar baby.

"ABC News Offers Barbara Walters $1 Million a Year," the headline on the front page of *The New York Times* read. The story explained why it mattered. "The contest between ABC and NBC for Miss Walters's services is significant in that it extends to the news realm of television the spectacular financial terms usually associated with entertainment stars." Among journalists, the concern was that adopting the financial rewards of the entertainment world inevitably would mean adopting its values.

There was also this red flag: Reasoner acknowledged he initially threatened to quit when he heard about the proposal to team him with her. "Nothing personal about Barbara," he said. "It's just that I'd rather continue to do the newscast by myself." He dismissed her credentials. "I was with her on Nixon's China trip, but I never actually saw her work," he told *Newsweek*. "All I know about her from that trip is that she rides a bus well."

The next morning, once the *Today* show had gone off the air at 9 a.m., she called Lee Stevens with her decision. She was ready to jump.

————

NBC said she had been pushed.

"NBC valued Barbara's service highly," John Chancellor intoned that night on the *Nightly News*, using the past tense, "but the negotiations for a renewal of her contract involved a million dollars and other privileges, and this afternoon NBC pulled out of the negotiations, leaving her a clear path to ABC. We wish her luck in her new job." His comments were a sign of the network's pique. Had such sensitive information about the salary demands and job negotiations of a network colleague been revealed on an evening newscast before?

Off the air, the quotes NBC officials were dishing were even less friendly. "It appeared yesterday that Miss Walters's departure from NBC might be effected on something less than amicable terms," *The New York Times* noted in yet another front-page story, quoting an NBC spokesman as decrying the "circus atmosphere" around the negotiations and her various demands. Those were presumably the ones Chancellor alluded to as "other privileges" beyond a million-dollar salary.

"There were things that one would associate with a movie queen, not a journalist, and we had second thoughts," the anonymous spokesman said.

Barbara fired back, saying the comments from "an uninformed, unidentified spokesman for NBC" were untrue. The decision to end negotiations had been hers, she said. The unnamed spokesman then retreated to higher ground. "It's a new day," he said. "We don't want to get into it any more. We wish her luck."

The million-dollar salary drew news stories, heated commentary, and the world's attention.

"The line between the news business and show business has been erased forever," wrote Charles B. Seib, the ombudsman at *The Washington*

Post. "That's entertainment money—up there with the likes of Johnny Carson and Catfish Hunter and the rock star of your choice. Tune in on the thrilling new soap opera, 'Barbara Walters, Barbara Walters,' soon to be seen on your local ABC outlet." That was a riff on *Mary Hartman, Mary Hartman*, a satirical soap opera of the day.

"Kobieta za 5 mlm dolarow" was the headline in Poland. There were stories in newspapers in Germany, France, Japan, and India. In an interview that aired on her second night on the evening news, Egyptian president Anwar Sadat teased her about it. "How do you like a million-dollars job?" he said as she smiled. "I must tell you quite frankly, you know the salary of my job. It is twelve thousand only—and I'm working day and night, Barbara!"

Reasoner also got a $100,000-a-year raise to match his new partner's $500,000 salary from the news division. He acknowledged his concerns on the *ABC Evening News*. "Some of you may have seen speculation about this in the papers," he said. "It's had more attention than Catfish Hunter, and Barbara can't even throw left-handed. [Actually, Catfish Hunter threw right-handed.] Many of the stories said that I had some reservations when the idea came up. If I did, they've been taken care of, and I welcome Barbara with no reservation." He said that having a woman as co-anchor "may well be an idea whose time has come."

His words sounded welcoming, but they had a double edge. Having a woman co-anchor "may" be an idea whose time has come, he had said, leaving open the possibility that maybe it hasn't. His reference to Catfish Hunter, the major league pitcher who had been baseball's first big-money free agent, was sly. The ballplayer's name was a joke in a new hit movie, *The Bad News Bears*, released two weeks earlier. When a Little League coach, played by Walter Matthau, tried to recruit a pitching prospect played by Tatum O'Neal, the imperious girl made ridiculous demands—imported jeans, modeling school, ballet lessons—before she would agree to play. The coach demanded, "Who do you think you are, Catfish Hunter?"

Besides the moniker of "Million-Dollar Baby," Barbara would soon gain another one of lasting fame.

On NBC's *Saturday Night Live*, comedian Gilda Radner introduced herself as "Baba Wawa," onstage to say farewell to NBC. "I don't wike weaving. Please trust me; it's not sowuh grapes, but wather that another network wecognizes in me a gweat talent for dewivewing wewevant news stories with crwstal cwarity to miwwions of Americans," she declared, the speech quirk so exaggerated that the words were hard to understand. "It's the onwy weason I'm weaving," she said to laughter. "Weally."

That comedic bit was introduced on April 24, 1976. The Baba Wawa character would appear dozens of times more on *SNL* over the four decades—*four decades*—that followed. Barbara was portrayed by Gilda Radner and Rachel Dratch and Cheri Oteri and others, the only consistency being an oversized wig and an inability to articulate "r's."

In public, Barbara laughed off the caricature, but in private she felt exposed and ridiculed over a speech impediment she had tried unsuccessfully to remedy. Others saw it as affirmation that she had entered the zeitgeist, though. "It's an incredible compliment about her career to be parodied that many times, and by that many actors," media analyst Brian Stelter told me. "Diane Sawyer hasn't been parodied by *SNL* that many times, in case anyone's keeping score."

When Radner died of ovarian cancer at age forty-two, Barbara sent a sympathy note to her widower, Gene Wilder. She signed it "Baba Wawa."

FAILURE

1976

"Good evening," Harry Reasoner began the evening news show, as always, then teased the day's top story. Agriculture Secretary Earl Butz had resigned amid a firestorm over telling a racist and obscene joke to, among others, former White House counsel John Dean. He had then revealed it to the world in an article he wrote for *Rolling Stone*. (Butz should have thought twice if he was counting on Dean to keep the vulgar comment quiet; the young lawyer's claim to fame was spilling the beans on President Richard Nixon in the Watergate scandal.) Dean didn't name the cabinet official who had been chitchatting in the first-class cabin of a flight leaving Kansas City after the Republican National Convention in August, but Butz was quickly identified as the culprit.

Without much of a segue, Reasoner then introduced the woman seated next to him. "Closer to home, I have a new colleague to welcome," he said with an expression that didn't exactly convey warmth. "Barbara?"

Her arrival on set was bigger news than Butz's demise—a media and a cultural milestone, although not everybody agreed whether it signaled a move in the right direction. Her picture was splashed on the covers of that week's editions of *People*, *Newsweek*, and *U.S. News & World Report*. President Gerald Ford sent a congratulatory telegram. "Good luck," rival Walter Cronkite of CBS told her in a phone call that day, "but not too much."

ABC's evening news show ran a perennial third place in the network ratings, but on this night, the first edition of *The ABC Evening News with Harry Reasoner and Barbara Walters* scored twice as many viewers as the competition on CBS or NBC. While a few women had filled in as evening network TV anchors in the past, Barbara Walters was the first to land the title and the permanent role. She had been waiting impatiently for this moment. She had been forced to spend the summer off the air after NBC declined to let her out of her contract early.

"Thank you, Harry," she replied. "Well, tonight has finally come for me, and I'm very pleased to be with you, Harry, and with ABC News."

After reports on Butz's resignation by the White House correspondent covering President Ford and the political correspondent covering Democratic presidential nominee Jimmy Carter, the two anchors engaged in something seen as revolutionary at the time: unscripted conversation. Give-and-take on the air was increasingly common during local newscasts but was generally dismissed by the national broadcasts as beneath their dignity, as "happy talk," not journalism.

This time, Barbara mentioned that she had talked to Earl Butz on the phone just before the show went on the air—a reminder of her legendary network of contacts with newsmakers. He had taken a jab at Carter, who two weeks earlier had sparked a furor of his own over an errant comment. He had told *Playboy* magazine that he had "looked on a lot of women with lust," committing adultery "in my heart many times." She quoted Butz: "Since I resigned for my indiscretion, I think Jimmy Carter should now step up to the plate himself and resign for his indiscreet remarks in *Playboy*."

Harry disputed the comparison. "I suppose, I suppose the Carter people would object to having one verbal indiscretion linked to a racial joke," he said. "Umm, let me tell you a little bit more about what Earl Butz said," she replied, although neither ABC nor any other network show quoted the offensive language in its entirety.

Earlier that day, Barbara had recorded two interviews by satellite to air on the first two nights of the new show. One was with Golda Meir, the first woman to be elected prime minister of Israel; she had led the government when the Yom Kippur War had begun on this date three years earlier. The other was with Anwar Sadat, the president of Egypt. She had promised Golda Meir her interview would go first, before Sadat, but ABC News president Bill Sheehan thought Sadat was more interesting; he decided to break his interview into two parts and to air the first one that night. Meir's interview would follow the next day. The Israeli leader was so furious about the broken commitment over timing that for the remaining two years of her life she refused to do another interview with Barbara.

At the end of the broadcast, Barbara told the audience that she was happy to be back on the air. "I missed you," she told those who had watched her on the *Today* show, and she welcomed others who might have tuned in because of "curiosity brought on by . . . my hourly wage." She said she wanted to offer a closer look at the people making the news and a deeper explanation of how the news affected viewers' lives. "I'd like to pause from time to time as we show news items to you and say, 'Wait a minute. What does this mean to my life and yours?'" she said. The program reported the Dow Jones Industrial Average as a matter of course, for instance; she wanted to explain "what it means to you, even if you don't own any stock." She said she would also focus on issues of particular concern to women.

What she outlined would become the norm for TV news—a focus on social trends as well as government edicts, and on the impact of news developments in the lives of those who were watching. But then and later, more traditional journalists worried aloud about the risks of reducing the emphasis on hard news in pursuit of more trivial matters and of higher ratings. "None dare call it show biz," *Time* magazine said, warning that the "new and less hard-newsy combination of interviews, news-you-can-use features and ad libbing is being watched closely by CBS and NBC, which now largely serve their news straight, thank you."

"She is changing our conception of news," a *New Republic* critic intoned, "I believe, for the worse." The *Los Angeles Times* published a front-page, multi-part series headlined "Crisis in TV News: Show-Biz Invasion." The tone could not have been more alarmist if the invaders had arrived from outer space. Barbara was featured in the opening paragraphs.

———

The first reviews of her performance on the air were reasonably positive, although they were often seasoned with sarcasm and sexism. "Miss Walters has not faltered or fumbled embarrassingly on the new job," *The New York Times* said, not quite a compliment. "In addition to being attractive, Miss Walters is a thorough professional, a remarkable woman who has risen to the top in what was once almost exclusively a man's world." *Newsday* said she had gotten off to "a good start," adding, "She didn't fall off her chair." *Time* magazine called her debut "as crisp as a new $100 bill," an allusion not only to her delivery but also to her paycheck. That was about the amount she was being paid for every minute of the newscast, the critic had calculated.

The review also sarcastically mentioned "Walters' weadily wecognizable deliverwy."

But the interaction between her and Harry was tense from the start. There were no signs of the spark that network executives had hoped for from the pairing. Executive producer Robert Siegenthaler's suggestion that they try for the sort of banter between Katharine Hepburn and Spencer Tracy in the movies went nowhere. On the second night, after Sadat had teasingly noted her million-dollar salary, Barbara turned to Reasoner and said, "But what I should have said to President Sadat is that he has better fringe benefits than we do, Harry." He gave her a silent, pained look. He seemed "as comfortable on camera with Walters as a governor under indictment," *The New Republic* observed.

Hundreds of women wrote personal letters to Walters relating their own experiences with workplace harassment and urging her to hang in there; she drafted a form letter to reply. Anita Colby, the supermodel and socialite whose *Today* show segments had given Barbara her first break, lodged a complaint with the president of ABC about Reasoner's attitude. "He made a remark that had some sexual connotation and I felt was very rude," she said. "I don't know how she could keep a stiff upper lip. It would have dissolved me into tears—but she's tough."

Actor John Wayne, whom she had never met, sent a telegram she would never forget. "Don't let the bastards get you down," it said.

On one early show, a news story aired about Henry Kissinger, the secretary of state and an occasional escort for Barbara at high-profile social events. "You know, Harry, Kissinger didn't do too badly as a sex symbol in Washington," she quipped to Reasoner. He replied icily, "Well, you'd know more about that than I would."

Both sides cited the exchange as evidence against the other. His defenders called her comment too cozy for a serious news program. Her defenders called his response nasty, a riposte that targeted her personal life.

The anchors' animosity behind the scenes was soon no secret to viewers on the air. Their body language became so hostile that Siegenthaler ordered the news director to avoid two-shots—that is, a camera angle that would show both of them at the same time. The risk was too high that one of them, usually Harry, would be looking disgusted at whatever the other was saying.

"It was cats and dogs; it was black and white," said Lynn Sherr, a groundbreaking correspondent herself who joined the show a year after Barbara arrived. "Harry wasn't always the world's nicest human being. This friendly 'Uncle Harry' image that he had on *60 Minutes* was kind of a joke. He was very smart, a wonderful writer, had a great delivery, but he could be very snarky." For her part, Barbara bristled at Harry's assertion that she hadn't earned the right to be there.

After the show each night, he would decamp to the bar at the Café Des Artistes around the block and loudly critique her performance. The camera crews and stagehands who had worked with him for years followed his lead in rebuffing her friendly overtures. Eventually, when she arrived in the newsroom each day, "she would come in with her head down; she wouldn't look left or right, and she wouldn't talk to anybody," Ellen Rossen, a producer at ABC who later married Av Westin, told me. "It was like an iceberg in there."

The rivalry between them intensified when ABC decided not to expand the nightly newscast from a half-hour to forty-five minutes or an hour, a prospect the network had used in convincing Barbara to sign a contract. That would have given her the breathing space to do her trademark interviews; it would have enabled Harry to get equal time for his commentaries.

But at a meeting with ABC affiliate stations in Los Angeles in May 1976, the first time Barbara and Harry appeared together, local TV executives were decidedly unenthusiastic about losing control to the national network of additional airtime and revenue. NBC and CBS had responded to the ABC initiative by discussing a similar move, but both decided against it. By that fall, so had ABC. A half-century later, there would be competing all-news cable stations but the network newscasts would still last only a half-hour.

Taking into account commercials, that meant Harry and Barbara had a grand total of twenty-two minutes each night to share on the air.

"He just hazed her," said Bob Iger, then a junior production assistant on the show who would rise to become president of ABC Television and CEO of the Walt Disney Co. "The tension was palpable . . . and I just remember thinking, how is the network going to get out of this one?" The only person Barbara Walters felt free to confide in was her makeup artist, and even her sympathy had its limits. "I would cry," Barbara said, "and she'd say, 'Stop crying, you're smearing the make-up.'"

The embattled Siegenthaler was replaced by Av Westin, who arrived with orders to negotiate a cease-fire on the set. Westin told me he was greeted at his new job by Bernie Cohen, a producer close to Harry. "You owe me," Cohen said. He had been using a stopwatch to time how long each anchor spoke, and he demanded an extra five minutes and fifteen seconds for Harry because on the previous day's show Barbara had scored that time advantage.

————

Their friction became fodder for humorists. In his Sunday column in *The New York Times*, Russell Baker offered his services as a counselor to resolve their differences. "We know, of course, that Barbara has the money, and it may be that Harry, a model of virility if there ever was one, resents having to ask her for $10 every time he wants to go bowling with the camera crew," he wrote. Art Buchwald of *The Washington Post* imagined a new "Babs and Hal Show" if they could only overcome their "domestic strife"; in his vision, they would deliver the news while holding hands and sharing a loveseat. The sarcastic headline: "Babs, You're One in a Million, Hawwy Weasoner, I Wuv You Too."

On *The Tonight Show,* Johnny Carson chatted with a large mustachioed man wearing a pink Cupid costume; he was holding an oversized gold-colored bow-and-arrow. "I have to shoot an arrow into Barbara Walters," Cupid explained. "Ah, you mean you're making her fall in love with Harry Reasoner," Carson replied. "No," Cupid said. "Harry just paid me to shoot her."

There was more serious speculation about who would survive. "The $1-million on-air marriage of Harry Reasoner and Barbara Walters is on the rocks," TV columnist Frank Swertlow reported in the *Chicago Daily News*. "Harry and Babs may be heading for the divorce court after only four months together." He quoted Sheehan as saying the network was considering sending Barbara to Washington to co-anchor the broadcast, which would mean the two of them would not have to sit side by side each night. She immediately told reporters she wasn't moving anywhere.

"The Showdown at ABC News" was the headline in *The New York Times*, featuring dueling interviews with the two co-anchors in their offices on either side of the newsroom. "Harry has been unhappy since the day the new show started," Barbara said. She pointedly asked, "And if he leaves where will he go?" As for Harry, "sources" were quoted in the story saying he "may seek a 'her-or-me' decision within a matter of weeks." Whether Barbara could sustain the show without him or a similar "credible" news figure, media reporter Jeff Greenfield wrote, "is a question very much in doubt."

The most troubling development for Barbara wasn't the reviews from the critics but the ratings from the audience. After that first night of record numbers, ABC's show remained stuck in third place. ("Welcome back," David Brinkley said in a wink to viewers when he opened NBC's newscast on the second night of the rival show.) During the last three months of 1976, ABC's share of the audience ticked up to 19 percent from 18 percent, but Cronkite's lead at CBS widened, to 29 percent from 27. NBC's show with John Chancellor and David Brinkley dipped to 25 percent from 26—still well ahead of ABC.

ABC got so many letters from viewers threatening to quit watching the show that a form letter was drafted to respond.

"We feel that the new co-anchor format with Barbara Walters and Harry Reasoner will add a very exciting dimension to newscasting, and we hope you will decide to continue to be one of our viewers," it said. "In that connection, we do ask that you keep an open mind and tune in for a reasonable period before making your decision."

———

The metrics mattered, for the networks' influence and their bottom lines.

TV newscasts were approaching the apogee of their influence. Forty million Americans tuned in to the nightly news each night to find out what had gone on in the country and the world that day. Cable TV wasn't prevalent yet, nor social media nor streaming services nor the other myriad options for staying informed that would emerge down the road. During that era, the three TV networks had as much control over defining the news and delivering it as any set of media outlets in U.S. history, before or after. The anchors on those shows reflected the assumptions about what voices Americans wanted to hear, about whom they would believe. In some households, "Uncle Walter" Cronkite was all but a member of the family, more trusted than any elected official.

Barbara aspired to that high ground, one that had never before been held by a woman—or, for that matter, by a Jew or a person of color or someone who was openly gay.

Growing up, she had seen in her father's career the risks of refusing to be satisfied with a success in hand, of gambling it all for some bigger prize. Now she worried she was following in Lou Walters's footsteps. "Everything I had worked for all these past years now was crashing down because of my bad judgment," she said. "I told myself that I should never have taken the chance. Was it ego? Was it too much ambition?"

Decades later, when she was named one of *Time* magazine's 100 most influential people in the world, she would call the episode the greatest learning experience of her life. By then, she had long regained her equilibrium and restored her career, although never again as the anchor of the evening news show. "Our program failed and I had to prove myself and work my way back," she recalled. "I think I did my best work then. From failure can often come success."

At the time, though, she wasn't sure she would ever recover. "I didn't know how she was going to live through it without having a breakdown," said Joyce Ashley, a psychoanalyst who had been one of her closest friends since high school. Barbara thought her career might well be over. "I was drowning," she said. "I was not only drowning, I was reading every day about people who were happy to put my head under the water."

Her mother, who had always doubted her husband's big ambitions, brought the same apprehension to her daughter. When Barbara would call her in Florida, Dena Walters would fret about every negative word she had read in the gossip columns. "Mom, what they wrote isn't true," her daughter would assure her. "She would respond, 'Oh darling, if it isn't true, why is it in the papers?'"

By then, Lou Walters was living at the Miami Jewish Home and Hospital for the Aged, the onetime high roller now dependent on his daughter's largesse. "He was very frail, and when I telephoned him, he struggled with the right thing to say," Barbara recalled. "He had always been afraid that my career might be over. Now that it looked as if it was happening, he tried so hard to cheer me up. He had a television set in his room and would say, 'You looked beautiful last night, darling. It will turn out all right.'

"And then he would add in a small voice, 'Do you want to come down here for a while?'"

In the end, it would turn out all right for Barbara. But that would take time and sweat and a boost from some powerful men. Fidel Castro, for one.

24

FIDEL

1977

Fidel Castro steered the jeep with one hand and gestured with his cigar in the other when he gave Barbara two things to hold as they splashed through the Sierra Maestra's rain-swollen streams. One was a tin of hard candies he kept on the dashboard to distribute to the children who would gather whenever he stopped in a town or village. The other was his revolver.

"My job was to hold the candy and the gun over my head to keep them dry," she said.

She had already interviewed the charismatic Cuban strongman for five hours the previous day and night about his regime's political prisoners, its crackdown on a free press, his communist ideology, and his personal life, which had long been shrouded in privacy. (He refused to even acknowledge that he had a private life.) The next morning, they flew in his presidential plane to Santiago de Cuba for a guided tour of the region where he and a band of insurgents had launched the revolution that overthrew dictator Fulgencio Batista in 1959.

As they drove, her hair pulled back under a bandanna, he taught her the lyrics in Spanish to one of his favorite songs, "Cielito Lindo," a familiar Mexican tune favored by mariachi bands.

Ay, ay, ay, ay,
Canta y no llores,
Porque cantando se alegran,
Cielito lindo, los corazones.

They ended the day at his mountain retreat, a complex of cabins with hot water, fresh towels, Algerian wine, and, for dinner, a roast suckling pig with the head still attached. Castro jokingly demanded payment for his services he had rendered—as an actor, perhaps. ABC producer Tom Capra protested that he had been a lousy actor, stopping in the middle of scenes to talk to children. What about as a director or producer? "You took us through swamps," Capra replied. "If that's your idea of directing, it's not very good. And don't think you're a producer, because we wasted hours and hours seeing absolutely nothing."

On the other hand, Castro, wearing his familiar olive-green military fatigues, had driven the jeep. They settled on five dollars in payment for that job. Capra wrote out a receipt for his expense account—"Payment to one driver, Fidel Castro, $5"—and Castro signed it with a flourish. He would give Barbara another note, scrawled in red ink on a copy of the constitution of the Republic of Cuba, and written after a very late night. "For Barbara as a remembrance of the most difficult interview that I have had in all the days of my life," he wrote in Spanish. "Fidel Castro, May 20, 1977. 1:29 a.m."

She framed it and hung it in her Fifth Avenue apartment, alongside photos and mementos of others she had interviewed, the respected and the reviled. They included a page of the questions she had prepared for the first joint interview with an Egyptian president and an Israeli prime minister; Anwar Sadat and Menachem Begin had both signed it. Yasir Arafat had inscribed his photo, "Revolution until victory." The long center hallway was a timeline of the conversations that had defined her life.

She called it her "Wall of Radicals." They had rescued her career.

Barbara's pursuit of Castro and the interview she delivered with him would be among the most celebrated and controversial. It would demonstrate her strategies and her tactics, some of them problematic, and her unrelenting drive to dominate the news. "A turning point in my career," she said. The nature of their relationship would become the subject of unending speculation, too.

———

Barbara had met Castro during a trip to Cuba in 1975, when she was part of a press contingent covering a four-day fact-finding trip by South Dakota senator George McGovern. She had made a point of wooing the Cuban dictator, and he rewarded her by promising her an exclusive interview for the *Today* show. She had been trying to schedule it ever since. She had sent letters to the Cuban mission of the United Nations and to the Czech embassy in Washington, which handled some Cuban affairs since the United States didn't have diplomatic relations with Havana.

Now she had moved to the *ABC Evening News*. The prospect of landing an interview with Castro loomed even larger, a way to counter the deluge of criticism she was enduring in her new job.

Then, suddenly, he agreed. Unknown to the public at the time, then–Secretary of State Henry Kissinger had secret exchanges with Castro during the final two years of President Ford's tenure about improving relations. When Jimmy Carter took office in 1977, he instructed his national security aides to build on the effort and explore establishing more normal ties. "The Cubans decided to do a full-court press at the beginning of the Carter administration," Peter Kornbluh, coauthor of a book about the back-channel negotiations, told me. The sit-down with Barbara was part of that behind-the-scenes campaign. "The interview helped basically humanize Fidel Castro," who had been demonized in the United States and was the target of a coup and covert assassination attempts during the Kennedy administration.

Important as it was, Barbara exaggerated the exclusivity of her interview.

"The mysterious Cuban leader hadn't given a television interview in sixteen years, except for little blips about some sports event," she wrote in her memoir. That would be news to Dan Rather, who had done his own extended interview with Castro for a *CBS Reports* special in 1974. Indeed, Barbara wasn't even the first female journalist from ABC to interview Castro. Lisa Howard, the network's first full-time female correspondent, had interviewed Castro on camera in 1963 for an ABC special called *Fidel Castro: Self Portrait*. It aired to some acclaim.

Lisa Howard isn't mentioned in Barbara's biography, though the journalist, three years older than Barbara, had gained a similar reputation for landing exclusive interviews with top newsmakers. As a radio reporter, she had gotten the first interview Nikita Khrushchev did with a reporter from the West. She interviewed President Dwight D. Eisenhower, Senator John F. Kennedy, and former first lady Eleanor Roosevelt. ABC hired her in May 1961, then fired her four years later for her leftist political activism.

At that point, Barbara had managed to get her first on-air job at *Today*, launching the career that would have her traveling to Havana in 1977.

————

When she arrived in Cuba, she and her producers met with Castro in his office. "Where would you like to go?" he asked, speaking in Spanish through his longtime interpreter, Juana Vera, known as Juanita. Barbara said she would like to see the Bay of Pigs and the Sierra Maestra. "We'll do both," he replied. The next morning, they rode a Cuban patrol boat across the bay.

"Is it true that we are the first Americans to cross the Bay of Pigs in sixteen years?" she asked—that is, since a small band of Cuban Americans had crossed it in a doomed CIA-backed attempt to overthrow his regime.

"As I remember, this is the first time," he replied.

"How do you feel when you come to the Bay of Pigs?" she asked.

"Before the invasion I usually came here to fish and to rest," he said. "After the invasion, I continued to come here, many times. I like this place. It is quiet, and there are good places for underwater fishing." So the bay that had become a symbol of America's failed Cold War coup was, in the target's mind, a pleasant spot for spear-fishing.

In their interview, Castro made it clear he was a communist, a question not then considered settled. He also acknowledged that Cuba's prisons held political prisoners, several thousand of them. "You allow no dissent," Barbara said. "Your newspapers, radio, television, motion pictures are under state control. People can dissent in their meetings, in their congresses, but no dissent or opposition is allowed in the public media."

"Barbara, our concept of freedom of the press is not like yours," he responded. "If you asked us if a newspaper could appear here against socialism, I can say honestly no, it cannot appear. It would not be allowed by the party, the government, or the people. In that sense we do not have the freedom of the press that you possess in the U.S. And we are very satisfied about that."

He was candid about his public policy but not about his personal life. "What is the importance of my being married or not?" he said when she persisted in asking. She pressed: Why should such a simple question be so difficult to answer? He paused and finally replied, "*Formalmente, no.*" "Formally, no." That was all. After the cameras were off, he led her and the crew into the kitchen, where he made melted cheese sandwiches for everyone.

When *Fidel Castro Speaks* aired on ABC in June, Cuba's state-controlled television broadcast nearly the entire interview, a step believed to be unprecedented. That presumably reflected an effort to prepare the Cuban people, too, for improved relations between the two countries. They showed the questions Castro parried about political prisoners and freedom of the press, apparently cutting only her queries about whether he was married.

In the United States, there was a flood of criticism from Cuban Americans, dismayed that she had given a friendly platform to a dictator whose regime they had fled. But the *New York Times* reviewer praised the skills she demonstrated in the hour-long prime-time special.

"Barbara Walters questions, confronts, flatters, cajoles, laughs, reprimands and, in general, turns in the kind of performance that has made her a major figure in television journalism, much to the consternation of many of her men colleagues," John J. O'Connor said, noting the connection she seemed to forge with her subjects. "For President Castro, as for President Anwar el-Sadat of Egypt and numerous other world leaders, Miss Walters is simply Barbara, and there is always the pronounced presence of man-women vibrations, which the interviewer skillfully uses to her advantage."

Barbara described her feminine wiles as a useful asset, appropriate to deploy—an approach that made some more traditional female journalists cringe, then and later. "I love to flirt and be flirted with," she wrote in her 1970 book, *How to Talk with Anybody About Practically Anything*. In her 2008 memoir, *Audition*, she said being a woman sometimes gave her an advantage. "Sex rears its happy little head, and a sought-after male subject chooses you to do the interview in the hope that somewhere along the line, the romantic side—or at least the flirtatious side—will surpass the professional," she wrote.

That wasn't the case with Castro, she insisted more than once. But others saw an unmistakable spark between them.

After she arranged the guest list for a dinner party at the Cuban mission when Castro visited the United Nations in 1979, then acted as his hostess, rumors swirled that their connection was romantic. Barbara blamed sexism. "I liked him a lot," she said. "Did we have a romance? Because how else could you, you know, what were you doing being a female reporter with Fidel Castro if you didn't have a romance?" The unmentioned evidence for that view: Castro a few years earlier had a sexual relationship with Lisa Howard.

"We did not have a romance," Barbara said flatly, though she acknowledged, "He is a magnetic personality." Her protestations, which turn on how to define the word "romance," didn't squelch the speculation. Whatever the parameters of her relationship with Castro, he was the sort of controversial, strong-willed man she found intriguing, along the lines of Roy Cohn and Richard Nixon.

David Westin, who became the president of ABC News, went to Cuba with Barbara for a second interview with Castro in 2002. "There was chemistry," he told me.

———

Castro seemed to feel an affinity for Barbara, too. He was willing to do what she asked. "I felt he liked me," she said. "Did he give me more of his time than he might have given a male journalist? Possibly."

Andrea Mitchell, NBC's chief foreign affairs correspondent, attended one of Barbara's small dinner parties in 2002 with her husband, Federal Reserve chairman Alan Greenspan, one of Barbara's old flames. Andrea mentioned proudly that, after months of effort, she had succeeded in scheduling an interview with Castro during an upcoming conference in Havana commemorating the fortieth anniversary of the Cuban Missile Crisis.

That disclosure turned out to be a mistake. The two women were friendly, "but nothing gets between Barbara and a 'get,'" Andrea said ruefully afterward.

Barbara turned around and arranged her own interview with the Cuban leader at the conference—and ahead of Andrea's, of course. But being ahead of Andrea wasn't enough: Barbara wanted the competition out of the way. When she met with Castro again in Havana, "I remember saying to him that he had gotten grayer and I had gotten blonder," she said. Castro told her, "So good to see you, Barbara. Andrea Mitchell's coming in two days." Barbara told Westin he had to convince the Cuban foreign minister, Felipe Pérez Roque, to cancel Andrea's interview. "They've got MSNBC," the cable network, she said. "They'll be able to get it on before *20/20* on Friday night."

The foreign minister demurred, saying the decision was up to Castro. Westin made his case at an impromptu meeting with the Cuban dictator. "Thank you, Mr. President, for your time and your candor," he began. "But the truth is that the way TV works in America, for you to reach as many people as possible, it's important that Barbara's interview be the first one to air in the United States. If you give another interview to someone else that airs around the same time, it will dilute the force of what you are saying, and neither of us would want that."

NBC had already sent out a press release touting the interview Castro had promised Andrea for the *Today* show, but Castro agreed on the spot to cancel it.

By now, Andrea had arrived in Havana, too. The *Today* show was planning two days of coverage around the conference and her interview, with host Matt Lauer flying in to anchor. Dan Rather of CBS had scheduled a session with Castro as well, or so he thought. They all learned from the New York tabloids that Barbara was getting the only interview Castro would do.

Castro tried to make amends, summoning Andrea to his office at the end of the conference and then giving her a ride to the airport, driving straight onto the tarmac for her to board her commercial flight. "Are you angry with me, Andrea?" he asked. "Yes, I am," she replied. Andrea would eventually get a sit-down with Castro that December.

For now, though, Barbara had her exclusive.

She followed up on a question he had dodged in their interview nearly a quarter-century earlier. What about his personal life? He was now said to have five children and many grandchildren, including triplets.

"It's prohibited to go into my personal life," he protested. "It's not our way."

"What's to hide?" she asked.

"It's my human right," he protested with a smile. "I cling to my human right to defend my privacy." He finally acknowledged, "Yes, we have descendants and all that." Triplets? "Well, I think there are some triplets around," he allowed. "I've heard they exist."

Castro, who died five years later, presented Barbara with a picture book of old combat photos from the Bay of Pigs, titled *Memories of a Victory*, with a note attached, written in Spanish: "For Barbara, in whose terrible hands I fell again after 25 years. I promise that I will never try to escape. It's impossible, and I think with affability about our next meeting, arranged for 2027."

The unlikely promise of another interview a quarter-century down the road was a joke but reflected a truth, something Castro recognized even if Barbara didn't fully acknowledge it. She lived for the get. She would feel a void in a personal life that was dominated by her needy parents and sister, her disappointing marriages, her estrangement from her only child. But her professional life could fill her with a sense of victory and vindication. She was addicted to the chase, the thrill of the scoop, the envy of her colleagues, the global headlines.

Woe to anyone, man or woman, who stood in her path.

25

COMEBACK

1977

Barbara was in Kansas City, interviewing Dolly Parton for one of her celebrity TV specials, when she heard that Walter Cronkite had scored a scoop—another one. He had been the anchor of the *CBS Evening News* for fifteen years and would stay in the job for four more, a journalist so trusted that his assessment in 1968 of a stalemate in the Vietnam War shook the nation and the Johnson White House.

Cronkite had developed a friendly relationship with Anwar Sadat since the Egyptian leader had taken power in 1970 after the death of Gamal Abdel Nasser. Cronkite managed to land the first TV interview by a Western correspondent with the new president. That initial interview made little news but the setting was memorable. The two men sat under a sprawling banyan tree on the banks of the Nile, smoking their pipes as they talked.

Now Agence France-Presse was reporting that Sadat was willing to go to Israel to discuss peace, an unprecedented gesture after three decades of enmity that dated to the founding of the Jewish state. The wire service moved the story on Friday, November 11, 1977. Cronkite assumed

Sadat's offer to Israel would be hedged with the usual preconditions designed to make a trip impossible. But he was intrigued enough that he arranged for another interview with Sadat, this one on the following Monday by satellite, then a cumbersome affair.

This time, there was news. In the 1977 interview, Cronkite asked Sadat about the AFP report. "I'm just waiting for the proper invitation," he replied. Under what conditions? "The only condition is that I want to discuss the whole situation with the 120 members of the Knesset and put the full picture and detail of the situation from our point of view." How soon? "In the earliest time possible," he said, perhaps even within a week.

As the interview was going on, Cronkite turned to a staffer and mouthed the words, *"Get Begin!"* As it happened, Israeli prime minister Menachem Begin was scheduled to deliver a speech that night at the Tel Aviv Hilton. The CBS News bureau in Israel scrambled to set up a temporary studio in an adjoining room for a satellite interview with him.

That interview made news, too. "Tell him he's got an invitation," Begin told Cronkite.

The back-and-forth exchanges dominated that night's newscast, surprised U.S. policymakers, and transformed the possibilities for peace in the Mideast. Cronkite interlaced the separate interviews in a way that made it almost seem as though the two leaders were talking to one another. *The New York Times* splashed the story with a three-deck headline across the top of the front page the next morning and published transcripts of both interviews. Cronkite had done what Barbara craved: advanced a diplomatic breakthrough and achieved a singular journalistic coup. No one questioned his gravitas or his right to sit in the anchor's chair.

CBS almost didn't have this exclusive to itself.

The new president of ABC News, Roone Arledge, had gotten a heads-up from an Israeli go-between that Sadat was ready to make news about an overture to Israel, if only a journalist would ask him. Arledge ordered Peter Jennings, then ABC's chief foreign correspondent, to fly to Cairo. Jennings, famously erudite and self-confident, seemed skeptical that his new boss really knew what he was talking about. Jennings met with Sadat, as instructed, but didn't bother to bring a camera crew with him.

As a result, CBS owned the exclusive. Jennings would pay for that miscalculation.

Roone decided to send Barbara to Israel as the lead reporter on the historic visit because, he noted, she had relationships with both Sadat and Begin from interviewing them before. Roone was also searching for a way to rescue the fortunes of his million-dollar anchor. It represented a rebuke for Jennings. His resentment about being bigfooted on the story would fester. "Peter held this against me for years," Barbara said. "I didn't blame him, but I didn't turn down the assignment."

Sadat announced he would fly to Jerusalem on Saturday, just five days after Cronkite's interview. Barbara flew to Tel Aviv on Friday, on the same commercial flight as NBC anchor John Chancellor; she was puzzled that Cronkite wasn't also on the flight. She soon learned why. The sixty-one-year-old CBS icon was one step ahead of her.

That night, after recording an interview with Israeli foreign minister Moshe Dayan, she was awakened from an exhausted sleep by Roone, calling from New York. "Cronkite's in Cairo," he told her. "He's got a seat on Sadat's plane tomorrow to Tel Aviv. Chancellor may be on that plane, too. Get on that plane."

Simply traveling to Cairo from Tel Aviv was no easy enterprise.

At the time, direct flights weren't permitted between Egypt and Israel; there weren't even phone connections between the two nations. Taking commercial flights through Cyprus wouldn't get her to Cairo in time. But CBS had chartered a French jet to ferry equipment from Paris to Tel Aviv. ABC hired that same charter to fly her and her crew to Egypt, with plans to make the requisite intermediate stop in Cyprus. Roone was working his contacts; he managed to convince the Egyptian ambassador to the United States, Ashraf Ghorbal, to get a direct flight approved, with no stop-off in Cyprus.

That would be historic in itself: The first civilian plane to take off in Israel and land in Egypt since 1948 would be ferrying Barbara Walters.

Then there was the question of getting on Sadat's plane. Barbara called Ghorbal, too, at his home in Washington, pleading for his help. "He said he would try but could give me no guarantees," she said.

Hours later, Walter Cronkite was boarding the Egyptian presidential plane in Cairo, preparing to make the historic journey with Sadat. Then, despite the airport's heavy security, he noticed a small French charter landing. His heart sank as he saw Barbara Walters disembark in a hurry. "She hopped out of it and ran across the field like a football player going into the play," he said. She was holding her hand up and waving it at his plane—as if to say "wait for me." "I couldn't have been unhappier," he recalled.

It was only the beginning of Cronkite's bad day.

He had a good relationship with Sadat, but it didn't compare to the warmth of the friendship Barbara had forged with him in her own previous interviews.

When the two men connected in that groundbreaking satellite interview on Monday, Sadat welcomed Cronkite with his customary query. "Good morning, Walter, and how is Barbara?" The Egyptian president opened every conversation with Cronkite with that question, as though the two Americans were partners, not competitors. Cronkite dubbed the standing exchange "our Barbara preliminaries," an annoyance he could hardly protest without seeming churlish. "Barbara is a friend of mine, but unless she falls ill—pray not—her health is not a burning issue with me," he grumbled.

The official plane flew from Cairo to Ismailia, near Sadat's weekend retreat, to pick him up for the flight to Tel Aviv. The TV anchors and *Time* magazine's veteran Mideast correspondent, Wilton Wynn, who had also gotten a seat on the plane, watched as Sadat walked slowly down a red carpet past an Egyptian honor guard and members of his cabinet.

Barbara held out her microphone and shouted a question. "Mr. President, what are your feelings at this moment?" she asked.

"Bar-ba-ra!" Sadat exclaimed, as always making her name three distinct and booming syllables. Then he turned to Cronkite. "Walter, what do you think of Bar-ba-ra making the plane?"

"Well, Mr. President," Cronkite replied. "It's not exactly what I had in mind."

On board, Sadat invited the journalists to his private cabin for a brief interview. They drew straws to determine who would ask the first question. She didn't get it, but she had "an ace up my sleeve," she said, or rather a small piece of paper. On it, she had written a question for Sadat: "Mr. President, would you agree to do an interview with me after you speak at the Knesset?" At the bottom of the page were four boxes: "Yes," "No," "Alone," "With PM Begin." As they left his cabin, she slipped the note to one of his aides.

After the gleaming white plane with the red-and-gold stripes landed at Ben Gurion Airport, Barbara ran across the tarmac to find a peeved Peter Jennings and the ABC setup. The network was broadcasting the arrival live, to the outrage of football fans who had tuned in for the kickoff of Ohio State vs. Michigan and had to watch seven minutes of history being made instead. (At stake in the game was a trip to the Rose Bowl; Michigan won, 14–6.) She pulled out the note Sadat's aide had handed back to her. "Yes," Sadat had checked. "Alone."

Sadat was welcomed by a twenty-one-gun salute and Israel's most esteemed leaders: Prime Minister Begin, President Ephraim Katzir, former prime ministers Golda Meir and Yitzhak Rabin, Foreign Minister Dayan, Agriculture Minister Ariel Sharon. Their previous encounters with Sadat had been through battle. Sadat had launched the Yom Kippur War with Syria against Israel in 1973, when Meir was prime minister. During the Six-Day War in 1967, when Sadat was speaker of the Egyptian National Assembly, Rabin was the chief of staff of Israel's armed forces. During both wars, Dayan was defense minister and Sharon commander of an armored division.

Barbara already had arranged for an interview later that day with Begin, with whom she'd also forged a friendship. She and her producer, Justin Friedland, drove to the prime minister's residence in Jerusalem. Sitting in his study, surrounded by photos of his family, Begin contemplated the history of the moment. He spoke with emotion about the Holocaust and the relatives he had lost in concentration camps. He hadn't prepared the remarks he would deliver to the Israeli parliament the next day; he told her that he never wrote anything in advance. He asked aide Yehiel Kadishai for a Bible to look up verses to cite. He was still talking after midnight when Kadishai urged him to go to bed so he would be rested for the busy day ahead.

Begin left the study and then popped back in. There was something he had forgotten to tell her. "On the ride from the airport I said to President Sadat, 'For the sake of our good friend Barbara, would you do the interview tomorrow with me together?' And Barbara, Sadat said yes. So we do it in the Knesset, when we're finished speaking." He delivered the momentous news almost as an aside.

The leaders of Israel and Egypt had never before done a joint interview, never sat side by side for an exchange that would be as remarkable in its way as their formal addresses to the parliament.

On Sunday, after the speeches in the main chamber of the Knesset and amid a commotion of Israeli security guards and Egyptian soldiers, the two leaders joined her in a small adjoining room. It began as though the three of them were old friends, having the most ordinary of conversations. "Mr. President, don't you think she's the prettiest reporter you've ever seen?" Begin said to Sadat. "Oh, Mr. Prime Minister, I can't say that," Sadat replied. "I have to go back to my country where we also have pretty reporters." Then he gave her a kiss.

All that underscored the personal style that Barbara brought to interviews, even with heads of state. It's hard to imagine such a cozy exchange between world leaders and, say, Cronkite or Chancellor. It was an approach that often gave journalists like them heartburn, but it was also one reason she had succeeded in persuading the leaders to talk, together, in front of the cameras.

For forty minutes, the two men expressed their admiration for one another and acknowledged the difficulties of achieving peace between their countries. Sadat said the Arab people would not concede one inch of occupied land. She pressed him on how an accord could be negotiated without compromise. "Barbara, politics can't be conducted like this," he finally protested. She cajoled, "I have to keep trying."

She asked Sadat if he planned to invite Begin to Cairo. "I am planning to invite him to Sinai," Sadat replied with a smile. The Sinai Peninsula was one of the prime disputes between them; Israel had occupied the Egyptian territory since the Six-Day War a decade earlier. Begin jumped in. "Well, I invite you," he said. She asked him about the creation of a Palestinian state. "My position is no," Begin replied. Sadat talked about how moved he had been by his visit that day to the Holocaust Memorial at Yad Vashem. She asked if he was concerned about his safety; other Arab leaders had condemned his outreach to Israel and some Egyptians saw him as a traitor. "Why should I be?" he replied. "I will not be taken one minute before God wants it." Four years later, he would be assassinated by Egyptian Islamic extremists.

It was a groundbreaking exchange. Friedland grabbed the two tape cassettes and rushed to the Israeli Television Broadcast Center to edit the footage and send it by satellite to New York.

But news of the interview began to leak. This time, it was Cronkite who was trying to catch up. He reached out to the two leaders and asked them to sit down for another joint interview, this time with him. They agreed. Now the competition centered on who could get on the air first. At 5:50 p.m. Eastern Time Sunday, ABC broke into the conclusion of an animated movie called *Gay Purr-ee*—a box-office bomb remembered mostly for Judy Garland as the voice of a cat named Mewsette—but aired just six minutes of the interview. Most of it would be broadcast in a special report at 10:45 p.m. CBS had an opening to use Cronkite's entire interview more quickly. *60 Minutes* was scheduled to start at 7 p.m. The show bumped a Mike Wallace investigation into the Central Intelligence Agency to air it.

After the interview was over, Cronkite could be heard making a final nervous comment on the raw satellite feed that CBS had rushed to send to New York. "Well, did Barbara get anything I didn't?" he asked.

———

For Barbara, it was a time of professional stress and personal loss. Lou Walters, the father with whom she had such a tangled relationship, had died of a heart attack a few months earlier, in August 1977, at age eighty-three. She was having lunch in New York with Yankees owner George Steinbrenner when the sad call from Miami came.

"I was heartsick but not surprised," she said. Dena was "emotionally prepared" for the death of her husband, the bon vivant she had married in a Boston banquet hall fifty-seven years earlier who had risen so high and fallen so hard. "Perhaps she was even relieved," Barbara said. "For a long time she had watched him become progressively weaker and more dispirited and, for just as long, she had felt helpless to do anything about it."

The family had never been observant Jews, and they didn't sit shiva, the seven-day Jewish ritual of mourning. Instead, Barbara and Dena and Jackie held a simple graveside service at Lakeside Memorial Park in Miami, where they had purchased a family plot. She didn't hold a memorial service in New York for fear, she said, that no one would come. That was surely a misjudgment, perhaps a reflection of her own insecurities.

On the day he died, she did notify the press. They gave Lou the sort of send-off he would have appreciated.

"Lou Walters, Nightclub Impresario and Founder of Latin Quarter, Dies," *The New York Times* reported the next morning, calling him "one of the nation's leading supper-club entrepreneurs in the 1940s and 1950s." United Press International described him as "the man behind the splashy chorus girl shows at the famed Latin Quarter." The obituary in *Variety* gave a showman's praise: "He believed in full lighting."

But with him gone, the situation with Dena and Jackie kept deteriorating. They were increasingly isolated and anxious about the future. Their arguments would end with doors slamming and Jackie in tears. Both had health scares that required hospitalization—Dena with a failing heart and lungs that had filled with fluid, Jackie with breast cancer that required a lumpectomy.

It fell to Barbara to manage their health care and their housing and their unhappiness. When she hosted a Thanksgiving dinner for her extended family at the Friars Club, she suggested they go around the table to say what each was thankful for on what was supposed to be a day of gratitude. When it was Dena's turn, she snapped, "I have nothing to be thankful for."

Soon after Lou died, Barbara interviewed show-biz legend Lucille Ball, an encounter that turned out to be piercing for both. The beloved star of *I Love Lucy* talked about her celebrated marriage with Desi Arnaz as she ignored efforts by her second husband, Gary Morton, to steer the conversation onto less sensitive ground. Lucy, then sixty-six years old, described her ex-husband as a high-stakes gambler, "a loser" who "constantly sabotaged his success." Her words could have been used to describe Lou Walters.

"He could win, win, high stakes; he could work very hard; he was brilliant, but he had to lose," she said. "Everything he built he had to break down."

———

Barbara was slowly, steadily staging her comeback.

"Barbara at that time was like a wounded bird," Ted Koppel, then ABC's diplomatic correspondent, told me. Some of the ABC executives who had championed her hiring already had been pushed out in a shake-up. Her career was not on steady ground.

But in the space of seven months, she convinced a string of world leaders to sit down with her for cutting-edge interviews: Fidel Castro in May, Yasir Arafat in September, and now Begin and Sadat in November. (The Arafat interview was marked by tragedy; ABC producers David Jayne and Larry Buckman were killed afterward when their charter flight crashed on takeoff from Amman, Jordan.) The interviews "put me back on the map as a serious journalist," Barbara said. "It didn't hurt that I'd gone head-to-head with Chancellor and Cronkite, the top men in broadcast journalism at the time, and, you should excuse the expression, beaten the pants off them. From that time on I was more or less accepted as a member of the old boys' club."

Chancellor didn't get a joint interview with Begin and Sadat until Monday; NBC News president Lester Crystal had to issue a written statement denying he had called him on the carpet for being the last of the network anchors to land one. In any case, two weeks later, Chancellor confirmed that he would leave his job as anchor of the evening news and become a commentator for the network.

Cronkite and CBS News, which had long viewed ABC News as an inferior operation, were stung by what Barbara had done. "[I]t was impossible during extensive watching over the weekend and yesterday morning not to notice a new aggressiveness at ABC News, while at the same time to be distressed by the almost spiritless and generally perfunctory coverage at CBS News," John J. O'Connor of *The New York Times* wrote. "This type of drive and commitment is new for ABC News and undoubtedly significant for all of broadcast journalism."

Barbara called her conversation with Begin and Sadat "the most personally thrilling interview I've ever done." It proved to herself, and everyone else, that her previous successes hadn't just been luck. It was evidence for Roone Arledge that she was a star worth protecting and promoting.

"The best interviewer in the business," he called her. It was getting hard to argue otherwise.

————

Barbara and Roone understood and respected each other, and their careers were inextricably linked.

They had met when they were twenty-somethings, just starting their careers at WNBT, the NBC affiliate in New York. They had kept in "quiet touch" when he ran ABC Sports, a relationship few of their colleagues realized. They would call one another to chat about this or that program, and she would relate her distress about dealing with Harry Reasoner. "I'm drowning," she told him. While many in ABC News viewed Roone's arrival as an alarming takeover by someone who knew sports, not news, she saw him as her salvation.

Indeed, in that roundabout way of life, her failure as an anchor had opened the door for his rise. Had the anchor team of Walters and Reasoner been a hit in the ratings, Bill Sheehan would have gotten much of the credit. Instead, when the show stumbled, he got much of the blame.

Amid rumors that Roone was about to add ABC News to his portfolio, he boosted Barbara and blamed Harry, the anchor for six years, for the broadcast's low ratings. "He has had his shot," Roone told TV columnist Frank Swertlow of the *Chicago Daily News*, calling Barbara "a great asset who has been mishandled," miscast in her current assignment. "It's like taking Elvis Presley and putting him in a choir," he said. "She doesn't fit the mold."

Roone took over Sheehan's job and replaced the show's executive producer, Robert Siegenthaler, with Av Westin. "Part of my job was to monitor the two of them, Harry and Barbara," Westin told me, at least until some more permanent solution could be negotiated. Roone set out to cast in new roles the broadcasters whose talents he respected—Peter Jennings, Ted Koppel, and Charles Gibson as well as Barbara—and to hire a new set of stars, among them Diane Sawyer, Lynn Sherr, and Chris Wallace.

First, he wanted to solve his biggest headache.

Watching the evening news co-anchored by Barbara and Harry "was like arriving for a dinner party at the house of a couple trying to maintain a truce in front of the world while waiting to claw each other's eyes out," he said. He already had signaled which one was going to be shown the door. "Barbara was the future of ABC News, Harry wasn't," he said. "Because while there were other Harry Reasoners in television, there was only one Barbara Walters."

Over the years, any number of her bosses would be intimidated by her drive and annoyed by her demands, but Roone "didn't care if she was a hundred-pound gorilla or an eight-hundred-pound gorilla," Richard Wald, an NBC veteran who was hired by Arledge for ABC, told me. "He simply accepted her as she was." They shared core qualities. Both had ferocious ambitions. Both were outsiders, scorned by some journalists because they lacked the industry's traditional credentials. Both had an instinctive sense of their audience and a flair for showbiz.

Roone wasn't deterred by a devastating assessment of her from Frank Magid Associates, a consulting firm known for championing the casual "Action News" format at local stations. "Many viewers are not comfortable watching her deliver the news," the report concluded. "Viewers often volunteered that she is not worth the money she is being paid, that she appears lofty, 'stuck-up,' extremely difficult to understand and follow, has a bad voice, is not able to effectively handle the anchor responsibilities and, quite simply, is not the type of personality that viewers can relate to as an individual."

But to Roone, those qualities weren't necessarily disqualifying. At ABC Sports, viewers hated the abrasive Howard Cosell but also tuned in to hear what he had to say. (Side note: In September 1975, Roone had launched *Saturday Night Live with Howard Cosell*, a prime-time variety show broadcast from the Ed Sullivan Theater that lasted only four months. In one of its eighteen episodes, Cosell and Barbara Walters, then co-host of *Today*, performed a duet of the anthem of competitive people, "Anything You Can Do I Can Do Better.")

For the rest of their lives, Roone would recognize Barbara's value and she would yearn for his approval. But straightening out the train wreck that was the *ABC Evening News* would be complicated.

———

Harry helped. He quit.

When ABC signed Barbara, Sheehan privately agreed to Harry's request that he could choose to leave after a year and a half, regardless of the provisions of his contract. "It was something that he wanted and the feeling was at the time, 'Well, if it isn't working by that time, then we'll be trying to do something else anyway,'" Sheehan said. When Reasoner exercised that option, Sheehan himself was history. In June 1978, after almost eight years as an ABC anchor, Harry returned to CBS.

Barbara was still triumphant a quarter-century later as she retold the story. "Then Roone Arledge decided to let Harry go back to *60 Minutes*, and keep me," she declared with satisfaction in what *The New York Times* described as her "exit interview," marking one of several retirements she would entertain. Roone believed in star power and he saw that in her, Bob Iger told me. "I think he believed that she could really help—meaning drive ratings, and win. Help [ABC] News win. Help Roone win."

She had prevailed.

Six weeks later, Roone unveiled a sleight-of-hand arrangement crafted to sideline her as the anchor without obviously demoting her. A trio of designated "deskmen" would deliver the news: Frank Reynolds in Washington, D.C., Peter Jennings in London, and Max Robinson in Chicago. They were anchors in all but name. Howard K. Smith would offer commentary from D.C. Barbara would remain in New York, heading an undefined "special coverage desk." The show would be renamed *World News Tonight*.

One problem with this plan was her contract, which guaranteed her the anchor spot for another three and a half years, plus the right to be consulted on co-anchors. By changing the nomenclature to "deskmen," Roone hoped semantics could skirt a showdown. Barbara chose not to press the issue; she may not have been sure she would have carried the day if she had. Indeed, she professed to be delighted. "We did all of that, really, to save Barbara," Roone said. In his memoir, Harry derided it as "the Arledge shell game." He described it this way: "By means of multiple anchors and other cosmetic devices, he more or less successfully concealed from the watching public the fact that Barbara was no longer any kind of an anchor."

TV critic Marvin Kitman noticed. In October, he wrote a column in *Newsday* detailing what he called "The Barbara Walters disappearing act," calculating how much time she was actually on the air during the newscast. "There are nights when Barbara Walters is on for barely more than a minute," he noted. "[I]t certainly is a smart way to get rid of a million dollar body without making a kerplunk in the water." A cartoon showed her on a ship walking the plank, a sword at her back.

Instead of being on the evening news five days a week, she began to appear three times a week, then once a week, then only when she had big interviews to air. Which was, after all, what she had always done best.

———

Almost a year after Sadat's groundbreaking journey to Jerusalem, President Jimmy Carter invited him and Begin to the presidential retreat at Camp David to try to hammer out the difficult details of a peace accord. It was two months after ABC had announced the "newsdesk" arrangement.

"By this time, she was digging her way back as somebody," Sam Donaldson, ABC's irrepressible White House correspondent, told me. The two of them and Ted Koppel had become fast friends—"the three Musketeers," Donaldson called them—after they all covered Carter's first major foreign trip at the beginning of the year. "There's no give-up there. There's no, 'Oh, I've been dealt a bad hand. It wasn't my fault. It's discrimination' and all that. No, she just was always a fighter and always a contender."

During the talks at Camp David, she joined White House reporters cooling their heels in the nearest town, Thurmont, Maryland, for any scraps of news. On the third day, they were taken to the presidential retreat by bus to see the leaders as they took a break from the negotiations. A military band played as a Marine squad conducted an orchestrated drill of bayoneted rifles. Then it was time for the reporters and photographers to return to Thurmont.

Marine guards stopped the two press buses at the gate and checked off the names of each person who had arrived an hour earlier. "I thought it was a little bit of overkill," Dale Leibach, then an assistant White House press secretary, told me. Who would dare try to surreptitiously stay behind in one of the most heavily protected places in the world? While fifty journalists had arrived on the press buses, however, only forty-nine were now on board to leave. Barbara was missing.

"We got a problem," Leibach told Gerald Rafshoon, Carter's communications adviser. "We loaded the bus and Barbara Walters isn't on it." Rafshoon climbed into the first bus and demanded answers. "Nobody's going. We're going to stay here until we find Barbara." He yelled at Donaldson: "Sam, where's Barbara?"

"Am I my sister's keeper?" Donaldson bellowed back.

During the search that followed, Rafshoon's wife, Eden, spotted a pair of feet in a stall of the visitors' restroom and ordered Barbara to come out and get on the bus. "It was vintage Barbara Walters, like just unrelenting in trying to get the story," Leibach said. Her plan—jaw-dropping in its audacity, given the security at a summit with the president of the United States and the leaders of Israel and Egypt—was to hide out and then somehow corner Israeli foreign minister Moshe Dayan and Defense Minister Ezer Weizman for interviews.

She boarded the bus, but she didn't apologize. She hadn't gotten where she was, and now rebounded from failure, by following the rules. Who could blame her for trying?

THE MAN SHE MARRIED
(BUT ONLY ONCE)

1984

After Lee Guber moved out of their apartment in 1972, Barbara provided gossip-column fodder for a decade as she was escorted around town by some of the most prominent men in the country.

For a time, she dated John Warner—a former Navy secretary who would later serve five terms as the senator from Virginia—although he later began to see, and then marry, actress Elizabeth Taylor. Over the years, she sometimes attended events with Henry Kissinger. "We became very good friends," the former secretary of state told me, but nothing more. When she was between marriages, she sent out feelers to Mike Wallace, a friend who was also between marriages, but that possibility between two of the most prominent journalists on television never went anywhere.

"When I talked to my father about it, he said there could only be one star in a marriage," his son, Chris Wallace, told me. "It was clear to me that he had no interest at all in being Mr. Barbara Walters."

Barbara wouldn't marry again until she met Merv Adelson. Who was, like Lee, cast in the mold of her father.

Mervyn Lee Adelson had separated from his second wife, but their divorce wasn't yet final when his friends began setting up the soon-to-be-eligible bachelor on dates in the summer of 1984. Leo-Arthur Kelmenson was neighbors with Barbara in Westhampton, the beachy enclave on eastern Long Island where she had rented a house. He had just sold his New York advertising agency to a "very successful man" from California, he told her. "He's recently separated from his wife and very attractive," Kelmenson said. "Would you like to meet him?"

They met for drinks at a New York bar, the cautious choice of blind-date veterans, then got on so well they agreed to go on to dinner. But neither was able to persuade the maître d' at the crowded Italian restaurant to seat them quickly. "I was teasing her, 'This is the kind of pull you have? You can't get a table?'" Merv said. Barbara teased him back: "'What are you talking about? You're the big Hollywood mogul and you can't get a table?'"

He was charmed. So was she.

When her father worked in Las Vegas, "there were these handsome suntanned men that I used to see with these gorgeous women, and I said, 'This is one of those men,'" she said. "It's the type, the California man, the open shirt, the blue eyes, the white hair." Back then, those men "didn't have any interest in me. Nor, I'm sure, would Merv have been interested if I hadn't become Barbara Walters." The aside was plaintive, even if she meant it as humorous self-deprecation. She would never stop fearing that it was only her success that made her attractive, that gave her value. That she wasn't enough just as herself; her name had to be so famous that she could refer to "Barbara Walters" in the third person.

Merv started with a confession of sorts. "So I told her, 'I want to see you again, but before I do, you have to know a few things,'" he said after they finally sat down for dinner. He had launched a successful real estate business by opening the first twenty-four-hour grocery store in Las Vegas. Then he cofounded Lorimar, an independent producer of such soapy TV hits as *The Waltons, Dallas, Falcon Crest*, and *Knots Landing*. She presumably knew all that already.

But he also wanted her to know he was battling allegations of being involved with organized crime. He and partner Irwin Molasky had built a luxury resort north of San Diego called Rancho La Costa, funded in part by a Teamsters pension fund then linked to the Mafia. The loan had been arranged by gaming kingpin Morris "Moe" Dalitz, also known as the Godfather of Vegas. The resort became a favored hangout for alleged Mafiosi—John "Jake the Barber" Factor, Louis "the Tailor" Rosanova, Anthony Giacalone of Detroit, Arnold Kimmes of San Diego, Anthony Spilotro of Las Vegas—as well as Hollywood stars alleged to be friendly with mobsters, among them Bing Crosby, Frank Sinatra, and Dean Martin.

"The Hundred-Million-Dollar Resort with Criminal Clientele" was the headline on an article published in *Penthouse* magazine in March 1975. Adelson was part of "the Moe Dalitz mob," it said, describing Dalitz as "a prime mover in transforming organized crime into a financial powerhouse." Adelson filed a libel suit against *Penthouse*—joined by Molasky, Dalitz, and La Costa executive Allard Roen—seeking a record $540 million in damages. The court proceeding that followed would break the record for the longest libel trial in legal history. In May 1982, after deliberating for two weeks, the jury found the magazine hadn't libeled Adelson or the others. That July, the judge granted Adelson and Molasky a new trial. Two years later, negotiations in the legal dispute were still dragging on when he had a blind date with Barbara.

She wasn't concerned. Merv didn't know about her own history with men alleged to be connected to organized crime. "Well, that's bull," she told him. It was "endearing" that he wanted to protect her reputation, she said. After dinner, she relayed Adelson's earnest admission to a confidante with amusement. He didn't understand how unlikely she was to be undone by rumors about being on the fringes of the Mob—not after the childhood she had lived. She had always been comfortable with men who had a reputation.

By now, her career was firmly back on track.

The disaster when she co-anchored *The ABC Evening News* was now six years in the past. She had been a correspondent for ABC's *20/20* almost from its start in 1978; in 1984 she was named co-host with Hugh

Downs. That October, she would moderate the first presidential debate between Walter Mondale and Ronald Reagan, a journalistic plum and evidence of stature. (She had also moderated a debate eight years earlier between Jimmy Carter and President Gerald Ford.) Her eponymous specials were landing hot guests, drawing huge ratings, and earning millions in ad revenue. Walter Cronkite, the man who was seen by millions as the voice of television news, left the anchor's chair in 1981 when he hit CBS's mandatory retirement age of sixty-five. Diane Sawyer, the rival she would view as a nemesis, wouldn't move to ABC News until 1989.

At this moment, Barbara's position at her network was unchallenged, her power to command the interviews she wanted at its peak. She was now the marquee name of television news.

It still wasn't enough.

———

Merv was "bigger than life," Barbara said. "He lived as if there were no tomorrow." He rode horses, skied and sailed, played golf and tennis. He had a mane of silver hair, a year-round tan, and a fortune estimated at $300 million. They began spending time with each other not only in New York, where he had an apartment at the Pierre Hotel overlooking Central Park, but also at his estate in Bel Air, his beach house in Malibu, and his ranch outside Aspen. The twenty-seven-acre spread was called the Lazy A, so lavishly decorated with a Western theme that *Architectural Digest* published a feature detailing just the horse barn and the three-bedroom guest quarters constructed above it.

In September 1984, the two were spotted at a Hollywood reception "dancing cheek to cheek," one gossip columnist reported. "Barbara prefers men who've by and large made it in life, or at least in their chosen careers," Robin Adams Sloan wrote, and Merv "fits that description to a 'T.'" In November, the syndicated columnist provided an update. "Tracking Ms. Walters' beaux is virtually a full-time job," Sloan said, but her current "attentions" were focused on Adelson. "He's mature, good looking in a non-flashy sort of way, powerful and very rich."

A year after they met, as they were strolling on the beach at Malibu,

Merv proposed and she accepted. He gave her a white diamond engagement ring from Harry Winston jewelers, 13.84 carats. It would be the third marriage for each. "Our life is going to be so bicoastal," she enthused to *The New York Times*. "We'll spend two weeks a month in Los Angeles and two weeks in New York." But she wasn't exactly starry-eyed. The marriage and the commute wouldn't affect her work schedule, she insisted, or her priorities. "Some nights, when one of his programs is up against '20/20,' we'll even be in competition," she said. The wedding was to be late that fall.

There was one complication, a familiar one—her troubled family.

After Lou Walters died ten years earlier, Barbara's mother and sister had begged her to move them back to New York, the site of happier days. "I anguished about it but decided there was no way I could continue my new relationship with Merv and have my mother along, with round-the-clock nurses in the apartment," Barbara said. "And what would I do with my sister?"

That question would be answered with the finality of loss. Jackie was diagnosed with ovarian cancer in 1985. Barbara went to Florida for the surgery but left to give a long-scheduled speech in Milwaukee. Jackie died a few days later. She felt "waves of guilt and sorrow" about not being by her sister's side at the end, Barbara said. "I gave a terrible speech and was criticized for it. I didn't give a damn." A complex mix of emotions was stirred by the passing of the sister she loved and hated, the sister she had protected and kept at a distance. "My difficult, temperamental, tragic, loving sister," she called her.

Dena, her mental decline continuing, was no longer lucid enough to be told that her older daughter was gone. Instead, Barbara told her that Jackie was staying with actress Carol Channing, who had always been kind to her.

As Barbara and Merv moved toward marriage, he dispatched one potential stumbling block, spurring negotiations to settle the long-running negotiations over the *Penthouse* article. In November, the two sides reached a settlement that included a conciliatory letter from the magazine, although it never printed a retraction. Neither side was awarded a penny for damages or legal fees. *Penthouse* "did not mean to imply nor did it intend for its readers to believe that Messrs. Adelson and Molasky are or were members of organized crime or criminals," the key sentence read. It noted their contributions to civic and philanthropic concerns and called La Costa "one of the outstanding resort complexes of the world."

But the bride was having misgivings, just as she had before her previous marriages, her *coulda-shoulda-woulda* uncertainties emerging again. She postponed the marriage from the fall, then canceled plans to hold a winter wedding over the holidays in Aspen. She conferred with Ann Landers, a friend accustomed to giving advice. The newspaper columnist, whose real name was Eppie Lederer, advised her not to go through with it. "Mother's response to that wedding was 'Oy,'" recalled her daughter, Margo Howard, skeptical that Barbara's third marriage would be any more successful than her first two. Eppie's cautionary counsel would cool the friendship between the two women for a while, despite Barbara's own doubts.

She worried about making a long-distance marriage work, and she had growing reservations about Merv. The qualities that attracted her also made her anxious. Like Lou Walters, he was in the volatile entertainment business, one that had brought her father both fortune and bankruptcy. Like Lee Guber, he had aspirations he would struggle to achieve.

Merv had flourished producing TV shows; now he wanted to expand his horizons to the more prestigious world of movies. Lorimar backed a few successful films, including *An Officer and a Gentleman*, but it had more flops, *The Fish That Saved Pittsburgh* and *Urgh! A Music War* among them. "I tried to convince myself that Merv was primarily a businessman," Barbara said, then acknowledged that was "the same rationalization I had adopted before marrying Lee." She had heard speculation that Merv's company might be in trouble. "How could I repeat that mistake?" she asked.

Rumors surfaced that the engagement was over. Liz Smith, the gossip columnist close to Barbara, tried to tamp them down. "You cynics who are counting out the Barbara Walters-Merv Adelson romance just because they didn't rush to the altar on somebody else's schedule, are wrong," she wrote in February 1986. "These two are more starry-eyed and involved than ever, together every available minute." She predicted, "One of these mornings we'll wake up and discover they are Mr. and Mrs."

On May 6, 1986, Barbara flew to California to break off the engagement. She would remember the precise date because, as it turned out, they would be married four days later.

It was an echo of her last-minute turnaround with Lee Guber. "Merv was charming and funny and tan and handsome," she thought once she saw him again. "What was the matter with me?" What's more, her eighteen-year-old daughter weighed in on his behalf. Jacqueline and Merv had become close while he was dating her mother. At the time, Jackie had been sent to a program in Idaho for troubled teens. The weight Barbara gave her daughter's views was a sign of how much repairing their frayed ties meant to her.

"Jackie said to her, 'Mom, this is the most wonderful man,'" said Wendy Goldberg, a California friend who was married to film and TV producer Leonard Goldberg. "'I don't know what's going to happen but I will always be, like, Merv's daughter.'" With that, Goldberg said, Jackie "precipitated the wedding."

"Her feelings for Merv meant a great deal to me and might even have tipped my decision," Barbara said years later of her daughter's influence. Even if it meant ignoring the growing unease she felt about the groom.

———

On May 8, 1986, Barbara called Wendy Goldberg with a question. Could she and Merv get married at the Goldbergs' mansion in Beverly Hills in two days?

The rush made it sound more like a shotgun wedding than a fairy-tale one.

"I became Mrs. Merv Adelson. Just like that. Fast, so I couldn't change my mind again," she said. She hadn't bought a wedding dress, so she donned a never-worn ivory lace gown encrusted with pearls from a friend in Beverly Hills; she and Shelby Saltzman Kirsch had been friends since they were high school classmates at Birch Wathen in New York. (She would later call her failure to order a wedding dress a sign she should have heeded. "It was because I *really* didn't want to get married," she would tell Arnold Scaasi, one of her favorite designers.) The gown would be "something borrowed." A blue garter would be "something blue." A lace handkerchief from Merv's daughter-in-law would be "something new." Barbara had a childhood Bible flown in from New York; it would be "something old."

Then she swallowed a Valium "and more or less zonked my way through the wedding."

Last-minute or not, the wedding had a certain California flair. Barbara descended the Goldbergs' grand staircase on the arm of her agent, Lee Stevens. The Goldbergs' twelve-year-old daughter, Amanda, was the flower girl. Jacqueline was maid of honor for her mother and Merv's daughter Ellie was matron of honor; his sons Gary and Andy served as the best men. Barbara and Merv exchanged vows under a chuppah of trellised ficus decorated with lilacs as Rabbi Jacob Pressman from Temple Beth Am officiated.

The collection of about eighty guests included Hollywood mogul Lew Wasserman, producer Sidney Lumet, and actress Linda Gray, who was then portraying the long-suffering wife of J. R. Ewing on the Lorimar drama *Dallas*. Beverly Sills, the celebrated soprano and a close friend of Barbara, read Elizabeth Barrett Browning's sonnet "How Do I Love Thee?" Jackie and a pal, Tracy Langsom, sang a duet of "That's What Friends Are For," the biggest song of the year. (A version by Dionne Warwick and others was *Billboard*'s top single in 1986 and won a Grammy.) Chasen's, Hollywood's favored restaurant, catered the dinner and the three-tiered wedding cake. The guests danced to a six-piece band in a garden tent until 2 a.m.

"It was all extremely touching and lovely," the bride said. During the toasts, she declared teasingly, "This is the way it will always be. Merv will always say the perfect thing, and I'll always get the last word." A photo from the party shows her standing behind her new husband, her arms draped around his shoulders, white orchids pinned to her hair. He is smiling. She looks pensive.

––––––––

Barbara and Merv married that Saturday in 1986. But for reasons that are puzzling to this day, over the years multiple news reports stated without attribution they had been married and divorced before, an error repeated so many times that it was often accepted as true.

One of the early inaccurate references, possibly the first, was in a 2014 *Vanity Fair* profile. The story included interviews with Walters and photos of her lounging in her Fifth Avenue apartment. "Walters has been married four times to three men," the story said. "[S]he married, divorced, re-married, and re-divorced her third husband, Merv Adelson . . . in an 11-year span." The author, Curtis Sittenfeld, told me she no longer had the files for the story and couldn't recall the source.

But the account that they had initially married in 1981 and divorced in 1984 would have been impossible, or at least illegal. At that time, Merv Adelson was still married to his second wife, Gail Kenaston; they married in 1978 and in 1982 were still being photographed at parties on the *Los Angeles Times* society pages. Their divorce wasn't yet final when Barbara met Merv in 1984.

Even so, the error proved persistent. When Barbara died in 2022, obituaries in *New York* magazine and CNN and elsewhere said she and Merv had been married twice. NPR said she was married five times to four different men, then corrected that error with another, that she had been married four times to three men. The error was repeated when Merv had died, too, in 2015, by CBS News, *TV Week, Entertainment Weekly, Parade* magazine, and elsewhere.

Barbara wanted to make sure *The New York Times* got it right in its obituary of Merv; she sent reporter Bruce Weber an email on the day Merv died saying they had married only once, despite reports to the contrary.

"Merv was a kind and gentle man with a great sense of humor," she told him. "We stayed friends long after our marriage."

That is, just the one marriage.

Not even that preemptive effort was enough to stop *The New York Times* from repeating the error a few years later, though. A story in 2023 about the auction of her estate described the engagement ring she had been given by Merv, "whom she married and divorced twice between 1981 and 1992."

THE RUNAWAY DAUGHTER

1985

Mother and daughter had been at odds for years, their relationship in a downward spiral. Perhaps that's no surprise, given Barbara's fraught relationships with her own mother and father. Neither had given her a particularly useful model of how to be a parent.

Jacqueline had been pulled out, or pushed out, of the exclusive Dalton School on the Upper East Side after the seventh grade. She was dispatched to boarding schools—in Maine one year, Connecticut the next—designed for the troubled teens of well-to-do families. Barbara Walters, who had yearned to have a child and delighted at adopting Jackie, was anguished about what had gone wrong, about whether it was her fault, about what to do next. She sought advice from everyone. Anita Siegenthaler, the wife of Robert Siegenthaler, an executive producer of the *ABC Evening News*, found herself sharing a ride with her to some network event. "She got into the cab and she said, 'Oh, my daughter is such an ordeal,'" confiding her motherly frustration even though the two women didn't know one another well. "'What do you do about your kids?'"

Things didn't seem to get better during the year Jackie attended the all-girls boarding school in Connecticut. She and a friend were caught off campus in a nearby town, high. The friend was expelled; Jacqueline wasn't. "The school obviously didn't want to lose Barbara Walters's daughter," Barbara sniffed; fairly or not, she would often view Jackie's ups and downs through the lens of her fame. She heard that Jackie had visited the friend at her home in Boston on another weekend; she ordered the school to prevent that from happening again.

"I didn't know what else to do," she said. "If I took Jackie out of the school, where would I send her?" There were those around her, including some who admired her most, who found that attitude perplexing. What about bringing her daughter home?

A twenty-something assistant who worked for Lee Guber's theatrical business found herself dealing with fractious phone calls between the divorced couple about their only child. "I found it very cold, and there was this little simmering of anger all the time," Amanda Butterbaugh told me, describing an incident she remembered clearly even decades later. "Lee was trying to arrange a cruise, a holiday cruise for her, but neither Barbara or Lee were going to go on the cruise with her," she said. "They were sending a companion." Lee was "bent out of shape" because Jacqueline had been bounced from one boarding school and had to be enrolled in another. "I don't get this kid," he complained. "We give her everything."

That was too much for Amanda. "I sat down and said, 'Lee, why would she behave for you or show you any kind of love and respect? You're not bringing her home for the holiday, and Barbara and you are putting her on a ship with someone who's not family and sending her away for her holiday break. What are you doing?"

He wasn't happy that she had spoken out. But to her relief he didn't fire her, and the next morning, he canceled the reservation for the cruise. Jackie came home to New York for that holiday. Still, from Amanda's viewpoint, Jackie's parents continued to see their daughter as a problem to be handled.

During the summer of 1985, Jackie celebrated her seventeenth birthday. Her mother enrolled her in a residential program for high school students at the Parsons School of Design in Los Angeles. She and Merv

Adelson were engaged and planning to spend some of the summer at his home in Malibu.

Two weeks after the program had begun, Parsons officials called Barbara. Jackie was gone. She had run away with the friend she had made at the school in Connecticut.

For four frantic days, Barbara had no idea where her teenage daughter had gone.

————

At Dalton, Jacqueline had been an indifferent student. She had few friends. She would host sleepovers at her apartment but rarely be invited back to other girls' homes. She towered over the other kids in her class, pushing six feet tall when she was twelve years old, making her feel even more like a misfit. "I felt like such an outcast," she said later. "I always felt, you know, if we had, I don't know, a housekeeper, that I could relate more to the housekeeper than I could the girls in my elite private school."

"It was really rough going when Jackie was in high school," recalled Kate O'Brian, a daughter of one of Barbara's closest friends. "Barbara at one point said, 'I should never have sent her to Dalton.'" For her part, Jackie didn't like people knowing who her mother was. "How do I know why people like me?" she asked. "I don't know if they like me because I'm me or because I'm Barbara Walters' daughter." Her last name was Guber; she would start by telling new acquaintances that her mother was a teacher, then that she was on TV, then that she was "kind of famous." (One friend finally guessed, "Wow! Your mom is Oprah Winfrey!")

Being the child of a very successful person carries its own assets and complications. "Particularly when you're young, you're aware of the fact that you are not a completely individual person in a lot of people's minds, that your identity and people's views of you—in relationship with you— is colored by who your parent is," journalist Chris Wallace, the son of Mike Wallace, told me. "I always had the feeling that if two phones rang at the same time and one of them was me and the other was CBS with a hot story, I had no doubt he would've picked up Line Two."

Fathers face less opprobrium than mothers for putting their careers first, though, especially in that era. Then the expectation was still that men would be the breadwinners while women, even professional ones, would rear the children. If things went awry, they would be seen as responsible, as the parent who had failed.

Barbara openly adored her daughter, and despite Jacqueline's discomfort she loved people knowing she had a child. In interviews, she talked about the joys and the travails of parenthood in ways that would make just about any preteen cringe with embarrassment.

She once told *Parents* magazine they had bathed together when Jackie was young; when she expressed curiosity about her body her mother took the opportunity to tell her she was adopted. "I said that breasts were used by mommies to feed their babies. And she asked about her vagina. I said, 'This is where a baby comes from. There are two ways that mommies who want babies have them—through this way and through adoption.'" She would tell Jackie she had been "born in my heart," meant to signal how much she had been wanted.

But in some ways Barbara was perplexed by Jacqueline, whose instincts and interests were poles apart from hers. It would take years of strain before she accepted her as her own person. "My blue-collar daughter," she eventually said dryly to a friend.

"She's a very different child from me," she told Gene Shalit, her mustachioed colleague on the *Today* show. At the time, Jacqueline was twelve years old. When they played Monopoly, Barbara would always win. Defeat didn't bother Jackie, a reaction her mother couldn't fathom. "She's too *good* a loser," she complained. "She's not competitive enough." Her conversation with Shalit was teased on the cover of *Ladies' Home Journal*, displayed on supermarket racks across the country. "BARBARA WALTERS talks about men, careers and her private struggle to raise a daughter," the headline promised beneath a photo of Barbara, wearing a ruffled lace collar and pearls, smiling.

In the article, Barbara expressed concern about movies like *Private Benjamin* that portrayed smoking marijuana as fun. When it came to drugs, "I'm not particularly worried about Jacqueline," Barbara said, then added, "It can happen with any child, I guess. I hope I don't eat my words."

She would, and soon. Within a year, Jackie was drinking booze, popping Quaaludes, and smoking pot. "I did marijuana," she said later. "It was called 'crank' then, but it's now methamphetamines. Quaaludes were all over the place. Valium." She said she would take just about any pill she could get. At thirteen, she would sneak out of the apartment in fishnet stockings and a miniskirt to party at Studio 54—her height helped mask her age—and return home at four in the morning. Neither her mother nor her live-in nanny seemed to notice.

"You are in fantasyland," Jackie said, describing the appeal of the famous club, a symbol of excess. "You have no idea where you are, and all of your problems supposedly seem to have gone away."

When her grades sank, her mother hired tutors in math and French. Then she heard that her daughter had been hanging out after school with a group of older boys on 84th Street. She found her with "a small gang of tough-looking boys, smoking and leaning against the cars on the street," Barbara said. They were not from Dalton. "Older boys from what was left of nearby Irish Yorkville," recalled a student at another elite Upper East Side school from the time. They were known as the 84th Street Gang.

Barbara dragged Jacqueline, then fourteen, home that day over her protests that she was in love with one of the boys. Barbara returned to the street corner the next day and warned the leader of the gang that she would have them arrested if her daughter was ever seen with them again. By now, Jackie often refused to get up in the morning and go to school; she would sleep in until the afternoon. Sometimes she couldn't be roused even after her mother would shake her and sprinkle her with cold water. Barbara sent her to a child psychologist; she refused to return after their first session.

Her mother worried about the course Jackie was on. She was also worried her daughter would make a scene in public that, given her own prominence, would make the tabloids.

Barbara, the fearless journalist who quizzed presidents and movie stars, professed to be clueless about what was going on in her own home, most of all her daughter's drug use. "I'm not saying that I shouldn't have known," she said. "I should have known." She would not be the first parent to be willfully blind toward a situation with a child that was too painful to see, or that seemed impossible to fix. She didn't want to cross-examine her daughter the way she would a newsmaker on TV, she said. Substance abuse never occurred to her; she wouldn't have recognized the smell of marijuana. "I took her to a doctor," she said. "I was afraid she had a brain tumor. I didn't think drugs."

She already had considered moving Jackie to a smaller school, one that was less high-powered. For a time, Dalton's administrators had urged that she stay. "Was this because I was a celebrity?" she would later wonder. Were they more interested in teaching their student or in being associated with her famous parent?

When Jackie was sent to boarding school in Maine, her mother downplayed the idea that anything was amiss. Her daughter was "going through what I guess is the usual adolescence," she shrugged in an interview. "There isn't anything for kids to do" in New York, she said, adding, "They start going to discotheques at fourteen."

Many teenagers experiment with drugs and nearly all of them fight with their parents, of course, and for a tangle of reasons. Jackie's behavior was hardly unusual among her classmates and her generation, although she would have a longer and more difficult time dealing with substance abuse than most. It's not hard to understand why she might feel disconnected, even abandoned. "I had a huge fear I was nothing inside, just an empty black hole," she said years later, when she was on the cusp of forty.

Her birth mother had given her up for adoption, apparently never seeing her again; her birth father may have never laid eyes on her. The couple who had contracted to adopt the baby chose not to because she turned out to be a girl. The couple who did adopt her separated when she was three years old. Her adoptive mother was consumed with her work. Her adoptive father passed away when she was nineteen.

On the day Lee Guber died, ABC producer Jessica Stedman Guff happened to come over to Barbara's apartment to deliver some work papers. She found Jackie sitting on a settee in the lobby, crying. "My father just died," she told her. "I said, 'I'm so sorry; that's so awful.' And she said, 'I don't really have anyone left.'"

Jackie felt increasingly isolated from her mother and her mother's life.

"I never felt like I fit into her world," she said. Jackie didn't really care if she herself lived or died. "I was just running."

———

When Jackie ran away, Barbara called Dr. Mitchell Rosenthal, a psychiatrist who had founded Phoenix House, the drug rehabilitation center. "Don't call the police," he told her. It would end up on the front page of every newspaper, he warned, which could make Jackie more determined to run or even target her for kidnapping. Instead, they devised a plan of what to do if and when she talked to Jackie. For four days, she waited.

She was close to notifying the authorities when a woman she didn't know phoned. Jackie and her friend had hitchhiked to New Mexico with the woman's brother; he had stolen Jackie's wallet and retrieved Barbara's phone number, and now she had it. She gave Barbara the number at the house where they were crashing.

Barbara called and reached Jackie, who said she was fine and didn't want to talk to her. Did she need money? Yes, she said. She and her friend wanted money to fly back to Boston. Barbara promised to send two airline tickets. Instead of sending the tickets, though, she sent a former Green Beret, a man who specialized in picking up runaways, by force if necessary. He arrived at 3 a.m. the next morning and carried Jackie to a waiting car. He reported that she seemed almost relieved.

After some consultation, Jackie was taken to an intervention program in Idaho, in a stretch of country so remote that running away would be all but impossible. She was allowed one phone call. "Don't leave me in this horrible place, please, please, please," she said to her mother, sobbing. She had learned her lesson. She promised she would never run away again. Barbara, crying, too, told her she had to stay.

Jackie wouldn't return to her boarding school in Connecticut. She remained in Idaho for more than two years, at first under angry protest and then voluntarily, even after she turned eighteen and could have checked herself out.

Barbara searched for anything that might relieve her daughter's sense of alienation. In the summer of 1986, Barbara and Merv went on their honeymoon in the south of France. While they were having lunch on a superyacht owned by a Saudi arms dealer, Adnan Khashoggi, their host offered her a private session with his onboard Hindu mystic, Shri Chandra Swamiji Maharaj. "The swami had such an aura of calm about him that I poured out all the trouble I was having with my daughter at the time, hoping for some swami wisdom," she said. He didn't have the answers, either.

Barbara concluded that being adopted was an important factor behind her daughter's travails. When she was at a photographer's studio in New York in 1982, posing for pictures that would be used in an ABC promotion, the photographer, Michael Raab, mentioned that he and his wife had just adopted a baby girl. Barbara asked her hair and makeup artists to step away to give them privacy. At the time, Jacqueline was fourteen and struggling. "Just remember this," she told him in a long and emotional conversation that he would remember and find helpful down the road. "All adoptive children have their own issues."

Still, Barbara never expressed regret about adopting Jackie, whatever their turmoil. She also remained forever grateful to the controversial friend who had played a key role in arranging it.

At the height of his influence, Roy Cohn had a wide circle among the powerful, the wealthy, the well-connected. In 1973, so many judges attended a party in the Grand Ballroom of the Biltmore Hotel celebrating the twenty-fifth anniversary of Roy's admission to the bar that *The New York Times* ran an editorial decrying their presence. "What conclusion should New Yorkers draw about the current state of political morality?" it demanded indignantly.

But at the end, he was terminally ill, mired in scandal, and shunned by many. Only his most loyal friends testified as character witnesses on his behalf in 1986, when he was battling legal disbarment hearings on charges of dishonesty, fraud, deceit, and misrepresentation. Donald Trump was one of them. New York representative Mario Biaggi. Yankees owner George Steinbrenner. Conservative columnists William F. Buckley Jr. and William Safire.

And Barbara Walters.

After Jackie earned her high school diploma in the Idaho program in August 1987, she moved to Portland, Oregon—just about as far from New York City as possible—and shared an apartment with a school friend. Barbara came with her to help her get settled; she was pleased that Jackie was talking about taking art classes at Portland Community College. They visited the wooded campus and the local ABC affiliate, KATU-TV. The station's public affairs director, Joella Werlin, was assigned to be their guide. She suggested that Jackie consider enrolling in the school's video production courses, and Barbara encouraged that idea.

If she did, Jackie would be eligible for an internship on a local children's TV program called *Popcorn*. The job was unpaid but highly sought by local college students eager to get their foot in the door at the station. "Barbara said that Jackie loves little children and she is good at photography, so she would really be perfect for this," Joella told me. She landed the internship in the spring of 1988.

Barbara bragged about Jackie's job, leaving the impression among a delighted audience at a Los Angeles event that her daughter might be thinking about following in her famous mother's footsteps. "My daughter Jackie—who is not here tonight—is about to become an intern at a TV station," she said on March 19, 1988, as she was being honored for lifetime achievement by the Museum of Broadcasting. Surely no unpaid internship had ever begun in a brighter spotlight.

But as it turned out, Jackie never enrolled in the community college, and she didn't do the work at her internship. After a one-month trial, the internship was canceled. To those at the station, Jackie seemed spoiled and entitled. She would sometimes disappear entirely; Barbara would call Joella to ask if she knew where she was. Arlene Schnitzer, a wealthy local philanthropist who knew Barbara, arranged for Jackie to enroll in Academy One, a sort of finishing school that taught modeling and makeup.

At the gala at the Museum of Broadcasting, Barbara said her focus on a career might have played a role in problems in her daughter's life. "So did I feel guilt?" she said. "How do I count the ways? Is there a working mother on earth who doesn't?" But she didn't express second thoughts, insisting that Jackie had turned out fine. Some of her daughter's issues were "because I wasn't home all the time," she acknowledged. Then she added, "I could have done it differently but then there wouldn't have been this."

That is, her remarkable career and the acclaim it had brought her. The award for lifetime achievement. She might as well have been quoting her father, celebrating his success and downplaying its cost to his family. To his daughter. To her daughter.

THE HONEYMOON
AND THE ARMS DEALER

1986

Sometimes the chase got her into trouble.

Barbara and Merv, taking a delayed honeymoon in the south of France, were invited to lunch by Saudi arms merchant Adnan Khashoggi aboard his superyacht, the *Nabila*. Merv had a friend who knew the flamboyant wheeler-dealer. It was a casual affair, or as casual as an affair can be aboard a 282-foot floating palace that featured a crew of seventy, gold bathroom fixtures, and its own helicopter pad. (A few years earlier, it had served as the ship of villain Maximillian Largo in the James Bond movie *Never Say Never Again*.)

They were invited back to the *Nabila* for dinner that night, with guests who included former Canadian prime minister Pierre Trudeau.

Four months later, the Iran-contra scandal broke and Khashoggi was in the headlines. He was reported to be the middleman who had brokered a deal for the Reagan administration to secretly sell weapons to Iran in return for the release of American hostages being held in Lebanon. The illegal scheme also involved funneling the profits to right-wing rebels in Nicaragua. Though President Ronald Reagan would recover, the scandal damaged his standing with the American public and even led to talk, which never really went anywhere, of impeachment.

She began pursuing an interview with Khashoggi, a process that involved meetings at La Costa, the California resort Merv had helped develop, and long conversations at Khashoggi's spectacular Fifth Avenue apartment. After finally agreeing, he insisted the interview take place aboard his private plane, a DC-8, as it flew from Newark Airport to Monte Carlo. When they landed, Khashoggi engineered another interview at his home there, this time with Manucher Ghorbanifar, a shadowy figure who had been involved in procuring the armaments.

The exclusives on the breaking story were featured on *20/20* and *Nightline*.

Then, complications. Ghorbanifar told Barbara he had to get a message to Reagan, warning her that the lives of American hostages hung in the balance. A hostage or perhaps two could be released on Christmas Eve, depending on what the president did; Ghorbanifar and his family in Iran could be killed if things went wrong. "I knew the rules: a reporter is not supposed to become personally involved in a story and certainly not be allowed to act as a messenger," Barbara said. But she hadn't gotten this far by following the rules. "I didn't want anybody's blood on my hands, so I decided to honor Ghorbanifar's demand for secrecy."

She called Jerry Zipkin, a dapper man-about-town who often escorted First Lady Nancy Reagan to society events—an unusual conduit for a national security message. Could he ask Nancy to call her? It was, she told him, "a very serious matter." Nancy called an hour later, and then Ronald Reagan got on the phone.

Barbara already knew the Reagans, of course. She had interviewed him at his beloved ranch in California, outside Santa Barbara, after he had survived an assassination attempt in 1981. She would interview him again at the White House. Barbara had also interviewed Nancy Reagan; she calculated that she conducted more interviews with her as first lady than any other reporter.

Now the president instructed her how to securely send a private letter and some notes she had gathered to him, and she did. In his diary, Reagan was excited by the information Barbara had described. "She is sending a lot of material obtained from a top Iranian figure re the money exchange," he wrote. "It sounds fantastic."

Months later, amid investigations by a special prosecutor and a select congressional committee, Barbara's role as an intermediary was revealed. The papers she sent included nothing new, officials concluded, but the fact that she had sent them created a firestorm.

"Iran Arms Dealer Used Barbara Walters to Secretly Pass on a Message to Reagan," *The Wall Street Journal* scooped. *The New York Times* followed: "Barbara Walters Gave Reagan Papers on Iran." In the *New York Post*, a cartoon depicted Ayatollah Khomeini sitting behind a news desk. "Good evening and welcome to *20/20*," the caption read. "Barbara Walters and I have swapped jobs."

David Burke, the ABC News vice president who oversaw the network's standards and ethics, was outraged. The network's biggest star was publicly reprimanded for breaking its rules. "Barbara Walters' transmission of her information to the president was in violation of a literal interpretation of news policy," the network's statement said. "ABC News policy expressly limits journalistic cooperation with government agencies unless threats to human life are involved." But the statement also noted, "Miss Walters believed that to be the case."

It was one of several episodes in which Barbara said "in retrospect" she should have chosen another course when she did this or that—when she seemed to undermine a colleague who had landed a big interview she wanted, or when she tried to help a controversial source win admission to an elite graduate school. But she also thought ABC was wrong to reprimand her, and she was wounded that not even Roone Arledge or Richard Wald defended her.

The furor spotlighted the intersection of money and politics and society in which she so easily moved. It reinforced the view of some that she was more celebrity chronicler than journalist. A UPI columnist dubbed it "Barbara Walters-gate" and said she had "damaged the credibility of everyone involved in delivering news to the people."

And the yacht? In short order, Khashoggi ran into financial problems and the yacht went to the Sultan of Brunei for nonpayment of a loan. He turned around and sold it to Donald Trump, who renamed it *Trump Princess*.

———

Barbara and Merv decided to buy a new apartment in New York, one that would be fully theirs. He sold his seven-room apartment at the Pierre and she sold her apartment at 555 Park Avenue, asking $3 million. Together, they bought the entire sixth floor of the building at 944 Fifth Avenue for $5.75 million—nearly $16 million in 2023 dollars. It had eleven rooms, two wood-burning fireplaces, space for a baby grand piano, and a breathtaking view of Central Park. Cindy Adams, the gossip columnist at the *New York Post* who was close to Barbara, said they "probably went Dutch" in buying the place; that is, they split the cost. Barbara would live there until the day she died, thirty-six years later. Then it would be listed for sale for $19.75 million.

Merv decided to buy a new home in Bel Air, too—actually, a house he had once owned and lived in with a previous wife. It had a pool and a fishpond and a tennis court on the grounds. "The 'vibes' seemed right for both of us," Barbara said. She added a professional dressing room to keep her clothes and have her makeup and hair done. He added a projection room to screen movies. *Architectural Digest* published an admiring tour of the house, describing it as "country-style" but the sort of country-style house that was decorated with a seventeenth-century English leather wing chair in the entry and a French limestone fireplace, circa 1720, in the living room.

Late that summer, they honeymooned in France, then hosted a grand dinner-dance in New York for three hundred of their closest friends. Most hadn't made it to the hastily arranged wedding ceremony in Los Angeles. The ornate invitations called it a celebration of their four-month anniversary, with a corny poem celebrating the union of "Big Apple" (that is, New York) with "Big Orange" (Los Angeles). The menu included "Los Angeles chili," a specialty of Chasen's, and New York strip steak. The guest list was eclectic New York royalty, from socialite Brooke Astor and the exiled Shahbanou of Iran to George Steinbrenner and Donald and Ivana Trump. Benjamin Netanyahu, then the U.N. ambassador from Israel, was there. The ballroom at the Pierre was filled with white roses, orchids, and tulips. Beverly Sills sang a version of "Oh, Promise Me" with joke lyrics written for the occasion. Michele Lee portrayed Barbara and Howard Keel portrayed Merv in a rendition of "Anything You Can Do I Can Do Better." (Both actors were then starring on Lorimar shows, *Knots Landing* and *Dallas*.) Keel then sang a love song dedicated to Barbara, although in a case of mistaken identity directed his performance at her cousin Lorraine, who looked a bit like her. "She was thrilled," Barbara reported afterward. Two top bands played that evening, the Count Basie Orchestra and the Jerry Kravat Orchestra.

Still, there was a shadow over the festivities. *The Wall Street Journal* had just published a blockbuster investigation on the front page, illustrated by a portrait of Adelson in one of the newspaper's distinctive stipple drawings. Lorimar had agreed to buy nine big-city television stations, six of them network affiliates, with plans to borrow as much as $2 billion to finance the purchase. The deal would make Adelson "a first-rank power in American communications," the story said—that is, if the Federal Communications Commission approved it. The agency was reviewing the pending purchase under a statute that called for it to examine the "character" and other qualifications of those who wanted to buy licensed broadcast stations.

The story raised questions about his character. "Seeds of Success: Two Lorimar Officials Have Had Ties to Men of Underworld Repute," the headline read. "Merv Adelson, Irwin Molasky Relied on Teamster Loans to Build Many Businesses."

The second paragraph: "And although Mr. Adelson isn't an on-air personality, in May he married one—Barbara Walters."

The sale would never go through. Lorimar eventually withdrew the offer to buy the TV stations; the price was deemed too high.

The rumors around Adelson weren't new. In 1963, a book titled *The Green Felt Jungle* tracked the role organized crime figures played in developing Las Vegas, including Moe Dalitz. "Merv Adelson and Molasky are known in Las Vegas as 'guys who fell into it' when they became socially acquainted with Dalitz at the Desert Inn Country Club," authors Ed Reid and Ovid Demaris wrote. As a result, "they learned much and prospered enormously." In 1966, an FBI report about Adelson and Molasky said that there was "no question as to their close association with the hoodlum element." In 1975, the *Penthouse* story about alleged mob connections had prompted the decade-long libel suit.

The *Journal* story included Adelson's denials of ties to the Mafia and noted he had never been charged with a crime. But it also detailed how he and his partner had gotten loans totaling more than $100 million from the Teamsters' Central States pension fund, described as "mob-run and notoriously corrupt" at the time. "A steady stream of Mafia men and racketeers" had stayed at La Costa as guests, sometimes for free, it said. One of them was Meyer Lansky, also known as "the Mob's accountant."

At the party, Barbara dismissed the story with a joke.

"I would like to thank *The Wall Street Journal* for underwriting tonight's party," she said in remarks that drew a laugh; she didn't have to explain the reference to anyone. The party ended with composer Jerry Herman performing "The Best of Times," a song he had written for his 1983 hit musical *La Cage aux Folles*, then playing at the Palace Theatre on Broadway.

> *The best of times is now,*
> *What's left of summer but a faded rose?*
> *The best of times is now,*
> *As for tomorrow, well, who knows?*

LOSS

1987

Barbara was back in Miami, where she had spent so much of her childhood. She was interviewing actor Don Johnson, who was starring in a successful TV show, *Miami Vice*, and promoting a less-successful film, *Sweet Hearts Dance*. In the interview, Walters asked Johnson when he lost his virginity (at age twelve) and to whom (the seventeen-year-old babysitter of his younger siblings) and whether he was going to remarry ex-wife Melanie Griffith (he said no, although in fact they did remarry the next year).

The segment's producer, Phyllis McGrady, wanted to film a "walk-and-talk," footage showing Barbara and her subject casually interacting that could be used to tease the segment. With Patrick Swayze, Barbara had danced; with Sylvester Stallone, she rode on the back of his motorcycle. With Don Johnson, she boarded a Scarab powerboat and he took off at seventy miles an hour across Biscayne Bay. He pumped his arms in the air triumphantly; her hair whipped in the wind. Another boat carrying her crew was speeding alongside them, shooting the picture and scanning the Miami coastline.

When they passed Palm Island, she began telling stories of her childhood there, pointing out the site of the Latin Quarter nightclub and the waterfront mansion where she had never managed to spot Al Capone. "She had great stories and she was in a wonderful mood," McGrady told me. "Those memories are very much a part of her persona—those years in Miami, living in Florida with her father and the club." Barbara described life with her father as a roller coaster, "the success and then the demise, and then the success again, and then the sad ending."

After the day of shooting was over, Barbara dropped by the Miami Jewish Home and Hospital for the Aged, where her mother was living. By then, Dena Walters no longer reliably recognized her or understood who she was. As it turned out, she was in the final months of her life.

It was a bittersweet day.

Soon afterward, Barbara agreed to bring Dena back to New York, as she had long requested. But she moved her not into her Fifth Avenue apartment, as her mother had wished, but to a suite in a nearby East Side hotel, with round-the-clock nursing care. A few months later, when Barbara was in California to celebrate daughter Jackie's twentieth birthday, her mother slipped into a coma and died before Barbara could make it back East to see her one last time. The pull of competing responsibilities meant she had missed the final moments of her father and her sister and now her mother.

Dena died in June 1988, at age ninety-one. She was buried in Lakeside Memorial Park, next to her husband and older daughter. The financial and emotional load Barbara had been shouldering for her family for three decades, ever since her father's suicide attempt in 1958, was over. Lou and Jackie and Dena were gone.

"I realized that, after all those years of worry and responsibility, I was finally, finally free," Barbara said, remembering the small graveside service. "There was a touch of relief, but mostly there was sadness and regret."

By now, she was fifty-eight years old. The loss of her childhood family changed nothing, and everything. Her drive and her success were firmly set; so was her sense of emptiness. But Lou would have one last surprise for his daughter.

———

It was years later that Barbara began to understand more fully the family forces that had shaped her, especially the impact her sister had on her.

In a book titled *The Normal One: Life with a Difficult or Damaged Sibling*, psychotherapist Jeanne Safer explored the lives of the siblings of families that had troubled or disabled children, a topic that had rarely been candidly explored before. At a dinner party soon after the book was published in 2002, Safer happened to meet Ene Riisna, a producer for Barbara Walters on ABC's *20/20*, and mentioned it. Riisna instantly saw the parallels with her boss; she picked up a copy from Safer a day or two later and delivered it to Barbara.

The slim, 204-page volume was a revelation. "I recognized myself on almost every page: 'the prematurely mature child; the looming responsibility for a sibling's care and well-being; the compulsion to be an overachiever; the fear of failure,'" she said after reading it. "Much of the need I had to prove myself, to achieve, to provide, to protect, can be traced to my feelings about Jackie."

Safer never met Barbara in person, but she told me that the traits Barbara displayed in public, especially her relentless drive, were shared by many of the "normal" siblings she had studied. They often believed they had an obligation to be perfect because their "problem" siblings were not, and to succeed because their siblings could not. They feared the consequences for everyone if they failed. "What a burden on this woman," Safer said. "She couldn't make a mistake without feeling like everything, my entire family, depends on me to stay up, to keep their heads above water."

Many such siblings faced an emotional conundrum, she concluded. They would feel shortchanged by their parents, whose attention was often dominated by their other child, but they would also believe they had no right to demand equal time, because they weren't the ones who especially needed it.

After Jackie died, her memory would remain close to the surface, precious and painful. Barbara was at Arthur Ashe Stadium, where the U.S. Open is played, setting up to do an interview in 1999 with a rising tennis star Alexandra Stevenson, for years the unacknowledged daughter of

Julius Erving. A group of special-needs children on a field trip were walking by. Barbara, usually all business, startled her producer, Katie Nelson Thomson, when she saw tears welling in Barbara's eyes. One of the little girls reminded her of her sister, she told her.

———

Anne Sweeney had a particular understanding of the impact a special-needs family member could have.

She became president of the Disney/ABC Television Group during Barbara's final decade at the network. One day, when *The View* was airing from Burbank, Barbara was making no secret about her displeasure for being booked at the Hilton at Universal Studios, a mid-level hotel she did not find up to her five-star standards. She was complaining to anyone who would listen about everything from the quality of the tissues to the brand of the bottled water. Trying to mollify one of the networks' biggest stars, Anne showed up at her door with a welcome basket of tissues and water and chocolates and apologies. Barbara invited her in for tea.

Barbara knew that Sweeney's son, Chris, was on the autistic spectrum. She had been open about his disability at a time many parents were not. That afternoon, they talked for four hours about the realities facing families that included someone—a sister, a son—with a disability. In their honest, sometimes anguished conversation, Sweeney saw a vulnerable, raw side of Barbara Walters that she rarely showed.

"I think Barbara recognized herself as a breadwinner, as a provider, very, very early on, probably before she had her first job," Anne Sweeney told me. Through her career, "I think that was rocket fuel for her, or a little bit of her rocket fuel was knowing she'd have to provide."

There it was: *the rocket fuel.*

30

DIANE

1989

Barbara could pinpoint precisely when she first encountered Diane Sawyer.

Hanging on the wall of her Fifth Avenue apartment was a photograph showing the two of them on the trip where they met. On the last full day of President Richard Nixon's tour of China in 1972, the eighty-seven reporters, photographers, and technicians in the traveling press corps lined up with a handful of staffers from the White House press and travel offices in the courtyard of the West Lake Guest House in Hangzhou for a picture to commemorate the historic journey.

The president is standing in the middle of the first row, a small smile on his face.

To his left side is his press secretary, Ron Ziegler, and then Helen Thomas, a correspondent for United Press International who would later become the dean of the White House press corps. Dan Rather of CBS is crouching at their feet. To Nixon's right side, so close their shoulders are touching, is Barbara. Unlike most of the other journalists on the trip, she was neither a White House correspondent nor a TV anchor. She appeared on *Today* but was not yet the show's co-host. Richard Wald, the network's executive vice president, had taken a gamble by sending her. Three other NBC correspondents were on the trip and scattered in the photo, each with more experience and higher status than she had.

Still, Barbara managed to plant herself in pride of place, closest of all to the president. She is beaming. Standing behind her is Walter Cronkite. The third female journalist credentialed for the trip, Fay Gillis Wells, a pioneering foreign correspondent then working for Storer Broadcasting Company, is halfway down the row, bundled up in a coat with a fur collar.

"There's Nixon," Barbara said two decades later, pointing out the president to *New York Times* reporter Bill Carter, who was then working on a profile of her for the newspaper's Sunday magazine. The photo was displayed in the long hallway that served as a gallery of her interactions with the biggest names in politics and entertainment. "Here I am, pushy cookie," she told him, using the self-deprecating description of herself that she favored. "And way over here, that's Diane," tracing her finger to the border of the frame.

"She was an assistant press secretary," Barbara said. "There were only two women on the trip who were reporters, Helen Thomas and me." That wasn't accurate. The slight to Fay Wells was presumably unintentional.

But the slight to Diane was unmistakably deliberate. Carter couldn't quite believe she was making her disdain so clear. As a reporter on the television beat, he had covered the rivalry between Barbara and Diane, typically including their pro forma declarations of how much they respected one another. Now she seemed determined to pick at that scab, even while a reporter was taking notes. "Got herself in the middle—very acknowledging the truth there," he told me, recalling the exchange. Then he mimicked her: "'But look, way over here in the corner of the picture— look who it is, way over here.' And she didn't have to do that. I'm writing an article. Wouldn't you resist that if you could?"

But she couldn't. "No way could she resist that," he said. She couldn't resist the comparison, the competition, not from the very start. Not later, at the height of her career. Not ever.

Diane always had it easy. At least, that's how Barbara saw it.

If Barbara's early career was a case study in the long slog, Diane's was a blueprint for how to soar. In 1978, after working for former president Nixon for four years as he wrote his memoir, she joined CBS News as a reporter. (Her prior media experience was a stint out of college as a weather girl at WLKY in Louisville.) Just three years later, she was named co-anchor of the *CBS Morning News*. In 1984, she became the first female correspondent on *60 Minutes*, another prestigious post.

Then Roone Arledge called. A chapter of his memoir is titled "Landing Diane," chronicling what he called "a clandestine courtship." For a year and a half, they would meet privately for lunch or dinner every few weeks, unbeknownst to Barbara or almost anyone else. He convinced Diane to make the jump to ABC; he persuaded executives at ABC reluctant about hiring her that it was a good idea. He pitched a newsmagazine called *Primetime Live* that would pair her with the network's boisterous White House correspondent, Sam Donaldson.

Roone saw it as a coup.

Barbara saw it as a betrayal.

"Roone Arledge, who was my savior, was also my nemesis because he brought Diane over from '60 Minutes' and pitted us against each other," she would say two decades later.

She had little warning that Diane's hiring was in the works and no say in whether it would happen. A few days before the announcement, when rumors began to swirl, Peter Jennings had called Roone to make sure any deal wouldn't affect his role as the sole anchor for the *ABC Evening News*. Then Roone called Barbara to give her a heads-up. "There's a fairly good possibility that the Diane Sawyer thing may happen, maybe even this weekend," he told her, using what he called his "softest soap," his smoothest persuasion. "I'm calling so you won't be taken by surprise if it does, number one, and number two, to assure you that, if it happens, it won't affect you in any way."

"That's terrific," she replied, though he noticed that her icy tone didn't match her warm words. "I'd be delighted to have Diane here. I think she's awfully good."

Half an hour later, she called back. "Now that I've thought it over, I'm totally opposed to her," she said, not even mentioning "her" name. This time, Barbara's words did match her tone. "It *has* to affect me. How is someone of my stature supposed to divide up things with *her*? With all the things I do for ABC, bringing in such an obvious competitor like her is going to make it very tough . . ." He assumed the unspoken conclusion of that sentence was "for me to continue working at ABC." He reassured her she was "foremost in my heart and would continue so everlastingly." He told her he wouldn't let her get hurt, that he would personally look after her interests.

When Diane's move was announced days later, the news shook the TV world in the same way Barbara's shift to ABC from NBC had. "The fact is that the people who run the network news divisions believe that Sawyer's defection from CBS was one of the most important events in broadcast journalism—perhaps *the* most important—since Barbara Walters was lured to ABC 13 years ago for $1 million," Edward Klein wrote in *New York* magazine. A close-up of a contemplative Diane was featured on the magazine's cover. The move signaled that "no longer CBS but ABC was the dominant network in news."

Both women were smart, ambitious, and extraordinarily hardworking. Neither had come up through journalism's traditional path. Barbara grew up in the show business world of her father's nightclubs in Miami and New York before moving into a hybrid of journalism and entertainment. Diane, the daughter of a Kentucky judge, had worked for the only American president ever to resign in disgrace, then managed the difficult maneuver of crossing over into the news media. The backgrounds of both were the subject of suspicion by some of their journalistic brethren.

In other ways, though, they could hardly have been more different. Diane was sixteen years younger, enough of an interval to benefit from gains that had been hard-won by Barbara and other groundbreakers. She was the most beautiful woman in TV news. As a teenager, she had been crowned America's Junior Miss; as an adult, she could seem almost ethereal. If Diane was cool and aloof, Barbara was hot, intense, in your face. Diane glided. Barbara charged.

If someone had built to order the woman most likely to set off Barbara

Walters, she would have looked a lot like Diane Sawyer. Their rivalry became the talk of the town, and the network.

"Barbara was wonderful; she was the smartest person ever; she was living in the moment every day; she never half-showed up. I mean, everything about her was wonderful, except she had this thing with Diane, which was very complicated," an ABC executive who worked with both told me. "Listen, we all speculated on, was it age? You know, the *All About Eve* thing," a reference to the 1951 movie in which an aging Broadway star, portrayed by Bette Davis, is undone by her ambitious assistant. "Was it because Diane was at the ascendancy in her career and that Barbara thought that she needed to hold on? . . .

"Both of them were tireless, but it is a zero-sum game in some ways," the ABC executive said—that is, the high-stakes business of landing the most desirable newsmakers for exclusive interviews. "I mean, yes, you can say to me there's a billion people on earth, why do you have to be a zero-sum game? But there's only three anybody wants to watch at one time."

Barbara suddenly faced new and more formidable competition in her own shop to get them.

"When I arrived, I'm sure it was confusing to her because interviews had been her sole terrain," Diane told me. "I was always working on some long-form, delving into violence in schools or something that had really intrigued me. So I never felt that shows I was on, or my career, depended on interviews solely, but I understood what they meant to her." The big interview was Barbara's bread-and-butter. "When I started doing some interviews, I think it must have thrown her."

Now Diane and her booker, Mark Robertson, were pursuing them, too; he was every bit as aggressive as Barbara, sometimes enabling Diane to stay above the fray. But to her surprise and dismay, Diane discovered ABC had no system to allocate prospective subjects, like the one that was used at *60 Minutes* to maintain some order among the famously competitive correspondents there. At ABC, it was a free-for-all. Whoever could land a big guest got them.

———

There was little sisterhood among the most ambitious women in TV news, at least at that point. "Television is a tough game," Barbara observed, "and you don't win by always being Ms. Nice Guy."

If it was a zero-sum game to land newsmakers, it was also a zero-sum game for women to get the on-the-air jobs to interview them. It would be decades before both co-anchors on a morning show would be female. Barbara had flopped as the first female co-anchor of a network's evening news show; the next woman wouldn't get a chance at the job for another fifteen years, when Connie Chung was named co-anchor with Dan Rather on the *CBS Evening News* in 1993. She would last two years—just a few months longer than Barbara.

Barbara was co-hosting an evening newsmagazine, *20/20*; now Diane would have one of her own on the same network. When Barbara had gotten her first on-air job on the *Today* show in 1964, NBC correspondent Nancy Dickerson saw her career prospects at the network decline. Barbara confided in friends her fear that the same thing could happen to her.

She had never viewed the protests that some of her more feminist-minded colleagues were organizing as being in her particular interest. When she was at the *Today* show, she had disappointed some of the other women at NBC News by declining to join a lawsuit charging discrimination. "Secretaries' and newswomen's careers were ended by that lawsuit—they were regarded as troublemakers," said Marlene Sanders, a groundbreaker herself who wrote a book about the history of women in TV. Barbara occasionally chipped in for fundraisers for the litigation, but she largely kept her distance when it mattered, Marlene said. Eventually, the network reached a settlement that included $2 million in compensatory back pay and an agreement to undertake affirmative actions to advance women at the network.

More than a decade later, when Barbara had moved to ABC, women in the network's Washington Bureau began their own push for more equitable treatment.

By then, the bureau had seven female reporters but none of them on the most prestigious beats—the White House, Congress, the Supreme Court, the State Department, the Pentagon. During informal get-togethers every month or so, they shared stories of discrimination and harassment and of a glass ceiling they saw. ABC had no women who were bureau chiefs, senior producers, or top executives. They began to quietly collect data on salaries, story assignments, and the diversity, or lack of it, in management. Reporter Carole Simpson was one of the leaders; her husband was a vice president of a computer company and helped them conduct a content analysis of every news broadcast on ABC.

Barbara didn't work in the Washington Bureau, and she seemed unaware of what was brewing. But she unintentionally provided the opportunity for them to air their grievances. She was receiving the Silver Satellite Award from American Women in Radio and Television at their annual dinner in May 1985, and Roone invited all the network's female correspondents from across the country—all fifteen of them—to New York for a luncheon that day to celebrate her. Over dessert, Roone rose to herald Barbara as a trailblazer and role model. She thanked him and praised management for employing such a talented group of women. Then she left because she had a story to finish for *20/20*.

After Barbara departed, Carole jumped to her feet, thanked Roone for inviting them, and offered a toast to her absent colleague. "Barbara, the best," she said.

Then she distributed the documents they had prepared. "We think we have a problem here," Carole said. "We have a problem of institutional sex discrimination. We don't think it's any conspiracy to keep us off the air. You're not bad people. . . . It just probably hasn't crossed your mind." She displayed a graph that showed the lack of women reporting and producing stories on the broadcasts. The conversation, some of it contentious, stretched for nearly three hours, until it was time for everyone to get ready for Barbara's awards dinner. "You know, I just really never had thought about it before," Roone said. "You're absolutely right."

By that evening, Barbara had heard what had happened after she left the luncheon. She revised her acceptance speech to endorse the women's efforts. Over the next few years, some progress was made, in part because ABC and its new owner, Capital Cities, wanted to avoid the sort of lawsuit that had hit NBC and *Newsweek*. In 1988, Carole became the weekend anchor of the evening news, though that was not the senior White House assignment she wanted.

Barbara supported their efforts, but she didn't really see it as her fight. She wasn't going to take a stand that might imperil her success. The only woman she wanted to move was Diane Sawyer.

Barbara welcomed Diane to ABC by trying to steal the first guest from her new show.

Thomas Root was at the center of a headline-grabbing mystery. On July 13, 1989, the communications lawyer took off from Washington National Airport in his Cessna 210 Centurion, flying to North Carolina to meet some clients. He radioed he was having trouble breathing; later, he would report he blacked out. The single-engine plane was tailed by military jets and helicopters as it headed down the Eastern Seaboard on autopilot for nearly four hours and eight hundred miles. When it ran out of fuel and crashed into the Atlantic Ocean near the Bahamas, Root bobbed to the surface and rescuers managed to pull him into a raft. Oh, and this: He had an unexplained gunshot wound in his stomach.

Primetime booker Maia Samuel persuaded Root to come to the New York studio for an exclusive, live interview with Diane for the first show. She checked him into a hotel on Central Park West and stationed herself in the lobby, on the lookout for mischief, presumably by some competitor at another network. Instead, it was an ABC colleague, Lynn Murray, an associate producer on *20/20*, who showed up. She had been dispatched to convince Root to ditch Diane and be interviewed by Barbara instead.

"It was a complicated internal ABC situation," Victor Neufeld, the executive producer of *20/20*, told me, an understatement. "It was very competitive, and I was in the middle." Working for Barbara was a privilege, journalistic "nirvana," he said, but it "wasn't for the faint-hearted." He took the fall for the stunt, saying he was the one who had suggested Murray pursue Root; at the time Barbara insisted she had nothing to do with it. But Neufeld confirmed to me years later that it was Barbara's doing. That's what everyone had assumed from the start.

Her producers on the show were "thunderstruck" by the audacity of the move, Diane told me, although she said she was too consumed with the other complications of launching a new show to pay much attention.

"None of us could get over the fact that she would actually attempt to steal the name [that is, the most prominent guest] for the premier show," Ira Rosen, a senior producer for *Primetime*, told me. "It was a sort of foreshadowing of what would be coming in the following months, years."

Soon afterward, Barbara tried to upend another interview that Diane had landed, this time with Katharine Hepburn. The crew from *Primetime* was already in Hepburn's New York apartment setting up the lights and cameras when Barbara called Hepburn, urging her to cancel Diane and talk to her instead, Roone biographer Marc Gunther reported. The famed actress declined.

Diane managed some payback for that one. When Barbara scheduled her own Hepburn interview a year later, *Primetime* rebroadcast Diane's interview just ahead of it. (A "management mistake," ABC's spokeswoman said afterward, a benign explanation that convinced no one.)

"There were no rules," Diane said. A year after she had arrived at ABC, she asked Roone to intervene, to set up some guardrails. To her frustration, he refused. "Roone felt that competition even in the family would be good," she said. "I really felt that it would be impossible for me to be put in a situation where I would be calling and Barbara would be calling, too. That's not what families do."

It was a classic Roone tactic, to hire the biggest names with the biggest ambitions and have them compete for the biggest prizes, the highest ratings, the most acclaim. "Roone loved pitting people against each other," producer Phyllis McGrady told me. "He thought it made everything rise to a new, different level." That was true not only of Barbara and Diane but also of men in his employ, of Peter Jennings and Ted Koppel and others.

Diane and Rosen demanded a meeting with Roone after Barbara managed to steal an interview, this one with John Hinckley Jr., who was confined to a psychiatric hospital for the attempted assassination of President Ronald Reagan. "How is thievery an honorable position to take in this and allowing it to happen?" Rosen asked him.

Roone, on a speakerphone, didn't share his outrage. "She outsmarted you," he said.

———

They were rivals, often bitter ones, but in some ways they were friends, too.

More than a thousand people attended the New York Friars Club tribute to Barbara in the ballroom of the Waldorf-Astoria on May 7, 1994. The dais had forty-two seats to accommodate all the speakers and the most prominent guests, among them Mayor Rudy Giuliani, opera star Beverly Sills, designer Oscar de la Renta, and comedian Sid Caesar. Barbara said she had agreed to be honored—presumably not such a painful idea—in memory of her father, who had been a member of the Friars Club for years, frequenting its bars and playing at its card tables. "My childhood was the world of show business, and my adult life is the world of news," she said, "and finally the two will meet."

Among those delivering toasts were Henry Kissinger, Sam Donaldson, Carol Channing, Sharon Stone. And Diane Sawyer.

Dressed in floating white pants and a sheer champagne-colored top that sparkled with sequins, she delivered a breathy, torch-song rendition of "You Made Me Love You." The lyrics had been rewritten with the help of Mike Nichols, Diane's husband and the award-winning theater and film director, producer, actor, and comedian. In short, someone who knew how to stage a performance.

The song drew howls of laughter through the ballroom, in part because the lyrics cut so close and everyone knew it—from Barbara's propensity to show off her legs in short skirts to her reputation for making those she interviewed break down in tears. To their own rivalry, including a reference to *All About Eve*.

The opening line was "You made me ruthless." Then the end of the song:

I even married a Jew,
Hoping to be more like you.

Barbara roared with laughter during the performance and embraced Diane afterward. "That was a sensation," she told her. Later that night, she called Diane because she wanted to hear the lyrics again.

Their relationship wasn't simple; it had layers. "I know that nobody, maybe, will believe this," Diane told me, "but we spent a lot of time laughing and forging a real friendship, and that was true even when I first arrived." The two of them understood more than anyone else the trials they had faced, the prices they had paid. While they had differences, they could recognize something of themselves in the other. "I could share anything with her, and I know she shared things with me, things that were very close to the bone," Diane said. She saw Barbara's wistfulness about her loving marriage to Mike Nichols. Barbara envied it, a reminder that she had never managed to sustain such a union herself.

———

They were also the most intensive competitors, a stronger strand in their relationship.

Two years later came the most explosive showdown of all between Barbara and Diane, one never before reported. It put Barbara on the defensive and blew up, at least for a time, the relationship she valued most, the one with Roone.

In 1996, every network was seeking an interview with President Bill Clinton as he pursued a campaign for a second term. After disastrous midterm elections in 1994 had cost Democrats control of the House and Senate, he had made a remarkable political metamorphosis, partly in concert with his leading antagonist, Republican House speaker Newt Gingrich.

The ABC brass decided it was Diane's turn to get the Clinton interview. "Roone Arledge made it very clear to me and told me specifically, and always on the phone with Joanna Bistany, who was his number two in managing the talent and all of that, that this one had to go to Diane, that I had to explain to the White House that ABC's priority was to get the interview and our priority for the interview was Diane Sawyer," Robin Sproul, the network's Washington bureau chief, told me. "I did, in fact, communicate that to the White House very clearly that that's what we wanted."

Barbara, who had conducted a White House interview with First Lady

Hillary Clinton about her new book in January, was supposed to stand down. That word reached everyone involved except, apparently, Barbara. To the bemusement of White House press secretary Mike McCurry, both Diane and Barbara were aggressively lobbying White House staffers for an interview with the president—not only explaining why they should get it but also why the other one shouldn't.

Sproul had driven her two young daughters to the Eastern Shore for a spring weekend when the White House press office pinged her beeper; it was before the era of smartphones. She called back. "Well, I have good news and bad news," McCurry told her. "You got the interview—and it's going to Barbara." He said he realized she would have "a hot one on her hands" with that. She called Roone and Joanna from the hotel. "Here's the situation," she told them. "We got the interview—yay!—but they're giving it to Barbara."

Roone was enraged. "How can they do that?" he demanded. She replied, "Look, they get to offer the interview to whoever they want to offer the interview to. That's what they get to do." "Well, you can tell them we don't want their interview," he replied angrily. "You call the White House and tell them we're not doing the interview."

Sproul, startled, warned that if ABC turned down a prized interview with the president because of a rivalry between two anchors, that would become the story, and a big one. "The White House knows that the two of them have been down there arguing it and fighting for this interview and if you turn it down, that will be leaked," she said.

"Call the White House now and you tell them, we're turning down the interview," Roone repeated.

Click.

An hour and a half later, Sproul was still trying to figure out exactly how to deliver that message to the White House when Joanna called her back. "Hon, you know that thing Roone asked you to do? Did you do that?" she asked. No, Sproul replied, not yet. Joanna said, "Don't do that. We're delighted to do the interview with the White House. Couldn't be happier. Thank you."

That would not be the end of it. Roone was so angry and the blowback so blistering that Barbara wrote a three-page memo to him offering her account of what had happened and why she was not at fault for any of it. For someone who was accustomed to being on offense, to plowing ahead, she suddenly found herself on her back foot. She had always had sharp antennae. It was a sign of the trouble she was in that she would feel compelled to write such an explanation, convincing or not.

"I am troubled, as I am sure you are, by the events concerning the background to the interview with President Clinton," she began in the memo typed on her *20/20* stationery, dated April 16, 1996. It was filed in the Roone Arledge archives at Columbia University. Joanna had never told her it was Diane's interview, she insisted, and besides, she was the one who deserved it. "Indeed, the only top ABC correspondent <u>never</u> to have interviewed President Clinton is me, so if anything, we would have expected ABC News to have asked for <u>us</u> to have priority, were there to be one," underlining words for emphasis.

She offered preemptive responses to whatever questions might be raised, in a word salad of explanation, finger-pointing, half-truths, random asides, and non sequiturs. The interview she recently had with Hillary was irrelevant, she wrote, and by the way only turned out to be newsworthy because of her acumen. She had never before met McCurry, so it was perfectly understandable that she went to see him, she said, and that she would request an interview with Clinton while she was in the press secretary's office.

She mentioned her pitch, the one that apparently had proved to be so persuasive. She had recently interviewed Colin Powell, she noted. "'Everyone knew what Powell's character was,' I said, 'but they didn't know how he stood on the issues until we asked,'" she told McCurry. "'With the president,' I suggested, 'everyone knows how he stands on the issues, but his character is being questioned.'

"McCurry then told us, to our astonishment, that ABC News was pushing hard for Diane," she wrote. "He thought we should know. We said, 'Oh,' and little more." Barbara blamed her apparent cluelessness on Joanna's failure to keep her informed. At one point, when they talked, Barbara wrote, "Joanna was ill and perhaps has forgotten some of the conversation."

Now, she complained, Joanna had delivered her a disquieting message. "She told us that you had 'washed your hands of the whole thing,'" Barbara wrote, and that "she, too, 'washed her hands of the whole situation' and that though she loved me as a 'human being,' from now on any discussions I had in the future should be with Alan Wurtzel." Wurtzel was the network's senior vice president for newsmagazine and long-form programming. Barbara was accustomed to having a clear channel to Roone, the boss at the top.

"I am also concerned about my relationship with Diane," Barbara continued. "She and I have had a wonderful relationship, considering our programs are still so competitive, and I would hate for her to have the impression that I knew of ABC News' position and deliberately undercut her." (For the record, Diane told me she remembered other incidents when they had clashed but not this one.)

That "wonderful relationship," and Barbara's concern about it, would surely have been news to everyone who had been caught in the crossfire between the two of them. The idea that she was "astonished" to learn the interview had been designated for Diane was less than credible, too. So was the notion that, even if she acknowledged knowing, she would have been deterred from trying to get the interview herself.

Whether they believed her version of events or not, though, Barbara closed with a threat. She was then in the midst of contract negotiations, she noted, suggesting that perhaps she might be better off at some other network. "All this dismayed me, to put it mildly," she wrote. "If this is what it is like before I sign a contract, I thought, what will the next years be like? How unhappy will I be?" She deployed, in effect, the nuclear option, that she would leave ABC.

That was a credible threat. Four years earlier, during the previous round of contract negotiations, CBS had pursued her. Howard Stringer, then president of the CBS Broadcast Group, and Laurence Tisch, the CEO and president of CBS, had offered her a staggering $10 million a year to anchor her own newsmagazine, promising a valuable time slot, 10 p.m. on Mondays. Anxious about having to prove herself yet again, she turned CBS down but let Bistany know about the rival's bid.

This time, the risk that she might take a walk was apparently enough to avert a showdown.

Barbara sat down with Clinton for the interview. As promised, she focused on questions about his character. At that time, the president had begun a sexual relationship with a White House intern named Monica Lewinsky, but neither Barbara nor almost anyone else realized that yet. "The American people have now had an adequate opportunity to judge me as president, to see my work, to make a judgment about whether I have the character to do this job, and they will do that," Clinton told her.

After all that, the interview didn't make news—nothing like the blockbuster interview she would have with Monica three years later. Barbara herself didn't think much of the sit-down with Clinton. "He never sparkled with me," she said dismissively. "Our conversation was not memorable to me."

———

There was a mantra in the hallways of ABC about the risks of crossing either of the network's top female stars in their drive to win a big interview or to get rid of an incommodious associate. "Diane will stab you in the back," the saying went, volunteered to me separately by three ABC veterans. "Barbara will stab you in the front."

"I was standing with Diane at the elevator once when she bumped into Barbara," Rosen recalled. "'How are you?' Barbara asked Diane. 'I'm fine, and you?' 'People say we don't get along, they should see us now,' Barbara said, reaching for Diane's hand. 'I know, I don't understand that,' Diane said and laughed. The elevator came and Diane said goodbye to Barbara. Inside the elevator, Diane looked at me and said, 'I hate that woman. Don't believe a word she says. She knifes me any chance she gets.'"

Diane could turn the tables. In 2000, Palestinian leader Yasir Arafat had been booked by Barbara for *20/20* when Diane flew to the Mideast, interviewed him, and got it on the air first, on *Good Morning America*. Barbara raised a ruckus. ABC News president David Westin, who had succeeded Roone, called them both into his office. He told them to stop undermining each other, that the Roone era of internal combustion was over. He then tried, with mixed success, to put in place a system to coordinate interview requests.

A year and a half later, that laying-down-the-law session provided the lead anecdote in a *New York Times* story about Westin's efforts. It said Westin's goal was to "bring together a newsroom set up under the system of his predecessor, Roone Arledge, which encouraged a roster of high-priced, superstar anchors and producers to bite, claw and hoodwink one another in the race for exclusive news." The story reported he was scoring some successes, including in brokering a cease-fire between Barbara and Diane. "These days, the rivalry is said to remain strong, though it has not been quite as tense," it said.

Or perhaps not. The week after that story was published, a new battle broke out between them. Rosie O'Donnell, the talk show host and co-median, was prepared for the first time to come out of the closet as she promoted her new book, *Find Me*. Diane had landed the interview to air on *Primetime Thursday* on March 14, 2002. But the day they taped the interview, on February 14, Barbara casually disclosed Rosie's sexual orientation on *The View*.

The show's panel was discussing a law in Florida that banned adoption by gay men and lesbians. Rosie had hoped to adopt a three-year-old girl named Mia, but was only allowed to become her foster mother. "What concerns Rosie is not just this case but that she has three adopted children and a foster child herself, and she, because she is gay, would not be al-lowed to adopt this child," Barbara said.

Because she is gay.

Diane had won the interview but Barbara had scooped the news. "The greatest TV diva duel since Joan Collins and Linda Evans slugged it out on 'Dynasty' back in the '80s," declared a *San Francisco Examiner* gossip columnist. Barbara claimed innocence but also offered a bit of a mea culpa. "This had nothing to do with getting an interview with Rosie," she insisted but then added, "I am sensitive enough now as I look back to see how it could be interpreted that way and how, if one didn't know the story and wanted to create a story, it could look as if I was trying to harm Diane."

Indeed, that was exactly how it looked to everyone involved.

"This is not the evil axis," Barbara said. "This is a little misunder-standing."

When David Bauder of the Associated Press called about the controversy, ABC's public relations chief, Jeffrey Schneider, urged the two women to agree to a joint interview with him. "I told them I thought that the only thing that would make the story go away would be for the two of them to sit and talk to him. They certainly wanted the story to go away. They hated, hated, hated the 'cat fight' story. For sure, more than anything they hated that."

They sat together in an ABC conference room to talk with Bauder on a speakerphone, "and they're both singing *Kumbaya* to him," Schneider told me. The headline on the AP story that followed: "ABC Stars Sawyer, Walters Deny Dispute About Story." But Bauder ended the story with an anecdote about the two women dining separately at the Four Seasons in New York on the same day as his interview. Diane had a scratch on her face that she had gotten when she ran into a tree while walking her dog over the weekend. "I'm going to tell everybody that I did it," Barbara was quoted as joking.

Barbara and Diane argued that the scrutiny of their disputes was fueled by a sexist trope about women clawing at women. "It was a constant battle royale, but so were the three anchormen, Peter, Dan, and Tom," Connie Chung told me, referring to Peter Jennings of ABC, Dan Rather of CBS, and Tom Brokaw of NBC. "They would battle it out and people would say, 'Fine, you know, that's guys, the Three Musketeers are fighting each other. They're fencing; they're shooting it out.'

"And when Barbara and Diane and I were fighting it out, they'd call it a cat fight."

Barbara argued that Jennings and Ted Koppel were "far more competitive" than she and Diane were, an assertion both men disputed. "That's nonsense," Peter responded at the time. Ted Koppel also disagreed. "There were times when we competed, but it was never at that kind of level and we really were friends," he told me. "Barbara and Diane were not friends."

Misogyny was part of it, but even allies acknowledged that the rivalry between Barbara and Diane had a fission as fierce or fiercer than the competition among anybody else in a business known for it. Barbara managed to be good friends with Ted Koppel and Sam Donaldson. But she became obsessed with Diane.

Everything had been hard for her, Barbara complained to her closest friends, while Diane had always had things easy. She was lovely and charming; even network executives, the male ones, sometimes seemed to melt in her presence. She had a successful marriage, something that always eluded the thrice-married, thrice-divorced Barbara. Diane and her accomplished husband moved in the most elite social circles. And the brutal truth was that Roone did favor Diane. For Barbara, it was like realizing that your father loved your sister more.

"Roone's beloved was Diane Sawyer," Koppel told me. "I don't mean that in a romantic sense, I just mean Roone was absolutely smitten by Diane and really saw Diane as the shinier of the two stars. He recognized Barbara's value to the network. He recognized that she was critical to the network and brought in a ton of money and a lot of viewers. But he was not enamored of Barbara; he was of Diane. That killed Barbara."

Roone was in Washington to attend a roast of Sam Donaldson and arranged a dinner in a private room at the Four Seasons for the ABC contingent there. "Diane, come sit by me here," he called out to Diane, loud enough for Barbara and everyone else to hear. Barbara, flinching, said in an aside, "Why does he always do that to me?"

What finally calmed their rivalry wasn't some sort of negotiated détente. The industry itself was changing. With the advent of cable television and then streaming services, with social media and new ways for celebrities and newsmakers to tell their stories, broadcast networks were no longer the only game in town. Ratings declined; so did advertising revenues. Even big interviews got smaller.

In January 2004, Barbara announced she was retiring from *20/20*, though she would still host specials on the Oscars and the year's *10 Most Fascinating People*. She was about to celebrate her seventy-fifth birthday, but her age wasn't the reason she gave for stepping back from the show that had featured her interviews for twenty-five years. The reason is that her bosses, under pressure to attract younger viewers, wanted fewer interviews with kings and prime ministers and more confessionals from celebrities and murderers.

"Newsmagazines in general are somewhat in jeopardy, I think," she said. "And I'll tell you the way it's going to be: we're going to hear that a woman had a love affair with a frog. The producers are going to come to me and say, 'Barbara, this woman had a love affair with a frog. Diane Sawyer already has the woman lined up. Do you want to do the frog?' And I will say, 'O.K., but only if I can get the frog and his mother.' And they'll say: 'But the frog wants an hour. And before you do the frog, the frog is going to do Oprah, O.K.?'"

For her last piece on *20/20*, ABC decided she should interview a teacher who had a sexual relationship with an underage boy—she had just been released from prison—rather than accept an offer to interview President George W. Bush.

"More frogs," as she put it.

———

When Ben Sherwood became president of ABC News in 2010, he was determined to ease the internal competition and forge a more collaborative work ethic within the network—to focus their energy against competitors at CBS and NBC, not at their colleagues down the corridor. "For years, it seemed that there had been roving gangs of anchormen and women and correspondents and producers roaming the halls and sometimes shooting each other in broad daylight," he told me. "We felt like we needed to restore law and order and bring the organization together peacefully. That was our goal."

In 1989, Roone had staged a celebrated publicity campaign featuring the network's biggest guns, informally dubbed "the Magnificent Seven": Peter Jennings, Ted Koppel, Barbara Walters, Diane Sawyer, David Brinkley, Sam Donaldson, and Hugh Downs. Now Sherwood scheduled a photo session at the ABC studio at Chelsea Piers including a much larger group of twenty-two anchors. His message: "This group, we'll win together, we'll win the championship together, and that's our mission together. It's not every woman and man for himself anymore. It's not me against you in the street: 'I'll kill you; I'll get that interview.' It's 'we're going to do this together.'"

Everyone was instructed to wear black or navy—not a uniform, exactly, but the colors of a unified team. Just about everybody complied, more or less. The fourteen men were all in dark suits, David Muir and George Stephanopoulos among them. Katie Couric and Christiane Amanpour dressed in dark gray; Lara Spencer and Elizabeth Vargas in quiet shades of blue; Robin Roberts in a muted maroon. Diane Sawyer, on the front row and just off center, was wearing a black suit and crisp white blouse, with just a touch of color in her narrow red belt.

Barbara arrived last and late, just in time to perch on her designated stool in the front. She was wearing not black or navy or gray or a color that was even slightly muted. She was wearing a red jacket over a black turtleneck, a brilliant combination that had the intended effect. With that red jacket, Barbara stole the spotlight. If this was a photograph of a team, there would be no question, visually at least, who commanded its center.

Diane's countenance in the photo is guarded, but she was furious. "See? It's all about her," she told others afterward. "She never follows the rules." Sherwood understood the power play involved, but at that point there was nothing to be done about it. The photo was taken and used for publicity. "She won that round," he told me with a rueful chuckle. "That was game-set-match."

In the picture, Barbara is in pride of place, in the precise center of the front row. Her expression is triumphant, remarkably like the one in the photo taken nearly two decades earlier in the courtyard of the West Lake Guest House in Hangzhou, China, where she had managed to park herself right next to President Nixon.

She is beaming.

YOU CAN'T HAVE IT ALL

1990

To almost no one's surprise, the notion that Barbara and Merv would happily split their time half-and-half between her New York and his California didn't last.

She was unable or unwilling to adjust her work schedule, which usually required her to be in New York City or on a flight to an interview. He preferred Malibu. Before they had managed to establish a workable long-distance routine for their marriage, he was staying mostly on his coast; she was staying mostly on hers. "She was at a point in her life where she wasn't going to give it up"—that is, to dial down her career—"and he was at a point in his life where he wanted more," Maurie Perl, an ABC News executive who worked closely with Barbara, told me. "He ultimately wanted a wife."

Connie Chung found herself seated next to Merv at one of Barbara's dinner parties. "Do you have an identity outside your job?" he asked her. She dodged the question with one of her own: "Why do you ask?" He said, "Because Barbara doesn't."

Before they had celebrated their fifth anniversary, Merv was having an affair with Thea Nesis, a lawyer from Los Angeles who would become his fourth wife. He thought nothing of it when a photographer snapped their photo as they were skiing in Aspen. He was in New York when Beverly Sills called the apartment. She warned Barbara that her husband's picture had just been published on the cover of *The National Enquirer*, cozying up in a ski lift with Thea. She was beautiful and athletic and more than thirty years younger than his current wife.

Barbara had seen her romances and marriages fail before—all of them, in fact—but this split was particularly painful and embarrassingly public. The other woman exposed Barbara's insecurities about her age, her looks, her ability to love and be loved. A close colleague told me the breakup was one of only a few times he ever saw her cry. "She never really forgave me, and I don't blame her," Merv said.

The breakup was announced in her friend Liz Smith's column, of course, with a version that didn't mention the latest tabloid furor. "It is with great sadness that Barbara Walters and Merv Adelson are announcing that they will be having a trial separation," the item read. "For the past five years, this glamorous and very nice couple has lived a high-intensity, bi-coastal wedlock, with each traveling from coast-to-coast at least once a month. But now, Merv's business interests require his spending most of his time in Los Angeles and Barbara's television assignments, instead of lessening, seem to have multiplied so that she is traveling all over the world or operating primarily from New York. The twain meets—but the effort is gigantic."

The account was about as candid as the item Barbara had leaked to the gossip columns three decades earlier about her father's "heart attack." In this case, there wasn't a trial separation; both knew the breach was permanent. The marriage hadn't lasted five years; it had lasted a little more than four. Merv's business interests weren't the new factor keeping him on the West Coast; his personal assignation was. And Barbara by that point had some say over her television assignments; she could have moderated her pace if she had chosen.

With her third marriage over and her relationship with her daughter as knotty as ever, she decided with some bitterness that her life offered proof it wasn't possible for a woman to have it all. After the latest divorce, she would date but never again marry. As humiliating as Merv's behavior was to her, she wasn't blameless in what had happened. No marriage ever matched the draw, the adrenaline of her work.

"You can have a great marriage and great children; great marriage and great career; great career and great children," Barbara told two thousand women gathered at a conference in Virginia Beach sponsored by Virginia senator John Warner in 1989; she and Warner had dated in the 1970s. "But I think it is so hard to have a great marriage, a great career—not a job but a career—and great children."

She urged the audience to have a life beyond getting up in the morning and going to work, but the aside she added was more revealing than her formal advice: "Although that can be pretty wonderful and intoxicating." It was, after all, the choice she had made.

———

A decade after the divorce, Merv was in financial trouble. He and his partners had sold Lorimar, their heavily indebted company, for $1.2 billion in stock to Warner Communications, which was about to merge with Time Inc. When the internet bubble burst in 2000, so did Merv's holdings in AOL Time Warner, costing him an estimated $114 million. He had invested much of his fortune in several other dot-com companies; that money vanished, too. He lost money on investments in real estate and insurance trusts.

He filed for personal bankruptcy in 2003. He owed his creditors a stunning $112.5 million. His fourth wife, Thea, had already begun proceedings for a divorce.

Yet Barbara didn't hold a grudge against him. A year later, in 2004, she called Jessica Stedman Guff, who had worked for her and was now the senior producer at ABC's *Good Morning America*.

"She says, 'Jessica, you have to put Merv on the show,'" Guff told me, recalling their conversation. "And I said, 'Why would I put Merv on the show?'" Once the titan of Lorimar, Adelson was now one of several producers for an obscure children's DVD series called *The JammX Kids*. The adventures of nine hip-hop friends were designed to combat childhood obesity by encouraging kids to dance.

Guff wasn't persuaded that the JammX Kids demonstrating their moves at Times Square really warranted a story on *Good Morning America*. But this was Barbara Walters asking. "Well, I suppose I could do like a minute and a half, two minutes, in the second hour," Guff said. "Well, you have to," Barbara said. "He's lost all his money. This is his only hope."

It was one more reprise of Barbara's relationship with her father. Then she was in her twenties, plowing her savings in his enterprises. Now she was in her seventies and still trying to rescue men who had disappointed her.

Guff sent an ABC correspondent and crew to Times Square to do a brief hit with Merv and the JammX Kids.

Near the end of his life, before he died of cancer in 2015, Merv acknowledged he had been aware of Dalitz's Mob ties in those early Las Vegas days—the suggestion he had spent so many years and legal action to combat. "I heard a lot about skimming," he said, but he insisted they had never discussed anything illegal. He had found it "exciting" to be associated with him. "The bow-downs you would get when I walked into a place with Moe. You began to enjoy that kind of thing—at least I did," he told *Vanity Fair*. "It's the way Vegas was."

By then, he was living in a five-hundred-square-foot studio apartment in Santa Monica with a kitchenette, a battered futon, and an aging dog named Teddy. His fourth wife would haul him into court over unpaid child support for their two daughters. One final humiliation: The headline over that news story identified him not by his name, not as the former multimillionaire titan of Hollywood. Instead, he was "Barbara Walters' bankrupt ex-husband."

After Barbara died, the items from her estate that were put up for auction included the engagement ring he had given her on that beach in Malibu.

32

THE YIN AND THE YANG

On the night Barbara Walters died, a string of notable female journalists phoned in to ABC's breaking coverage to talk about her role in their lives and their careers—Katie Couric, Joan Lunden, Connie Chung, Elizabeth Vargas, and Deborah Roberts. "Journalistic royalty," Roberts, who had joined *20/20* as a correspondent during Barbara's last decade on the show, called her former colleague.

She was a generous mentor-by-example, Roberts said. But she also never stopped being a competitor.

"Barbara often would ask, 'What are you working on? What are you working on?'" Roberts told me later with a laugh. "Every now and again, I was hesitant to say because I thought if it was an idea of something she liked, next thing I know, my story would be shut down and Barbara would be doing it." An interview Roberts had once worked to line up with Kelly Ripa suddenly became Barbara's interview. "She would tell you in a flash if there was something you were working on and she thought it was not that interesting. But if it was something interesting, she might not say much, and then the next thing you know, she's doing it."

That yin and yang—the empathy and the rivalry—continued to the end.

When Roberts was expecting her first child, she felt a bit of trepidation when she went in to tell Barbara she was pregnant and planning to take maternity leave. Barbara's work ethic was legendary; would she disapprove of her going off the air, even temporarily? She was stunned by Barbara's response. "When you've had the baby, take the time because you'll never get that time back," she advised. "And I have to say, that's one thing I probably should have done a little bit better. I should have focused a bit more on my family."

———

Barbara was a pioneer, but she insisted her goal had been to prove herself, not to make a point. Whether she intended to or not, though, she became an inspiration for generations of girls and women who thought they could aspire to the most prominent, powerful positions because she had.

"She inspired me," Norah O'Donnell, who in 2019 took Walter Cronkite's old seat as anchor of the *CBS Evening News*, told me. As a middle-schooler growing up in Texas, Norah would call her best friend, Shauna Calhoun, and leave joke voicemail messages. "This is Barbara Walters," she would say, mimicking Barbara's voice. "I'm calling to talk to you, if you have time for an interview."

"For me, to see someone like that made me imagine the possibilities," said Katie Couric, who in 2006 became the first female solo anchor on a network evening newscast, at CBS. In high school in suburban Virginia, she had grown up watching Barbara interview newsmakers. "TV news was an exciting, relatively new field for women, and I thought, 'Hey, if my face doesn't stop a clock, it's much more lucrative than radio or print, and why not?'" Couric told me. "I don't know if I would've said, 'Why not?' if it hadn't been for Barbara Walters."

She credited her predecessor with rattling cages "before women were even allowed into the zoo."

The fact that Barbara had broken through a glass ceiling—more than one, in fact—and endured wounds from the shards gave her a special standing among many of those who became her competitors. She could be fierce in fighting for interviews, said Connie Chung, but she added: "She earned the right to be a diva."

Barbara would send notes of congratulations when other women landed a big job or a major interview, handwritten on her cream or light blue stationery, and she regularly fielded calls from them when they sought advice during tough times. She hired women as well as men for the top jobs on her staff—Phyllis McGrady and Jessica Stedman Guff and Katie Nelson Thomson among them—and she promoted their careers even after they left her employ. She would give her female friends generous gifts and unvarnished advice, including things she had learned the hard way, especially on the perils of balancing a career and motherhood.

"There was a great loyalty gene in Barbara," Louise Grunwald, one of her closest friends, told me.

Her manner was never maternal, not in the traditional way, but she could be, at times, a mother hen.

"She mom'ed the correspondents whom she liked," Chung told me. She was the second woman, after Barbara, to co-anchor a network newscast, and the two were colleagues for a while at *20/20*. "Anytime I did something, she would actually write me a note, or in some way bring it to my attention that she saw it." When Connie received one of her missives, "it was always, 'Oh, boy, I got a handwritten note from Barbara.'"

In 1970, an unemployed writer named Pat Mitchell had fled to the ladies' room at NBC and was fighting back tears when Barbara walked in. She was famous; Pat was not. Still, Barbara said hello and introduced herself—a kind gesture not required by ladies'-room etiquette—and Pat blurted out her woes. She was a single mother who had moved to New York to work for *Look*; nine months later, the newsmagazine had folded. She had just auditioned for WNBC as a reporter, but it hadn't gone well. Bernie Shusman, head of the local news operation, said her thick Georgia accent made it unlikely she could get a job on the air.

"Don't listen to anyone who gives you the reasons you will fail," Barbara told her in their brief exchange. "Just prove them wrong." Only in retrospect did Pat realize how often Barbara must have heard that dismissal herself, about her peculiar speech patterns making a broadcast career impractical. When Pat finally landed a job at WBZ in Boston, she wrote Barbara a letter, thanking her for the words of encouragement at a crucial moment.

Pat Mitchell would have her own remarkable career in television news. She worked as a reporter and talk show host, became the first president of CNN's division for documentaries, then the first female president and CEO of PBS. Years later, when she was interviewing for the job of CEO and president of the Paley Center for Media in New York, Barbara was on the search committee. Pat was offered the job, and Barbara encouraged her to take it. She did.

Finding female mentors was nearly impossible in the early years, Pat said. "At that time, it was very difficult to show up for other women because of the absolute dictate—maybe not always stated but nonetheless understood—that there was generally one place in every network or one place in every production company for a woman."

But she and Barbara eventually became friends and allies, she said. "In what we both often referred to as our 'third act,' Barbara became more vocal and public in her support for other women in the media business. That wasn't her reputation, but that was the reality of what I experienced with her."

————

Lynn Sherr had a different attitude than Barbara did about the women's movement. She had been an outspoken advocate for women in journalism from her early days as a reporter for the Associated Press. When she joined *20/20* as a correspondent in 1986, she and Barbara got along well—a cordiality facilitated, she acknowledged, by the fact she was typically interested in stories that didn't appeal to Barbara. "Once you were her friend, you were her friend," she told me. "She could be a real girl's girl. You could gossip; you could dish. You could be in trouble and she would be there to help you."

In 1997, Lynn was in trouble. She had been rushed to the hospital with stabbing abdominal pain that doctors misdiagnosed as appendicitis. When they operated, they discovered she had colon cancer. "They took out a foot and a half of colon," she said. "I wound up in chemo for the better part of the year." While she would eventually recover, it was a terrifying time.

Soon after the operation, Barbara called to check on how she was doing. A few days later, she would be the first person to visit her in the hospital, wearing the baseball cap she donned when she didn't want to be recognized. She mentioned that gossip columnist Liz Smith had heard Lynn was in the hospital and wanted to run an item about it. Would that be okay? "I told Barbara I wasn't sure," Lynn said. "I didn't know the complete diagnosis yet. I didn't want to go public until I had all the facts." She didn't want to make "a publicity thing" out of her health.

"But people are talking," Barbara replied. "They've heard something. Better to get out the facts than to let the rumors grow." They drafted language that struck a casual tone and skirted the messy truth.

"ABC's ACE reporter Lynn Sherr, who toils for '20/20' and recently published a wonderful book about her love of giraffes, 'Tall Blondes,' is *hors de combat*, but it's temporary," the item read. "She thought she had appendicitis and went into the hospital, where they found a growth in her colon. It was removed. She has a clean bill of health now and will be back at work in a few weeks. Her friends are rejoicing."

The word "cancer" was nowhere to be found—apparently a growth of who-knows-what had been removed from her colon—and she didn't have a clean bill of health, not yet. She wouldn't be back at work in a few weeks, either.

"Was it a little premature?" Lynn said. "Oh, yeah. Did I have any idea if I was going to be fine? I certainly did not." But the item in Liz Smith's column served to protect her public image and her job. "That was the end of my worries about ABC, about anybody looking at me askance in that regard," she told me. "That was a friendship thing. It was also a wise TV thing. It was just a smart thing to do."

She didn't fault Barbara for not being an early advocate for other women. She understood Barbara's view that her success on its own would eventually make room for others, though the realization was sometimes bittersweet. "She was surprised, shocked, envious, as we all were, that after a certain point, all the things she had fought for were out there for other people," Lynn said. Barbara expressed some resentment when, doing a spot on *Good Morning America*, she saw that a room had been designated for co-host Joan Lunden to use for her young children while she worked. No one had done that for her when she adopted a newborn.

"I'm not suggesting Joan didn't deserve it," Lynn said. "But sometimes it is hard not to say, 'Wait a minute. I had a fight for that, and you just get it.'"

———

There were times Barbara was the best of friends, and times when she was not.

She stepped in to help when Nancy Shevell McCartney, her cousin and a generation younger, was going through a difficult patch—the death of her mother, then a diagnosis of breast cancer while in her mid-thirties. Barbara paved the way for her to see the top specialist at Sloan Kettering, where she had connections. She gave her a notebook that she took to many appointments, to track what the doctors were saying. She went with her to some appointments and visited her in the hospital. Just her presence made a positive difference, she told me.

"She completely quarterbacked it," Nancy, who later married Paul McCartney, told me. "I think that one of the reasons that I survived all these years is because of the care that she orchestrated for me."

Her relationships with her closest girlfriends outlasted any of her marriages.

She and columnist Cindy Adams, who had met at the Latin Quarter when both were teenagers, would vacation together with Judith Sheindlin, better known as Judge Judy, on her yacht. Barbara sat on the front row of couture fashion shows with Annette de la Renta, wife of the renowned designer whose clothes she often wore, alongside Nancy Kissinger and *Vogue*'s Anna Wintour. She joined a luncheon of powerhouse women in New York media every month or two for gossip and laughs. The original group included columnist Liz Smith, *USA Today* columnist Jeannie Williams, Clinton White House veteran Lisa Caputo, ABC correspondent Cynthia McFadden, CNN executive Jennifer Maguire Isham, and top publicists Maurie Perl of Condé Nast, Beth Kseniak of *Vanity Fair*, and Peggy Siegal. Barbara and author Nora Ephron later became regular members. Liz would occasionally bring celebrity guests—Bette Midler for one lunch, George Clooney for another—and she dubbed the group The Harpies.

But even women whose friendship with Barbara spanned decades learned the same lesson that her husbands had. Her career came first, even if they were in the midst of some crisis and wanted her attention. One of her closest friends told me this reality would always create "a certain distance" between them.

And don't cross her. "She could carry a grudge like a .44 Magnum," media writer Bill Carter told me.

Mary Alice Williams had known Barbara for years. She had helped launch CNN and worked as an anchor and correspondent at NBC; she was later an anchor for NJTV, the public television network in New Jersey. When Barbara was creating *The View* and casting the women who would serve on the original panel, she asked Mary Alice to audition to be the moderator. Meredith Vieira got the job instead, but Barbara wrote Mary Alice a personal note leaving the door open for a role down the road.

Then Mary Alice performed a song that teased her—and that crossed a line, in Barbara's view.

The Inner Circle is an annual benefit at which journalists spoof pols and the New York City mayor enlists Broadway stars to spoof them back. Mary Alice was on stage portraying Fox anchor Greta Van Susteren. In a cover story in *People* magazine a few months before the April 2002 show, Greta had discussed her recent cosmetic surgery, typically a taboo topic; the change in her appearance had prompted comments. Mary Alice held aloft an oversized photo of Greta and sang lyrics that began, "Who Am I Anyway?" the plaintive song from *A Chorus Line*.

> *"This is a picture of a person I don't know.*
> *My face behind my ears, I'll work a thousand years.*
> *Dan, Tom and Peter had their faces lifted, too,*
> *And Barbara Walters, she's had eighty-two."*

When she finished, she blew a kiss in Barbara's direction in the ballroom as the audience roared.

In fact, while Barbara had cosmetic surgery earlier in her career, she had relied only on Botox, facial fillers, and excellent makeup and lighting since the early 1990s, according to her longtime makeup artist, Lori Klein. Barbara was outspoken in her umbrage at a joke she saw as inaccurate and mean-spirited.

"Extremely insulting," Barbara declared on *The View* the next Monday. She didn't cite Mary Alice by name, but she did complain that the woman involved had recently called her for help in setting up a job interview at ABC News. She had done so much to help her; why would she hurt her in this way? Mary Alice, who happened to be watching the show that morning, sat down and immediately sent an apologetic "Dear Barbara" email. "I'm so sorry you took offense at it," she wrote. "I meant the opposite." Barbara never responded; the two women would see each other only one more time, in public and in passing.

Barbara's friends knew she could be mercurial. Susan Mercandetti, who had been a colleague at ABC, had admired an elaborate bracelet that Barbara had gotten in Syria during the 2011 trip to interview Syrian president Bashar al-Assad. Later, when the two women were having lunch, Barbara pulled the bracelet out of her bag and gave it to her. "I want you to have this," she said.

She could be considerate one moment and cutting the next, Susan told me. "She'd surprise you with her sharp tone and she would surprise you with her kindness."

Sometimes she would combine both those traits. Her kindness, or at least her good advice, could be delivered with a sharp edge.

Cynthia McFadden arrived at one of Barbara's famous dinner parties straight from the airport; she had changed clothes on the plane. "Darling, hello, how are you?" Barbara greeted her ABC colleague. "I'm exhausted," McFadden replied and began to complain. Barbara abruptly stopped her. "No one is interested," she snapped. "You must never do this again, ever."

McFadden was taken aback, but later she decided Barbara was right. "No one is interested" that you're tired, she told me. "If you're going to come, come! Put on your game face and do it."

The first time Deborah Roberts had a story on *20/20*, she brought a stack of notes on set, where she would introduce it and then chitchat with Barbara and Hugh Downs about it afterward. "During the piece, Barbara looked at me and she grabbed my notes and she tossed them on the floor," Deborah told me. "I almost had a heart attack. I was like, what is she doing? Why is she so rude? Is this hazing? And Barbara looked at me and said, 'You don't need those. You know your story. Talk to me.'"

THE BARBARA WALTERS INTERVIEW

Barbara Walters didn't invent the TV newsmaker interview, the most intimate of portraits on the biggest of platforms. Edward R. Murrow pioneered them, hosting *Person to Person* on CBS in the 1950s with an eclectic mix of guests from Washington and Hollywood who sat in their living rooms and chatted with him at a studio in New York. But it was Barbara who nurtured, expanded, perfected, promoted, and finally defined the form, the conversation-on-camera with headliners who were trying to make a splash, stage a comeback, promote a movie, or, occasionally, influence a jury.

Everyone understood what "the Barbara Walters interview" meant and the cachet it carried, even her rivals. "Nobody calls it the 'Peter Jennings interview,'" admitted Peter Jennings, the ABC anchor who occasionally viewed Barbara and her work with a certain disdain. When one of her interviews was over, "I always had the sense that she squeezed the sponge dry," said Chris Wallace, who admired her as "a star and an icon, a legend" when he was a rising journalist at ABC before working at Fox News and CNN. "One could argue about the order of the questions or the framing of the questions, but I always felt that when she was doing one of those big newsmaker or celebrity interviews, she got everything out of them."

Years later, that would seem like a relic from another era. The advent of social media and online streaming meant politicians like Donald Trump and entertainers like Taylor Swift no longer needed an interlocutor to connect with the audiences they wanted to reach. But in her day, Barbara persuaded the powerful, the celebrated, and the notorious to sit down with her. Then she commanded huge ratings as she subjected them to her distinctive inquisition.

If Mike Wallace at CBS (the father of Chris Wallace) was the generation's interviewer-as-bad-cop, aggressive and confrontational, Barbara was the interviewer-as-Jewish-mother, sympathetic but probing enough to make you talk about the places where it hurt. "Almost single-handedly, Barbara Walters turned TV interviewing into the weepily empathetic kudzu that has swamped broadcast journalism," *Vanity Fair* wrote in 2001, the sort of backhanded compliment often aimed her way. "Weepily empathetic kudzu" doesn't sound like praise. On the other hand, she did succeed in reshaping some of the broadcast industry's fundamentals in her image.

At her best, she revealed the core of those she profiled, exposing aspects of them that hadn't been fully seen or understood before. She cared more about people than policy, more about the feelings and motivations of the powerful than their ten-point plans. "She is a reporter, and she reports what you are like," said Richard Wald, a broadcast executive who worked with her at NBC and at ABC. Her subjects understood that, he told me. "Nobody ever complained to me in the two networks we worked together in that she drew a false picture of them."

How did she do it?

This is how.

I. THE "GET"

First, land the guest.

To the dismay of some in the business, Barbara raised the art of the "get" to a contact sport. She was unencumbered by the rules, including those a string of bosses tried to impose. "Barbara didn't deal with management or channels," said Robin Sproul, the longtime Washington bureau chief for ABC, who would find herself surprised to learn Barbara was about to sit down with this president or that first lady. "There was no confronting Barbara on anything. She was going to do what she did."

Barbara wrote letters on her personalized stationery, circulated at cocktail parties, hosted intimate lunches and dinners, and cultivated the parents and friends and lawyers of those she wanted to interview. She was interested not only in political leaders but also in actors and authors and those caught up accidentally in the headlines, as criminals or victims. The combinations could be dizzying. "The Shah blurs into Anwar el-Sadat and then turns into Mr. T," a *New York Times* critic teased.

She also played the long game. If someone wouldn't talk to her now, maybe they would later. Her campaign to interview Mark David Chapman, the man who killed John Lennon, took twelve years.

After Chapman pleaded guilty to murder and was sentenced to prison, she wrote to him each year in advance of the anniversary of the day, on December 8, 1980, when he stood outside The Dakota, Lennon's apartment building on the Upper West Side, and shot the iconic musician in the back. He had never explained why he did it. Finally, in 1992, he agreed to talk with her. She met with him in a small room at Attica Correctional Facility in upstate New York for his first television interview.

The *20/20* program caused a furor, enraging some who accused her of exploiting a tragedy and others who said it was unconscionable to give a killer such a platform. But Chapman's bizarre reverie to her was unquestionably newsworthy. Among other things, their exchange raised questions about whether the judge in the case should have allowed him to withdraw his lawyer's insanity defense.

Barbara was indefatigable in her pursuit of a big interview.

She was in Jerusalem in March 1979 as President Jimmy Carter was negotiating the final sticking points of the Camp David accords. She had already scheduled an interview with Israeli prime minister Menachem Begin. That done, she flew to Cairo through Cyprus in hopes of getting Egyptian president Anwar Sadat on the fly, but it was almost 11 p.m. when she finally arrived, unannounced, at his residence on the Giza, overlooking the Nile.

When the security guard on duty declined to convey a message that she was there, Barbara wasn't deterred. She threw pebbles at Sadat's window, trying to raise his attention. "Why we weren't arrested I can't imagine," she said later. When another guard finally agreed to take in a note from her, Sadat sent back word that she couldn't interview him then but that he would sit down with her when he went to Washington soon to sign the final peace treaty—a trip that was news in itself. She immediately stood outside his house and recorded a stand-up reporting it.

Six months later, she was in Cuba to cover the Sixth Summit of the Non-Aligned Movement, a gathering of ninety-three countries that had proclaimed their interest in keeping distance from both the United States and the Soviet Union. Barbara became increasingly impatient with the lack of action; she began to fret that she was wasting her time in Havana. Then she looked around the huge convention center.

"We were seated in essentially the mezzanine, and down below in the orchestra was the King of Jordan," said Ellen Rossen Westin, a producer from *World News Tonight* who was with her. Barbara pulled her stationery from her bag and, in recognition of her generally indecipherable handwriting, dictated a letter to Ellen. Barbara had interviewed King Hussein and the American-born Queen Noor a year earlier at their palace in Jordan.

"Dear Your Majesty," Barbara began. "I'm seated in the balcony and I have on a red scarf, and I'd like to talk to you. Wave if you can see me." A few minutes passed as a summit staffer was given the letter to deliver. "Up pops the King of Jordan and suddenly he's waving to Barbara in the balcony," Ellen told me. "And of course she got the interview."

And, of course, she got on the air.

2. THE CARDS

Then, prepare the questions.

She called it her homework. "I do so much homework, I know more about the person than he or she does about himself," she said, describing the research amassed by her staff. "Then, I write—I can write fifty or a hundred questions, on little three-by-five cards. I put them in order. Then I throw some away. Then I put others in. I can spend hours, days changing the order of questions. But here's the important thing: You've got to know your questions, so you can throw them all away, if you have to." That is, if the interview took a surprising turn.

She would sit down in her office with her assistant and the producers to brainstorm. She would cast a wider net, too. "Before she'd do an interview, I don't care if it was Henry Kissinger or Joe, the elevator operator, she would call everybody in New York City" to get ideas for questions, Av Westin, an executive producer at ABC, told me. What were Kissinger's ideas? What did Joe want to know?

The wording would be revised until the cards were virtually unreadable; her longtime assistant Monica Caulfield would type a clean copy with the latest version to resume the process. Barbara would throw discards on the floor, though staffers would gather those cards for a reject file, just in case. The final versions would be typed on larger, five-by-eight-inch index cards. Before her second interview with Fidel Castro, she had more than two hundred cards in her deck, recalled ABC News president David Westin. "On the plane, we just kept going over it," he told me. "In the hotel, we kept going over it, winnowing them down. Which ones are we going to ask? Can we combine these two questions?"

Her approach was different from some other top broadcast interviewers. Radio and TV host Larry King bragged that he didn't prepare before interviews, that he didn't want to have read the author's book or to delve into the details of their story before his listeners did. "I never write down a question, ever," Ted Koppel, the longtime anchor of ABC's *Nightline*, told me. "To me, an interview is a conversation, and a conversation gains momentum based on the answers." Otherwise, the risk is that an interviewer will be focused not on the answer being given but on the next questions they had prepared.

"It clearly works for some people," he acknowledged. "It works for Barbara."

For the broadcast, she wanted every interview to have a strong beginning, a tantalizing bit to use in promotion, and a memorable end. "A hooker, a teaser and a conclusion," as she put it. Rick Klein, an ABC political director who helped her prepare for some interviews late in her career, likened her to the best point guards in professional basketball, the ones who seemed to have eyes in the back of their head and an ability to see the whole court. "She knew this question is going to be part of Act One; this question is going to be part of Act Two," he told me. "She was moving these things around in her head, looking to upgrade, looking to make sure that they all fit."

When the interview ended, she already had a sense of what she wanted the final edit to be—the result of her early training behind the scenes on the mechanics of television. "It was like *bang, bang, bang* through the whole thing," said Rob Wallace, one of her senior producers. She would mark what to cut and what to feature with a clarity she lacked in her personal affairs. "She once joked to me . . . that this is what she knows how to do better than anything," he recalled. She told him, "'Not life, not how to handle life. I don't know how to do that. This I know how to do.'"

In 2009, she was getting ready to interview Sarah Palin, the former Alaska governor who had been John McCain's running mate on the Republican ticket in 2008 and was now promoting her book about the experience. "She had a question in there that was, just, 'Are you going to run for president?'" Klein said. "I was, like, look, she's already said she's not. You know how she's going to answer."

"That's for the promo," she replied—that is, for a clip released beforehand that would show Barbara asking the question but not Palin answering it. It would be a teaser. Indeed it was. "Here's the big question," Barbara was shown asking in an ad that teased the segment. "Do you ever want to be president of the United States?"

Only later, on the show, was Palin's response shown. "That certainly isn't on my radar screen right now," she said, though she added that she couldn't predict what might happen down the road. Palin's answer wasn't particularly newsworthy, but Barbara had succeeded in creating an expectant moment that just might draw in viewers.

Michael J. Satin, a white-collar defense lawyer in Washington, once dissected Barbara's interview with Monica Lewinsky in the *American Bar Association Journal* as a case study in effective questioning, with lessons for attorneys in the courtroom. "It is this interview that lawyers should watch to learn how to conduct an effective direct examination," he wrote. "[I]t is how Ms. Walters plans, structures, and executes the interview that merits attention."

Barbara managed to be both empathetic and skeptical, he wrote—just like many of those who would be watching. When Monica said testifying before the grand jury about intimate details of her relationship with Clinton was "very, very violating," Barbara shot back, "There is the question of why you offered so many intimate details to the prosecutor. I mean, why, for example, tell them about the cigar business?" Monica replied that the grand jury already knew that salacious anecdote from prior testimony by her friends, an explanation that enhanced her credibility. Their exchanges had "the appearance of a private conversation between two people," Satin wrote, while the audience "is like a fly on the wall, observing the interaction."

There was a less scholarly description of her technique that Barbara liked. Early on, *Newsweek* described her questions as "dumdum bullets swaddled in angora." That is, seemingly cozy questions that hit their mark, then expanded on impact.

3. THE BIG QUESTION

Ask the question everyone wants answered.

"Why did you kill John Lennon?" she asked Mark David Chapman at the start.

"John Lennon fell into a very deep hole, a hole so deep inside of me that I thought by killing him I would acquire his fame," he replied. He recalled "turning to Satan for the strength" to pull the trigger; once he had, the "movie stopped."

"And with Satan, you exorcized Satan yourself?" she followed up, as matter-of-factly as if she was asking him to spell his middle name. It was not a question typed on one of her cards. "Tell me about that."

Sitting face-to-face with someone and posing a question that has the potential to embarrass or enrage is harder than it looks. Barbara would agonize beforehand over the wording—typically making the question shorter and simpler and thus harder to dodge—and over its placement in the interview. She often asked it at the end, as the climax of the conversation, and sometimes at the start, as the ignition.

Her manner may have been soft—swaddled in angora, say—but she rarely shied from going where no one else would dare.

Barbara asked former first lady Mamie Eisenhower, in a roundabout way, about rumors that she drank too much. (The problem, Mamie replied, was that inner ear problems meant she "couldn't walk a straight line and everybody thought I was inebriated.") She posed the same question, more directly, to Russian president Boris Yeltsin; he denied the reports, too. She asked Chinese leader Jiang Zemin what had happened to the Tiananmen Square demonstrator known as "tank man." "I think never killed," he replied, though he didn't deny the young protester, an icon of bravery and defiance, had been arrested.

When she interviewed ex-president Richard Nixon in 1980, she sparked headlines with the question she had saved for the end: Did he regret not burning the White House tapes that had sealed his fate, his resignation? Yes, he responded. "They were private conversations, subject to misinterpretation, as we have seen." She asked Robin Givens if she was physically afraid of her husband, heavyweight champion Mike Tyson; she said was "very, very much afraid." She asked actress Katharine Hepburn why her head visibly shook. The actress denied it was Parkinson's disease, as many had assumed. She said it was instead a trait she inherited from her paternal grandfather, treatable by drinking enough whiskey.

In late 2001, Barbara sat down in the Kremlin with Vladimir Putin for his first interview with an American journalist since the September 11 terror attacks on the United States. The big question she wanted to ask the former KGB agent was so sensitive that she didn't write it down for fear his spies might somehow manage to see her cards beforehand.

She waited until the end of the allotted time in case he took such offense that he walked out.

"Did you ever order anyone killed?" she asked him, through a translator.

"Nyet," he replied, his face impassive, betraying neither offense nor any other emotion.

4. THE TEARS

Make them cry.

That was not her goal, she insisted, especially after it happened so often it became a cliché. There would be a moment in many of her interviews when tears would well in the eyes of the person she was interviewing, sometimes streaming down the cheeks. Some guests declared at the start she was not going to make them cry. That provided no guarantee that they wouldn't eventually succumb.

The fact was that whatever prompted them to be newsworthy enough to be interviewed meant it was probably an emotional time. "She interviewed everyone at that moment, whatever that moment was for them, whether it was a success or a failure or a screwup," said Betsy Shuller, who worked for Barbara's production company, Barwall, which produced the Barbara Walters specials for ABC. "She had everyone at that moment." They had agreed to an interview aware of "the intensity of talking to her." They knew she would be asking personal questions.

What would most often prompt people to cry?

"I would ask questions about their childhood, relationship with their parents," Barbara said. "I'd very often ask people about their father and get a more emotional answer than I do if I ask about mothers." She could have been talking about herself; memories of her father struck the strongest emotional chord in her.

Patrick Swayze cried in a 1988 interview when he said he hoped he would have made his late father proud. "He thought crying was weak—Texas mentality," the actor said as he brushed tears from his cheeks. Norman Schwarzkopf Jr., the commander of forces in the First Gulf War, began to cry when talking about his father. Generals weep, too, he said. "Frankly, any man that doesn't cry scares me a little bit," he said. Goldie Hawn's eyes filled with tears when she recalled advice from her father. "My dad used to say, 'You start feeling too big for your britches, Goldie, just go stand out there and look at that ocean, and you won't feel so big.'"

The personal question and the watery response became such a trope that it was used, to her surprise and delight, in an "interview" with the Teenage Mutant Ninja Turtles in 1991. The actors portraying the comic superheroes, clad in green plastic heads and bodysuits, were promoting the series' second movie, *The Secret of the Ooze*, a commercial success though not a critical one. In their backstory, the Turtles had been taken in and reared by Master Splinter, a mutant rat who taught them martial arts.

"Do you know who your parents were?" she asked Donatello, purportedly the smartest of the turtles, named after the Italian sculptor and identifiable by his purple bandanna. She hadn't been warned beforehand about what would happen next. He gasped, apparently overcome by emotion. Then a cascade of water began to spurt from his eyes, soaking her skirt and the set.

When she retired in 2014, she joked about her propensity to draw tears.

She joined a send-off on NBC's *Saturday Night Live*, which through the years had parodied her voice, her name-dropping, her sappiest questions. On the "Weekend Update" segment, she offered faux anchor Cecily Strong some tips on interviewing celebrities. "It is fine to make people smile, but the real money is in making them cry!" she advised. "Nothing brings in the viewers like seeing a celebrity reduced to tears. You may think, 'Aww, I'm feeling really bad for them,' but all I'm thinking is, 'Ka-ching!'"

5. THE MISSTEPS

Like every human enterprise, it didn't always work.

For one thing, she could be too cozy with her subjects, and she occasionally pulled her punches. In 1976, First Lady Betty Ford seemed inebriated during a tour of the White House and a joint interview with her husband; Barbara deliberately didn't air the audio that showed her slurring her words—journalistically, not a defensible decision. "If she had a drinking problem, I wasn't going to be the one to expose her," she said later, although of course that sort of revelation was the basis for her reputation and the underpinnings of journalism. Eventually Barbara conceded she had made a mistake. "If I were interviewing a first lady today, and she was obviously inebriated, I would certainly air it," she said.

Sometimes the people she was interviewing refused to engage, despite her best efforts and the most carefully prepared questions. Warren Beatty was her least favorite interview; his responses were close to monosyllabic. She cited Al Gore, too; he resisted any efforts to talk about the disputed presidential election he had won-but-lost, the reason she was interested in interviewing him. Others who seemed tantalizing in advance turned out not to have much to say. "It gets harder and harder to interview the twenty-one-year-old star whose most meaningful experience was winning a surfing contest," she said.

Then there was the tree question.

In fairness, it wasn't one she had planned to ask, written on her cards. It was a follow-up to a comment Katharine Hepburn made. Asked how she had become a legend, the actress said, "I'm like a tree." Barbara followed up with a question she came to regret: "What kind of tree are you?" The answer would be forgotten (an oak, Hepburn said) but the question would be forever remembered, and ridiculed.

Barbara had only herself to blame for another comment that became ammunition for hecklers. A month after the 1976 election, she went to Plains, Georgia, to interview President-elect Jimmy Carter and Rosalynn Carter in their hometown. During the interview, she asked, "Do you sleep in a double bed or twin beds?" an odd query that might have attracted more commentary if she hadn't closed the interview with an earnest, out-of-nowhere plea that prompted even more derision. (For the record, Carter said a double bed.)

"Be wise with us, Governor," she intoned solemnly. "Be good to us."

"I'll try," he responded.

The criticism from her journalistic colleagues was brutal. "It is as if Mr. Carter had just become Louis XIV and, without Pope Barbara's admonition, he might be dumb with us and mean to us," Morley Safer of CBS raged in his radio commentary. Later, she admitted it had been an inexplicable lapse of judgment. "How dare I say something so corny, so personal, and, of course, so female?" she said.

Sometimes the misstep wasn't that her questions were too soft but that they were too intrusive, especially when she was interviewing young people. Under the standards of a later era, some would have created more furor than they did at the time.

When she was fifteen years old, actress Brooke Shields starred in a Calvin Klein TV commercial with a sultry slogan: "You want to know what comes between me and my Calvins? Nothing." Years later, as an adult, she said she had been so naive at the time that she hadn't understood the erotic innuendo behind the ad. But in her interview Barbara underscored the sexual tease with questions surely inappropriate to ask a teenage girl. "Brooke, what are your measurements?" she said. Looking perplexed, Brooke replied, "Um, I'm five-ten and 120." Then Barbara urged her to stand up and stood up next to her, comparing their heights and pivoting as if to compare their figures.

"And I thought, 'This isn't right. I don't understand what this is,'" Brooke said years later. "But I just behaved and just smiled and felt, like, so taken advantage of in so many ways." She called the exchange "practically criminal" and added, "It's not journalism."

When Barbara interviewed pop star Ricky Martin in 2000, his sexual orientation was the subject of speculation, although he wouldn't come out of the closet for another decade. "You could stop these rumors," she said. "You could say, 'Yes, I am gay or no, I'm not.'" Martin looked stunned. "I just don't feel like it," he finally replied. Two decades later, the memory of that moment still made him uncomfortable. "When she dropped the question, I felt violated because I was just not ready to come out," he said. "There's a little PTSD with that."

His refusal to answer the question prompted some to assume he was gay, and it hurt his career, Barbara said later. "When I think back on it now I feel it was an inappropriate question." What she didn't say: It was, however, the big question viewers wanted to hear.

BETTE DAVIS AND THE DALAI LAMA

In Barbara's memoir, the endpapers front and back are covered with hundreds of names in small italic type, one after another, divided by dots and in alphabetical order. They are some of the people she interviewed over the decades, from A (King Abdullah of Jordan, King Abdullah of Saudi Arabia) to Z (Renée Zellweger, Catherine Zeta-Jones). Most of them didn't rate a mention in the 612 pages of text in the book. Still, they were notable not only for their individual prominence but also for their collective number. In her prime, it might have been easier to list the headliners she hadn't interviewed than those she had.

For Barbara, interviews were where she shone, spotlighting her ability to put the newsworthy at ease and get them to dish, and sometimes to cry. They became her signature soon after she was hired for her first on-air job with NBC's *Today* show in 1964. She did interviews as *Today's* co-host, then as co-anchor of ABC's evening news and later of *20/20*; as host of the Barbara Walters specials on ABC and eventually of her Oscar night specials each spring and the *10 Most Fascinating People* franchise each December.

She became more prominent than many of those she was interviewing.

"First, may I say that is it both an honor and a privilege for you to be interviewed by me," Cheri Oteri, portraying Barbara, said to the real

Barbara in a comic bit aired on her last regular appearance on *The View*. Cheri was one of a string of comedians who depicted Barbara on NBC's *Saturday Night Live*. The faux Barbara reminisced about purported good times from her past, among them at the Black Sea in 1981. "I was at a Russian hotel with Mikhail Gorbachev, R.J. Wagner, Smokin' Joe Frazier, Dom DeLuise, and an already liquored-up teenager by the name of Vlad Putin," Cheri-as-Barbara mused.

That recollection was a joke, but it did reflect the eclectic range of those who interested Barbara. She had a broad view of who, exactly, could be worth talking to—not only presidents but also movie stars and singers, not to mention people who had gained notoriety through corruption or crime. "She was a populist," Jeff Zucker, a former president of CNN Worldwide and NBC Universal, told me. She was willing to pursue interviews that those he described as "journalists with a capital J" thought beneath them.

"During my twenty-five years at *20/20* I interviewed almost every important murderer, alleged or convicted," she said. Peter Jennings, say, might not have seen that as an achievement. She saw it as a brag.

The range of her interests was reflected in the chapter titles of her memoir: "Finally, Fidel." "The Historic Interview: Anwar Sadat and Menachem Begin." "Presidents and First Ladies: Forty Years Inside the White House." "Heads of State: The Good, the Bad, and the Mad." "Murderers." "Uncommon Criminals." "Monica."

Then there was the category she labeled "Celebrities Who Affected My Life."

———

The seven interviews she cited as changing her life weren't her most notable, the ones that generated the biggest headlines or drew the highest ratings. In this group, she listed three actresses, Bette Davis, Katharine Hepburn, and Audrey Hepburn. Two families that dealt valiantly with disabilities—Robert and Michelle Smithdas, a blind and deaf couple, and actor Christopher Reeve, paralyzed in a horseback-riding accident. Comedian Richard Pryor, brilliant and addicted, who attempted suicide by setting himself on fire. And the Dalai Lama.

Barbara offered little explanation of why she chose these seven people out of the thousands she had interviewed, of what exactly linked Bette Davis and the Dalai Lama. "I don't think Barbara . . . was deeply introspective," one of her closest friends demurred when I speculated about the message she was sending with these choices. Of her many interviews, "few stick to my bones, as it were," Barbara said in passing. "There were some, however, which because of my own inner needs, have stayed with me, affected my life, and perhaps even changed me."

That's the thread: They were people who were working through the roadblocks that Barbara herself struggled with, even though she was generally loath to admit that. Balancing a career with marriage and children. Dealing with disabilities in a family, as she did with her sister. Substance abuse, a challenge her daughter faced. Assessing the rewards and costs of a life that had given her fame and fortune but not peace.

In these interviews, she often seemed to be trying to sort out those issues. The questions she posed resonated not only with many viewers but also in her own life, though she typically didn't acknowledge that personal dimension on the air. If she was looking for guidance, she got conflicting advice. Katharine Hepburn declared it "impossible" to balance work and family; she had no children and no regrets. "If I were a man, I would not marry a woman with a career and I'd torture myself as a mother," she said. In contrast, Audrey Hepburn gave up her successful movie career to raise her two sons, though she called the tradeoffs agonizing. "I was miserable both ways," she said.

When she interviewed Bette Davis in 1987, Barbara was fifty-seven years old and in her third marriage, which would end in another divorce. Her daughter was living at a school in Idaho for troubled teens, where she had been taken after abusing drugs and running away from home.

Bette, at seventy-eight, was a generation older than Barbara. She was promoting her autobiography, *This 'N That*, written in part as a response to a scathing memoir by her older daughter. In *My Mother's Keeper*, published two years earlier, B. D. Hyman had portrayed her mother as a bully and an alcoholic. The actress had also survived a mastectomy and a stroke that left her smile askew and her iconic raspy voice labored, but she was still feisty and unapologetic.

"Did you get mellow, mellower, as you got older?" Barbara asked her.

"I'm afraid that would be a good change, but I don't think it's happened," Bette replied, waving her cigarette in the air. She dismissed her four ex-husbands as unworthy of comment. "One day we wake up and we see very clearly and we wonder what in hell we saw in that person," she said, saying she had been "tricked" by the appeal of sex. In the most emotional part of the interview, Barbara asked her about her daughter. Their relationship had been "shattered" by her book, Bette said. She denied any fault in their estrangement.

"Were you a good mother?" Barbara asked. She might as well have been interviewing herself.

"Yes, I think I was," Bette replied. "I think basically I love my children very, very much. My impression as a mother, yes, I think I was a good mother." But her response was halting, as though she wasn't quite sure, and she acknowledged that she had refused to speak with her daughter for three years. When Barbara asked her what "sustained" her, Bette, who would die two years later, mentioned neither family nor friends nor faith.

"Really and truly what sustains me is work," she said. "I think the work is it. And when you sort of realize that as you get older, you've made a big discovery." Part of your legacy, she said, is to display enough distinctive characteristics to be impersonated. In her interview, Bette then offered a rendition of "What a dump," the scornful line often used to caricature her. The 1949 movie in which she had delivered it, *Beyond the Forest*, was forgettable, but years later those three words had become forever identified with her in the opening scene of Edward Albee's *Who's Afraid of Virginia Woolf?*

Barbara remarked that she had been hurt by being caricatured. She had been stung by those who mocked her difficulty in pronouncing "r's"; the *Saturday Night Live* moniker of "Baba Wawa" had stuck.

"You must be pleased," Bette Davis insisted, more animated than she was at any other time during the interview. "It's very, very important for longevity. And on your way to becoming a legend, I think the caricatures are a great big help, a big help."

On your way to becoming a legend.

The life lessons from the Dalai Lama were, unsurprisingly, different from those offered by Bette Davis.

Barbara interviewed the spiritual leader of Tibetan Buddhism in Dharamshala, his mountain sanctuary in India, for a 2005 special titled *Heaven: Where Is It? And How Do We Get There?* The Dalai Lama, wearing his burgundy robes and sitting face-to-face with her, explained the Buddhist theory of reincarnation. "I'm certainly not a Buddhist, but part of me believes that someone like my sister, Jackie, or others who had very difficult lives, could come back to something better," she said years later. "On some spiritual level that reaches me."

He told her that the purpose of life was "to be happy." How does one accomplish happiness? "I say warmheartedness," he replied. "Compassion gives you inner strength, more self-confidence. That can really change your attitude." As she was leaving, she had a request she rarely made with those she interviewed. "Is it possible to kiss you on the cheek?" she asked. He laughed and agreed, then showed her how the indigenous Maori kiss in New Zealand, lightly rubbing the tips of their noses together.

Barbara took his advice about the importance of warmheartedness and compassion to heart. For a while.

"It was a few days later; we were heading home," Rob Wallace, the senior producer working on the special, told me. "She said, 'I felt very, very different. I felt very, very happy.'" She didn't feel anger or jealousy or ambition. But she also felt, well, boring.

"Little by little the old emotions seeped back in," she said. The characteristics more likely to be extolled by Bette Davis.

THE VIEW

1996

Barbara Walters and Bill Geddie were at the River Café, the Brooklyn Bridge in the background, to shoot footage for one of her TV specials. They chatted as the crew set up lights. "We should do a daytime show," her executive producer said to her, and not for the first time. He was a fan of daytime talk shows in general and of host Regis Philbin in particular; he had always wanted to produce one himself. She had an idea about a fresh approach. "My conversations with my daughter are so interesting," she said. "We come at life from a completely different angle." What about a show that featured a panel of women from different generations?

That seemed to be that.

The next year, in 1997, Patricia Fili-Krushel, the president of ABC Daytime, called Geddie to say she was in search of a show to air at 11 a.m. Eastern Time, a time slot where a series of efforts had flopped. *The Home Show* had been canceled in 1994; *Mike and Maty* had been canceled in 1996. Now *Caryl & Marilyn: Real Friends* was going into reruns in June until something could be found to replace it. David Westin, then president of the ABC Network, had given her an ultimatum. (Westin later became president of ABC News, succeeding Roone Arledge.) "We had failed in that daytime, that time period again and again and again," Westin told me. "I said, 'Pat, this is the deal: You got deadlines. I think you got six months to come up with something, or I'm going to give it to News." That is, ABC News would take over the 11 a.m. hour to air a show of its own.

She called Geddie. "You're always talking about doing a daytime show," she told him. This was his chance.

Geddie and Barbara wrote a pitch for a show that he dubbed *Everybody's a Critic*. She would cite two inspirations for it. One was *Girl Talk with Virginia Graham*, a daytime talk show that featured celebrity guests. Barbara had occasionally appeared on it during her early years at the *Today* show. But the syndicated show had been canceled in 1969, nearly three decades earlier. The other was the political roundtable on ABC's Sunday morning program, *This Week with David Brinkley*, which she regularly joined. What the two shows shared was candid conversation, the sort of lively exchanges among opinionated people that you might overhear at a dinner party or a bar.

Fili-Krushel had reservations. Barbara wanted to engage on serious topics. Fili-Krushel wanted to keep it light. The show's featured headlines should be ripped from the tabloid New York *Daily News*, she said. "*The New York Times*," Barbara countered. "I want to talk about Syria." But she was persuaded otherwise after watching focus groups of daytime TV viewers. The experiences of her impresario father, his roots in vaudeville and nightclubs, had ingrained in her the imperative of keeping the audience in mind. "I got it," she said. "*USA Today* and the *Daily News*. This is our audience." Less Syria; more celebrities.

One problem: Roone Arledge was against the whole idea.

The idea for the new show was "frivolous," he told her, one of those dismissive adjectives often deployed against women. He warned it would undermine her hard-won reputation as a serious journalist. "Roone felt it was potentially dangerous, and it would be canceled within a year or so, and it would be very bad for her reputation," Geddie said. "Completely unworkable," Roone said.

But Fili-Krushel didn't work for Roone. She called Westin, their mutual boss, with the proposal for *Everybody's a Critic*. "And I said, 'You know what? That's a great idea. Why don't we do that?'" Westin told me. "But Barbara was under contract to ABC News. And I went to Roone and he said, 'No way. I'm not doing that because once she does that, she'll be distracted. She won't be paying attention to *20/20* and things like that.'"

It was the only time Westin could recall flatly overruling Roone. The two were close; they worked together for years in various roles. At the crucial meeting, they talked on a conference call. "I said, 'I'm making the decision. This is too good an idea. We've got to make this. We're doing it,'" Westin said. "He was furious, furious. I said, 'I'm sorry; it's just too good an idea.'"

ABC rented a suite at the Essex House hotel on Central Park South, near the network's headquarters. Crew members set up a makeshift TV control room in the bedroom and arranged the furniture in the living room in front of a curtained window. In an adjoining suite, models and motivational speakers and TV personalities and would-be TV personalities waited for a chance to try out for a new daytime talk show that no one was sure would succeed.

Cameras began to roll for the first audition—three prospects and Barbara, arrayed on a couch and some chairs. Talking.

"We've all seen it: '39 Dead in Cult Suicide,'" said Meredith Vieira. The veteran journalist had arrived that morning a bit wary of this prospective enterprise. She held up a copy of the *New York Post* from a few days earlier with the headline in screaming type. Thirty-nine people had been found dead at an estate in a San Diego suburb, members of a group that believed the Hale-Bopp comet then streaking across the sky was their ticket to heaven. "Heaven's Gate," they called themselves.

"These young people are obviously searching for something," said Star Jones, a former prosecutor in Brooklyn who was trying to get a toehold on TV as a legal affairs commentator.

Debbie Matenopoulos, a senior at New York University whose TV experience consisted of a part-time job as a production assistant at MTV, chimed in. "This UFO thing doesn't strike me as odd," she said breezily.

When Barbara called the mass suicide a senseless tragedy, Meredith challenged her, albeit teasingly. How do you know? she asked. You haven't been to heaven.

For the audition's second take, Meredith, Star, and Debbie stayed in their seats. Joy Behar, a stand-up comedian who had hosted a cable TV variety show, was summoned to take the place of Barbara. Barbara went into the bedroom to observe on the TV monitor with Geddie.

The conversation that followed among the group on the audition tape was engaged and engaging. "Barbara and I looked at each other and we thought, 'We are geniuses! Look what a great show it's going to be!'" Geddie told me. They began to try different combinations, swapping in the women waiting in the next room. "It never worked again, the entire day of these people coming through," he said. "It was tedious. Nobody had anything to say."

They ended up with the cast they had started with.

There was still a tentative tone to the handwritten letter Barbara sent Mary Alice Williams, telling her she didn't make the cut. "This is a very difficult note for me to write, for you know I think you are absolutely terrific," she wrote to Mary Alice, who had been an anchor on programs at CNN and NBC. Barbara had urged her to try out. "It came down to a choice between you and Meredith, and since Meredith is already an ABC employee, the weight was on her side. Who knows? Things can possibly change."

At the beginning, though, the lineup would be the even-keeled Meredith, a working mother in her forties, as moderator. On the panel would be the outspoken Star and the quirky Debbie, a member of Gen X. When Barbara couldn't be the fourth member on the set because of her other obligations, Joy would step in; she soon became a standing member of the panel, too. "The ladies," Barbara would call them, viewing them as her TV daughters, although not all of them would last as members of the family.

"I wasn't sure if it would be a success," Joy told me. She had other projects in the works, including a sitcom; she had already recorded the pilot for that. "But I wanted to live in New York; I didn't want to be in L.A. at all. And I also felt that it would be a smart show because of Barbara." Her agent advised against taking the gig, arguing it didn't pay enough. "And I said, 'Well, it's in New York, and it really uses my abilities to talk off the top of my head. And it's Barbara Walters.' And so that's why I took the job." A quarter-century later, she would be the only original panelist still sitting at the table.

Debbie would be let go two years later; what were generally derided as her goofy comments had made her a regular target on *Saturday Night Live*. "We hired her because she wasn't intimidated by the rest of them, and she should have been," producer Jessica Stedman Guff told me. Star would be pushed out in 2006 amid a flurry of recriminations. Meredith would leave that year, too, to become co-host of *Today*, the job Barbara once held. Joy would outlast even the show's founders. There would be friction and fame, shouted arguments and tearful dramas. Eventually, even the august *New York Times* would call it "the most important political TV show in America" and put the co-hosts on the cover of its Sunday magazine.

It would be called *The View*.

———

Barbara didn't need the work when *The View* was launched, and yet she did.

She was already the best-known broadcaster on the air. That said, she was now sixty-seven years old. While older men might be seen as distinguished-looking, the working assumption of the day was that no woman would be allowed to age on the air. Geddie recalled a conversation he had when he joined Barbara's team in 1991, when she was sixty-one. "One of the male executives at ABC said, 'It's a great job, kid, but you're only going to have it for another year or two.' I said, 'Oh, why?' He says, 'Nobody wants to see a woman over sixty on television.'"

"She saw the writing on the wall," Joy told me. "She knew about ageism, sexism in the industry. She didn't want to retire like Walter Cronkite was forced to retire at sixty-five. She saw that, and she said, 'They're not going to put me out to pasture,' and she came up with this show. I mean, it was brilliant. It was a show to go into her nineties, if she wanted. And she almost did."

There would soon be some troubling signals for her at ABC News. In 1998, the network merged *20/20* and *Primetime* and made Diane Sawyer and Barbara co-hosts on a Sunday night edition of the expanded *20/20* franchise. Diane had lobbied for the change "as only Diane can lobby," Roone would recall; she thought it would ease the war between her and Barbara for big interviews. But Barbara opposed it. Despite the name change, the editions on other nights of the week, hosted separately by her and by Diane, continued to compete. Ratings fell. The Sunday program wouldn't last.

"We hadn't taken lemons and made lemonade," Barbara complained. "We'd taken lemonade and made lemons."

Two years later, Westin split them back into two separate shows, each with its original name. But the next year, in 2001, ABC moved *20/20* out of its traditional Friday nighttime slot to make way for a dramatic series, *Once and Again*, that would end up surviving just one more season. Media analysts interpreted the schedule change as a slight for Barbara; so did she. She was "amazed and disappointed," she told *The New York Times*, suggesting it might prompt her to reconsider her contract with the network.

She would retire from *20/20* in 2004, at age seventy-four. By then, *The View* was going strong. She would be a mainstay on it for another decade. "She loved to be on the air; she really did," Alexandra Cohen, the supervising producer of *The View* known to everyone as Dusty, told me. "It was really like oxygen for her. And the more it became water-cooler conversation, the more she loved it."

Over time, she became more willing to reveal herself on the show, even to make fun of herself. On this, Roone had been right. On *The View*, Barbara became less the journalist, more the personality. It was a chance to demonstrate that she wasn't only the relentless inquisitor. "I think there was a time when I was considered too serious and without a sense of humor because I was always in charge, especially asking very strong men questions," she said. "It was considered rude or pushy." But on *The View*, "I could be funny; I had women whom I could joke with, and I could show—good, bad, or indifferent—my personality."

For the Halloween show in 2003, she dressed as Marilyn Monroe, sporting a tousled blond wig, a strapless pink gown, a feathered boa, elbow-length satin gloves, and oversized faux diamond jewelry. She sang a breathy version of "Diamonds Are a Girl's Best Friend" in a performance that made some on the set cringe. A year later, *The View* was being shot in Las Vegas on a set outside Caesars Palace, designed to resemble the Roman Colosseum. She arrived atop a throne being carried by four muscular men scantily clad as gladiators.

"Move over, Cleopatra," Meredith declared to laughter.

Four years later, *The View* was back in Las Vegas. This time, Barbara climbed into illusionist Lance Burton's magic box and, to all appearances, was sawed in two—her blond hair visible at one end of his table and her apparently disembodied feet sticking out of the other.

Walter Cronkite never did that.

———

At the start, the executives at ABC Daytime weren't entirely confident this show would break the losing streak for its late-morning time slot.

"They wanted it to work, but they didn't expect it to work," Geddie said. Here's how he knew that: They decided against investing in a new set. Instead, the show was assigned to use the set that had been constructed for a soap opera called *The City* that lasted for a year and a half before being canceled in March. It depicted a loft apartment in SoHo with an enormous paned window that would have provided a magnificent view of New York City, if it hadn't been just a faux window on a TV set.

"It's got a view," Geddie thought when he saw it. With that, he had the perfect name for the new show; his initial proposal of "Everybody's a Critic" hadn't survived. It should be called "The View from Here," he proposed. But a trademark search found that a Canadian show had already copyrighted that name. So the American version would be shortened.

The show would have to win over its early doubters. After the turbulence in the time slot, some of ABC's biggest affiliate stations had chosen to air other shows then. Barbara began calling station managers in Boston, Philadelphia, Miami, Pittsburgh, Milwaukee, and Washington, D.C., to woo them back. She also persuaded some big-name actors to join the new show as guests despite its low initial ratings, a favor for its celebrity booker. The first week on the air, *The View* managed to score appearances by Tom Selleck, Sylvester Stallone, and Michael J. Fox.

Barbara developed a routine for the days she was on the show. Hairdresser Bryant Renfroe and makeup artist Lori Klein would arrive at her Fifth Avenue apartment in a chauffeured car provided by the network; she would dump her bags in the back seat and then lead her small entourage in a morning march across Central Park. When they emerged on the West Side, the car would be waiting there, and she would climb in to ride to the studio on West End Avenue. ("A few more steps to your right and you'd be in the river," she said.) The co-hosts would gather in the makeup room about 8:30 a.m. to choose a half-dozen issues for the "Hot Topics" segment that started the show.

"I was always saying, 'Make sparks,'" Geddie told me. He wanted to avoid subjects on which they all agreed, dismissing them as "ladies who lunch" conversations. He finally had a sign printed up—"MAKE SPARKS"—and hung it in the small holding room just off stage.

They made sparks, not always intentionally. *The View* was groundbreaking, the start of a wave. Barbara, who had defined the big TV interview a quarter-century earlier, was now at the forefront of the new age of reality TV. The show blurred the lines between news and opinion. It showed women—forceful women, loud women—in charge. It opened the door for candid conversations about marriages and miscarriages, about identity and sex. ("I sometimes said, 'Enough with the penises,'" Barbara recalled, describing herself as "the panel prude.")

This was not the chitchat among the well-mannered ladies on NBC's *Not for Women Only*, which she had moderated in the 1970s, or on the syndicated *Girl Talk with Virginia Graham* in the 1960s. These discussions were supposed to be revealing even if they were painful, perhaps especially if they were painful. It was a reality show and a news program and a soap opera. "A genius bit of television," *Vanity Fair* declared.

"We didn't create a new format," Barbara said. "We created a new atmosphere."

The View reflected the rising tide of feminism across the country. "The idea of women talking to one another on daytime television is not exactly radical," *The New York Times* wrote in its review when the show began. "The idea that those women should be smart and accomplished is still odd enough to make 'The View' seem wildly different. It actively defies the bubbleheads-'R'-us approach to women's talk shows."

In the years that followed, a string of talk shows would be launched in the image of *The View*, tinkering mostly with the precise gender makeup of the co-hosts. NBC premiered *Later Today* (with three female panelists) in 1999; it lasted a year. Dick Clark Productions started a syndicated show called *The Other Half* (with four male panelists) in 2001; it lasted two years. CBS debuted *The Talk* (with five female panelists) in 2010; each show began with a segment on a headline of the day called "Everybody Talks," its version of "Hot Topics." In 2014, Fox News launched *Outnumbered* (with four female co-hosts and one male), a conservative-leaning version of the genre. Tyra Banks's *FABLife* (with one male and four female panelists) debuted in 2015 for a single season.

None of them achieved the lifespan, the ratings, or the buzz of *The View*.

In time, the show had an effect not only on the broadcasting industry but on American politics. It became a floating focus group, part of the national conversation, and a destination for ambitious pols. The back-and-forth seemed more casual than, say, *Meet the Press*, but in fact it demanded more authenticity and tolerated fewer canned answers than traditional political shows. It gained credibility with women just as they were becoming an increasingly powerful force in elections.

In 2010, when Barack Obama became the first sitting president to appear on a daytime talk show, it was on *The View*. Joe Biden appeared on the show as vice president and as a presidential candidate. So did John McCain and Mitt Romney and Donald Trump.

But the biggest ratings she ever got—indeed, the biggest ratings any such show had ever gotten—weren't for an interview with a president but with someone else who worked at the White House. With an intern named Monica.

MONICA

1998

Barbara was in Seattle to interview software magnate Bill Gates for *20/20* when the ABC News assignment desk called with an astonishing alert: A special counsel appointed by the Justice Department was investigating whether President Bill Clinton had urged a former White House intern to lie under oath about their alleged sexual liaison.

Her name was Monica Lewinsky. Could Barbara get an interview with her?

Her sit-down that day with Gates was interesting enough. He criticized the Justice Department's efforts to rein in Microsoft, the company he had founded, and he broke his customary public reserve to demonstrate how he sang "Twinkle Twinkle Little Star" to his toddler daughter at bedtime. But it was Monica's emergence into the public spotlight that would lead to the most watched interview in the history of television news, before or since. "The biggest 'get' of my career," Barbara said afterward—the highest praise she could imagine.

She wouldn't be the only one trying. At ABC, Diane Sawyer and Connie Chung were also in the mix, along with Oprah Winfrey and Larry

King and the biggest names at every other network in the United States and many of them around the world. For more than a year, Barbara used every skill and strategy she had honed in decades in the business to land it. Her pursuit of Monica and the interview she then delivered would be the epitome of the era when the big TV interview could cause an earthquake. For better or worse, in the view of some journalists.

But it wouldn't be easy, and it wouldn't be fast. It would be a case study in how relentlessly and how shrewdly Barbara worked.

———

By the time the story broke, Barbara knew just about everyone in the community of boldfaced names and the lawyers who represented them. For decades, she had been accumulating their phone numbers and their trust. But that wasn't Monica's world, not yet. She would enter it later, well after FBI agents ambushed her at Pentagon City Mall in suburban Washington—where she thought she was meeting Linda Tripp, a co-worker she thought was a friend. Actually, Tripp had tipped off the FBI to Monica's affair with Clinton. After hours of questioning, the twenty-four-year-old was finally allowed to call her mother. Her parents were divorced; they called her father that night. Bernard Lewinsky, a doctor in Los Angeles, reached out to a trial lawyer he knew, though William Ginsburg's specialty was medical malpractice.

Ginsburg was a character who favored bow ties and publicity. "Her lawyer was on TV more than I was," Barbara marveled. He would be immortalized in media history for a feat that became known as "the full Ginsburg," appearing on all five Sunday TV interview shows on a single morning. (The shows, which prefer exclusive interviews, almost never had the same guest unless they were red-hot; Ginsburg was thermonuclear.) He was in such high demand that even Barbara and her unrivaled Rolodex were having trouble getting through to him.

Finally, her longtime producer, Katie Nelson Thomson, saw him appearing live on a show at NBC's Washington headquarters. One of Thomson's first jobs had been in that massive building, working for John McLaughlin, a Catholic-priest-turned-TV-host. She knew Ginsburg almost certainly would be leaving through the door that led to the circular front drive. She called the NBC switchboard and convinced an operator to connect her with the security guard stationed there. Then she sweet-talked the guard into stopping Ginsburg on his way out and handing him the phone. "I might have said, 'I have a really urgent call for William Ginsburg,'" she told me.

Ginsburg agreed to meet Barbara in Washington the following Saturday. He suggested the Cosmos Club, a private club just off Embassy Row.

Barbara Walters didn't know William Ginsburg, but of course William Ginsburg knew Barbara Walters. "A bit of a fan," she recalled. They had another connection: Ginsburg had attended Alexander Hamilton High School in Los Angeles with Joel Siegel, then ABC's film critic. Siegel told Ginsburg he could trust Barbara, and he took that assurance to heart. Even at their first meeting, speaking off the record, he told her the essential outlines of one of the biggest political scandals of the century, including some details that wouldn't be revealed publicly for months.

At the time, Clinton allies had begun portraying Monica as a stalker and a liar, an attention-seeker whose preposterous story couldn't possibly be believed. Some suggested she might be mentally ill. Hillary Clinton seemed to initially believe them, confiding in a friend that the young woman was a "narcissistic loony toon." But Ginsburg told Barbara that Monica and Bill Clinton had been intimate, though their relationship had "never been consummated"—that is, that they had never had intercourse. (He told her to draw her own conclusions about that.) Clinton had called her dozens of times on the phone late at night for long conversations, he said. The president had given her gifts, among them a special edition of Walt Whitman's *Leaves of Grass* and a pottery frog.

That odd detail—a pottery frog—would prove important in affirming the nature of their ties. Later, Barbara mentioned it to George Stephanopoulos, the ABC anchor who had once been one of Clinton's closest advisers. He told her that very few people knew the president had a "thing for frogs." The ceramic frog, the book of poetry, the late-night phone calls bespoke a personal relationship, not the imaginings of the mentally ill.

At the time, though, Monica's public image was being defined by a Clinton team that had years of experience in managing accusations by women of misbehavior. She was in legal peril as well. She had lied in an affidavit in early January, swearing that she hadn't had a sexual relationship with the president. Ginsburg was trying to negotiate a grant of immunity, which would have made it feasible for her to speak out, but that deal wouldn't be struck for months. Meanwhile, she was being followed everywhere by paparazzi and ridiculed about her weight. The tabloids dubbed her the "Tubby Temptress" and the "Portly Pepperpot."

Monica was staying with her father in Los Angeles when her mother was subpoenaed to testify before the independent counsel's grand jury in Washington on February 11. They watched on television with dismay as a phalanx of news cameras outside the courthouse showed Marcia Lewis emerging after four and a half hours of questioning. She was red-eyed and distraught; she looked close to collapse. It was time to tell their side, at least some of it, Bernard Lewinsky and Ginsburg agreed. Barbara was the one they chose to hear it.

Lewinsky didn't want the cameras and the commotion at his house, so ABC rented a suite at a nearby hotel. They kept it secret until it was done. It was the first big exclusive interview of the scandal.

"This must be every parent's nightmare," Barbara told Bernard when they met, although in fact it's unclear how many parents worry that their child might be swept into a sex scandal with a president. Still, Monica's father warmed to her, and during their twenty-minute interview he unleashed an attack on the special counsel, Ken Starr, who had originally been appointed to investigate alleged financial misdealings in Arkansas by the Clintons. "To pit a mother against a daughter, to coerce her to talk, to me it's reminiscent of the McCarthy era, or the Inquisition and even, you know, you could stretch to the Hitler era," he said.

After the interview aired on *20/20*, on February 20, Monica called her father afterward to congratulate him. The comparison to the Holocaust would draw criticism, but he had at least gotten everyone's attention, and portrayed his daughter not as a stalker but as the victim of an overzealous prosecutor.

———

The courtship of Ginsburg continued.

The mainstream networks prohibited their news shows from paying money for an interview, but there was no rule against currying favor. Ginsburg was offered tickets to the theater and meals at fancy restaurants. Diane Sawyer volunteered to introduce Bernard Lewinsky, an avid amateur photographer, to the famed Richard Avedon. Once, when Barbara called to chat, she discovered Ginsburg was having dinner with Mike Wallace of CBS's *60 Minutes*.

Katie Nelson Thomson came up with the idea for a prize she knew Ginsburg would relish: to be Barbara's escort at a black-tie gala in New York being thrown by *Time* to celebrate the magazine's seventy-fifth anniversary. The guest list had an almost ludicrous range, from former Federal Reserve chairman Paul Volcker to actress Raquel Welch to three-time heavyweight champion Muhammad Ali. Louis Farrakhan and the singer Jewel. Dr. Jack Kevorkian and John F. Kennedy Jr. Mikhail Gorbachev.

And Bill Clinton.

At the dinner, Barbara, accustomed to being seated at the best seat in the best table in the house, found herself consigned to the back of the room—an effort, she realized, to keep her companion as far as possible from the president, a featured speaker that evening. "Most of my colleagues were seated ringside," she grumbled. "So I had a lousy time."

Ginsburg, however, had a wonderful time, which had been the point. He managed to leave the misimpression with a *New York Times* reporter that he had been invited on his own, and that he had considered bringing Monica as his guest but decided against it. He said he was most excited about spotting "James Bond"—that would be actor Sean Connery—and General William Westmoreland. "I've learned very, very quickly that people are people," he opined.

For Barbara, there would be a payoff for her seating in Siberia that night. A few weeks later, in April, Ginsburg told her if she was in California, he might be able to arrange for her to drop by Bernard's house and meet Monica—an off-the-record opportunity to begin building a relationship. She went to California, of course, and he took her to the house in the Brentwood section of Los Angeles to see Bernard; his second wife, Barbara; and Monica.

"When Monica entered the room, you would have thought she had nothing pressing on her mind," Barbara recalled. "She was smiling and cheerful. My first thought was that she was prettier than she appeared in photographs. She had beautiful skin, shiny black hair, and although she was somewhat heavy, she was far from obese. She was what my grandmother would have described as zaftig, which sort of means plump in a good way."

They quickly fell into the conversation of friends, or perhaps of a niece with a favorite aunt. Monica had been shopping that day; she modeled some hats she had bought. She said her stepmother had taught her how to knit, which helped occupy her time as she waited for her legal fate to be settled.

She knew how difficult all this must be for her, Barbara said.

"I was basically a good kid growing up," Monica told her. "I didn't smoke or take drugs. I had good grades and never shoplifted."

"Next time, shoplift," Barbara advised, drawing a laugh.

Monica said Barbara's compassion seemed authentic, and she appreciated her quip. "Humor has always been very important to me and how I connect with people," she said later. "It's one of the ways we all got through 1998." She trusted her to do a respectful interview with "more nuance and different angles" beyond the salacious. She hoped that talking to one of TV's biggest names would somehow help her to get her old life back. "Barbara was one of the most respected voices in news at the time," she said. "It felt appropriate to sit down with her."

But an interview with anyone was off the table until Ken Starr had granted Monica immunity from prosecution. After six months with no deal, and with Ginsburg loving the spotlight too much, Monica's team fired him. They hired two new lawyers, Washington insiders who, of course, Barbara already knew from high-profile interviews she had negotiated in the past.

Plato Cacheris had represented Fawn Hall, the striking secretary to Colonel Oliver North; she famously had smuggled documents out of the White House in her undergarments during the Iran-contra affair. Jacob Stein had represented Oregon senator Bob Packwood, accused by more than two dozen women of sexual misconduct.

Finally, in July, the independent counsel gave Monica transactional immunity. She would be shielded from prosecution in the case in exchange for cooperating with prosecutors and testifying truthfully. She turned over to them the notorious blue Gap dress; FBI analysts determined that it was stained with Clinton's semen, a crucial confirmation of her account of their relationship. In August, she testified to the federal grand jury that she did have a sexual relationship with the president. Eleven days later, Clinton testified, too, then delivered a remorseful, four-minute confession to the nation. Finally, in September, Starr released a nearly five-hundred-page report that described every encounter between them in what Barbara Walters would call "virtually pornographic fashion."

Now the legal risks of sitting down for an interview seemed to be settled. "[W]hen you finally decide to do an interview, you won't find a more sympathetic friend in the Fourth Estate than me," wrote Jake Tapper, a future CNN anchor who was then a reporter for the *Washington City Paper*; the two had once dated before all this happened. Larry King sent an ingratiating letter to her stepfather, R. Peter Straus, whom he knew, saying that with him Monica would "be able to tell her story without any time constraints or the fear of editing."

Barbara was months ahead of them already. But there would still be hurdles ahead, financial and otherwise, before the two women would finally sit face-to-face in front of the cameras.

———

Oprah Winfrey said she had landed the interview nearly everybody wanted—but declared she was no longer willing to do it.

"I was told that I did have it but then the conversation moved in a direction that I did not want to go," Oprah said in September 1998. She announced the news on her syndicated talk show and released a written statement. "I do not pay for interviews, no matter what the payment is called. So, I have now taken myself officially out of the running and I no longer want the interview."

Monica's representatives had promised her the interview, she said, then called back to demand the international rights to the tape, which they could then sell in other countries. She considered that a pay-for-play move. She called the question of who would own foreign rights of the tape "really the turning point" that ended their talks.

Monica's team said Judy Smith, a public relations consultant who briefly advised her, had led Oprah to believe she would get the interview before Monica had signed off on that. Soon after Oprah's announcement, Smith was gone. (She would later be the inspiration for the lead character of Washington fixer Olivia Pope in ABC's series *Scandal*.) At ABC, there was skepticism about whether Oprah had the interview nailed down. "I never say we have the interview until the person's in the chair because, I mean, you never know," Katie Nelson Thomson told me. "But I told Barbara that, based on my continued interaction with the family, I really didn't think Oprah had sealed the deal, and we were still very much under consideration." They believed Barbara's outreach to Monica and her parents had given her the inside track. In her memoir, Barbara doesn't mention Oprah's claim in the twenty-page chapter titled "Monica."

In any case, Barbara still wanted the interview, and she was willing to be innovative in negotiating the financial terms to get it.

There were other competitors. One was Australian-born media baron Rupert Murdoch, whose company offered Monica a deal totaling more than $5.5 million that included an interview, a potential movie or miniseries, and a book deal with HarperCollins, the publisher that was part of his empire. The TV special might also be broadcast on Britain's BSkyB and other News Corporation outlets around the world. David Hill, chairman and CEO of Fox Broadcasting Company, was handling the negotiations.

Monica needed money, lots of it, and a blockbuster interview was the most promising and perhaps the only way to get it. By now she owed more than a million dollars to her lawyers, a bill her father was refusing to pay; her mother's new husband didn't want to be responsible for it, either. Monica was going to be on her own to foot it. What's more, she wanted to pay back the legal bills that her mother and four of her friends had accumulated during the Starr investigation. She also needed to finance her living expenses now and down the road. She understood that it would be difficult for her to get a regular job anytime soon, and possibly forever. Her mother was encouraging her to strike a big deal that would get her out of debt.

Meanwhile, Barbara found a connection to Monica's mother. On April 4, two months after her tearful testimony before Starr's grand jury, Marcia Lewis had quietly married R. Peter Straus. She was a forty-nine-year-old divorcee; he was a seventy-four-year-old widower. The owner of a chain of eleven radio stations and five newspapers in the Hudson Valley of New York and in northern New Jersey, he was a radio pioneer and a ranking member in the Washington–New York nexus of the noteworthy. Of course Barbara knew him.

Barbara called Straus, and he agreed to put her in touch with his new wife. The two women arranged to meet with Richard Carlson, another of the well-connected, a former journalist and diplomat who knew Straus. Each had served as director of the Voice of America; Straus had been appointed by President Carter in 1977 and Carlson by President Reagan in 1986. Behind the scenes, Straus had arranged for Carlson to act as Monica's agent, sifting through the real and ridiculous offers she was getting to do interviews and endorse products. (In one of those small-world oddities, Carlson is the father of Tucker Carlson, later the right-wing *provocateur*.)

Barbara enlisted David Westin, the president of ABC News and a lawyer himself, to go with her. At the meeting, Marcia Lewis called her daughter, then in Los Angeles, and put her on speakerphone.

"I understand why you want this money," Westin told Monica. "Understand why we cannot pay that money—because if we pay that money, it undercuts any credibility," for the network and for her. "Now, you have to decide what's best for you. But from your point of view, I'll just tell you if you want to have an interview that people believe in, getting paid a lot of money from Fox is not going to get you there. That undercuts the very purpose of what you're trying to do."

Then he proposed an arrangement, one he told me he had thought of on the fly. She would do the interview with Barbara, but ABC would agree not to distribute it outside North America. That would preserve her ability to reach a lucrative deal with an international broadcaster to do a separate interview. The idea broke the impasse. In the end, Monica was interviewed by Jon Snow of Britain's Channel 4 for a payment of about $660,000 and 75 percent of distribution sales; it was sold to stations around the world. *Hello!* magazine, sort of the European version of *People*, paid her another half-million dollars for a photo spread. She also received the lion's share of a $1.5 million advance for her authorized biography, *Monica's Story*, to be written by Andrew Morton and published by St. Martin's Press close to the interview.

The arrangement with ABC wasn't exactly the same as the one Oprah had rejected, to give Monica foreign rights to their interview. But it was still "a little atypical, a little unusual," one that raised some eyebrows and cost ABC millions in potential revenue, a senior ABC executive from the time acknowledged to me. "Very unusual, actually."

At the moment, though, there was no firm commitment for any interview. Barbara and Monica continued to chat on the phone. Barbara invited her to come to her apartment for dinner. Monica arrived wearing dark glasses and bringing a scarf she had knitted as a gift. "Are you knitting the names of people you want to destroy?" Barbara asked, smiling, but Monica didn't seem to catch the reference to Dickens's *A Tale of Two Cities*; in it, Madame Defarge had stitched in the seams the names of those she was targeting for execution during the French Revolution.

The evening was all about building trust. Barbara walked her down the long hallway that displayed dozens of photographs of her with the famous newsmakers she had interviewed; she showed her a picture of her late father, Lou Walters, the impresario. When they sat down, she reiterated the arguments Westin had made on the phone. Taking payment for her big first interview would affirm the judgment of those who saw her as "an opportunist greedy for fame and money," she said. But an interview with her would be a chance for Monica to present herself with dignity, as "a woman who cares about the truth and has tried to be honest."

Barbara followed up, as she often did, with a letter, this one written on her personalized ABC News stationery and dated November 3, 1998.

"Believe me, I know how difficult this decision is for you," she wrote. She noted other interviews she had done with young women enmeshed in controversy—with Donna Rice, who had a fling with Colorado senator Gary Hart that undermined his presidential campaign, and with Desiree Washington, who had accused boxer Mike Tyson of rape. "In both cases, the young women chose to simply tell their story to me in a most dignified fashion," she said. She noted that Donna was now married, Desiree in graduate school. She suggested that Monica could also be able to "once again walk outside with your head held high," that she could find a future after scandal.

"I fully believe that no one else can possibly do the kind of interview that I could do," she wrote. "It isn't only my own reputation for fairness and integrity. It is also that you and I have a trust and respect for each other that will permeate the screen."

She signed the letter "Fondly" and sent a copy to Carlson with an odd handwritten note. "I believe every word of it," she wrote.

That was enough. Monica called and asked to meet with the ABC team who would be working on her interview.

They gathered in Barbara's apartment for lunch: Phyllis McGrady, then the ABC News vice president of special projects and a trusted colleague; longtime producer Martin Clancy; and Katie Nelson Thomson. The conversation ranged from the dishy—why Monica had never had the notorious blue dress dry-cleaned—to the practical. The network would promote the interview with a sense of decorum and discretion, they promised. For one thing, the promo would show Barbara's questions and Monica's face, but not her answers. That was "a stunt" to build suspense, Westin told me; at that point, Americans had never heard Monica's voice. It also preserved cachet for her to negotiate a second interview with a foreign broadcaster, the one that came with a check.

When the lunch was over, the deal was done. Monica agreed to do her first interview on ABC, with Barbara.

———

There would be one final snag. Monica's immunity agreement included a gag order. She had to get Starr's approval to speak to the news media until there had been "a final resolution of this matter." When the interview was announced in November, the special counsel's office hadn't agreed. If Monica went ahead with the interview anyway, the immunity deal could be considered broken and she could be liable for prosecution.

Westin was ready to hire Floyd Abrams, the nation's most prominent

First Amendment attorney, to file a lawsuit on behalf of ABC seeking to overturn the interview ban on constitutional grounds. Carlson was skeptical whether a lawsuit would succeed, and he cautioned that it almost certainly would take time. Instead, he proposed hiring Theodore Olson, a former assistant U.S. attorney general who had friendly connections with Starr in conservative legal circles. They had been colleagues at the legal firm of Gibson, Dunn & Crutcher. Westin agreed that ABC would pay Olson's bill for reaching out to Starr's team.

When the arrangement was disclosed a year later in *The New Yorker*, critics said ABC's payment to Monica's lawyer smelled suspiciously like "checkbook journalism." *The Washington Post* called it "an unorthodox step." The *New York Post* demanded, "Did ABC Pay to Get Monica?"

Westin defended the $25,000 payment as proper. "I agreed to pay her lawyer's fee to get the permission," he told me. "I said, 'Well, listen, she wouldn't be owing the money if she wasn't doing it for ABC News, so I think it's a reasonable expense. She's not going to do the interview in order to get her lawyer's fee.'" It was because of ABC's desire to interview her that she was incurring the cost.

Carlson was able to make his case directly to Starr; the two men were both at a Christmas party and slipped into a side room to talk. Carlson noted that Starr himself had been the victim of bad publicity; he had done an interview (with Diane Sawyer on *20/20*, in fact) to try to present himself in a more favorable light. Shouldn't Monica be allowed to do the same after a year of attack and speculation? On February 16, four days after the Senate acquitted Clinton in the nation's first presidential impeachment trial in a century, the independent counsel sent Monica's lawyers a letter approving the interview. But they forbade her to say anything about the prosecutors and their investigation, including the day they had intercepted her at Pentagon City Mall.

The interview was back on track, just in time to air on the final night of a "sweeps" month when Nielsen ratings were used to set advertising rates for the next quarter. The two-hour, prime-time special was set for Wednesday, March 3, 1999.

———

Barbara was calculating what to ask. Monica was practicing how to answer.

For months, Monica's team had been trying to prepare her for the interview. A memo titled "Key Messages/BW Interview" and dated October 22, 1999, listed more than fifty possible questions and suggested answers. One of them—"Who is Monica Lewinsky?"—turned out to be similar to the opening query Barbara would pose. Another was close to Barbara's final question. The memo's version: "How will you explain to your children why you had an affair with the President of the United States?" There was a separate section about parrying questions about her weight and extolling the virtues of Jenny Craig, the weight-loss company that had hired her as a spokeswoman. (Suggested language: "I've tried a lot of programs in the past, but this one has really worked for me.")

Carlson had long experience in Washington and the news media; he had been a wire service reporter before becoming a documentary filmmaker and director of the Voice of America. At kitchen-table sessions that included members of Monica's family, they ran through the questions he thought Barbara was likely to pose.

They battled the most over how to answer this one: "Do you still love him?"

Monica agreed that question was all but inevitable, but she didn't have a ready, clean answer. She said she didn't love Clinton and yet she did—a response that risked making her look like a sap to Americans who already didn't think much of her. She finally agreed that she wouldn't say she still loved him. Even though, she added, that she did. In a way.

————

Barbara had been writing and rewriting her cards with questions for months.

She read *The Starr Report*, skimmed the supplemental evidence that the independent counsel had released, and reviewed the hundreds of pages of transcripts of the tapes Linda Tripp had surreptitiously recorded of her conversations with Monica. She read the grand jury testimony that had been released and the speeches President Clinton had made.

She enlisted Chris Vlasto, an award-winning ABC producer who with correspondent Jackie Judd had helped break the story at its start and had covered the investigation ever since.

Vlasto played, essentially, the role of Monica in hours of discussion in Barbara's ABC office with her inner circle. He knew the material more deeply than anyone else. If I ask this, Barbara would say, how would Monica answer? If she responds that way, what would be a smart follow-up?

For Barbara, the goal of this interview was different from many of the others she had done over the years. After a $52 million investigation by a special counsel, armed with the power to subpoena even the president, it seemed unlikely there was some revelation still to be unveiled, some news that hadn't already been broken. What Americans didn't know, though, was what Monica sounded like, why she did what she did, how she came across in person. Was she a scorned temptress, or was Clinton a sexual predator, or did something entirely different explain their relationship? Who was she, really?

For Monica, that was one reason she had chosen Barbara to do the interview. "She takes her work very seriously and approached this interview with the journalistic professionalism one would expect," she said later. "But not far behind, was an intention to introduce me to the world as more than a headline or punchline—as a human being and a young woman. People tuned in to the interview not just because they were curious about me, but because it was going to be through Barbara Walters's trusted perspective."

This was Barbara's opening question: "Monica, you have been described as a bimbo, a stalker, a seductress. Describe yourself."

"I think I'm very loving; I'm very loyal; I think I'm intelligent," she answered, then chuckled self-consciously. "I think I certainly feel that I have been misportrayed in the past year, and unfairly so."

Katie Nelson Thomson's comment at an early planning session formed the basis for another key question. "I've been in the White House many times and I don't understand how someone could flash her underpants to the president," Katie had puzzled. In the interview, Barbara posed that question this way: "You lifted the back of your jacket and showed the president of the United States your thong underwear. Where did you get the nerve? I mean, who does that?"

"It was a small, subtle, flirtatious gesture, and that's me," Monica replied. Barbara asked, "Was it saying, 'I'm available'?" Monica put it a bit differently. "I think it was saying, 'I'm interested, too. I'll play.'"

Barbara's assistant, Monica Caulfield, initially typed about two hundred possible questions on the three-by-five index cards Barbara liked to use as she prepared for an interview, to revise and to shuffle. She devised a way to get around Starr's edict that Monica couldn't talk in the interview about that terrifying first interrogation session by the FBI. There was no restriction on what Barbara could say, so she would read that passage from Monica's book. In their negotiations before the interview, ABC had agreed to help publicize *Monica's Story*, the authorized biography by Andrew Morton that was being published the day after the interview aired. They repeatedly showed a close-up of the cover during the two-hour show.

Talking about sex would be trickier.

During her lunch at Barbara's apartment, Monica had mentioned that after she had been moved to a job at the Pentagon, she had a three-month fling with an older man there, had gotten pregnant, and had "a termination procedure"—an abortion. Should Barbara ask her about that? Monica had included it in her book. Barbara decided to pose a question, but when Monica seemed too taken aback to answer, Barbara backed off and read that passage from the book, too.

The most difficult sticking point in the strategy sessions beforehand was how explicit to be in describing what actually happened between Bill Clinton and Monica Lewinsky—the oral sex, the lewd use of a cigar. Barbara was no prude, but she was cautious about giving too many details; viewers who wanted more could read *The Starr Report*, she reasoned. But Clinton had testified that he hadn't had sex with Monica, and Vlasto wanted to make sure it was clear that the president had lied about that, by any reasonable definition of what "having sex" meant.

During the interview, Barbara would walk around that subject more carefully than any other, although at one point she said the words "oral sex." She referred without explanation to "that cigar business." She also asked Monica what "phone sex" was. (During the prep sessions, a perplexed Barbara had asked her team that question.) "The impression that the president gave was that this was a one-way street, that he was gratified, and you were not," she said. "But the truth is that you were gratified."

"Yes, yes," Monica said.

Barbara followed up with what was surely the most carefully crafted description possible of a female orgasm, worthy of the Victorians. "And that there were things that were done that made you feel as a woman happy and contented?" she asked.

"Yes," Monica said.

Despite the lack of details, that certainly sounded like sex.

The interview was recorded on a Saturday, on February 20, just four days after the special counsel had given its approval and one year to the day since her father's interview with Barbara had aired. Monica entered the garage at ABC headquarters and was escorted to the *20/20* studio amid intensive security. "It was terrifying for me," she recalled. "I'd never done an interview with a reporter, much less on television and with such high stakes. The only interviews I'd done at that point were job interviews and interviews with the independent counsel's office." She was still "somewhat shell-shocked" by all that happened to her, "and the full import of being interviewed by her—and as my first—did not sink in until years later."

The set was decorated to look like a living room, with seven cameras in place to record every question, every answer, every reaction, every interaction. The design was deliberately staid: upholstered couch, faux fireplace, generic leather-bound books in matched sets. Barbara wore a soft blue suit with a subtle plaid on the jacket and skirt. Monica wore a black suit and lilac shell and small drop earrings, her hair combed behind her ears. Her glossy lipstick caused a brief sensation; Club Monaco's "Glaze" would be sold out within days. She was sensitive about whether she would look heavy, so they sat in upholstered chairs with high arms that shielded her sides. The temperature on the set was kept low, at her request. At one point, during a break, Monica worried about whether she was visibly perspiring; Barbara reassured her that she wasn't. "I remember very kindly she acquiesced to my request of the room being cold, because when I get nervous, I often flop sweat," Monica said. "It was freezing."

To one side, Chris Vlasto was sitting next to Richard Carlson and one of Monica's lawyers. There was a phone between them to put Marcia Lewis on the line; Carlson was keeping Monica's mother up to date on what was happening.

Near the start, Monica volunteered an apology to the country, to her family, and to Clinton's family "for my part in this ordeal," something Marcia Lewis had urged her beforehand not to do. "I wouldn't dream of asking Chelsea and Mrs. Clinton to forgive me, but I would ask them to know that I am very sorry for what happened and for what they've been through," Monica said.

During the first break, Monica came over to chat. "How am I doing, guys?" she asked. They reassured her that she was doing "great." Then Carlson said, "Well, your mom would love to see if you could ask Barbara to take it back"—that is, to agree not to use the apology she had just given. Monica threw what two people who saw the exchange on the set described to me as a tantrum, a reminder of her youth. "This is my day!" she snapped. "Why does she have to ruin my day?"

Toward the end of the four-and-a-half-hour session, she seemed relieved. "It isn't as hard as I thought it would be," Monica said at one point, off camera. Barbara replied, "You've had much worse happen to you."

The interview was personal and sometimes painful. Barbara asked Monica why she repeatedly had affairs with married men. "What I've come to see is that that happened because I don't have enough feelings of self-worth, so that I didn't feel that . . . I was worthy of being number one to a man," she replied. Clinton was willing to have oral sex and phone sex with her, she said, but unwilling to say he loved her. She wanted to have intercourse; he almost always refused and they never did. "When you get to be my age, you'll understand that there are consequences for those kinds of things," he told her.

"Monica, are you still in love with Bill Clinton?" Barbara asked—the question Monica had struggled with most beforehand.

"No," she replied, as she had promised during her practice sessions. But she also acknowledged that she was still sorting out her feelings about him. They were complicated. "Sometimes I have warm feelings, sometimes, I'm proud of him still, and sometimes I hate his guts and he makes me sick," she said.

Barbara's final question, just ten words long, had been drafted in hours of discussion and debate in her office. She asked, "What will you tell your children, when you have them?"

"Mommy made a big mistake," Monica replied with a rueful smile.

Barbara was nervous.

The day before the interview aired, the first hour of the unedited, three-hour audio tape was leaked to the New York *Daily News*, which splashed the contents over four pages. ABC insiders suspected some disgruntled employee from the National Association of Broadcast Employees and Technicians was responsible; the network and the union had been locked in contentious contract negotiations. Would the tabloid's disclosure take the shine off her scoop? A week earlier, *The Washington Post* had plastered on its front page an account from an unnamed source who had sat in on the interview; it paraphrased some of her newsiest comments but didn't have direct quotes. Without identifying his source, *Post* media writer Howard Kurtz, later host of Fox News's *MediaBuzz*, told me he thought the leak was likely an authorized one, designed to build interest and boost ratings for the broadcast.

Barbara had heard chatter from the high-minded who insisted, "Oh, I'm not going to watch Monica Lewinsky; that's beneath me." Would they really stay away?

The evening had an unpromising start. She was throwing a watch party at her apartment, as she usually did for her big specials. But she had started a fire in the fireplace without realizing the flue was closed. The room filled with smoke; the fire department was called.

At the party were both ABC colleagues and East Side pals. Glitterati sporting leopard skin and jewels mingled with British broadcaster David Frost. Dominick Dunne, chronicler of the elite and their unwelcome interactions with the law, kept shouting at the others to be quiet while the interview was on the air; he wanted to hear every word. *New York Times* columnist Frank Rich insisted that Barbara look out the window at the paucity of traffic heading down Fifth Avenue. It was a sign, he teased, that everybody in America was inside, watching *20/20*.

"What do you think, Chris?" Barbara asked Vlasto during the evening. "How many millions of people do you think are going to see it?" They agreed on a guess of twenty to twenty-five million. Then he went outside the building, to the sidewalk on Fifth Avenue, to smoke a cigarette. He looked around the corner and could see into a stack of living room windows in the apartment building on the corner. On floor after floor, there was the glow of television sets. He went back upstairs and insisted that Barbara peer out a window to glimpse it, too.

"I think this is going to be a little bigger," he told her. It was. The show attracted an average of 48.5 million viewers, and an estimated 70 million people watched all or part of it. (To compare, Oprah's blockbuster interview with Prince Harry and Meghan Markle in 2022 drew an average of 17.1 million viewers.) The Nielsen rating of 33.4 for *Monica: In Her Own Words* smashed the record for a news program on a single network—a record that had been held by Diane Sawyer's interview of Michael Jackson and Lisa Marie Presley. Of the nation's TV sets that were on during those two hours, almost half were tuned to ABC. In a *USA Today*/CNN/Gallup Poll afterward, nearly six in ten Americans said they had seen at least a little of the interview; one in five had watched it all. The advertising revenue set a record for a network news program, too. Industry executives estimated ABC pulled in $20 to $25 million in commercials.

The interview aired more than a year—406 days, to be precise—after the ABC News assignment desk had called Barbara in Seattle with an astonishing alert: A special counsel appointed by the Justice Department was investigating whether President Clinton had urged a former White House intern to lie under oath about their alleged sexual liaison.

Her name was Monica Lewinsky. Could Barbara get an interview with her?

Why, yes. Yes, she could.

TRUMP

They were friends, in the way the rich and famous can be friends, especially when it is to their mutual benefit. Donald Trump attended the party celebrating Barbara Walters's wedding to Merv Adelson in 1986 in New York; she attended his wedding to Melania Knauss in 2005 in Palm Beach. Both were frequent names in the New York tabloids. Both had an entertainer's instincts, comfortable in celebrity circles. They shared a friendship with Roy Cohn, to the dismay of many in their social set who found the notorious lawyer reprehensible.

Their chummy, occasionally volatile relationship said a great deal about both Barbara Walters and Donald Trump. They each could be transactional. He was one in a long line of controversial men who intrigued her. For his part, she offered what he craved the most: status. If Trump was a worthy subject of "the great Barbara Walters," as he sometimes called her, that meant he must matter.

The first time she interviewed Trump on the air was in 1987, for *20/20*, when he was encouraging speculation that he might be presidential material. His speech to the Portsmouth Rotary Club in New Hampshire drew hundreds of people. She filed a glowing story about his trip to the state that every four years hosted the first presidential primary, introducing him as a "master builder" and a "man who seems to have everything."

She asked his wife, Ivana Trump, about her view of her husband's political future. "How many tall buildings you can build and how many casinos you can own?" Ivana mused. In another ten years, she predicted, "He's definitely going to look for something or some other business or another thing for him to do."

Ivana was right about that, although it would take more than ten years for him to make the leap to politics, and by then she would no longer be his wife.

In that first *20/20* interview, her portrait of Trump was all roses. "Jacuzzi journalism," scoffed the TV reviewer for *Newsday*. "Apparently, Walters is more concerned with her credentials as an A-list party-goer—the kinds of parties where she schmoozes with people like Donald and Ivana Trump—than with her credentials as a reporter." She raised no questions about his business acumen and didn't push back to his startling boast that his ability to lie, to bluff, was a key to his business success. Looking back, Trump was probably right about that, and perhaps Barbara didn't contest his claim because, growing up in show business, she was familiar with the trait.

In that first interview, Trump offered other glimpses of the character Americans would get to know well years later. He was clearly more drawn by the idea of winning the White House than he was by how he might govern once he got there.

"If you could be appointed president and didn't have to run, would you like to be president?" she asked.

"Well, wouldn't that be an interesting concept," Trump, then forty-one, replied. He called it something "a lot of people" would like. But in a comment that in hindsight seemed particularly revealing, he said, "Interestingly, you know, part of the enjoyment of something and part of the whole, the whole thing is the battle. If you could be appointed, I'm not sure that would be the same ball game. . . . It's the quest that really I believe—it's the hunt, that I believe I love."

In 1990, when news of his split from Ivana hit the tabloids, Barbara sent Trump a sympathetic letter. It was on his birthday, June 14, a birthdate she noted he shared with her daughter. "I am very fond of Ivana, and good women have a tendency to support each other," she wrote. "But I remember all the years when you and I had a trust and friendship that was very much our own. And since this may be a time when 'a fellow needs a friend,' I wanted you to know that my feelings for you remain the same."

Friends or not, though, two months later she would take a tough tack when she interviewed him as he was promoting a new book, *Surviving at the Top*.

"There are many people who would say, 'Failing at the Top,'" she began, noting the heavy debt he had assumed to buy the Plaza Hotel. He responded by previewing the denunciation of the press as "fake news" that would become familiar during his presidency a quarter of a century later. "I hope the general public understands how inherently dishonest the press in this country is," he said.

"Being on the verge of bankruptcy, being bailed out by the banks, skating on thin ice and almost drowning—that's a businessman to be admired?" she demanded.

"You say on the verge of bankruptcy, Barbara, and you talk on the verge, and you listen to what people are saying," Trump shot back. She replied, "I talk to your bankers." They had told her the only way he could pay back his loans would be to sell the Plaza. He waved that idea away. Everyone was saying what a "great deal" he had struck in buying the iconic hotel, he said.

"No, they're not," she persisted.

Afterward, he was furious. "I'm gonna get that woman," he said of Barbara in an exchange with BBC host Selina Scott during a flight to Miami from New York. "Watch me."

But the hard feelings apparently didn't last, not when their interests aligned again. When *The View* was launched seven years later, Trump's daughter Ivanka was a guest during its first few weeks; she was fifteen years old at the time and plugging her modeling career. He appeared on the show eighteen times even before he launched his presidential campaign in 2015. "He was on all the time," Joy Behar, one of the regulars on the panel, told me. "We all felt that he was like this very picaresque character; he was like this New York character who acted crazy and had women and headlines that say, 'Best sex ever.'" He was always willing and eager to talk up his latest project, as a real estate developer or as a reality

TV host. After he was elected president in 2016, some of Barbara's colleagues at ABC grumbled that she had played an early role in building unwarranted credibility for him by giving him so much airtime.

"You needed a guest, someone dropped out at the last moment, you could actually get him," Geddie told me. Trump would even take a cameo role in a comedic skit. "Barbara's a short-order cook at the diner, and who's her first customer?" Geddie said, recalling one of them. "Donald Trump."

———————

The headlines from *The View* on December 20, 2006, were supposed to be about Hillary Clinton, but in the end, the show became all about Trump.

Hillary had appeared on *The View* just once before, although she had been a regular topic of conversation, often with admiration. During the show's tenure, she had gone from embattled first lady to U.S. senator from New York. Now she had trounced her Republican opponent to win reelection, though many assumed she wouldn't complete her new six-year term. With that race behind her, she was considered the all-but-certain Democratic presidential nominee in 2008. When the show opened, the announcer declared that Hillary would be "revealing everything, from whether she wants to move back to the White House in '08 to what she really thinks of the war in Iraq."

As she waited to be introduced onto the set, comedian and actress Rosie O'Donnell began to mock Trump. Her disdain for him, and his disdain for her, were no secret.

Rosie's fury had started to build the night before. Trump had called a news conference to make a dramatic announcement. The winner of the Miss USA Pageant, a contest he owned, had been caught using cocaine and partying at bars. Then twenty years old, she had violated not only laws restricting underage drinking and illicit drug use but also the pageant's code of ethics. Those rules required upstanding behavior by those who aspired to the Miss USA title, along with no previous marriages or visible tattoos. But Trump declared he was going to give Tara Conner a second chance, sending her into rehab but not taking her crown. (She would later credit Trump for her decade of sobriety that followed. "He saved my life," she would write.) In front of the TV cameras that night, she wept. He preened. Rosie, watching on TV at home, steamed.

On the show the next morning, Joy Behar teased the story. "We'll talk about Trump when we get back," she said.

"Oh, jeez," said Rosie, who at Barbara's request had succeeded Meredith Vieira as the show's moderator that September. "I'm getting nauseous. I don't enjoy him in any capacity. We'll be back talking about Donald and his hair loop."

When the show came back on the air, Rosie roasted Trump as "a snake-oil salesman" and ridiculed his distinctive comb-over, flipping her own long black hair over the top of her head to demonstrate. "He's the moral authority?" she demanded. "Left the first wife; had an affair. Left the second wife; had an affair." She dismissed the argument that he had been a success in business. "He inherited a lot of money, and he's been bankrupt so many times, where he didn't have to pay."

She seemed to realize she might have gone too far. "Here comes a lawsuit," she quipped.

The events that followed presaged those a decade later, when Hillary Clinton and Donald Trump would compete for the White House. The way he dominated coverage of her. His coarse language toward women, as in the *Access Hollywood* tape that would threaten his campaign. His particular hatred of Rosie; he would disparage her during debates. His sensitivity toward questions about his business smarts and personal wealth.

Finally, Hillary came on the set. "I was laughing so hard backstage, I didn't think I'd get out," she told the panel. Joy replied, "Every day, we're in trouble on this show."

"Isn't that interesting," Hillary said. "I wonder why that happens."

"I don't know," Joy said. "We're just women."

On that day, Barbara wasn't on the air; she wasn't even watching. She was cruising the Caribbean aboard a 152-foot yacht named *Triumphant Lady* and owned by her friend Judith Sheindlin, who had earned a fortune as TV's Judge Judy. But Trump was watching. By the time Geddie returned to his office after the show ended, an enraged Trump was on the phone from Trump Tower, threatening to sue *The View*, ABC, Rosie, and

Barbara. He didn't mention Rosie's gibes about his hair loss or his marital infidelities. What he took offense at was the attack on his financial record. While he had led businesses that had declared bankruptcy, he had never personally filed for bankruptcy.

Geddie called Barbara. Given her history with Trump, maybe she could smooth things over. Geddie conferenced him in for a three-way conversation. She was conciliatory. She promised to correct the misstatement that he had filed for bankruptcy.

She also may have expressed regret over hiring Rosie in the first place.

That was how Trump interpreted the conversation. He wrote an open "Dear Rosie" letter on company stationery that said Barbara had told him working with Rosie was "like living in hell." According to him, there was more: "Donald, never get into the mud with pigs," he claimed she had said of Rosie. And this: "Don't worry, she won't be here for long."

Barbara issued a written statement denying that she had regretted "for one moment" hiring Rosie as moderator of *The View.* But the statement also called Trump "a personal friend" and "a good friend to *The View* for many years."

By now Trump was denouncing O'Donnell in appearances on TV and radio shows. He called her fat, stupid, ugly, a degenerate, a "wacko." On CNN, he called her "a loser" and "a bully." On Fox News, he referred to her as "that animal."

During the days that followed, over the holiday break, Barbara didn't call Rosie to commiserate or offer her support. Rosie didn't feel she adequately defended her when she was under attack. She also didn't accept at face value Barbara's carefully worded statement about what she had said to Trump in that phone call.

"I was hurt now. I was wounded," Rosie said. "As for me, the worst part of it was that I knew, from the get-go, twisted though he was, I knew in my heart that Barbara had said those things. In one way or another, she had betrayed me." They were "in the club of women together," she said. "But she was also in the rich money club, the designer gowns and gilded mirrors and yachts in the Riviera club. And when the shit hit the golden fan, she tossed the women's club aside and cast her allegiance with the wealthy guy."

The two women finally saw one another face-to-face again in the makeup room before the show on January 8, 2007. The ferocious argument that followed was detailed in the *New York Post* the next morning. Barbara said she had done everything she could to quash the story. Rosie called her a liar—actually, the *Post* reported, "a (bleeping) liar." "I definitely yelled," she said later. "I said how disappointed I was and how shocked and hurt I was that she wouldn't stand up for me. I felt very betrayed about her going behind my back and speaking to Donald Trump in Trumpian language."

In a rain of invective, Rosie told Barbara that she was a bad mother. "No wonder Jackie can't stand you," she said, a reference to her strained relationship with her only child. "Do not speak about my daughter," Barbara angrily replied.

The show went on that day, and two days later the two women made a public show of unity. "Well, he's at it again," Rosie said after another attack from Trump. "That poor, pathetic man," Barbara offered. That got Trump's attention. He issued a statement calling Barbara a liar and a "sad figurehead dominated by a third-rate comedian." He said he wished she hadn't chosen him as one of the *10 Most Fascinating People* for her annual special in 2004. (Most Trump observers doubted that assertion.)

A few months after the blow-up on *The View*, in April, Rosie announced she would be leaving the show in June after failing to settle on an extension of her one-year contract. Geddie already had told Barbara that he wouldn't stay with the show if Rosie's contract was renewed; Barbara had agreed. Rosie would go off the air in May, earlier than planned, after heated words on the air about the Iraq War with co-host Elisabeth Hasselbeck. Then, in the fall, Rosie published a book, *Celebrity Detox*, detailing her version of what had happened and her harsh assessment of the woman she had considered an icon and a mentor.

"Barbara Walters, arguably the most poised person on this planet" was "all rough-edged and unfinished inside," she wrote.

In her book, Rosie wrote what almost no one dared to say out loud. She suggested it was time for Barbara, then seventy-eight years old, to retire.

"At some point, a person gets tired. It's inevitable, the aging process," she said. "Barbara Walters is almost twice my age and she's been doing this for nearly half a century; at some point it becomes necessary to step back. I hope when the time comes for me to do this, I will be graceful and go. Everyone has to go. Going is part of the gig."

Nothing could have enraged Barbara more than the expression of sympathy that sheathed a stiletto.

"I'll bet behind the glam and glitter it hurts to be Barbara, some-times," Rosie went on, "because, while you can hide aging, you can't erase it; it leaves its grainy footprints, its smears." Rosie was already off *The View*, though she would return for a season after Barbara had retired.

For now, Barbara stayed on the show. In fact, she expressed interest in becoming the moderator when Rosie left, only to be dissuaded by those who thought that wasn't a good idea. Whoopi Goldberg joined the cast as moderator instead. For Barbara, the "grainy footprints" of aging were beginning to show.

ONE MORE TIME

2011

The Hollywood celebrities drew bigger ratings, but Barbara's favorite interviews, and the ones that made her reputation in history, were of a more serious sort. She was "driven to interview world leaders and icons," she said. Anwar Sadat and Menachem Begin were on that list, winners of the Nobel Peace Prize for their negotiations in the Mideast. So were an array of dictators and despots, many considered enemies of the United States, some accused of corruption and brutality.

Late in life, at a forum at Harvard's Institute of Politics, a student asked if there had been anyone she had refused to interview, on principle. Someone who was just too notorious. She seemed perplexed by the question.

"I've done more murderers than presidents," she replied. "I'm very unjudgmental." In 1997, when Hugh Downs refused to interview sportscaster Marv Albert on *20/20* after he had been accused of sexual assault, she did the interview. That attitude presumably reflected the experiences of her childhood. She had grown up in a world that welcomed or at least tolerated mobsters and rumrunners and folks who might have spent some time in prison, or were at risk of going there.

Figures like Saddam Hussein and Muammar Qaddafi didn't intimidate her. They interested her. "Dictators and generals, that's my speed," she joked.

Barbara gave Americans an up-close-and-personal introduction to the Shah of Iran in 1977 from his palace in Tehran; on the air, he questioned the intelligence and competence of women as his wife, the empress, quietly protested, her eyes filling with tears. Barbara talked to Saddam at the presidential palace in Baghdad in 1981, his first interview for American television. In 1986, she sat down with the recently deposed dictator of Haiti, Jean-Claude "Baby Doc" Duvalier, and his wife, Michele, who denied stealing millions from their country. The setting didn't bolster their credibility; they spoke from their sumptuous villa in the south of France.

She flew to Libya to sit down with Qaddafi in his tent in the center of Tripoli, amid palm trees and roaming camels; he laughed when she asked him about rumors he was crazy. She twice interviewed Russian president Boris Yeltsin, then returned to Moscow to talk to his successor, Vladimir Putin. She interviewed Saudi Crown Prince Abdullah, Chinese leader Jiang Zemin, and Venezuelan strongman Hugo Chávez.

In 2011, at eighty-two, she would conduct her last session with the sort of notorious foreign leader she loved to encounter. The interview had the hallmarks of the ones she had been doing for decades: the indefatigable competition to land it, the relentless work to prepare for it, the keen performance once the cameras began to roll. And the controversy afterward.

———

Syrian president Bashar al-Assad was supposed to be Diane Sawyer's interview, assigned under the arbitration system that Ben Sherwood had set up after he became president of ABC News in December 2010 to impose more coordination and civility in the competition for big guests. Christiane Amanpour was pushing to land him, too. Barbara had been slowing down, anyway, albeit a decade or two later than most her age. In 2004, at seventy-five, she had stepped down as co-host of *20/20*, the TV newsmagazine she had been appearing on for a quarter-century. In 2010, she aired the last of the Oscar night specials that she had been hosting for nearly three decades.

But she was still appearing regularly on *The View* and hosting her *10 Most Fascinating People* specials each December. There were few signs that Diane was making headway with Assad as the "Arab Spring" uprisings ousted leaders in Egypt, Libya, Tunisia, and Yemen. Syria had responded to protests with crackdowns and brutality, the beginning of a long and bloody civil war.

"This is a very important moment in Syria and all of a sudden Barbara announces that she's got Assad," Sherwood told me. "I don't know how it happened. I think that she knew somebody somewhere."

Of course she did. Barbara had held an off-the-record meeting in the Mideast with Assad and his influential wife, Asma al-Assad, years earlier, and in 2008 she had gone to Syria expecting an interview with him that didn't happen. Then, in March 2011, Barbara attended a cocktail party hosted by the Syrian ambassador to the United Nations, Bashar Jaafari, and met the ambassador's daughter, Sheherazad Jaafari, also known as Sherry. Then twenty-one years old, she was working as a junior press aide in Syria's U.N. mission and, as it turned out, had a close and friendly relationship with Assad himself. Somehow, Syria then offered Barbara the interview everyone wanted.

Diane protested that the interview was supposed to be hers, but Sherwood recognized the news value of the booking. Assad, an ophthalmologist by training who had succeeded his father as president of Syria in 2000, had never before done an American television interview. So much for ABC's new orderly system for distributing the big interviews among the top talent.

As ever, Barbara's preparations were meticulous. Tom Nagorski, then ABC's managing editor for international news, was enlisted to give her a crash course on Assad and Syria. He was repeatedly summoned to her office, regardless of what other world news was breaking. "I soon learned that my role—apart from sorting out the various details for the trip—would be to sit for mock interviews and play the role of Assad," he told me.

She would use her index cards, building a stack and reordering them. "She was both remarkably thorough and insecure, I thought," Nagorski said. The card-shuffling continued all the way to Damascus. He called it "a chess player's vision of the interview, thinking through various questions and potential answers and counters."

Traveling to Damascus wasn't simple, given the impact of the civil war that was raging. Nor was it safe for journalists once they were there. Security consultants employed by ABC warned Barbara not to leave her hotel except to do the interview. When she and her entourage were in Amman, Jordan, waiting to fly to Damascus, their flight was delayed because the Jordanian airline they were flying didn't want its pilot and crew to risk staying overnight in Syria. They took off in the morning instead.

But she ignored the warnings to stay in the hotel. In New York, Sherwood got a security alert when she headed out to shop in a souk. "The lady just did what she wanted," he said.

"We walked around the old city doing some filming and shopping," recalled Alexander Marquardt, a thirty-year-old ABC correspondent covering the Mideast who accompanied her. "It was right before Christmas, and she was buying presents, including a vest for Whoopi Goldberg." At one point, she scolded him for saying too much in front of Sherry, who had been assigned as their Syrian minder. Barbara didn't want to give Assad a heads-up on what she was going to ask him.

———

Ten days earlier, Sherry had sent an email to Assad's top aides with advice for the interview, including how to respond to questions about the regime's violence toward its own citizens.

She outlined the language he might expect to hear. "The idea of violence has been one of the major subjects brought up in every article," she cautioned. "They use the phrases 'The Syrian government is killing its own people,' 'Tanks have been used in many cities,' 'Airplanes have been used to suppress the peaceful demonstration,' and 'Security forces are criminals and bloody.'" Indeed, those turned out to be points Barbara pressed during the interview.

Sherry offered suggestions on how to respond.

"It is hugely important and worth mentioning that 'mistakes' have been done in the beginning of the crises because we did not have a well-organized 'police force,'" she wrote in one of a series of emails later leaked by the hacker collective known as Anonymous. "American psyche can be easily manipulated when they hear that there are 'mistakes' done and now we are 'fixing it.'"

She suggested trying to turn the tables, citing controversies in the United States. "It's worth mentioning also what is happening now in Wall Street and the way the demonstrations are been suppressed by policemen, police dogs and beatings," she said. The Occupy Wall Street movement had begun staging protests in September 2011. Assad could say that Syria "doesn't have a policy to torture people," she advised, "unlike the USA, where there are courses and schools that specialize in teaching policemen and officers how to torture."

———————

Barbara Walters and Bashar al-Assad sat face-to-face, almost knee-to-knee, in identical chairs carved of dark wood. The backdrop was a wall of burnished gold curtains, with a flag of Syria on a stanchion behind him. A small table held two crystal glasses of water and an ornate silver box. There was none of the on-air bonhomie that marked her interviews with Castro and Qaddafi. Afterward, when they stood side by side for a joint portrait, neither would smile.

She started with a softball. "Mr. President, you have invited us to Damascus and you have not given an interview to the American media since this crisis began. What is it you want us to know?"

Then the hardballs.

For nearly an hour, she posed the toughest questions, reordering some cards and skipping others, pursuing follow-ups on the fly. Foreign affairs scholars who had been skeptical beforehand praised her fearlessness. "Everyone who made snarky questions about Walters' lack of qualifications to conduct this interview should be eating crow (and that includes me)," David Kenner of *Foreign Policy* magazine wrote in a favorable article with an insulting subhead, "Barbara Walters: Not Awful!"

"Much of the world regards you as a dictator and a tyrant," she told Assad. "What do you say to that?

"You don't have the support of your people. You know, sir, that many leaders in the region have been overthrown. You have seen, I am certain, the pictures [from] Egypt [of] President Mubarak in jail, pictures of, in Libya of Moammar Gadhafi killed. Are you afraid that you might be next?"

She ticked off alleged atrocities and showed him the horrific photos as evidence: A thirteen-year-old boy, arrested in April, whose body was returned to his family bearing scars of torture, his face bruised and swollen. A cartoonist who was beaten, his arms broken. A singer who wrote a song calling for Assad's ouster, found with his throat cut.

"You have seen these pictures, have you not?" she asked as she showed them to him and to the world. "Are you remorseful?"

Assad, speaking fluent English, denied it all, calm and impassive in a dark suit and gray tie. He denied that he and his government had been involved in any wrongdoing. He expressed no guilt and no regret. "There was no command to kill or to be brutal," he said. He disputed the news accounts by Western reporters and the investigation by a United Nations commission that concluded the Syrian government had committed torture, rape, and crimes against humanity.

He also used some of the tactics Sherry Jaafari had suggested, declaring that perhaps mistakes had been made by individuals, and countering that the United States didn't come to this debate with clean hands. "There is a difference between having policy to crack down and between having some mistakes committed by some officials, there is a big difference," he said. "For example, when you talk about policy it's like what happened in Guantanamo when you have policy of torture."

What is the biggest misperception that Americans have about what's happening in Syria?

"OK, we don't kill our people, nobody kill," Assad said. "No government in the world kills its people, unless it's led by a crazy person."

Barbara Walters never had a formal interview with President Lyndon Johnson, though they met several times, including this White House visit in 1967. She said he was outgoing and gregarious in private but awkward and ill at ease using a teleprompter, despite advice she gave him when he asked. *(LBJ Library photo by Frank Wolfe, White House Photo Office)*

Barbara with President Richard Nixon and George Romney, secretary of housing and urban development, in the Oval Office in 1969. The desk is stacked with mail in response to Nixon's speech defending the Vietnam War and appealing to a "Silent Majority" in the U.S. She forged a friendly relationship with him.

(White House Photo Office; Richard Nixon Presidential Library and Museum)

After President Gerald Ford lost the 1976 election, Barbara conducts a farewell interview with him and Betty Ford in the White House. The way she handled her encounter with a visibly inebriated first lady led to one of her few professional regrets. *(Gerald R. Ford Presidential Library)*

For her first ABC special, Barbara interviews Jimmy and Rosalynn Carter at their home in Plains, Georgia, a month after he had been elected president in 1976. "Be wise with us, governor," she said in closing. "Be good to us." She later agreed with critics that her remark was "stupid." *(© ABC/Getty Images)*

Eight months after Ronald Reagan was shot by a would-be assassin in 1981, Barbara interviews him at his ranch near Santa Barbara. "I don't want to hurt your feelings, but this is the scroungiest jeep," she teased. He replied, "Yes, but remember, we have an austerity program going on." He would be involved in one of the biggest controversies of her career. *(© ABC/Getty Images)*

Barbara interviews George H. W. Bush at the White House in 1992. They met before he was in politics; his brother Jonathan knew her second husband, Lee Guber. He called and dropped by her apartment one morning. She was in her bathrobe, drinking coffee, when he told her he had decided to seek the GOP presidential nomination in 1980.

(George H.W. Bush Presidential Library and Museum)

Barbara beat ABC colleague Diane Sawyer in landing an interview with Bill Clinton at the White House in 1996, but afterward she wasn't impressed by the interview or him. "He never sparkled with me," she said. "The most interesting member of that family is Hillary Clinton."

(Terry Ashe/© ABC/Getty Images)

Two days before George W. Bush's inauguration, Barbara interviews him at his ranch in Crawford, Texas. They sat down to talk in his muddy barn. Was he nervous about being president? "I can't wait to get up there," he told her. "I can't wait to get started." *(Virginia Sherwood/© ABC/Getty Images)*

Barbara interviewed Barack Obama several times in the White House, and she suggested a question to Jimmy Fallon before the president appeared on *Late Night with Jimmy Fallon* in 2012. "He lives in the White House with his wife, his mother-in-law, his two daughters. Besides the dog, he's the only male in the family at the White House. What is that like?" Fallon made it his opening question. *(George Burns/© ABC/Getty Images)*

Barbara's first TV interview with Donald Trump, in 1987. The blustery real estate developer discussed the prospect he might one day want to be president. Here, aboard his private plane. (Donna Svennevik/© ABC/Getty Images)

Barbara's final interview with Donald Trump in 2015, when he was running in a presidential campaign he would win. Their transactional relationship had dramatic highs and lows. *(Ida Mae Astute/© ABC/Getty Images)*

Barbara with Joe Biden on *The View* in 2014. The future president was then vice president. *(Lou Rocco/© ABC/Getty Images)*

LEFT: Barbara crosses the Bay of Pigs with Cuban president Fidel Castro in 1977, part of an interview on ABC that helped rebuild her reputation.

(© ABC/Getty Images)

BELOW: Barbara interviews Egyptian president Anwar Sadat, left, and Israeli prime minister Menachem Begin in 1977 after Sadat's historic address to the Israeli Knesset. She would call it her proudest interview.

(© ABC/Getty Images)

Barbara interviews King Hussein of Jordan in 1975 on ABC's *Issues and Answers*.

(© ABC/Getty Images)

Barbara interviews Libyan leader Muammar Qaddafi outside his tent in Tripoli, Libya, in 1989. He laughed when she asked him about reports he was crazy.

(Kimberly Butler/© ABC/Getty Images)

Barbara shakes hands with Russian president Vladimir Putin in 2001. She saved a final, provocative question for the end of their interview in case he walked out in protest.

(AP Images/Mikhail Metzel)

Barbara interviews Syrian president Bashar al-Assad in Damascus amid his government's brutal crackdown of the Arab Spring protests in 2011.

(Rob Wallace/© ABC/Getty Images)

ABOVE: Barbara's interview with Monica Lewinsky in 1999 drew the largest audience of any news division interview in the history of television.

(Virginia Sherwood/© ABC/Getty Images)

The front page of the New York *Daily News* on March 2, 1999.

(NY Daily News Archive via Getty Images)

Barbara tries a soft-shoe dance with entertainer George Burns during an interview in 1979. *(ABC/Courtesy: Everett Collection)*

Actor Sylvester Stallone gives Barbara a ride on the back of his motorcycle—and loans her his leather motorcycle jacket—during their interview in 1988. *(John Bryson/Getty Images)*

Barbara interviews actress Katharine Hepburn in 1981; she offered blunt advice on balancing children and a career.
(© ABC/Getty Images)

BELOW: Actor Don Johnson crosses Biscayne Bay in a powerboat with Barbara during a 1988 interview in Miami. She pointed out her childhood stomping grounds on Palm Island.
(Lynn Pelham/© ABC/Getty Images)

In a joint interview with heavyweight boxer Mike Tyson, her husband, actress Robin Givens tells Barbara that their eight-month marriage has been "pure hell." A week after the interview aired, she filed for divorce.

(Robert Maass/© ABC/Getty Images)

Barbara called her 2005 interview with the Dalai Lama one of the most meaningful of her career. After they talked, they rubbed noses and he gave her some life advice. *(Rob Wallace/© ABC/Getty Images)*

Barbara interviews Walter Cronkite on Martha's Vineyard in 1983, after he had retired as anchor of the *CBS Evening News.*

(ABC Photo Archives)

The original cast of *The View* when it premiered in 1997. From left, Star Jones, Joy Behar, Meredith Vieira, Debbie Matenopoulos, and Barbara. Behar began as a fill-in for Barbara but soon became a regular co-host.

(ABC/Courtesy: Everett Collection)

In 2010, Barack Obama became the first sitting president to appear on a daytime talk show. From left, Whoopi Goldberg, Barbara, Obama, Joy Behar, Sherri Shepherd, and Elizabeth Hasselbeck. *(Courtesy Barack Obama Presidential Library)*

The nation's leading female broadcast journalists surprised Barbara in 2014 for a tribute on the set during her final regular appearance on *The View*. *(Ida Mae Astute/© ABC/Getty Images)*

When Barbara retired in 2014, the Walt Disney Company named the ABC News headquarters building after her—though she would later complain the plaque was too small. *(Slaven Vlasic/Getty Images)*

The marker on Barbara's grave in Miami. *(Photo by Romina Ruiz-Goiriena)*

"No regrets": Barbara Walters in 2012. *(Donna Svennevik/© ABC/Getty Images)*

ABC aired the interview with Assad on December 7, 2011, starting with *Good Morning America* at 7 a.m. Eastern Time, then on *The View*, then on *World News with Diane Sawyer*, and finally on a special edition of *Nightline*. Insiders at the network noticed that Diane chose not to anchor the evening news that night; David Muir subbed for her. Her absence meant she didn't have to introduce the exclusive interview that was supposed to have been hers.

"Good evening. Diane is on assignment tonight and we begin here with two major stories this evening," Muir said. "Barbara Walters and her exclusive one-on-one with Syria's embattled president, face-to-face as she asks, why the deadly crackdown? She's right here tonight."

A month later, Sherry sent a chatty email to Barbara.

"I applied for Columbia and hope to get accepted," it read. "If there is any way you think you can give my application a push, I would really, really appreciate it. You did mention you knew a professor there." She called Barbara her "adopted mother." Two days later, Barbara did try to give her application a push in an email to Richard Wald, the former ABC executive then teaching at Columbia's Graduate School of Journalism.

"This young woman, whose resume is attached, is the [daughter] of the Syrian Ambassador to the UN. She helped arrange my interview with Assad. She is only 21 but had his ear and his confidence," Barbara wrote. She noted she had applied to Columbia. "She is brilliant, beautiful, speaks five languages. Anything you can do to help?"

Wald replied the next day. He had checked: She was applying not to the graduate program at the Journalism School but to the School for International Affairs. He said he would "get them to give her special attention," although Wald told me he in fact didn't do anything to intervene. When the emails were hacked and released by Anonymous, a furor erupted both about Barbara's coziness with a source and about the university possibly giving special treatment for someone associated with Assad's brutal regime. By then, Sherry had been admitted to Columbia but in the wake of the controversy decided to attend the New School instead.

Barbara released a brief written statement. "In retrospect," she said, "I realize that this created a conflict and I regret that."

Despite the mea culpa, it wasn't at all clear she had regrets. She had none about landing the interview, however messy the road had been to get there. It was thirty-four years after her reputation-making interview with Fidel Castro, one that helped put her career back on track. Now Bashar al-Assad would close a record that no journalist was likely to ever break.

39

THE FALL

2013

She was the center of attention that evening, holding court at the party the British ambassador traditionally hosted in Washington on the eve of a presidential inauguration—in this case, the night before Barack Obama would be sworn in for a second term. Barbara Walters had interviewed Obama, of course, and more than once. She had sat down with him and Michelle Obama four times since he was first elected president, in 2008. Most recently, she had interviewed them over the Christmas holidays in 2011.

As usual, she was dressed to the nines. When she was ready to leave the British embassy, she and Susan Mercandetti, an ABC vice president, walked down the broad, curving marble staircase that gave the building's foyer its grandeur. Barbara had offered Mercandetti the use of her chauffeured car after it had ferried her back to her hotel. "Take my arm," Mercandetti said, holding it out, knowing how treacherous marble steps could be, especially for an eighty-three-year-old woman. Barbara gave her a look that made it clear she had no need of help from anyone. She ignored her when the younger woman offered her arm again near the bottom of the staircase.

Then, out of the corner of her eye, she saw Barbara's orange coat flash by as she fell forward, landing flat on her face. "Her earrings went one way; her shoes went the other way, and I saw a trickle of blood," Mercandetti told me. "And I said, 'Oh my God, she's dead.'"

Barbara wasn't dead, of course, though she was unconscious for a few seconds. When she came to, she was wounded, and she was mad.

"Do not call an ambulance, Susan," she ordered in the tone of someone accustomed to having her edicts obeyed. "Do not call an ambulance," she repeated. Mercandetti was gathering her scattered belongings and trying to shield her from the gaze of other partygoers walking down the stairs behind her. A phalanx of embassy aides quickly formed a sort of human shield around her. Even in the age of smartphones, not a single photo of the incident would surface; Barbara's allies would later give Mercandetti props for that. "You're bleeding," she told her, insisting, "We have to call an ambulance."

By now Barbara was sitting up and collecting herself. "I'm fine; I'm fine," she insisted. "Susan, I told you I don't want to go to the hospital." But there was no question that was precisely where she needed to go. Miraculously, she hadn't broken any bones, but the cut on her forehead would require six stitches to close. Two women leaving the party handed Mercandetti the names of cosmetic surgeons for the delicate job of stitching the gash without leaving a disfiguring scar. When she tried to pass on the doctors' names, Barbara impatiently waved her away. "I have my own," she said brusquely.

When the ambulance arrived to take her to George Washington University Hospital—the downtown trauma center where President Ronald Reagan had been treated after a would-be assassin shot him in 1981—she sent Mercandetti a final glare.

Mercandetti's first call on that night was to ABC News president Ben Sherwood, who was already on his way to Washington for the inauguration. "Barbara's in the hospital," she told him. "Come right to the hospital." She went there herself and stayed for hours, though Barbara had barred almost everyone from coming into her room. Mercandetti tracked down the head nurse to clear the way for Sherwood.

"The president of the network is coming and he needs to see her," she said.

"No one's going in there," the nurse replied. "She doesn't want to see anyone."

"I know, I know, but it's her boss," Mercandetti replied. "It's Barbara Walters and he needs to know that she's okay, and he's her boss." By now, she was chasing the nurse down a hospital hallway. "No, no, you don't understand. He's got to get in there. He's the president of the network." The nurse then stopped so abruptly that Mercandetti barreled into her back.

"Oh, honey," she replied, unswayed. "We have real presidents here."

When Sherwood arrived in Washington, he headed straight to the hospital. Barbara wouldn't relent. He was turned away by an unyielding guard at the entrance. He wasn't worried about her recovering "because I think she is indestructible," he told me, but he took the accident as a warning that the network had to be more "protective" of her.

By then, word already was circulating about the fall.

Peter Brown, a debonair fixture of New York society who sometimes accompanied Barbara to events, heard the news from a friend who had been at the party. He called Amanda Downes, the longtime social secretary at the embassy, on her cell phone. "Which hospital has Barbara gone to?" he asked. "You're not supposed to know anything," she replied. He pressed her. "You know how friendly I am with Barbara," he said. Indeed, he was British and had attended affairs with her at the embassy. Finally, Downes told him where she had been taken.

Then Brown called George Pineda, the majordomo who had long run Barbara's household and much of her life. He happened to be in California visiting relatives. "I said to George, 'Get on the plane to Washington now because Barbara is in the hospital and we don't know what's happened to her and how serious it is and everything,'" Brown told me, relating the conversation. "'So you need to be there fast.'"

The next morning, Mike Allen of *Politico* broke the news. "Barbara Walters Falls, Cuts Forehead," it said, a story that would be followed by wire services and TV shows and tabloids across the country. The ABC spokesman, Jeffrey Schneider, issued a written statement that used a bit of humor. "Out of an abundance of caution, she went to the hospital to have her cut tended to, have a full examination and remains there for observation," it read. "Barbara is alert (and telling everyone what to do), which we all take as a very positive sign."

But the accident turned out to be serious indeed. It would be a pivot point in her life, with repercussions from which she would never recover. In contrast, an earlier heart scare that had worried her and gotten public attention turned out to be a breeze in comparison, dealt with and done.

————

Her cardiologist had diagnosed her with aortic valve stenosis in October 2009. She delayed surgery to replace the failing valve in hopes that an experimental technique, one that was less invasive than traditional open-heart surgery, might be approved. By the next spring, though, she began to feel pressure in her chest during her regular morning walk across Central Park—at the midpoint of the park, where she would climb down and then up the steps that surrounded the Bethesda Fountain. She was understandably not enthused about undergoing open-heart surgery. She had been bragging for decades that she had never missed a day of work because of illness. She sought a second opinion from Dr. Craig Smith, the cardiologist who had performed heart surgery on Bill Clinton and Mike Nichols, then a third from another cardiologist, Dr. Jerry Gliklich.

They all advised surgery, and soon. Her condition was getting worse, Dr. Gliklich cautioned. He told her not to walk across the park anymore. The exertion could be too much. She could die.

That was enough to persuade her to schedule the surgery, but she was determined to minimize her time off the air. The operation was set for Wednesday, May 12, 2010, at the Columbia campus of New York-Presbyterian Hospital. She didn't inform David Westin, then the president of ABC News, or Bill Geddie, the cofounder and executive producer of *The View*, until that Sunday. On Monday morning, she told the world, choreographing a rosy message, just as she had for her father's health crisis decades before.

"Later this week, I am going to have surgery to replace one faulty heart valve," she announced on *The View*. She hadn't given her co-hosts a heads-up for fear someone would leak the news. "Lots of people have done this. I have known of this condition for a while now, and my doctors and I have decided that this is the best time to do the surgery. Since the summer is coming up, I can take a nice vacation."

Despite her nonchalant tone, she took steps behind the scenes that acknowledged the seriousness of the surgery. She updated her will. She wrote personal letters to her daughter, Jackie; to her longtime house-keeper, Icodel Tomlinson; and to George Pineda, with instructions to open them only if she didn't make it through the operation. She walked Jackie through her apartment, with its lifetime of artwork and memora-bilia. She told her daughter to feel free to choose anything she wanted, if the worst happened. If she died. Jackie told her she would take only a few mementos. Nothing more.

————

Jackie, at forty-one, finally seemed to have found her footing.

She had moved from Seattle to Maine—now living on the same coast as her mother, although still five hundred miles and a world away from the East Side of New York. In 2001, Jackie bought 308 acres of fields and woods off a rutted dirt road near Springfield, Maine, and hired a staff of licensed therapists. She opened a small residential program called New Horizons for New Women, designed for at-risk girls—girls with chal-lenges like those she had faced. They would stay for six to nine weeks, at a cost of $20,000 to $30,000. Then the counselors would meet with their parents to discuss what should happen next. "A blend of Outward Bound and Dr. Phil," one reporter wrote.

The program had enrolled more than three hundred girls by the time it closed seven years later.

There was still turmoil in Jackie's life, though. Like her mother, she had married more than once—first in 1996 in Blaine, Washington, to Scott Pontius, a construction worker, then in 2001 in Maine to wilder-ness guide Mark Danforth. Both marriages ended in divorce. She would then form a long-term relationship with Dennis (Tony) Pinkham, a postal worker. She and Barbara had finally reconciled. In 2001, she appeared for the first time on TV, in a joint interview with her mother for an ABC special on adoption. "Maybe it's because she has enough self-esteem,"

Barbara suggested about their rapprochement, given her daughter's new marriage and her work to launch New Horizons.

Their relationship was no longer so fraught. Some parents and children "have mutual acceptance from the beginning," Barbara said in 2008. "We didn't. We are at that point now, but it took a long time."

"We have come to appreciate each other's quirks," Jackie said.

Now, in 2010, she had flown to New York from Maine to be with her mother for the operation. "I just wanted to keep quiet and be there for her," she wrote on the day of the surgery in a small diary she was keeping. Then, at 7:30 that evening, another entry: "Dr. Smith called. I heard him say you were out of surgery, you were in recovery, and you were OK. There was something angelic about you. I have always loved you. But that moment, it was like a different connection was formed."

Jackie would snap a picture on her smartphone of her mother propped up in a hospital bed, a mass of tubes and wires draped over her right shoulder, a blood pressure cuff on her left arm. She is reading *The New York Times*.

———

The surgery had gone precisely as planned: Barbara's chest was cracked open; her heart was stopped for thirty minutes, and a heart-lung machine took over pumping her blood for more than an hour. Her failing valve was replaced with one from a cow.

She spent ten days in the hospital, then went home to recuperate. She wasn't sorry when a paparazzo staking out her apartment building snapped photos of her just two weeks later, on June 3, taking a walk. She was wearing a sleek black sweater and pants, sunglasses, and a chunky four-strand necklace of turquoise beads with matching earrings. Her hair was uncharacteristically unstyled, flat against her head, but she raised her hand in a chipper wave and there was a smile on her face. "Are you feeling OK?" the photographer shouted. "How do I look?" she replied. "You look great," he said. "That's how I feel," she said.

The pictures proved that she was alive and well—so remarkably recovered that the photo was posted not only on Celebrity-Gossip.net but also on HeartValveSurgery.com. The New York *Daily News* ran the photograph under the headline, "HELLO, GORGEOUS!" Columnist Liz Smith wrote that Barbara was "having the time of her life strolling out each day down Fifth Avenue and having truck drivers and taxi cab guys yell out, 'How ya doin', Barbara!'"

She was scheduled to make a grand return to *The View* after Labor Day, but then Obama agreed to an appearance on July 29, the first time a sitting president would go on a daytime talk show. No one was surprised when she decided to come back early for that. There was a bit of stagecraft to her entrance, to avoid the appearance that she was wobbly. When Whoopi Goldberg introduced her onstage, Jenny McCarthy moved toward her and took her arm to help her up the two steps to the platform. After Barbara thanked them for the applause and good wishes—"from the bottom of my new heart!"—she was the one who introduced Obama. "This is a historic day for *The View*," she said. "We are honored to welcome the 44th president of the United States, Barack Obama."

"Well, this is fun," Obama said as he settled on the curved yellow couch next to her. "Well, we hope so," she replied. "But you know you have, you've gone through a little bit of a beating the past month." His job-approval ratings had dipped into the mid-40s as he dealt with the repercussions of the 2008 financial meltdown and the historic Deepwater Horizon oil spill in the Gulf of Mexico. "Do you really think that being with a bunch of women, five women who never shut up, is going to be calming?"

"Look, I was trying to find a show that Michelle actually watched," he replied to laughter.

Despite the conviviality, some of those close to her were concerned that she had "less clarity" than before. There was speculation it might be an after-effect of spending hours under anesthesia; some medical studies had found elderly patients especially susceptible to cognitive decline after surgery. Sharp focus was a bigger imperative for *The View*, which aired live, than it was for the specials she was still hosting. Those shows were prerecorded and edited.

Even those who worried most were struck by how she would snap to attention when the red light of the camera went on. It was a phenomenon she had displayed since her first time on camera, on the *Today* show decades earlier, when she talked teasingly about her trip to Paris for the fashion shows with little of the nervousness she felt before and after the show.

"When the light was on, boom! She just exuded smartness and enthusiasm and energy," Deborah Roberts, a correspondent on *20/20* during Barbara's final years on the show, told me. But at the end of the day, when she was leaving the building, "all of a sudden, she just became this very quiet, almost a shell of a figure."

"She wasn't maybe quite as quick as she was seventeen years before," said a longtime producer, Alexandra (Dusty) Cohen. That said, "once she got on the air, she never missed a step, ever—ever, ever, ever. I never worried when she was on the air," she told me. "Whatever she had to do to prepare herself to be on the air, she did. I don't know what that was, but she did."

Even so, she did start to miss a step or two, even when the camera was on. At times, she had trouble tracking the conversation; she'd make a non sequitur that the others would talk past, sometimes signaling one another with a nudge under the table. She could seem uncertain when the chatter turned to young, emerging celebrities. When Jenny McCarthy, a co-host during the 2013–2014 season, told a story about meeting a fan and referred to herself in the third person, Barbara asked on the air, "Who is Jenny McCarthy?"

McCarthy treated it as a joke and moved on. "I totally brushed it off," she said later. "That's where Barbara's head was. She was spacing out. She was checking out." Backstage, Barbara would target McCarthy for criticism, the younger woman told author Ramin Setoodeh in his 2019 account of the show, *Ladies Who Punch*. She likened it to the movie *Mommie Dearest*, which portrayed actress Joan Crawford as unhinged and abusive to her adopted daughter.

Barbara already had been confiding with Anne Sweeney, then the president of the Disney/ABC Television Group, about when she should retire. "She was constantly assessing herself," Sweeney told me. "She held herself to a very high standard." Everyone remembered the embarrassing episode that had tainted the end of David Brinkley's illustrious career. On election night 1996, he said Americans could expect four more years of "goddamned nonsense" from President Bill Clinton, who had just won a second term, calling him "a bore."

Four days later, the seventy-six-year-old broadcaster apologized to Clinton and hosted his final show on *This Week.*

During one of their conversations, in 2010 or 2011, Barbara handed Sweeney a slip of paper, which she promised to keep. "If you ever ask me, wherever we are, 'Should I retire?' I will pull out the piece of paper and hand it to you," Sweeney assured her. She told me, "I carried that piece of paper for a few years."

It read: "Barbara Walters, re retirement year: 2014."

She wasn't ready to stop—in some ways, she would never be ready—but she understood the time would come. Her tumble at the British embassy that Saturday night in 2013 would make it clear just how close that time was.

It turned out that the fall was caused not by a stumble but by a fever.

She had been at a New Year's party in Florida when she gave a smooch to actor Frank Langella, who was then dating Whoopi Goldberg. He didn't realize that he was coming down with a case of shingles, a disease caused by the same virus as chickenpox. When she was getting ready for the festivities in Washington, her longtime makeup artist, Lori Klein, told her she felt feverish. So did her hairdresser, Bryant Renfroe. "You sure you're okay?" he asked her. She brushed off their concerns.

At the embassy, though, she told Jennifer Maguire Isham, a friend from the "Harpies" luncheon group, that she didn't feel well, "which is not something Barbara ever said," Maguire told me. "She said she felt hot." Later, Barbara said she fell because she was "woozy" from the fever, not because she was unsteady on her feet.

The next morning, on Sunday, she couldn't join ABC's coverage of the inauguration as planned, of course. But the network's statement that day suggested she would be off *The View* only for the better part of a week. On Tuesday, she sent word that her release from the hospital had been delayed because she was running a low-grade fever. "The doctors stitched her up and she is doing fine," Whoopi Goldberg said on *The View*, "but they want her to take it easy." They didn't disclose that she had suffered a concussion, or that she was undergoing CAT scans to monitor the risk of bleeding near her brain.

Later they reported on *The View* that she had gotten chickenpox; in fact, according to a close source, her medical diagnosis was shingles. Everyone made light of it. "We are telling you, Barbara, no scratching," Whoopi said. "We love you, we miss you. We just don't want to hug you."

"This is what you get for interviewing Honey Boo Boo," the brash child beauty pageant contestant then featured on a reality TV series, Joy Behar added to laughter.

Barbara was able to move to a New York hospital, but she was still there ten days after the fall. Despite the public reassurances, it was a sign of how serious her condition was when she missed not only the rest of January but also all of February, during crucial sweeps, when bigger audiences for a show mean higher advertising rates. She wasn't back on the air until March 4, six weeks after her fall. She walked out on the set arm in arm with Joy—a friendly gesture, and also a steadying one—and lifted her bangs to show a faint scar from the stitches and a single pockmark in the middle of her forehead.

Her return was considered so newsworthy that *ABC World News with Diane Sawyer*, ran a story about it that night by one of its top correspondents, David Muir, who would later anchor the evening news show himself. The headline was "Her Comeback," but in fact rumors were already swirling that Barbara would announce her retirement soon. Two months later, she did. She would retire from TV entirely a year later, in 2014, she announced on *The View*—the same year she had written on that slip of paper for Anne Sweeney.

"In the summer of 2014, I plan to retire from appearing on television at all," she declared. (That was a promise she would not entirely keep.) "I've had an amazing career—beyond anything I could have imagined, and I hope I have inspired some other women both in front of and behind the camera," she said. At one point, she wiped tears from her cheeks. "I want to leave while people are still saying, 'Why is she leaving?' Instead of, 'Why doesn't she leave?'"

Even so, she was never quite ready to go. As her tenure on *The View* was about to end, a colleague asked if there was anything she wanted. "More time," she replied. After the goodbye show, as women broadcasters who had lined up to honor her began to disperse, Lisa Ling asked, "Barbara, in a couple of months, are you going to be lounging in a hammock in Tahiti?" she leaned over and whispered, "They're making me quit." That wasn't quite true. It was her friends at ABC, anxious to protect her reputation and her legacy, who had quietly, carefully made the case that it was time for her to choose to retire. They would have to make one final intervention when an unexpected job offer arrived from a competing network.

———

As Barbara was recovering from the fall, another family crisis erupted. Her daughter, Jackie Guber Danforth, was struggling with substance abuse again.

She had moved to Florida from Maine when, in May 2013, she was charged with driving under the influence. Collier County sheriff's deputies had pulled over an SUV that other drivers had reported was endangering traffic on Interstate 75. Both she and her passenger, longtime boyfriend Dennis (Tony) Pinkham, appeared inebriated, the police report said, and the situation deteriorated. They said they tried to handcuff Pinkham to keep him from running into traffic. Then Jackie began shouting and tussling with the officers. "I was afraid that the suspect may run into traffic on the highway, so she was taken to the ground due to her unpredictable behavior, then secured in handcuffs," the police report said. Jackie refused to take a field sobriety test but a breathalyzer given at the jail showed her with a blood alcohol level of 0.218, a reading associated with severe impairment and more than double the Florida limit of .08.

Her mug shot, hair disheveled and cheek scraped, was splashed on news sites across the country. The mug shot for Tony, who was charged with possession of marijuana, showed an unsmiling man with salt-and-pepper hair and a mutton-chop beard. She had to post a $1,000 bond to be released, court records show, and in September was found guilty of a DUI, of driving under the influence. Her driver's license was suspended for a year.

There was one final hiccup to Barbara's carefully scripted exit from television.

Jeff Zucker had become president of CNN Worldwide a few months earlier, in January 2013. He had been hired to shake things up, and fast. He had an idea: What about landing Barbara Walters? That would be guaranteed to command attention.

He had tried to hire her from ABC once before, in 2010, when he was president and CEO of NBC Universal. "She did not, I think, feel fully appreciated" at ABC, he told me, and her celebrated tensions with Diane Sawyer were at their height. He offered her a deal to do everything she was doing at ABC. "She could have been eighty years old, but she was still the biggest star in television," he said. The move was a long shot, and it didn't work out. He wasn't sure how seriously she considered it. "My guess is she used it as leverage in her renegotiations with ABC," he said without rancor. "If I made them pay a little bit more, so be it."

Three years later, just after he moved to CNN, she announced her retirement. Once again, the chatter was that she was feeling unappreciated, "that she didn't really want to retire—that this wasn't really her choice," he said. He tried again. CNN "needed some wattage; we needed some star power; we needed some firepower."

Once again, he wasn't concerned about her age. "I don't care how old she is. She could still walk and talk, and she was Barbara Walters," he said, then added: "It was still better than most of the stuff I had."

This time, the negotiations became more serious. Zucker and two other CNN executives, Allison Gollust and Michael Bass, met twice with her and her agent at her Fifth Avenue apartment. She could do four to six interview shows a year—or however many she wanted to do—and participate in their live coverage of big events. "We were in a talent-grabbing mode," Amy Entelis, a former ABC executive who had moved to CNN to lead the talent and content development team, told me. For Barbara, it would keep her in the mix, in the news. She was flattered, and she was interested.

But those closest to her, the ones who had helped convince her it was time to step away, were alarmed. Jeffrey Schneider, the ABC spokesman who had often served as Barbara's escort to big events, called Entelis, whom he knew well.

"I was like, 'Do you think we would want her to be off the air if there wasn't a sufficiently great reason for that?'" he told me. Barbara was beginning to make missteps. There had never been a disastrous moment that went viral, but those who cared about her worried that one day soon there might be. "I mean, honestly, we would love her to do this forever, but the reason we're doing this is because we love her," he said to Entelis, who had her own decades-long friendship with Barbara.

Barbara asked Geddie what she should do. No one had worked more closely with her, and for so long. "I was absolute about it," he told me, and she finally took his advice. "It's time. Don't take another job. Your legacy is secure and complete. Don't be one of those quarterbacks that goes to some other team and doesn't make it to the Super Bowl and then retires. You've already done it. It's over."

40

THE END

2014

Oprah Winfrey stepped out from backstage first.

On Barbara's final day on *The View*, the show she had cofounded and fostered for seventeen years, she already had been feted by Hillary Clinton and Bill de Blasio. The New York mayor had proclaimed it "Barbara Walters Day" in the city. The show aired a recorded segment of Barbara Walters interviewing Barbara Walters; the faux Barbara was played by Cheri Oteri, the comedian who was the latest to impersonate her on *Saturday Night Live*. The two women wore identical neon fuchsia jackets, oversized pearls, and mops of brassy curled hair.

Word was out that the current and previous co-hosts of *The View*, all ten of them, were going to show up for her last day. That turned out to be the least of it.

"Of course I'm here; of course I'm here," Oprah said after hugging an astonished Barbara and taking a seat at the center of the table. (In fact, Oprah was said to have initially demurred when invited to appear, on the theory Barbara would never really retire from TV.) "Like everyone else, I want to thank you for being a pioneer, and everything that that word means," Oprah said to her. "It means being the first, the first in the room, to knock down the door, to break down the barriers, to pave the road that we all walk on."

What followed was a procession onstage of more than two dozen of the nation's leading female broadcasters from every network, friends and frenemies: Diane Sawyer. Robin Roberts. Lara Spencer. Elizabeth Vargas. Amy Robach. Deborah Roberts. Juju Chang. Katie Couric. Savannah Guthrie. Natalie Morales. Tamron Hall. Maria Shriver. Cynthia McFadden. Meredith Vieira. Kathie Lee Gifford. Hoda Kotb. Jane Pauley. Gayle King. Elisabeth Hasselbeck. Gretchen Carlson. Lisa Ling. Deborah Norville. Paula Zahn. Connie Chung. Joan Lunden.

They created a high-heeled traffic jam, like the stalled receiving line at a wedding, as each took a moment to embrace the star of the day, the leading woman of their industry, their fiercest competitor. They clustered onstage, applauding. Diane, wearing a neon yellow dress, claimed the prime position just behind Barbara's right shoulder and never budged, a lesson in placement she could have learned from her. "We all proudly stand on your shoulders, Barbara Walters," Oprah declared.

Producers Bill Geddie and Alexandra Cohen had engineered the extraordinary scene. "The Mount Rushmore moment," Tamron Hall called it. No one invited to appear had declined to be there, Cohen told me. (Carole Simpson, a groundbreaking anchor herself, complained to others afterward that she hadn't been included, an inadvertent oversight.) They had managed to keep their plan secret. Barbara was rarely overwhelmed on the air, but this time, she seemed almost speechless.

"It was a shock to her," said Whoopi Goldberg, who had a bird's-eye view, sitting just across the curved table from her. "I think Barbara never really was convinced that she was as good as she was," she told me. "I think it took her a long time to understand that people really meant what they said the way they said it."

"I just want to say, this is my legacy," Barbara finally declared, gesturing to the high-powered women all around her. "These are my legacy."

Oprah's initial instinct turned out to be right. Barbara's official send-off included that tableau of top journalists, a two-hour prime-time special, and a plaque in the lobby naming ABC News headquarters after her. But she wasn't quite ready to step away.

Just three weeks passed before ABC announced she would be back to interview filmmaker Peter Rodger for *20/20*. He had asked that she be the one to talk with him about his son, Elliot, who in May had killed six people in a rampage near the University of California, Santa Barbara. It was a good "get," especially at the moment, but it was no historic sit-down with Sadat and Begin, no Monica Lewinsky exclusive. Still, it was enough to draw her back on the air.

A few months later, she called Geddie, who had been pushed out as executive producer of *The View* after she left. "I think I could do another *Fascinating People*," she told him, the year-end specials they had launched in 1993. ABC was happy to accommodate; the 2013 show had dominated its ninety-minute time period with total viewers and in key demographics, although perhaps in part because it had been billed as the final one. "I was absolutely delighted when ABC approached me to do another year of *10 Most Fascinating People*," she was quoted as saying in the official announcement, a less-than-candid explanation of its resurrection. "I know we said last year was our last, but there are just too many fascinating people out there."

Her list for 2014 included human rights lawyer Amal Clooney, singer Taylor Swift, billionaire Elon Musk—and, of course, Oprah. But the ratings tumbled from the previous year, especially among the sought-after group of 18-to-49-year-olds.

A year later, Geddie had moved to the West Coast and was working on new projects when Barbara called again. "I think just one more," she said.

By then, in 2015, she was eighty-six years old and showing her age. One of her choices of the ten most fascinating people of the year was actor Bradley Cooper. "I find you very screwable," she told him during a discussion of his sex appeal, a quip that didn't make it on the air. He was forty, young enough to be her grandson. "Thank you," he replied politely. During taping for the show, she asked comedian Amy Schumer if she ever faked orgasms, a topic explored in her latest movie, *Trainwreck*. The comedian responded, graphically, and then turned the question around. "Have you ever faked it?" she asked. "I'm not going to tell you," Barbara replied. Why not? "Because I have this image of myself as being dignified and so on." That was precisely the problem, some friends worried—that she was putting her dignity and her hard-won reputation at risk by being unable to leave the spotlight.

At the top of her list that year was Caitlyn Jenner, but she declined to sit down with Barbara. It was Diane Sawyer who got the interview in which she confirmed that she was no longer Bruce and identified as a woman. Another of the "most fascinating" people Barbara chose that year was Donald Trump.

She had repeatedly interviewed Trump on *20/20* and on *The View* when he was a New York real estate developer, then a reality TV host of *The Apprentice*. Now he was on more serious terrain, running for the Republican nomination for president of the United States, an office he would unexpectedly win a year later. He was controversial. Journalists weren't sure how seriously to take his most outrageous remarks. In other words, he was a ripe target for a classic Barbara Walters Interview.

That's not what she delivered. Their conversation lacked the crispness, the crackle that characterized her best sit-downs. She seemed to be reading down a list of prepared questions on a sheet of paper; it trembled in her hand. He was the one leaning forward, trying to give the interview energy. Does he regret his call for a ban on Muslim immigrants? "Not at all," he said. Is he a bigot? "Probably the least of anybody you ever met," he declared. Could he defeat Hillary Clinton? "She doesn't have the strength or the stamina." Was that because she's a woman? He didn't respond to that question, and she didn't follow up.

Barbara may not have been ready to move on, but Americans were. The ratings dropped. "Barbara Walters' Picks Prove to Be 29% Less Fascinating," the headline in *TVLine* read. It would be the last of the twenty-two-year *Most Fascinating* franchise. After a half-century since she was hired as the "girl writer" for the *Today* show and began pitching stories to the producer, she was finally off the air.

———

Barbara was all too familiar with the cognitive decline that can come with age. Her mother had suffered from dementia for years before she died, at times unable to recognize her own daughter. It was the final, frustrating chapter in their complicated relationship. Socialite and philanthropist Brooke Astor had been a good friend; when she was in her nineties, Barbara watched her slip into the fog of Alzheimer's disease. She ended up being a witness at the trial of Astor's only child, Anthony Marshall. Accused of taking advantage of his mother's illness to trick her out of millions of dollars, he would be convicted of first-degree grand larceny.

Brooke was "in and out" mentally at her hundredth birthday party in 2002, Barbara testified in his trial in state Supreme Court. A few months later, when Barbara dropped by to see Brooke again, she was confused. Then she stopped recognizing her at all. "After that last visit, I felt that there was no purpose in my visiting," Barbara told the court. "I wasn't bringing her any pleasure, and it was painful." Painful for the visitor to see a friend so diminished, and no comfort for the patient—a lesson she would take to heart in her own life.

By now, she was putting her financial house in order. Her wealth, accumulated through a lifetime of hard work and tough negotiation, meant she could ensure her own financial well-being for the rest of her life, however long it might be. She settled an inheritance on her daughter, Jackie, now living in Florida. She began to bestow some significant charitable contributions. In October 2014, she completed three contributions totaling $10 million to New York-Presbyterian/Columbia Medical Center, where she had undergone her heart valve surgery; they named the Acute Care Treatment Center after her. The size of the gift was the result of "working a very long time," she joked. "I've been working since Abraham Lincoln."

The following February, in 2015, she donated $15 million to Sarah Lawrence, where she had graduated from college, to build the Barbara Walters Campus Center. It was the largest single contribution in the school's history. A year earlier, she had donated her archives there. But when construction on the new building began in 2018, Sarah Lawrence said without explanation that she "could not join the groundbreaking festivities." By then, Barbara was almost never seen in public. Instead, college officials, students, and the Bronxville mayor lined up on a clear, cold January day with shovels to turn over spades of dirt on the site.

Like her friend Brooke, friends said Barbara began to be "in and out."

Six months after she retired from *The View*, the supermarket tabloids were already starting to report that she suffered from dementia. For years, it would be a trope in their coverage of her and her disappearance from the public scene. That wasn't the real story, though. Even in her declining years she managed to avoid disclosure of a painful truth. Only a few in her innermost circle knew her actual diagnosis.

The fall on the steps at the British embassy had been the source of her long decline. According to three knowledgeable sources, the traumatic injury to her brain over time led to a case of hydrocephalus, sometimes called water on the brain. With this condition, a buildup of fluid in the ventricles within the brain puts harmful pressure on the brain's tissues. The neurological disorder can affect patients' balance and make it hard for them to walk, prompting some to use a shuffling gait. As it develops, it can change their personality, impair their cognition, erode their memory, and lead to dementia.

Barbara was cared for by some of the most highly regarded doctors in the field. With reluctance, she agreed to have a shunt inserted in her brain to drain the excess fluid. But while the symptoms can sometimes be controlled and even reversed with treatment, the condition can't be cured, and its effects can be progressive.

Just a month after her official goodbye on *The View*, she attended a party hosted by *The New York Times* for its Opinion section; when an aide in the Carter White House who had worked with her through the years greeted her, she had no idea who he was. But in October, she was sharp and clear in an interview with David Gergen at the John F. Kennedy School at Harvard that stretched for more than an hour. A year later, in 2015, there was no flash of recognition when a *New York* magazine reporter who had interviewed her several times came up to say hello at a book party. At the New York premiere of Woody Allen's *Café Society* in 2016, a society photo showed her in a pantsuit that looked too large for her frame; the pants puddled around her shoes. She was wearing Chanel shoes, but they were flats; she no longer risked wearing more fashionable high heels. She smiled for the camera, looking a bit lost.

That year, Lynn Sherr met Barbara for lunch at Michael's, a favorite bistro on West 55th Street. "She was already not the same person," the former *20/20* correspondent told me. "She was not playful and fun. She seemed angry and there were long pauses. I had never in my life sat with Barbara and there were silences."

Another former colleague, Susan Mercandetti, took her to lunch at Bistro Chat Noir, a cozy restaurant a half-block off Central Park. The two women had worked together at ABC and later, when Mercandetti was working for a publishing house and Barbara was writing her memoir. "She was in her glass-half-empty mode," Mercandetti told me. "She was unhappy about how she never got her due." Her successors, from Diane Sawyer to Katie Couric, had an easier time than she did, she said, thanks to her. She couldn't be coaxed out of her funk. "No matter what I said—'You're the biggest star, you're Barbara Walters'—she wasn't hearing anything. She was just angry at the world."

She seemed unable to take comfort in the career she had, the life she lived. She had always been determined and competitive—breaking ground demanded that—but now she became increasingly angry and bitter. She was resentful and dismissive of some of the women who followed her, even the ones who paid her homage. Only Oprah seemed to be a worthy successor. None of the awards and accolades would be enough.

She had always believed that if she wasn't in the spotlight, if she wasn't in command, that she would no longer be welcome at the intimate dinners and splashy galas that meant so much to her. Now she turned those fears into a self-fulfilling prophecy, pushing away friends and isolating herself, even from those who reached out. Only a handful of people were allowed to visit. Her makeup artist, Lori Klein, was one of them. After decades of working together, they were close. "I'd go over there; we'd put *The View* on, and I would reminisce about stories to make her laugh," Lori told me.

But Barbara's world, once so large, was fast contracting.

"The tragedy is that she got herself into this isolation that she now suffers by not being able to bear the thought that she was not a central figure publicly," Henry Kissinger, a close friend, told me in an interview in his New York office six months before she died. "That was unbelievably hard for her." She stopped going to an annual Christmas celebration hosted by Oscar and Annette de la Renta in Punta Cana, in the Dominican Republic, "because she didn't want to be seen and not recognized."

"We all loved her for her special qualities," Kissinger said, but "towards the end, her public persona became her real persona."

New York Post columnist Cindy Adams, long her booster, became her protector as rumors of dementia circulated. "Everyone now interviews anyone . . . but before today's Lilliputians, only one giant existed. Barbara," Adams wrote in her column on April 16, 2018. "Today, looking great, she lives grandly with assistants, antiques, paintings, scrapbooks, files, friends and chief of staff over 20 years, George Pineda." The column wasn't true. The woman who had delighted in going out, in being seen, had become a recluse. She had times of clarity but also times of confusion.

Louise Grunwald, one of her closest friends, tried to coax her to go outside, to enjoy Central Park, even if it meant using her wheelchair. "I said, 'Barbara, you and I have walked down the street with your baseball cap and your sunglasses. Nobody can recognize you.'" She was unpersuaded. "'What if the paparazzi are there?'" she would reply. Grunwald told me: "It was always about the paparazzi."

Cindy Adams's column prompted a good friend of Barbara to send her one last email. Lorinda Ash was a generation younger than Barbara, but they had become confidantes who had lunched, shopped, and gone to shows together. Both were friends with Woody Allen. "She gave me a lot of great advice," Ash told me, "including not to neglect my personal life and to get remarried because growing old alone was no fun."

But Barbara had stopped responding when she reached out. "Dear Barbara, I think of you every morning when I walk the dogs in the park, across from your apartment," Ash wrote. "I loved Cindy Adams' column about you yesterday. I hope you are doing well. Can I come visit you perhaps this weekend for a few minutes? I'd love to catch up. Are you up to coming over for dinner or just the two of us or perhaps with the Allens one night? With love, Lorinda."

Barbara sent an email in response, the last note Ash would receive from her.

"Dear Lorinda, I myself love the column too. Even though I am not going out yet, I keep myself very busy. Keep in touch. Much love, Barbara."

As time passed, friends said their invitations weren't acknowledged, their calls not returned. George Pineda had worked as a butler for Merv Adelson, her third husband, and then ended up in Barbara's employ after the couple divorced. Now he was the chief of staff managing most of her personal affairs, to the annoyance of some of those who could no longer get through to her. Even her trusted hairdresser and confidant Bryant Renfroe stopped hearing from her. For her ninetieth birthday in 2019, he sent her the ninety front pages of *The New York Times* from September 25, the day of her birth. The pages were bound in a red spiral cover, modeled on the book of contacts and phone numbers she had always carried with her. By then, he hadn't seen her in two years. There was no response.

In March 2016, she did manage to attend the funeral of Carol Guber.

Carol had been a teenager when her father, Lee Guber, married Barbara. The two immediately hit it off, with an easier relationship than Barbara had with daughter Jackie. Barbara would jokingly sign her letters to Carol as "your evil stepmother." More than once, she gave her instructions about what to do when she died; both assumed the older woman would pass away first. She wanted their kinship recognized, even if her marriage to Lee hadn't lasted. "At my funeral, you've got to be in the front row, and you say, 'I was her daughter.' You make sure you're up there," she told her. Carol's son, Noah Shachtman, remembered how determined she had been about that. "She was like, 'I want you to be at my funeral and say, "I was your daughter," "I was your grandson."'"

But Carol died first, and suddenly. She was sixty-nine years old; Barbara was eighty-six. "Barbara was already in really declining health by then, and still came to the memorial, which nobody expected," Shachtman, a journalist who has been editor-in-chief of *The Daily Beast* and of *Rolling Stone*, told me. The services were held on a Sunday evening at the Or Olam synagogue on the East Side.

"It was the first time I had seen her in a while," Shachtman said. "It was pretty intense." He believed she had "willed herself" to be able to handle the service, to remember the girl who had in better days been as close as a daughter.

The glimpses of Barbara Walters, of the old Barbara Walters, became rare.

She had always admired the blunt-spoken Arizona senator John McCain, and the feeling was mutual; he had encouraged his reluctant daughter, Meghan, to accept an offer to be a co-host on *The View*. When her father died in 2018, she went off the show for weeks, then returned. An email from Barbara arrived, the font size blown up to an enormous 24 points, presumably to make it easier to read as she wrote it.

"Dear Meghan, I am so sad for you, but like a trooper you are back at work," she wrote. "Your father was a giant of a man and you have inherited his stamina and sense of purpose. I send you a big hug. Barbara Walters."

———

Michael Bloomberg had been a frequent guest over the years at Barbara's dinner parties, renowned for their mix of extraordinary guests and for the conversations she would direct. (It was at one of her dinners in 1977 that an inebriated Hamilton Jordan, then the White House chief of staff, created an international furor when he plucked at the low neckline of the wife of the Egyptian ambassador, looked down, and announced, "I have just seen the twin pyramids of the Nile.") Barbara had begun inviting Bloomberg before he was a big name on the city's social scene, before the billionaire businessman would run and win three terms as mayor of New York.

"To be a friend of Barbara Walters added to your star power, your luster, your résumé—to be seen with Barbara, to have Barbara mention you or to have Barbara invite you to her table," he told me. She had described him as an appealing guest. "He's straight, intelligent, and attractive," she said. They would make a public show of flirting, although they never had a romantic relationship. "I have always teased that if I could meet Michael ten years older, this would be the man I'd run off with," she said.

(She was a dozen years older than he was.) He replied, "When Barbara needs a walker, she calls me"—that is, an appropriate man to escort her to big events.

In 2003, the co-hosts of *The View* chose their perfect husbands for a "fantasy wedding" series. While some of the others settled on movie stars, she picked Bloomberg. "Because I thought he's cute as can be and he's rich," she explained. "Who wouldn't want that?" For a comic bit, she carried a gaudy oversized torch and wore a rhinestone tiara as she stood next to his cardboard cutout. Bloomberg, then in his first term as mayor, showed up onstage. "Did you really think I was going to miss my own wedding?" he asked. He was back on *The View* a decade later, on the day she announced her retirement. By then, he was in his last term at City Hall. "I would like to tell you, it was never consummated," she said of their "marriage." "Hope springs eternal," Bloomberg replied.

Her dinners had introduced him to a heady mix of politicians and business leaders and movie stars and journalists, some of them new to him. Ten or twelve guests would be invited, or perhaps summoned, to sit around the table in her dining room. "What you would call in the *New York Post* 'boldfaced names,'" Bloomberg told me. "Interesting people who had accomplished things and really had something to say, whether you agreed with them or not." She would always start the dinner by going around the group, posing some provocative query. "She would get one conversation going around the table and insisted, if anybody had a side conversation, she would stop them," he said, a practice he would adopt when he hosted small dinners of his own.

After her retirement, she stopped hosting the dinners at her apartment or accepting invitations to dinners at his. As she became increasingly isolated, rumors about her well-being swirled. Bloomberg wanted to check in on her in person; he had the stature to insist. "I remember thinking she was a friend and had included me in dinner parties that I was honored to be in. Particularly in the beginning, when I was less jaded, maybe, was thrilled to be at. And I thought it'd just be a nice thing to do."

He visited her on August 30, 2018. By then, she was seeing few people outside of family members and caregivers. When he arrived, she was sitting quietly in the living room. "She was on a couch, I remember, and didn't move very much," he said. "She nodded and said 'hello,'" but he wasn't sure whether she knew who he was. He asked Pineda if she knew him, if she would remember that he had visited. Probably not, Pineda told him.

"I wouldn't use the word 'shocking,'" Bloomberg said of that last visit. "I would use the word, 'sad.'"

He could glimpse into the dining room, decorated in soft peach and green, the big round table at its center, a portrait of herself from happier days on the wall. Now the room was empty and still.

For years, her closest friends maintained a conspiracy of silence about her decline, even after she had disappeared from public view. Cindy Adams's column in 2018 insisting that she was "looking great" and living grandly was part of that. After all, Barbara had always believed that when it came to her private life, she had the right to tell her own version of the truth.

A few days after Barbara died, Cindy wrote a column that described with more honesty the final years of her lifelong friend. Her disclosures prompted an unhappy stir among some of those who wanted to protect Barbara's reputation, even at the end. "Barbara then . . . slowly . . . inch-by-inch . . . inexplicably began frazzling," Cindy wrote in the *New York Post*. "She fell faint. A fall. Forgetful. Repetition." A hospital room was set up in her apartment. She stopped receiving guests or venturing outside. "Then walking became a wheelchair. Then her conversation stopped."

The interviewer who had built her career on talking—on posing hard questions and drawing out surprising answers—was silent. She died in her apartment on Friday, December 30, 2022, on the cusp of a new year.

———

Barbara would have liked this: ABC News announced her death at age ninety-three by breaking into an edition of *20/20*, the newsmagazine she had co-hosted for twenty-five years, the program that had broadcast some of her most memorable interviews. But she surely would have preferred a moment with better ratings than the night before New Year's Eve. And she might well have been annoyed that Pope Benedict XVI died a day later, stealing some of the weekend's obituary thunder.

"We are interrupting regular programming to bring you some sad news," ABC correspondent Phil Lipof somberly declared. "Legendary newswoman, friend, and colleague to so many here, Barbara Walters, has died at the age of ninety-three. She died peacefully at her home earlier this evening."

Lipof wasn't one of the many who had been her friend and colleague. Hired at ABC News a year earlier, he happened to be on duty during the holiday weekend. He had already anchored a newscast on the network's streaming service and was taking a break to eat take-out barbecue for dinner before going back on the air to introduce *Nightline* at 11 p.m. Then the call came to the newsroom that Barbara had died. "I was just thinking, we need to get on air; we need to do this right," Lipof told me. "We need to do right by Barbara and be as compassionate, as comprehensive as we can be."

For the next hour and a half, Lipof conducted a stream of phone interviews on the air with those who did know her: David Muir, Deborah Roberts, Katie Couric, Joan Lunden, Connie Chung, Elizabeth Vargas, and producer David Sloan. Lipof did a competent, respectful job on the fly. But critics would snipe that one of the network's stars, Muir or George Stephanopoulos or Robin Roberts, should have been called in to make the announcement. "Barbara Walters would not have been pleased," media critic Dylan Byers wrote on the website *Puck*. "News of her death was reported on ABC, her near life-long home, by Phil Lipof, a little-known correspondent who was filling in on one of the least-watched days of the year."

It was, after all, the passing of one of the most famous and influential TV journalists in history, a figure who for decades had defined the network.

There was an outpouring on Twitter, the platform on which @barbarajwalters hadn't posted in years yet still had 1.4 million followers. "Barbara Walters has always been an example of bravery and truth—breaking barriers while driving our nation forward," President Joe Biden tweeted. There were tributes from politicians and journalists and actors and athletes and viewers. "She cared about the truth and she made us care too," Kareem Abdul-Jabbar posted.

"The greatest of them all, by far," said Donald Trump. "I knew her well, was interviewed by her many times, and there was nobody like the legendary Barbara Walters—And never will be!"

———————

Friends were dismayed when there was no grand memorial service, nothing like the 2005 celebration honoring Peter Jennings after he died, held in Carnegie Hall, across the street from the apartment Barbara had once occupied. That two-hour service had featured actors (Alan Alda), musicians (Yo-Yo Ma, Wynton Marsalis), journalists (Ted Koppel), the Royal Canadian Mounted Police, bagpipes—and Barbara in the audience.

After attending events like that, she would banter about who would speak at her memorial, but by the end of her life those in contact with her said she cared less about that. Daughter Jackie, who had always been so private, rebuffed ABC's proposals to hold a big event, according to network insiders, and company executives decided it wouldn't be appropriate to proceed without her.

Barbara's remains were cremated and buried, with no word even to some of her closest friends, next to Dena and Jackie and Lou at Lakeside Memorial Park in Miami. Their small black and gold markers sit in narrow marble frames, flat to the ground alongside a quiet path. Jackie's marker remembers her as "beloved daughter and sister," Dena's as "beloved wife and mother," Lou's as "beloved husband and father."

Unlike the others, Barbara's marker doesn't call her "beloved," and it doesn't mention her role as a daughter or a wife or a mother. She has a distinctive parting message of her own.

"No regrets," it reads. "I had a great life."

THE RULEBREAKER

It's no fun being nobody, not having enough money to enjoy life, being trapped. It's wonderful to be somebody.

Barbara Walters had only started her journey on the road to being some-body when she made that declaration of intent in 1972. By then, she had managed to move from behind-the-scenes to on-the-air at NBC's *Today* show, but other women had held a role on the show before. It would be two years before she was named the first female co-host of a network's morning show, four years before she became the first female co-anchor of an evening news show, twenty-five years before she would create a day-time talk show that reinvented television conversation.

By then, there would be no denying she was somebody. No other woman had risen as high as she did in the world of TV news. No other person had done more to shape and rule what stands as its golden age. She redefined whose stories were considered worthy of telling and what questions they could be asked. She interviewed a wider range and a larger number of the world's political leaders than anyone else, before or since, giving Americans a personal introduction even to despots and dictators. She had an impact on the country's evolving culture, too, on the willing-ness to explore sensitive topics from rearing transgender kids to consider-ing the afterlife. Her questions and the emotional reactions they often provoked—even an Army general with the moniker "Stormin' Norman" cried when she asked about his father—helped open the door for the powerful to express their vulnerabilities in public.

In the process, Barbara earned the highest ratings in the business, commanded the attention of the country, and became one of the most famous faces on the globe. Over the decades, she appeared a dozen times on The Gallup Poll's list of the most admired women of the year, in the company of Queen Elizabeth II and Mother Teresa.

Yet she never stopped battling journalism's traditionalists—the "Capital J Journalists"—about whether she really belonged in their ranks. "Even though they've seen everything she's done, they still don't give her the gravitas," Whoopi Goldberg told me, then corrected herself. "Women do. Men do not." Over decades of proving herself, Barbara faced sexism, at first blatant and then more subtle. She got her first writing job in TV "mostly because she had a darling ass," a CBS producer would recall. Even after she had achieved iconic status, Peter Jennings would at times be so slighting of her on the air when they co-anchored breaking news events that it sparked public comment. "Rude and peremptory," columnist Liz Smith called his manner during coverage of O. J. Simpson's two-hour car chase down Los Angeles freeways in 1994. Barbara was privately wounded by *Saturday Night Live* caricatures that mocked her speech, her mannerisms, the pronunciation of her name. She exulted in tributes from female journalists who followed her but also resented the easier path they walked because of the price she had paid.

"When I talk to the old guys in the business, they see her as someone who has cast-iron testicles, you know what I mean?" Bill Geddie, her longtime executive producer and co-creator of *The View*, told me. Those closest to her, though, said she was propelled not by her strength but by her uncertainties. "I think she woke up every day saying, 'Have I done enough? Do they still like me? What do I have to do to extend this? How do I make this work?' I think that's who she really is."

"While she could be dishy and funny and irreverent and all those wonderful things with her girlfriends, there was a hole that I think never got filled, an itch that never got scratched," Cynthia McFadden, an ABC colleague and friend to Barbara, told me. "My standard line to her was,

'If only you could appreciate your success as much as the rest of us have benefited from it.' But she wasn't able to."

She was, oddly enough, afraid of heights. She was also the most driven person most of her friends and co-workers had ever met.

Her distant father, her disabled sister, her up-and-down childhood left Barbara feeling both responsible for her family and unsure whether she was up to the task. She remembered, like a scar that wouldn't heal, the single sentence Lou Walters had written in his daughter's college application for Sarah Lawrence. "Barbara is a very normal girl with normal interests," he had said. What could be more impersonal? More dismissive?

She was nearly eighty years old and researching her memoir when she read the actual application for the first time. That nine-word sentence turned out to be the conclusion of a four-page evaluation by her father that was laced with warmth. She took "good interest" in her schoolwork, he said; he was proud of her "good work and good marks." She was able to make "friends easily and hold them." She read "a great deal" and was "literary-minded." She had both "initiative and creative ability." She had "no trait" that dismayed him and not "any bad habits."

That was the sort of affectionate praise he had rarely expressed to her in person, feelings that she had never been entirely confident he held. It was as though she had discovered a sled labeled "Rosebud," too late to make a difference. She had always assumed that his perfunctory assessment of her was "proof that he didn't know me at all," she wrote. "Reading now what he actually wrote, I realize that it's quite the opposite—I didn't know him."

———

Despite her coiffed hair and society pals, Barbara Walters was at heart a rulebreaker, even a revolutionary. Sometimes she didn't exactly break the rules; she simply ignored them, as though they couldn't possibly apply to her. Women can't do serious interviews? Just watch her. Reporters can't hide in the bathroom at Camp David in hopes of landing an exclusive? Send out a search party. Seniors in their sixties and seventies and eighties should quietly step back and let the next generation grab the spotlight? Forget it.

At a time when ambition was seen as unladylike, Barbara plowed into a profession that wasn't ready to welcome her. She ignored the edict that female voices didn't sound authoritative enough to deliver the news, that female temperaments made women unsuited for the rigors of the highest ranks of the field. She dismissed any conflict about being interested not only in Washington but also in Hollywood—after all, wasn't the audience intrigued by both?—and with that blurred the line between entertainment and news. To the tsk-tsking of the graybeards, she commanded higher salaries than any journalist had ever made, though their high-minded objections didn't prevent them from demanding raises themselves. She became a brand.

She broke barriers not only as a woman but also as a woman who dared to age on the air, defying the expectation that while men gained authority, women became obsolete. (Admittedly, that defiance only went so far. Her hair got blonder as she aged, and her face remained remarkably free of wrinkles.) She was sixty-seven when she started *The View*, eighty-four when she finally relinquished her seat at the table.

"Without Barbara Walters there wouldn't have been me—nor any other woman you see on evening, morning, and daily news," Oprah Winfrey said when Barbara died, posting a photo on Instagram that showed younger versions of themselves sitting on a bench, arms around each other, smiling. At the audition for her first TV job in the 1970s, long before the two had met, Oprah consciously imitated the manner she had seen Barbara display on the *Today* show. "For the first year of my television career, I thought I was Barbara—Black," she said. "I just had her in my mind, for inspiration."

For decades, Barbara would be a role model for thousands of women, most of whom she would never meet. By the time she passed away, no network morning show would have dared field an all-male team of anchors. A woman, Norah O'Donnell, sat in Walter Cronkite's chair at the *CBS Evening News*. A woman, Kim Godwin, was president of ABC News, and the first Black woman to lead a major network's news division. Women were the head or co-head of NBC News, CBS News, and Fox News.

But seeing Barbara only as a groundbreaking woman in broadcasting underestimates her legacy. She was one of the most influential journalists of either gender in an industry that was just beginning to understand its possibilities when she got her first job. She is on the short list of those who have left the biggest imprints on television news, a group that also includes Edward R. Murrow, Mike Wallace, Walter Cronkite, Roone Arledge, Roger Ailes, and Oprah Winfrey.

"Barbara Walters is the patron saint of TV news," said Steven D. Stark, author of a book exploring television's impact on American culture. "For better or worse, she created what we now think of as television news."

———

Achieving that distinction wasn't free, and it didn't happen by accident.

She divorced a trio of husbands and struggled with her only child from adolescence into adulthood, although they eventually made their peace. "I don't think you can have it all," Barbara said when daughter Jackie was twelve, saying the women's movement had exaggerated the possibility of having both a demanding career and a rich personal life. "[I]f I am the epitome of the woman who has it all, let me tell you something. There are many things that tear me apart. I pay a price."

After retirement, as she began to lose her mobility and her memory, she pushed away even many of her closest friends. For the final years of her life, she was tended to by her chief-of-staff and paid caretakers in her Fifth Avenue apartment, permitting few others to see her. After a lifetime of being at the center of almost everything, the solitude was poignant, the silence resounding.

"It would have been nice to have had several children, you know," she said at age seventy-eight, looking back. Her daughter had rejected her entreaties to give her grandchildren. "It would be nice to have, you know, a marriage now in its 40th year. I mean, you're asking me if I'm happy, yes, but you know, those are things I don't have."

She loved her job and savored her success. She exulted in the power and the praise, the multimillion-dollar fortune she had earned and the accolades she had won. But I asked dozens of her friends and colleagues a knottier question: Was she happy?

"I think she was very happy with many, many aspects of her life, including her career, motherhood, and strong, loving friendships," Nancy Shevell McCartney, a second cousin so close that she came to consider Barbara a surrogate mother, told me. "Maybe for a minute, she thought to herself, 'I should have a more domestic side to my life.' But I think after that minute she realized that her life was complete and fulfilling."

But most of the others I asked concluded, some reluctantly, that the answer was "no," or at least not exactly "yes." "Happy-ish," suggested Joy Behar, the panelist on *The View* with the longest tenure. Not one described her as content. "She was essentially restless," Diane Sawyer told me. "Happiness or not, I do think the restlessness kept her moving."

"I didn't know her to be happy," said Ben Sherwood, a former president of ABC News. "I knew her to be hard-charging and driving and relentless and insatiable and unquenchable and indestructible." But even after her biggest triumphs, her most celebrated interviews, she would seem to feel satisfaction only for a moment. "I knew her to be empty almost immediately afterwards, trying to figure out: How do we top that?"

Near the end of her career, she sometimes wondered whether it had all been worth it.

"What does being 'Barbara Walters' mean?" Oprah asked her in 2004.

"Sometimes it's okay—and sometimes I can't drive," Barbara replied, a comment that may be more revealing than the non sequitur it seems to be. *Sometimes it's okay—and sometimes I can't drive.* She was shorthanding a comment Jackie had once made in describing her: "My mommy can't cook. My mommy can't drive. My mommy can only do television." In more direct words, perhaps, she relished what "being Barbara Walters" meant, but she realized that she had missed out on some of life's fundamentals. She had never learned to drive a car, or to sustain an intimate relationship. "Most of the time when I look back on what I've done, I think, 'Did I do that?' And you know what I say to myself? 'Why didn't I enjoy it more? Was I working too hard to see it?'"

She gestured toward the gallery of photographs in her apartment showing her with the most famous people in the world. "Look at all those pictures in the hallway," she said. "Look at what I accomplished. Yet I was always on to the next thing."

When she retired in 2014, ABC News named its headquarters after her, the building at 44 West 66th Street where she had worked for nearly four decades. (Nothing lasts forever: A decade later, ABC was poised to move to newly built Disney headquarters on Hudson Square, in lower Manhattan.) "I want to make something very clear, that each and every one of you, from the desk assistant to the producers to the correspondents and anchors, each of you who walk through these doors every day, yeah, my name is going to be on this building, but this building belongs to you," she said during a ribbon-cutting ceremony that included Walt Disney Company CEO Bob Iger and Ben Sherwood, Diane Sawyer and George Stephanopoulos.

"The Barbara Walters Building," the brass plaque declared, gold letters on a black background. "In recognition of Barbara Walters' historic achievements and contributions to the fields of journalism and broadcasting for the past five decades."

Still, she soon complained to a *Variety* reporter that the plaque was too small. "You have to really search to find it," she told Ramin Setoodeh, demanding, "Tell me where it is. You don't even know. I'm not being humble. I do not know where it is."

The plaque may have been smaller than she wanted, but in fact it was in the middle of the main wall of the lobby, framed in gold and surrounded by photos of herself and the ABC stars who hadn't had the building named after them. It was where every visitor had to pass, where it was impossible to miss. Where she was impossible to miss.

Acknowledgments

When it comes to acknowledging appreciation, let me start with Barbara Jill Walters.

Her groundbreaking life was extraordinary both for her determination and her demons, creating a legacy that continues to resonate today. I am sorry that her health made it impossible for me to interview her in person for this biography. Fortunately, she had lived her life out loud. The hundreds of interviews she gave and the thousands of interviews she conducted provided a window into the hurdles she faced and the mountains she climbed.

Many of those who worked with her and those who were close to her provided important information and insights. I'm grateful to them for their trust and their time. In particular, my thanks to Kerry Smith and the leadership at ABC News and to Cindi Berger, Barbara's longtime publicist, for their cooperation. Two previous books, *Barbara Walters: An Unauthorized Biography*, by Jerry Oppenheimer, published in 1990, and *Ladies Who Punch: The Explosive Inside Story of The View*, by Ramin Setoodeh, published in 2019, were especially useful resources, as was Barbara's 2008 memoir, *Audition*. I appreciate the help of Abby Lester and Christina Kasman, archivists at Sarah Lawrence's Esther Raushenbush Library, which houses Barbara Walters's papers.

My agents, Matt Latimer and Keith Urbahn of Javelin, once again were invaluable every step of the way, starting with the notion of Barbara Walters as a subject. They have made every aspect of this project possible and better. My researcher, Lillianna Byington, was a crucial partner, as she has been before. This account is richer and more accurate because of her intelligence and her diligence. Romina Ruiz-Goiriena delivered remarkable research assistance in Miami. My editor, Priscilla Painton of Simon & Schuster, is an author's dream, with smarts and skills that are threaded through this book. My thanks to the entire Simon & Schuster team, led by Jonathan Karp and including Hana Park, Lisa Healy, Fred Chase, Carolyn Levin, Julia Prosser, Elizabeth Herman, Stephen Bedford, Elizabeth Venere, Jackie Seow, Amanda Mulholland, Paul Dippolito, Joy O'Meara, Debbie Friedman, and Catherine Foster.

Of course, any errors are mine alone.

I am proud of my association with *USA Today* and grateful for the support of my bosses there, among them Maribel Perez Wadsworth, Nicole Carroll, Kristin Roberts, Terence Samuel, and Caren Bohan. Family members and friends helped at key moments. Kevin Bohn and Leslie Bennetts shared their encyclopedic knowledge and endless enthusiasm. Mimi Hall and Lee Horwich were early and perceptive readers. Dr. Lynn Montz gave guidance on medical passages and Michael Dee on legal ones. Carl Leubsdorf Jr. provided tech support, even at inconvenient times.

As always, Carl Leubsdorf Sr. was my first, my last, my most demanding, and my most appreciative reader.

Thank you.

Source Notes

Persons Interviewed

My thanks to those who agreed to be interviewed for this biography. They include:

David Adler

Mike Allen

Lorinda Ash

Robert Barnett

David Bauder

Joy Behar

Geoffrey Bennett

Leslie Bennetts

Cindi Berger

Brad Blakeman

Michael Bloomberg

Bill Boggs

Peter Brown

Kimberly Butler

Amanda Butterbaugh

Bill Carter

Chris Christie

Connie Chung

Alexandra Cohen

Richard Cohen

Ann Compton

Paul Costello

Katie Couric

John Dickerson

Bob Dole

Sam Donaldson

Susan Douglas

Carol Edgar

Stuart Eizenstat

Amy Entelis

Jimmy Finkelstein

Lola Finkelstein

Steve Friedman

Bill Geddie

Wendy Goldberg

Whoopi Goldberg

Meryl Gordon

Rex Granum

Lloyd Grove

Allen Grubman

Louise Grunwald

Jessica Stedman Guff

Tammy Haddad

Kathryn Harris

Sharon King Hoge

Bob Iger

Christopher Isham

Jennifer Maguire Isham

Sara Just

Christina Kasman

Jay Kernis

Suzanne Kianpour

Henry Kissinger

Lori Klein

Rick Klein

Ted Koppel

Peter Kornbluh

Brooke Kroeger

Howard Kurtz

Brian Lamb

Dale Leibach

Abby Lester

Phil Lipof

Barbara Lustig

Richard Lustig

Alexander Marquardt

Meghan McCain

Nancy Shevell McCartney

Mike McCurry

Cynthia McFadden

Phyllis McGrady

Mary McNamara

Susan Mercandetti

Andrea Mitchell

Pat Mitchell

Barbara Mutterperl

Victor Neufeld

Bridget O'Brian

Kate O'Brian

Norah O'Donnell

Jerry Oppenheimer

Norman Ornstein

Norman Pearlstine

Maurie Perl

Pam Pisner

John Podesta

Charles Ponce de Leon

Jen Psaki

Sally Quinn

Michael Raab

Gerald Rafshoon

Paul Richter

Marie Ridder

Deborah Roberts

Charlie Rose

Ira Rosen

Jeanne Safer

Diane Sawyer

Linda Peek Schacht

Jeffrey Schneider

Noah Shachtman

Lynn Sherr

Ben Sherwood

Betsy Shuller

Peggy Siegal

Anita Siegenthaler

Curtis Sittenfeld

David Sloan

Kerry Smith

Robin Sproul

Steven D. Stark

Brian Stelter

Donna Svennevik

Anne Sweeney

Katie Nelson Thomson

Chris Vlasto

Richard Wald

Chris Wallace

Rob Wallace

Bruce Weber

Joella Werlin

Betsy West

Av Westin

David Westin

Ellen Rossen Westin

Jeannie Williams

Mary Alice Williams

Alicia P. Q. Wittmeyer

Julian Zelizer

Jeff Zucker

Note: Some of those interviewed asked not to be identified by name.

Notes

Introduction: Million-Dollar Baby

xiii *"Barbara Walters: Million-Dollar Baby?":* Jack E. Anderson, "Barbara Walters: Million-Dollar Baby?," *Miami Herald,* April 22, 1976, p. 1.

xiii *"A Million-Dollar Baby Handling 5-and-10 Cent News?":* Art Buchwald, "A Million-Dollar Baby Handling 5-and-10 Cent News?," *Washington Post,* April 29, 1976, p. B1.

xiii *Richard Salant, the president of CBS News:* "Out Takes," *Ithaca Journal,* May 1, 1976, p. 28.

xiii *Walter Cronkite said he had experienced "a first wave of nausea":* Bob Foster, "Cronkite; News; Walters and Money," *San Mateo Times,* May 7, 1976.

xiv *Despite that queasy feeling:* Douglas Brinkley, *Cronkite* (New York: Harper-Collins, 2012), 524.

xiv *Smith was her predecessor on the show:* "The Murrow Boys" were CBS radio reporters associated with Edward R. Murrow. During World War II, Howard K. Smith was one of the last American reporters to leave Berlin before the U.S. and Germany went to war. Stanley Cloud and Lynne Olson, *The Murrow Boys: Pioneers on the Front Lines of Broadcast Journalism* (Boston: Houghton Mifflin, 1996), 135–41.

xiv *"Be strong and stand up to it":* Interview with Howard K. Smith, quoted in Douglass K. Daniel, *Harry Reasoner: A Life in the News* (Austin: University of Texas Press, 2007), 164. Smith died in 2002 at the age of eighty-seven.

xiv *On the Friday night before Barbara's debut: ABC Evening News,* October 1, 1976.

xv   *He had already described himself on the air as a chauvinist:* Daniel, *Harry Reasoner*, 158.

xv   *He endorsed a bride's vow to "obey" her husband:* Harry Reasoner, *The Reasoner Report* (New York: Doubleday, 1966), 167–68.

xv   *He called the first issue of Gloria Steinem's Ms. magazine "pretty sad":* Harry Reasoner, *ABC Evening News*, December 21, 1971.

xv   *He questioned whether the advent of the first female anchor:* Daniel, *Harry Reasoner*, 158.

xv   *When female flight attendants were battling sexist stereotypes:* Harry Reasoner, *Reasoner Report*, ABC News, March 10, 1973.

xvi *In a commentary at the close: The ABC Evening News with Harry Reasoner and Barbara Walters*, October 4, 1976.

xvi *After those early shows, Victor Neufeld:* Author interview with Victor Neufeld. Neufeld would later become executive producer of *20/20*. "What I experienced with those walks with her is the torture she had to go through and the rejection and the humiliation and all that pain," he told me.

xvi *A powerful congressman weighed in, outraged:* "The Supersalaried Superstar: Eyebrows Are Up Everywhere over Walters's High Price Tag," *Broadcasting*, May 3, 1976, p. 30.

xvi *"Doll Barbie to Learn Her ABC's":* Kay Gardella, "Doll Barbie to Learn Her ABC's," New York *Daily News*, April 23, 1976, p. 1.

xvii *"I would pick up the paper every day":* Interview with Barbara Walters on *Larry King Live*, CNN, November 19, 1999.

xvii *"She was so brilliant":* Author interview with Diane Sawyer.

xviii *"I want to be like Barbara Walters":* "Oprah Talks to Barbara Walters," *O, The Oprah Magazine*, October 2004.

xviii *Jen Psaki would negotiate with her parents:* Author interview with Jen Psaki.

xviii *She had a stock response:* Barbara Walters, *Audition* (New York: Alfred A. Knopf, 2008), 5 (hereinafter: Walters, *Audition*).

xviii *"On the other hand, maybe I should have lived":* Walters, *Audition*, 143.

xviii *"Given everything she's accomplished":* Elisabeth Bumiller, "So Famous, Such Clout, She Could Interview Herself," *New York Times*, April 21, 1996, Section 2, p. 1.

xviii *A quarter-century later, after Barbara had passed away:* Author interview with Diane Sawyer.

xix *Barbara titled her 2008 memoir* Audition: Walters, *Audition*, 111.

xix *They were almost precisely the same age:* Av Westin was born in New York on July 29, 1929. Barbara Walters was born eight weeks later in Boston, on September 25, 1929. Westin died on March 12, 2022, Walters on December 30, 2022.

xix *"I used to characterize her":* Author interview with Av Westin.

Chapter 1: A Glass Eye and a British Accent

1 *Louis Abraham Warmwater was born:* His gravestone and some obituaries said he was born in 1896, but his certified Whitechapel birth certificate gives the date as January 26, 1894.

1 *"It made me":* Sidney Fields, "Only Human," *New York Mirror*, November 9, 1951.

1 *Before they left, he was playing when he fell:* Jerry Oppenheimer, *Barbara Walters: An Unauthorized Biography* (New York: St. Martin's Press, 1990), 9–10 (hereinafter: Oppenheimer, *Barbara Walters*). Walters, *Audition*, 7.

2 *As a schoolboy:* Walters, *Audition*, 10. Oppenheimer, *Barbara Walters*, 10.

2 *When the bosses announced:* Walters, *Audition*, 9–10.

3 *At a weekly salary:* In *Audition*, p. 12, Barbara Walters said her father's first salary was $6 a week. In a 1951 interview, Lou Walters said it had been $4 a week. Fields, "Only Human."

3 *When one of the agency's owners:* Oppenheimer, *Barbara Walters*, 13.

3 *He asked Quigley:* Fields, "Only Human."

4 *His new agency represented:* Oppenheimer, *Barbara Walters*, 14.

4 *He represented a young:* Oppenheimer, *Barbara Walters*, 13.

4 *"He wasn't one":* Interviews with Ed Risman in 1988, quoted in Oppenheimer, *Barbara Walters*, 15.

4 *Lou's personal bookie*: Interview with Ben (Ford) Abrams in 1988, quoted in Oppenheimer, *Barbara Walters*, 15.

Chapter 2: Roots

5 *Barbara couldn't remember:* Walters, *Audition*, 22.

5 *"I had no religious education":* Interview with Barbara Walters on PBS's *Finding Your Roots*, hosted by Henry Louis Gates Jr., April 1, 2012.

5   *"So someone says"*: While Barbara Walters said being Jewish hadn't governed her life in any way, Jewish organizations sometimes embraced her. When she announced her retirement in 2013, the *Atlanta Jewish Times* (May 20, 2013) ran an item about it under the headline, "Jews Making News." The story said, "Although her parents were not religious, Walters still openly identifies with her Jewish heritage."

6   *At least, that was the story told*: Walters, *Audition*, 8.

6   *"My father told me"*: Oppenheimer, *Barbara Walters*, 9.

7   *In England*: *Finding Your Roots* with Henry Louis Gates Jr.

7   *Celia Sacovich*: Immigration records spell her last name as "Sacovich," but in her memoir Barbara Walters spelled it "Sakowitz." Walters, *Audition*, 9.

8   *grandmother Celia*: Walters, *Audition*, 9.

8   *On the morning*: Walters, *Audition*, 11.

Chapter 3: Lou and Dena

9   *Lou Walters was twenty-five*: In an interview in 1951, Lou Walters said he was earning $1,000 a week at the time he got married. Sidney Fields, "Only Human," *New York Mirror*, November 9, 1951.

9   *At twenty-two, Dena was*: Dena Seletsky was born in Boston on January 31, 1897. Henry Louis Gates Jr., *Finding Your Roots* (Chapel Hill: University of North Carolina Press, 2014), 53.

9   *For their engagement*: Oppenheimer, *Barbara Walters*, 14. Walters, *Audition*, 13.

9   *"Both the bride and groom"*: "Walters-Seletsky Wedding Tonight," *Boston Post*, May 31, 1920, p. 31.

10   *Not everyone*: Gates Jr., *Finding Your Roots*, 53.

10   *They soon moved into a lavishly decorated mansion*: Oppenheimer, *Barbara Walters*, 15, described it as an eighteen-room house. Walters, *Audition*, 13, said it had fourteen rooms.

10   *At one point*: Walters, *Audition*, 13.

10   *Lou was a soft touch, "a hell of a guy"*: Interview with Herman Seletsky in 1988, quoted in Oppenheimer, *Barbara Walters*, 15.

10   *Lou and Dena's first child*: Walters, *Audition*, 16.

10   *The family was forced to move*: Jim Bishop, "Heart Attack Wasn't the End for

Show Producer," Harlingen (Texas) *Valley Morning Star*, April 20, 1961. In *Audition*, p. 14, Barbara Walters said they moved to a two-family house in Brookline.

10 *"My mother was sure things":* Walters, *Audition*, 18.

11 *"For a fast two years":* Maurice Zolotow, "Breath-Taking Boniface," *Saturday Evening Post*, February 20, 1943, p. 48.

11 *During the 1930s, there were times:* "Barbara Walters—Star of the Morning," *Newsweek*, May 6, 1974, p. 59.

11 *Barbara later saw her father:* Walters, *Audition*, 183.

11 *He started booking acts:* Walters, *Audition*, 15.

11 *"Not very glamorous":* Walters, *Audition*, 15.

12 *"Stop. Look. And Listen":* Walters, *Audition*, 16.

12 *Lou could envision:* Oppenheimer, *Barbara Walters*, 20.

12 *"Latin Quarter":* "The Latin Quarter," from *Gold Diggers in Paris*, Warner Bros., 1938. The movie musical was directed by Ray Enright with musical numbers created and directed by Busby Berkeley.

12 *At age eighty-two:* She sang during a taping of PBS's *Finding Your Roots*, which aired on PBS on April 1, 2012.

12 *He had borrowed money:* Interviews with Ed Risman in 1988, quoted in Oppenheimer, *Barbara Walters*, 21.

12 *He paid a local artist $250:* Walters, *Audition*, 27.

13 *"What if it fails?":* Walters, *Audition*, 26.

13 *On opening night:* Walters, *Audition*, 27.

13 *By one estimate, the Boston Latin Quarter:* Walters, *Audition*, 28.

13 *"Just let me get my hands":* Zolotow, "Breath-Taking Boniface."

13 *For the grand finale:* Walters, *Audition*, 28.

Chapter 4: Never Young

14 *Her family's affectionate nickname for her was "Skinnymalinkydink":* Walters, *Audition*, 24.

15 *Jackie had briefly attended Lawrence:* Walters, *Audition*, 20.

15 *Years later, Barbara wondered: Audition: Barbara Walters' Journey*, ABC News Special, May 7, 2008.

15 *"Behind these fantasy figures were real people":* Curtis Sittenfeld, "View from the Top," *Vanity Fair*, May 8, 2014.

15 *"When you see her":* Sittenfeld, "View from the Top."

16 *"She'd sit in":* Interview with Ed Risman in 1988, quoted in Oppenheimer, *Barbara Walters*, 23.

16 *"She sees the seams":* Walters, *Audition*, 17.

16 *"On paper, they seemed ideally suited":* Walters, *Audition*, 8.

16 *His infidelity was not exactly a rarity:* Oppenheimer, *Barbara Walters*, 22.

16 *Lou was said to have an extended and serious affair:* Walters, *Audition*, 48–49.

17 *"My mother should have married":* Elisabeth Bumiller, "So Famous, Such Clout, She Could Interview Herself," *New York Times*, April 21, 1996, Section 2, p. 1.

17 *"I don't know":* Interviews with Shirley Budd in 1988 and 1989, quoted in Oppenheimer, *Barbara Walters*, 6.

17 *"I can't remember":* Walters, *Audition*, 16–17.

17 *She bought a watercolor:* "The Estate of American icon Barbara Walters at Bonhams," Bonhams auction house, Sept. 29, 2023.

17 *"To this day":* Walters, *Audition*, 25.

18 *Her days were dominated:* Jackie Walters was briefly enrolled in the Lawrence School in an "ungraded group," a class for children with developmental disabilities. Walters, *Audition*, 20.

18 *"My mother really took care":* Author interview with Peter Brown.

18 *Barbara grew up with "tension in the air":* Martin Clancy and Christina Caron, "Walters' Personal Revelations," ABC News, May 7, 2008. The quote was from Joyce Ashley.

18 *"It did not seem odd to me":* Walters, *Audition*, 18.

18 *"I ask you":* Interview with Barbara Walters on *Larry King Live*, CNN, May 12, 2008.

Chapter 5: "The Strongest Influence in My Life"

19 *Still, the first paragraph:* Walters, *Audition*, 3.

20 *"I loved my sister":* Walters, *Audition*, 4.

20 *Barbara's earliest memory:* Walters, *Audition*, 5.

20 *A few years later:* Walters, *Audition*, 21.

20 *"This meant I had my parents all to myself":* Walters, *Audition*, 33.

20 *Broadway legend Carol Channing:* Walters, *Audition*, 112.

21 *That experience gave him a stronger need:* James Fox, "Johnnie Ray," *Oregon Encyclopedia*, Oregon Historical Society.

21 *"Johnnie is working in Chicago":* Walters, *Audition*, 46.

22 *"It makes me so sad for her":* Walters, *Audition*, 18–19.

22 *If her pretenses had persisted:* "Factitious disorder," Mayo Clinic, Health Information: Diseases and Conditions.

22 *"A very serious pupil":* Walters, *Audition*, 20.

23 *"To other people":* Barbara Walters' 25th Anniversary Special, ABC.

23 *"When I was about seven years old":* Walters, *Audition*, 20.

23 *"He was handsome":* Barbara Walters interviewed on *Masterclass*, Oprah Winfrey Network, June 29, 2014.

24 *"Not necessarily better":* Walters, *Audition*, 22–23.

Chapter 6: The Fifth-Grader and the Bootlegger

25 *"I was in love":* Walters, *Audition*, 31.

26 *It was painted pistachio green:* Walters, *Audition*, 30.

26 *During Prohibition, he had been known as "king of the bootleggers":* "Bill Dwyer Dies; 'Bootlegger King'": *New York Times*, December 11, 1946, p. 32.

26 *But he had encountered a spot of trouble:* "U.S. Wins $3,715,907 in 10-Minute Trial," *New York Times*, May 26, 1939, p. 18.

27 *"They say your life passes in front of you":* Walters, *Audition*, 31.

27 *"He took a shine to me":* Walters, *Audition*, 33–34.

28 *Later, Barbara would wonder if Dwyer was gay:* Walters, *Audition*, 34–35.

28 *The $6 minimum promised:* Ad in the *Miami Daily News*, December 22, 1942.

28 *The club's second winter season:* Geoffrey Tomb, "Behind the Gatehouse, Island Thrives in Casino's Wake," *Miami Herald*, July 25, 1993.

29 *"He would walk up to the standing microphone":* Walters, *Audition*, 37.

29 *She could also re-create on demand the patter of a Spanish ventriloquist:* Richard Severo, "Señor Wences, Ventriloquist Who Was a TV Regular, 103," *New York Times*, April 21, 1999, p. 21. At age eighty-four, he reached a younger audience with an appearance on *The Muppet Show*.

29 *"This place puts on perhaps the most elaborate show in the Miami area":* FBI memo written by the Miami field office, dated May 11, 1944.

29 *Al Capone had bought:* Geoffrey Tomb, "Behind the Gatehouse, Island

Thrives in Casino's Wake," *Miami Herald*, July 25, 1993. www93palm.com. "Al Capone's Miami Villa Death Home!" TopTenRealEstateDeals.com.

29   *More than a decade later:* Gilbert Sandler, "Al Capone's Hide-out," *Baltimore Sun*, August 30, 1994.

30   *"He never interfered with anyone":* Lou Walters unpublished memoir, quoted in Walters, *Audition*, 36.

30   *"Free-associate," Hamlin said:* Chris Chase, "First Lady of Talk," *Life*, July 14, 1972, p. 56.

Chapter 7: Another Opening, Another Show

31   *The Latin Quarter was doing so well:* Peggy Simmonds, "On the Night Side: Lou Walters the Fabulous Comes into His Fabulous Own as Satevepost Goes Overboard," *Miami Daily News*, February 20, 1943, p. 8A.

31   *"One of the outstanding clubs in the country":* Hal Pearl, "The Night Watch: Meet the Host," *Miami Daily News*, January 24, 1941, p. 14A.

31   *He took his "Midnight in Paris" revue to Nassau:* "Duchess of Windsor with Boston Couple," *Boston Daily Globe*, April 3, 1941, p. 30.

31   *Lou was eager to expand:* Oppenheimer, *Barbara Walters*, 27.

31   *he was sitting alone:* Walters, *Audition*, 39.

32   *He would provide the capital:* Interviews with Sonja Loew in 1988, quoted in Oppenheimer, *Barbara Walters*, 27.

32   *The Broadway correspondent:* Bob Musel, "Big Town Medley," Clinton (Illinois) *Daily Journal and Public*, April 30, 1942, p. 2.

32   *Barbara enrolled at Fieldston:* Note: The author's husband, Carl Leubsdorf, is a Fieldston graduate.

33   *"It was coed and full of cliques":* Walters, *Audition*, 40.

33   *She made mostly:* Jill Robinson, "The Real Barbara Walters," *Vogue*, September 1978, p. 48. She said, "I flunked gym, flunked home economics. I am not visual and can't draw. But, I'm compulsive. Whatever it is, I must do it today. And must do it over until it's right."

33   *The only recognition she recalled winning:* Walters, *Audition*, 49.

33   *"Okay, so I'm bragging":* Walters, *Audition*, 40–41.

34   *"I remember very clearly":* Walters, *Audition*, 49.

34   *An ad for the show:* Afton (Oklahoma) *American*, June 13, 1957.

34 *A local newspaper:* "Fabulous Show for Exposition," *Okemah* (Oklahoma) *Daily Leader*, June 9, 1957, p. 3.

34 *"Walters has conceived":* "'Artists-Models' a Lush Nitery," *Billboard*, November 13, 1943, p. 29.

34 *But Walters's other Broadway shows:* Walters, *Audition*, 48.

35 *Comic and singer Martha Raye:* Earl Wilson, "It Happened Last Night," Madison (Wisconsin) *Capital Times*, September 2, 1945, p. 2.

35 *a local columnist later wrote:* Tony Weitzel, "Along the Trail," *Naples* (Florida) *Daily News*, February 26, 1974. Weitzel had previously worked as a journalist in Detroit, Chicago, and elsewhere.

35 *A year after:* "Detroit L.Q. Sold; Morelli Fronts Buyers," *Billboard*, September 15, 1945, p. 33.

35 *Lou would even lose:* Interviews with Ben (Ford) Abrams in 1988 and 1989, quoted in Oppenheimer, *Barbara Walters*, 37–38. The Latin Quarter in Boston would close in 1952.

35 *Years later,* The Boston Globe *reported:* "Ask the Globe," November 6, 1992, p. 52. Michael Redstone's role with the Latin Quarter in Boston is also mentioned in UP, "Latin Quarter Boston Night Club Closes," *Burlington* (North Carolina) *Daily News*, January 11, 1952.

35 *Regulars at the Friars Club:* Barbara and Dan Lewis, "They Call Her Barbara, or Is It 'Babwa'?" *San Antonio Express*, February 20, 1977.

35 *Broadway columnist Dorothy Kilgallen:* Dorothy Kilgallen, "Voice of Broadway," Pottstown (Pennsylvania) *Mercury*, August 31, 1943.

35 *Looking back, she said those years reminded her:* Kiss Me, Kate, a musical version of William Shakespeare's *The Taming of the Shrew*, premiered in 1948.

36 *In each of them, "she had to start cold":* Elizabeth Peer, "Barbara Walters—Star of the Morning," *Newsweek*, May 6, 1974, p. 60.

36 *"She was always afraid":* Walters, *Audition*, 47–48.

37 *The Latin Quarter grossed:* Louis Calta, "Lou Walters, Nightclub Impresario and Founder of Latin Quarter, Dies," *New York Times*, August 16, 1977, p. 36.

37 *"I knew Lou Walters":* Walters, *Audition*, 55.

37 *In 2019, the four-bedroom penthouse sold:* City Reality via www.cityrealty .com/nyc/central-park-west/91-central-park-west/5533#/goto-sec_closing.

37 *"The whole thing looked like a huge Easter egg":* Walters, *Audition*, 56.

38 *She was teased:* Oppenheimer, *Barbara Walters*, 42.

39 *"What has meant the most to you"*: Walters, *Audition*, 60.
39 *She seemed to be appropriating:* Interview with Enid Kraeler Reiman, quoted in Oppenheimer, *Barbara Walters*, 29.
39 *"Barbara, even at the young age of sixteen"*: Interviews with Joan Gilbert Peyser in 1988, quoted in Oppenheimer, *Barbara Walters*, 45.

Chapter 8: The Ostrich

41 *As a freshman at Sarah Lawrence:* Deborah Katz, "Aisle Seat," *The* (Sarah Lawrence College) *Campus*, March 3, 1948, p. 2. *The Bronxville Reporter* ran a photo of the cast in costume and onstage with the headline, "A Bit of Old Ireland," and the *Daily Times* in Mamaroneck published a picture of a tense-looking Barbara and two fellow actresses getting ready for the show. "Make-up in Bronxville," the cutline read. *Bronxville Reporter*, December 15, 1949, p. 4. "Make-up in Bronxville," (Mamaroneck, N.Y.) *Daily Times*, April 1, 1950.
42 *"I remember the thrill"*: Walters, *Audition*, 63.
43 *she was elected president of her dorm:* "Chang, Hoeber, Solomon, Class Presidents," *The* (Sarah Lawrence College) *Campus*, May 11, 1949, p. 1.
43 *"What we did was talk"*: Walters, *Audition*, 63.
43 *she was part of the college debate team:* "SL=Victor/Yale in Battle/Education," *The* (Sarah Lawrence College) *Campus*, November 22, 1950, p. 1.
44 *But the lead story in that edition:* *The* (Sarah Lawrence College) *Campus*, May 11, 1949, p. 1.
44 *"I don't remember having"*: Walters, *Audition*, 66–67.
44 *In her senior yearbook:* Sarah Lawrence College yearbook, 1951, p. 30.

Chapter 9: The Speedwriting Secretarial School

45 *"All my friends seemed to know"*: Walters, *Audition*, 70.
46 *She and two friends:* One of the friends was Anita Coleman. Walters, *Audition*, 71.
46 *She described her boss as a "pink-faced man"*: Walters, *Audition*, 72.
46 *A friend, Rhoda Rosenthal:* After a traditional start of marriage and children, Rhoda Rosenthal would cut a new path as the women's movement devel-

oped. In 1979, she graduated from Yale Law School, groundbreaking in her age and her gender. Gloria Cole, "A Second Start at Yale Law," *New York Times*, April 9, 1978, p. 11. "Rhoda Rosenthal Obituary," Santa Barbara *Independent*, December 10, 2019.

46 *She met first with Ted Cott:* Andy Lanset, "Ted Cott, WNYC Wunderkind," NYPR Archives & Preservation, December 11, 2013.

46 *"Ted was at least ten":* Walters, *Audition*, 73.

47 *"Can you imagine":* "Roone Arledge Funeral Service," C-SPAN.org, December 9, 2002. Richard Sandomir, "Journalism Stars Recall Idiosyncratic Arledge," *New York Times*, December 10, 2002, p. C19.

47 *"we would make sure that somebody":* Interview with Barbara Walters in Jack Huber and Dean Diggins, *Interviewing America's Top Interviewers* (Birch Lane Press, 1991), 130–31.

47 *"I learned how":* Oral history with Barbara Walters by the Television Academy Foundation, conducted by Don Carleton, May 23, 2000.

48 *"She may be the youngest":* Joan Nielsen, "Young Producer," *TV Guide*, May 15, 1953. The article identifies her as twenty-three; she was twenty-four at the time. She would begin to claim she was born in 1931; she was born in 1929.

48 *"Ted had become":* Walters, *Audition*, 76. Ted Cott, who later became president of the National Academy of Television Arts and Sciences, died in 1973 of a heart attack at the age of fifty-five. Associated Press, "Rites Set for Ex-Head of TV Academy," *Fort Worth Star-Telegram*, June 15, 1973, p. 34.

48 *Liberace once played:* "Liberace on Eloise McElhone Show on WPIX Plays Mini Piano."

48 *Barbara even filled in:* Ben Gross, "What's On?," New York *Daily News*, April 10, 1954, p. 23.

49 *he would later be identified:* "Head of Foreign Policy Magazine Named Ambassador to Denmark," *New York Times*, May 27, 1978, p. 22.

49 *He became an investment banker:* "W.D. Manshel, 66; Magazine Publisher Was an Ambassador," *New York Times*, February 27, 1990, p. B8.

49 *The local mayor:* "Anita J. Coleman Married in Italy; Sarah Lawrence Graduate Is Bride of Warren D. Manshel, an Alumnus of Harvard," *New York Times*, October 10, 1954, p. 104.

49 *Her picture:* The photo is in the second picture section of *Audition*.

50 *"I was free, free, free!":* Walters, *Audition*, 77.

50 *"Okay, Barbara, you get your choice":* Author interview with Phyllis McGrady.

Chapter 10: The Most Forgettable Husband; The Most Notorious Friend

51 *"I remained":* Walters, *Audition*, 79.

52 *He quoted her:* Ken Auletta, "Don't Mess with Roy Cohn," *Esquire*, December 5, 1978.

52 *But she would deny even that limited cordiality:* Walters, *Audition*, 80.

52 *Some accounts have said Barbara and Roy dated:* Oppenheimer, *Barbara Walters*, 55. She attended Sarah Lawrence College from 1947 to 1951. During that period, the account says, they were seen together at the New York Latin Quarter. But both Walters and Cohn say they met in Florida in 1955, and a search by this author found no contemporaneous accounts in Broadway columns or elsewhere during Walters's college years reporting them as together.

52 *Roy called her the next day:* Auletta, "Don't Mess with Roy Cohn."

52 *"Two of a kind":* James Conaway, "How to Talk with Barbara Walters About Practically Anything," *New York Times Magazine*, September 10, 1972, p. 40.

52 *She said he looked:* Walters, *Audition*, 80.

52 *"I think she was his beard":* Author interview with Jessica Stedman Guff.

53 *"How could you possibly":* Walters, *Audition*, 103.

53 *the* Miami Herald *headline:* "Mr. Katz, Bride Go to Europe," *Miami Herald*, June 21, 1955, p. 2B.

54 *"Young women like me":* Walters, *Audition*, 82.

54 *Matchboxes had been printed:* Some accounts of Barbara Walters's life incorrectly say the wedding was on June 21, 1955. According to the divorce papers filed in Alabama three years later, it took place on June 20, 1955.

54 The Miami Herald *described:* "Mr. Katz, Bride Go to Europe," *Miami Herald*.

54 *"During many of these days":* Walters, *Audition*, 83.

55 *"I hired Barbara":* Interview with Charlie Andrews, quoted in Oppenheimer, *Barbara Walters*, 83.

55 *The journalists in the room:* Oppenheimer, *Barbara Walters*, 89.

55 *"She came to me":* Author interview with Av Westin.

56 *"I don't look"*: Walters, *Audition*, 86. Barbara Walters included the photo in her memoir.

56 *"At that point, we probably were sending"*: Author interview with Av Westin.

56 *"What a horrible experience"*: Walters, *Audition*, 86.

56 *"We scooped everybody"*: Interview with Jim Fleming, quoted in Oppenheimer, *Barbara Walters*, 91.

57 *On May 21, 1958, Circuit Court Judge Bob Moore Jr. signed the papers:* A decade later, the Alabama State Bar Association sought to discipline Circuit Court Judge Bob Moore Jr. for running a divorce mill out of the Marion County Courthouse. The Alabama Supreme Court ruled that the association didn't have jurisdiction over judges, but in 1970 a federal grand jury indicted Moore and another judge on charges of using the mails to defraud out-of-staters seeking divorces. They were allegedly charging nonresidents a fee of $465 to be notified when to make a quick visit to the state to pick up their divorce papers. "Two State Judges Indicted," *Montgomery* (Alabama) *Advertiser*, August 21, 1970, p. 1. "Alabama Indictments Cast Doubt on Legality of 'Quickie' Divorces by Mail," *New York Times*, August 23, 1970, p. 53.

57 *On the final decree:* Alabama Department of Health, Bureau of Vital Statistics, Circuit Court of Marion County, Trial Docket No. 6037.

57 *He ended up remarrying himself:* "Rita Katz," paid death notice, *New York Times*, April 18, 2021. Some accounts of Barbara Walters's life misspell the maiden name of Bob Katz's second wife. It is Kupsick, not Krupsick. They had two daughters.

57 *When he died:* "Katz, Robert H. (Bob)," paid notice, *New York Times*, August 30, 2005.

57 *"She never talked about it"*: Author interview with Bill Geddie.

57 *Her denial of the incontrovertible truth was reminiscent:* See Chapter Two: "Roots."

58 *When she married:* UPI, "Barbara Walters Weds Television Producer," *Columbia* (South Carolina) *Record*, May 12, 1986.

58 *A fan paperback:* Barbara and Dan Lewis, *Barbara Walters: TV's SuperLady* (New York: Pinnacle, 1976), 18.

58 *Later, in a lavish spread in* Newsweek: Elizabeth Peer, "Barbara Walters—Star of the Morning," *Newsweek*, May 6, 1974, p. 60.

58 *She saw a psychiatrist:* Walters, *Audition*, 84.

58 *A quarter-century after her quick trip:* Walters, *Audition*, 87.

Chapter 11: Catastrophe

59 *His family said:* Walters, *Audition*, 16. "He played for money and usually lost, in part because a lot of his cardplaying friends were in on the secret of his half blindness and, it was said, would often discard to his fake eye to confuse him."

59 *"Don't worry":* Walters, *Audition*, 88.

60 *Walters got $500,000:* Walters, *Audition*, 88.

60 *"Lou Walters and E.M. Loew":* Lee Mortimer, "Walter Winchell," *Wilkes-Barre* (Pennsylvania) *Times Leader*, January 14, 1958, p. 16.

60 *Another associate, Cass Franklin:* Irving Slossberg, "On and Off Broadway," *Coney Island Times*, August 3, 1957.

60 *Onstage were:* Lee Mortimer, "New York Confidential," Eureka (California) *Humboldt Standard*, August 21, 1957, p. 4.

60 *the Morlidor Trio:* A 1966 performance by the Morlidor Trio at the London Hippodrome can be seen on YouTube at https://www.youtube.com /watch?v+ytLEVnATEx8.

60 *"No swan song":* Lee Mortimer, "New York Confidential," *New York Mirror*, July 24, 1957.

60 *The syndicated columnist:* Lee Mortimer, "New York Confidential," *New York Mirror*, New Logansport (Indiana) *Pharos-Tribune*, July 26, 1957.

61 *The club's first reservation:* Lee Mortimer, "New York Confidential," Eureka (California) *Humboldt Standard*, August 21, 1957, p. 4.

61 *the Hope School for Retarded Children:* Walters, *Audition*, 182, 368.

61 *he hired:* Lee Mortimer, "New York Confidential," Eureka (California) *Humboldt Standard*, August 21, 1957, p. 4.

61 *When the Café de Paris opened:* Leonard Lyons, "Uncle Miltie Taking It Real Easy," *St. Louis Globe-Democrat*, February 9, 1958, p. 3F.

62 *An economic downturn:* Walters, *Audition*, 89.

62 *Lou recognized:* Earl Wilson, "It Happened Last Night," *The Progress-Index* (Petersburg-Colonial Heights, Virginia), May 9, 1957, p. 18.

62 *But he encountered problems:* Earl Wilson, "It Happened Last Night," Long Beach (California) *Press Telegram*, February 21, 1958, p. A7.

63 *Walters instead put up:* Interviews with Chickie James in 1988, quoted in Oppenheimer, *Barbara Walters*, 99.

63 *The feud with his former business partner:* Earl Wilson, "It Happened Last Night," (Fayette County, Pennsylvania) *Morning Herald*, April 28, 1958, p. 4.

63 *A swimming tank:* Earl Wilson, "It Happened Last Night," Endicott (New York) *Daily Bulletin*, May 24, 1958, p. 8.

63 *"Lou Walters' new Cafe":* Earl Wilson, "It Happened Last Night," Endicott (New York) *Daily Bulletin*, May 28, 1958, p. 7.

63 *The review:* Dorothy Kilgallen, "Dorothy Kilgallen's Broadway," *Salt Lake Tribune*, June 10, 1958.

63 *He was paying a premium:* "Lou Terras—in Show Business," Kings County (New York) *Chronicle*, August 26, 1958, p. 1.

63 *"I'm really in a fix":* Lou Sobol, "New York Cavalcade," *New York Journal American*, June 3, 1958.

63 *The last-minute replacement:* Hy Gardner, "Night Letter," North Hollywood (California) *Valley Times*, June 20, 1958.

64 *She gave Lou all of it:* Walters, *Audition*, 90.

Chapter 12: "A Halo of Fear"

65 *The two young women:* Four months later, in October 1958, Marilyn Landsberger, a fellow classmate of the Fieldston School, married Seymour Herskovitz. She became a residential real estate broker and died in 2015. "Marilyn Landsberger Is Married at Plaza," *New York Times*, October 24, 1958. "Marilyn Herskovitz" obituary notice, *New York Times*, August 1, 2015.

66 *"A sorcerer of magic and fantasy":* Walters, *Audition*, 38.

67 *"Not then":* Walters, *Audition*, 92.

67 *"Everything I had always dreaded":* Walters, *Audition*, 87–95.

67 *"I think a halo of fear":* Elizabeth Peer, "Barbara Walters—Star of the Morning," *Newsweek*, May 6, 1974, p. 59.

68 *The first mention:* "Walter Winchell of New York," *New York Mirror*, June 15, 1958, p. 6.

68 *"Cafe de Paris chief":* "With Walter Winchell on Broadway," *Pocono* (Pennsylvania) *Record*, June 17, 1958, p. 4.

68 *In the same issue:* Lee Mortimer, "Stars Offer Help to Lou Walters," *New York Mirror*, June 16, 1958, p. 31.

68 *A few days after that:* Hy Gardner, "Night Letter," North Hollywood (California) *Valley Times*, June 20, 1958.

68 *Two decades later:* Louis Calta, "Lou Walters, Nightclub Impresario and Founder of Latin Quarter, Dies," *New York Times*, August 16, 1977, p. 36.

68 *"Lou Walters' sad plight":* Dorothy Kilgallen, "Voice of Broadway," Shamokin (Pennsylvania) *News-Dispatch*, June 19, 1958, p. 6.

68 *"The fight to keep":* Hy Gardner, "Show People Rally, Help Lou Walters Recuperation," Ogden (Utah) *Standard Examiner*, June 28, 1958.

69 *On June 20:* "Cafe de Paris Asks for Help," *Billboard*, June 23, 1958, pp. 4, 20. In filing in New York Federal Court for Chapter 11 bankruptcy, the club listed $500,000 in debts and $451,000 in assets. The liabilities included $7,000 in back wages, $29,000 in federal taxes, $6,000 in municipal taxes, $90,000 in secured claims and $368,000 in unsecured claims. Among the 150 unsecured creditors were actress Betty Hutton and Rod Alexander, a well-known choreographer.

69 *Creditors and vendors:* Dorothy Kilgallen, "Around New York," Mansfield (Ohio) *News-Journal*, August 28, 1958, p. 37. The bankruptcy in New York complicated the bankruptcy already in process for the Café de Paris in Miami Beach, she wrote. "The receiver who took over the assets of Lou Walters' Cafe de Paris in Miami Beach is in a swivet. He released costumes from the show for use in Walters' Broadway cabaret, and since that went bankrupt, the elaborate dresses and suits have been impounded here. Now the Miami receiver has the unpleasant problem of explaining to the Florida courts just how he happened to let the assets get away from him."

69 *the jewel Lou had launched:* Herb Kelly, "Latin Quarter Drops Curtain on Golden Era," *Miami News*, August 28, 1959, p. 5B.

69 *He became chairman:* Lucian K. Truscott IV, "Hollywood's Wall Street Connection," *New York Times*, February 26, 1978, p. 288.

70 *Chesler's profitable enterprises:* FBI files obtained through Freedom of Information Act requests filed by the author. Memo from the Special Investigation Division, Miami, to the FBI director, June 22, 1967.

70 *Chesler was said to have won:* Joe Williams, "Kefauver Committee to Scrutinize Nation's 'High Rollers,'" Evansville (Indiana) *Press*, March 3, 1960, p. 39.

70 *In 1981, Chesler was reported:* FBI files obtained through Freedom of Information Act requests filed by the author. Memo from the Special Investigation Division, Miami, to the FBI director, April 24, 1981.

70 *He owned the building:* Dorothy Kilgallen, "Voice of Broadway," South Carolina *Index-Journal*, August 11, 1958.

71 *"We were suddenly bereft":* James Conaway, "How to Talk with Barbara Walters About Practically Anything," *New York Times Magazine*, September 10, 1972, p. 40.

71 *Chesler's version:* Interviews with Irving Zussman in 1988 and 1989, quoted in Oppenheimer, *Barbara Walters*, 100–101.

71 *Four years later:* Walters, *Audition*, 112.

72 *After he read her book:* Author interview with Bob Iger. His memoir, *The Ride of a Lifetime: Lessons Learned from 15 Years as CEO of the Walt Disney Company*, was published by Random House in 2019.

72 *"the big question":* Walters, *Audition*, 95–96.

72 *Four decades after her father attempted suicide:* Jennet Conant, "Major Barbara," *Vanity Fair*, March 1999, p. 262.

Chapter 13: Sunrise

73 *A narrow wooden door behind the box office:* The door was spied by the author's husband at the Hudson Theatre in 2022. In a 2017 interview, general manager Eric Paris called the door "one of the coolest things we found" during the renovation. Frank Dilella, "Finishing the Hat . . . and Finishing the Theatre," *Broadway Direct*, February 28, 2017.

74 *McCrary gave her:* Interview with Tex McCrary, quoted in Oppenheimer, *Barbara Walters*, 104–5.

74 *"I didn't have":* Interview with William Safire in 1988, quoted in Oppenheimer, *Barbara Walters*, 102.

75 *In those days before payola got a bad name:* Walters, *Audition*, 100.

75 *her "Dark Ages":* James Conaway, "How to Talk with Barbara Walters About Practically Anything," *New York Times Magazine*, September 10, 1972, p. 40.

75 *"Barbara, there are":* Interview with William Safire in 1988, quoted in Oppenheimer, *Barbara Walters*, 104.

75 *He said she should be:* Walters, *Audition,* 101.

75 *By now, Barbara had turned thirty:* In her memoir, published in 2008, Barbara Walters said she was "born around the time my grandfather Abraham died of a heart attack in 1931." In fact, she was born in 1929. Walters, *Audition,* 11.

75 *"There still seemed":* Walters, *Audition,* 104.

76 *"She had class":* Walters, *Audition,* 105.

76 *"Then, one absolutely wonderful day":* Walters, *Audition,* 105.

76 *She had kept in touch:* Fred Freed's daughter, Kayce Freed, was herself a producer who later worked with Barbara Walters at ABC's *20/20.* In 1997, she married ABC anchor Peter Jennings, whose life would also intersect with Walters's.

76 *When he took the job at the* Today *show:* Walters, *Audition,* 108–9.

76 *At her request:* Oppenheimer, *Barbara Walters,* 109.

77 *"I had good judgment":* Interview with Judy Freed in 1989, quoted in Oppenheimer, *Barbara Walters,* 109–10. Fred Freed died in 1974 at the age of fifty-three. "Fred Freed, N.B.C. Producer of Prize Documentaries, Dead," *New York Times,* April 1, 1974, p. 34. Judy Freed died in 2016 at the age of ninety-four. "Freed, Judith," *New York Times,* March 29, 2016.

77 *Freed assigned:* Interview with Craig Fisher in 1988, quoted in Oppenheimer, *Barbara Walters,* 110.

78 *"Anita was very much a lady":* Walters, *Audition,* 106.

78 *Movie mogul David O. Selznick:* "Cinema: Cover Girl," *Time,* January 8, 1945.

79 *"Had I been the same age as Barbara":* Interviews with Anita Colby in 1989, quoted in Oppenheimer, *Barbara Walters,* 112–13.

78 *"Anita may have been fine with being fired":* Walters, *Audition,* 106.

80 *"I never saw anybody who covered so much territory":* Interviews with Anita Colby in 1989, quoted in Oppenheimer, *Barbara Walters,* 114.

80 *Her identity would be so wrapped up:* Walters, *Audition,* 145.

Chapter 14: A Godfather of the Mafia Sort

81 *"Happy, Happy":* Lee Mortimer, "Walter Winchell," *Wilkes-Barre* (Pennsylvania) *Times-Leader,* August 2, 1960.

81 *Cohn headed a syndicate:* Martin Kane, "A Real Crown for Floyd," *Sports Illustrated,* July 4, 1960.

81   *Six months later:* Lee Mortimer, "New York Confidential," *Terre Haute Tribune*, January 17, 1961.

82   *He was "the first person":* Oppenheimer, *Barbara Walters*, 55. Joan Gilbert Peyser became a prominent musicologist and award-winning biographer.

82   *Near the end of Cohn's life:* Lois Romano, "He'd Rewrite the Epitaph," *Newsday*, January 14, 1986; Part II, p. 3.

82   *One friend said Roy and Barbara were engaged for a time:* Nicholas von Hoffman, *Citizen Cohn* (New York: Doubleday, 1988), 256.

82   *The wife of Hearst columnist George Sokolsky:* von Hoffman, *Citizen Cohn*, 104–5.

82   *Dorothy Sokolsky said:* Dorothy Sokolsky was married to George Sokolsky, a Hearst columnist, a mentor to Roy Cohn, and a conservative defender of Joseph McCarthy. When George Sokolsky died in 1962, it was a sign of his influence that the honorary pallbearers included former president Herbert Hoover, Attorney General Robert Kennedy, FBI director J. Edgar Hoover, General Douglas MacArthur, New York mayor Robert F. Wagner, and Senators Everett Dirksen of Illinois, Thomas Dodd of Connecticut, and Barry Goldwater of Arizona—and Roy Cohn. Source: "Leading Americans Attend Funeral Services for George Sokolsky," Jewish Telegraphic Agency, December 17, 1962. von Hoffman, *Citizen Cohn*, 278.

82   *"No Pain, but Plenty of Fun":* Lee Mortimer, "Winchell's Column," *Columbia* (South Carolina) *Record*, March 27, 1961, p. 6A.

82   *Later, Roy delayed the purchase:* After Roy Cohn died, the townhouse at 39 East 68th Street was sold for $3.7 million; the proceeds became enmeshed in a tax dispute. Cohn or his law firm had purchased the house in 1967 for $325,000, nearly $3 million in 2022 dollars. Arnold H. Lubasch, "Town House Used by Cohn Is Purchased," *New York Times*, October 17, 1987. In 2022, the real estate website Zillow.com estimated the house's value at $21 million or so.

82   *It was the closest she came:* Walters, *Audition*, 114.

82   *She dismissed her as:* Oppenheimer, *Barbara Walters*, 154.

82   *Barbara and his mother "never got along":* Ken Auletta, "Don't Mess with Roy Cohn," *Esquire*, December 5, 1978.

83   *He teasingly inscribed a copy:* Auletta, "Don't Mess with Roy Cohn." During the luncheon with Barbara Walters and her mother at Windows on the

World, Roy Cohn said the bouncer from the nightclub Studio 54 tracked him down by phone. "We have a guy here who says he's the president of Cyprus. What should we do?" After asking several questions, Roy said, "Let him in."

83 *Roy and Barbara and another friend:* Author interview with Kate O'Brian.
83 *On his deathbed:* Jack Anderson, "Roy Cohn AIDS Story Had to Be Revealed," *Newsday*, August 25, 1986, p. 56.
83 *A square for him:* National AIDS Memorial, AIDS Quilt, Block 0104.
83 *In retrospect:* David Wiegand, "This Time, It's Barbara Walters' Turn to Speak," *San Francisco Chronicle*, May 6, 2008.
84 *"He had strong connections":* Walters, *Audition*, 103.
84 *"Roy was like a godfather":* Walters, *Audition*, 113.
84 *"I knew all his faults":* Walters, *Audition*, 112.

Chapter 15: Becoming Barbara Walters

85 *"[I]t never occurred to me":* Walters, *Audition*, 111.
85 *"Barbara was nagging":* Interview with Jane Murphy Schulberg, quoted in Oppenheimer, *Barbara Walters*, 156. Jane Murphy was a production assistant on the *Today* show; she later married Stuart Schulberg, who succeeded Al Morgan as the show's producer.
86 *"You don't have the right looks":* Walters, *Audition*, 127.
86 *"We forced our staff writer":* Stephen Battaglio, *From Yesterday to TODAY: Six Decades of America's Favorite Morning Show* (Philadelphia: Running Press, 2011), 63.
86 *Less than a year later:* During her trip to India, Jacqueline Kennedy visited New Delhi, Agra, Udaipur, and Jaipur. In Pakistan, she visited Lahore, Rawalpindi, Peshawar, and Karachi. "Jackie in India on 40 Sunday," *Binghamton* (New York) *Press*, March 31, 1962, p. 6.
86 Life *magazine called her:* Ben Cosgrove, "Jackie Kennedy: The First Lady Wows India in 1962," *Life*, February 9, 2012.
86 *Indian prime minister Jawaharlal Nehru:* Andy Glass, "Jacqueline Kennedy Begins South Asia Trip, March 12, 1962," *Politico*, March 12, 2015.
87 *Every outfit Jackie wore: Life* magazine calculated that Jacqueline Kennedy wore twenty-two different outfits during nine days in India; on a single day

in New Delhi, she changed five times. Anne Chamberlin, "It Just Had to Be a Fashion Show," *Life*, March 30, 1962, p. 32.

87   *Sander Vanocur, NBC's White House correspondent:* The one-hour special, which aired on April 1, 1962, was titled *Jacqueline Kennedy's Journey.* It preempted a show called *1, 2, 3—Go!* and an episode of *Bullwinkle.* "Jackie's Tour Is NBC Special," *Daily Reporter* (Dover, Ohio), March 24, 1962, p. 17.

87   *correspondent Welles Hangen:* In 1970, while covering the war in Southeast Asia, Welles Hangen and his TV crew were seized by Viet Cong and Khmer Rouge guerrillas in southern Cambodia and killed three days later. His remains weren't recovered until 1993. He was then buried at Arlington National Cemetery. Ronald Sullivan, "A Journalist Killed in Cambodia in '70 Buried with Honors," *New York Times*, January 30, 1993, p. 11.

87   *"It's a terrific story!":* Interview with Robert (Shad) Northshield, quoted in Oppenheimer, *Barbara Walters*, 129.

87   *"A woman's story":* Walters, *Audition*, 116.

87   *"I know I can swing this":* Interview with Robert (Shad) Northshield, quoted in Oppenheimer, *Barbara Walters*, 129.

87   *She enlisted a mutual friend:* Letter to Letitia Baldrige from Lester Cooper, dated February 19, 1962; John F. Kennedy Library. Cooper's wife, Audrey, had attended Vassar with Baldrige.

87   *Forty-five reporters were credentialed:* Walters, *Audition*, p. 16. She identified the other female reporters as Fran Lewine of the Associated Press, Anne Chamberlin of *Time*, Gwen Morgan of the *Chicago Tribune*, Molly Thayer of *The Washington Post*, Joan Braden of *The Saturday Evening Post,* and Marie Ridder. In an interview, Ridder told me she was working on the trip for *The Washington Star*; Barbara Walters incorrectly wrote that she was working for the Ridder newspaper chain.

88   *Her grandfather, B. W. Fleisher, had been the publisher:* When Japan entered World War II in the fall of 1940, B. W. Fleisher was forced through a systematic intimidation campaign to sell the newspaper to Japanese interests. The new owner merged it with *The Japan Times and Mail,* aligned with the Japanese Foreign Office. Fleisher died in Minnesota in 1946. "B.W. Fleisher, 76, Ran Tokyo Paper," *New York Times*, May 1, 1946, p. 25.

88   *On a stop in Pakistan:* Author interview with Marie Ridder. Also: Walters, *Audition*, 117.

88   *The standard rough-and-tumble of the traveling press corps:* Marie was the sort of woman with a commanding presence unlikely to be terrified, then or later. I interviewed her at her sprawling house in suburban McLean, Virginia, on a cliff with a spectacular view of the Potomac River. It was the place she had reared her four children after marrying Walter Ridder, a third-generation newspaperman and a member of the family that owned Ridder Publications. (In our phone call scheduling the interview, she offhandedly volunteered to serve "a sandwich," since we were meeting at midday. When I arrived, she poured us glasses of sherry before we sat down to a luncheon on fine china of roast chicken with chutney, and homemade angel food cake for dessert.)

88   *She brought a wig with her:* "Have Wig, Will Travel with the First Lady," *Burlington* (Iowa) *Hawk Eye*, March 15, 1962, p. 8. A gossipy White House column by the North American Newspaper Alliance noted Jacqueline Kennedy's "secret" wig on the trip. "The wig is for those occasions when Mrs. Kennedy needs a shampoo and new waveset and has no time for same." Dorothy McCardle, "Next Birthday Is a Milestone for President," *Chattanooga* (Tennessee) *Times*, March 18, 1962, p. 36.

88   *She fumed when Sandy Vanocur declined:* Walters, *Audition*, 119.

88   *She filed radio reports but complained to other journalists:* Interview with Anne Chamberlin, a correspondent for *Time* magazine on the trip, quoted in Oppenheimer, *Barbara Walters*, 131.

89   *She described Joan:* Walters, *Audition*, 117.

89   *To be fair, some other female reporters, including Marie:* During the trip, Joan Braden and Marie Ridder were the only reporters invited to one black-tie affair, but Braden picked up both invitations and never passed on the one for Ridder. Ridder discovered this only when she asked afterward why she hadn't been included. "She wanted to be the exclusive," Ridder told me. Author interview with Marie Ridder. Braden's family of eight children was the basis for the book and ABC television series *Eight Is Enough*, written by her husband, Tom Braden.

89   *"The hard-bitten male reporters":* Walters, *Audition*, 117.

89   *In the NBC press release:* "Have Wig, Will Travel with the First Lady," *Burlington* (Iowa) *Hawk Eye*.

89 *Barbara begged and pleaded:* Interview with Letitia Baldrige, quoted in Oppenheimer, *Barbara Walters*, 132. In this account, Baldrige said she had given Barbara Walters a chance to ask a few questions of Jackie Kennedy. But Walters said she never got that opportunity. Walters, *Audition*, 118.

89 *Years later, Barbara called that:* Sitting down for an interview with Jacqueline Kennedy Onassis was a goal Barbara Walters would never achieve, though not for lack of trying. For decades, when their paths crossed in East Side circles, she would ask her for an interview, to no avail. Jackie was on her lifetime short list of near-misses and big regrets, the others including royals and popes. Walters, *Audition*, 491.

90 *"My first with a head of state":* Walters, *Audition*, 122.

90 *"An Exclusive Chat with JACKIE KENNEDY":* Joan Braden, "An Exclusive Chat with Jackie Kennedy," *Saturday Evening Post*, May 12, 1962.

90 *"She hadn't really done":* Robert Metz, *The Today Show* (Chicago: Playboy Press, 1977), 186.

90 *Barbara once said:* Walters, *Audition*, 73.

91 *A federal grand jury indicted him:* "Waldorf Officer Indicted on Taxes," *New York Times*, October 3, 1958, p. 20. Also: "Arbiter of Good Food: Claudius Charles Philippe," *New York Times*, October 3, 1958, p. 20.

91 *Journalist Edward R. Murrow visited Philippe's country home:* Edward R. Murrow visited Watch Hill Farm to interview Claudius Charles Philippe and his wife, French actress Mony Dalmès, for an episode of CBS's *Person to Person* that aired on June 8, 1956. "Waldorf Man on 'Person,'" TV listings in *Des Moines Register*, June 3, 1956, p. 10.

91 *The New Yorker published a profile of him:* Geoffrey T. Hellman, "Profiles: Very, Very Cordial," *The New Yorker*, February 19, 1955, p. 37.

91 *"I guess his indictment":* Walters, *Audition*, 98.

92 *Philippe eventually pleaded guilty:* "Ex-Waldorf Aide Fined in Tax Case," *New York Times*, September 20, 1960, p. 80.

92 *Barbara never told her parents:* Walters, *Audition*, 99.

92 *Philippe's assistant recalled:* Interview with Jeremyn Davern, quoted in Oppenheimer, *Barbara Walters*, 124.

92 *"Magical," she called them:* Walters, *Audition*, 99.

93 *"TV's equivalent of a geisha":* Oppenheimer, *Barbara Walters*, 115.

93   *"The one writing job"*: Beryl Pfizer interview, quoted in Oppenheimer, *Barbara Walters*, 117.

93   *She went to the office:* Leonard Lyons, "The Lyons Den: Theater Walls a Salmon Color to Avoid Clashes with Ladies," *Lawrence* (Kansas) *Daily Journal-World*, June 13, 1962, p. 4.

93   *The final posting:* @BarbaraJWalters retweet of a tweet posted by @TheView, September 28, 2017.

94   *It was not the exposé about the exploitation:* Gloria Steinem, "A Bunny's Tale," *Show* magazine, May 1963, pp. 90–115, and June 1963, pp. 66–68, 110–116. The first story billed itself as "Show's First Expose for Intelligent People."

94   *"I can still do the 'bunny dip'":* Walters, *Audition*, 128–29.

94   *"Hope springs eternal":* "A Night in the Life of a Playboy Bunny," *Today*, NBC, December 31, 1962.

94   *In 1963, after John F. Kennedy was assassinated:* Walters, *Audition*, 132.

95   *"the female interest":* Neil Hickey, *TV Guide*, August 1, 1964.

95   *"[T]here were mornings":* Walters, *Audition*, 127.

95   *Morgan hired actress Maureen O'Sullivan:* Walters, *Audition*, 135–37. Maureen O'Sullivan's daughter is actress and activist Mia Farrow.

95   *Columnist Jack O'Brian:* Jack O'Brian, "Dawn Greets Barbara, a Girl of 'Today,'" *New York Journal American*, October 11, 1964, p. 8.

95   *"They asked me":* Betty White, interview on March 19, 2020, for the Archive of American Television.

96   *she would work cheap:* Walters, *Audition*, 144.

96   *"Why not take someone":* Hugh Downs, *On Camera: My 10,000 Hours on Television* (New York: G. P. Putnam's Sons, 1986), 121.

96   *"I always tried to promote Barbara":* Stephen Battaglio, *From Yesterday to TODAY: Six Decades of America's Favorite Morning Show* (Philadelphia: Running Press, 2011), 79.

96   *"The three of us were his insurance":* Walters, *Audition*, 141. Note: Aline Saarinen became an NBC correspondent and the network's Paris bureau chief.

97   *"A frivolous and sexist idea":* Downs, *On Camera*, 123.

97   *"I started in my new role":* Walters, *Audition*, 141.

97   *"Dawn Greets Barbara":* Jack O'Brian, *New York Journal-American*, October 11, 1964, p. 8.

Chapter 16: The Runaway Bride

98 *"I have been married"*: Barbara Walters: Her Story, 25th Anniversary Special, ABC News special, May 16, 2014. The quote was pulled from a comment she made during an episode of *The View*.

98 *She was "always questioning herself"*: Author interview with Diane Sawyer.

98 *"He's nice"*: Walters, *Audition*, 124.

99 *"Oh no. Not another one!"*: Walters, *Audition*, 124.

99 *Its club, the Rendezvous*: "Jazz Venues," *All That Philly Jazz*, phillyjazz.us.

99 *"I managed to convince myself"*: Walters, *Audition*, 125.

99 *She was the one who pursued him*: Interview with Frank Ford, Lee Guber's business partner, quoted in Oppenheimer, *Barbara Walters*, 139. "She would call him every night at our hotel," he said. "After Lee got off the phone he'd say to me, 'Jeez, I don't know what to do. She's really after me. She wants to get married and I've had one bad marriage and I don't know whether I should marry her or not.' . . . She persisted. She chased him. She was the main pursuer."

99 *"I knew right away"*: Sally Quinn, "Barbara Walters: Woman of 'Today,'" *Washington Post*, January 30, 1972, p. E1.

99 *Lou Walters landed contracts*: Walters, *Audition*, 102.

100 *"It wasn't Broadway"*: Walters, *Audition*, 112.

100 *"ALL NEW! SAUCY! PERT!"*: *Miami Herald*, December 30, 1963, p. 14D.

100 *"In the lavish costuming and production tradition of Lou Walters"*: George Bourke, "Paree Is Lavish and Exciting," *Miami Herald*, December 25, 1963, p. 9F.

100 *The evening's entertainments "have been compared"*: George Bourke, "Nightlife," *Miami Herald*, August 8, 1964, and November 25, 1964.

101 *"A show is a show"*: Walters, *Audition*, 130.

101 *"What would you do"*: Walters, *Audition*, 131.

101 *Walters had leased*: "Aqua Show Owner Plans New One," *Miami News*, July 21, 1964, p. B1.

102 *a "noisy and proprietary" woman*: Walters, *Audition*, 57.

102 *"I don't usually do this"*: Interview with Sonja Loew, quoted in Oppenheimer, *Barbara Walters*, 181.

102 *"Loew made me a flattering proposition"*: Herb Kelly, "Walters Sought for Old Top Job at Latin Quarter," *Miami News*, February 23, 1965, p. 7B.

102 *"When Loew said"*: Leonard Harris, New York *World-Telegram and the Sun*, quoted in Oppenheimer, *Barbara Walters*, 181.

102 *he still owed $100,000 to the Internal Revenue Service:* "Lou Walters Is Bankrupt," *New York Times*, December 6, 1966, p. 60. The cabaret listing noted that comedian Totie Fields was performing at the Latin Quarter.

103 *A few days after President Kennedy's assassination:* Walters, *Audition*, 133.

103 *"We wanted to cling together stormily":* Quinn, "Barbara Walters: Woman of 'Today.'"

103 *"Pretty, perky, popular Barbara Walters":* Jack O'Brian, "On the Air," *New York Journal-American*, December 3, 1963, p. 20.

103 *The night before the wedding:* Ken Auletta, "Don't Mess with Roy Cohn," *Esquire*, December 5, 1978. Chez Vito was a posh Italian restaurant on the Upper East Side that featured opera singers and serenading violinists.

104 The New York Times *notice:* "Lee Guber Marries Barbara J. Walters," *New York Times*, December 9, 1963.

104 *"I felt trapped and restless":* Walters, *Audition*, 134.

104 *"The hardest part":* Quinn, "Barbara Walters: Woman of 'Today.'"

104 *"You're ecstatic at the high point":* Walters, *Audition*, 138.

Chapter 17: The "Pushy Cookie"

106 *"Exhilarated," she said:* Walters, *Audition*, 141.

106 *"I'm very bold on camera":* Ron Reagan, "Barbara Walters: She's Candid Off Camera," *Ladies' Home Journal*, June 1984, p. 24.

106 *"I'm a Lord-Knows-What":* "Barbara Walters' '*Today*' Job," New England *TV Guide*, January 2, 1965.

107 *keeping them hungry beforehand:* Walters, *Audition*, 140.

107 *Some said she had a speech impediment:* Sally Quinn, "Barbara Walters: Woman of 'Today,'" *Washington Post*, January 30, 1972, p. E1.

107 *Now that she was going to be on the air regularly:* James Conaway, "How to Talk with Barbara Walters About Practically Anything," *New York Times Magazine*, September 10, 1972, p. 40. Al Morgan said actor Boris Karloff "had the same kind of lisp."

107 *For three months, she was drilled in exercises in enunciation:* Judy Bachrach,

"Barbara Walters Made It the Hard Way," *Baltimore Sun*, December 14, 1970, p. B6.

107 *Even some viewers wrote:* Walters, *Audition*, 142.

108 *Marlene Sanders of ABC:* Marlene Sanders, then a vice president at ABC News, supported hiring Barbara Walters as co-anchor but was privately skeptical "because she didn't have the news credentials." She was also "rueful" that she missed the opportunity herself. "I thought if I had kept my nose to the grindstone and stayed on the air maybe it could have been me." Interview with Marlene Sanders in 1988, quoted in Oppenheimer, *Barbara Walters*, 253.

108 *"Once Barbara Walters started co-hosting the* Today *show in 1964":* John Dickerson, *On Her Trail: My Mother, Nancy Dickerson, TV News' First Woman Star* (New York: Simon & Schuster, 2006), 217.

109 *After writing the memoir:* Author interview with John Dickerson.

109 *Barbara would accuse her:* Walters, *Audition*, 146.

109 *Six years later, when Barbara got the job as co-anchor:* Oppenheimer, *Barbara Walters*, 258.

109 *"[I]f you didn't watch her mouth":* Elise Chisholm, "Reporter Nancy Dickerson Adds Another 'First' to Her Stable," Baltimore *Evening Sun*, February 15, 1978, p. B1. In the article, Chisholm wrote of Dickerson, "You get the feeling she thinks Barbara Walters is overrated and overpaid."

109 *In a* New York Times *article:* Gloria Steinem, "Nylons in the Newsroom," *New York Times*, November 7, 1965.

109 *Women viewers "identify with me":* Conaway, "How to Talk with Barbara Walters About Practically Anything."

109 *The producers had to coach her:* Walters, *Audition*, 128.

109 *"They don't want me to be a glamour puss":* Steinem, "Nylons in the Newsroom."

110 *Asked what she disliked most:* "Barbara Walters Answers the Proust Questionnaire," *Vanity Fair*, October 1, 2004.

110 *"The woman now receiving":* Steinem, "Nylons in the Newsroom."

110 *"I think probably at this stage it would have happened with or without the women's movement":* Rhoda Amon, "Barbara Walters: TV Hostess and Interviewer Is Interviewed," Louisville *Courier-Journal & Times*, June 16, 1974, p. G9.

110 *"Barbara Walters for Women's Lib, but Not Violently":* Philip Nobile, "Barbara

Walters for Women's Lib, but Not Violently," Gannett News Service, *Elmira* (New York) *Sunday Telegram*, March 12, 1972, p. 9A.

110 *"I think that a little of a woman goes a long way on television":* Cynthia Lowry, "Barbara Walters Fills 'Today Girl' Spot on TV," Associated Press, *Wisconsin State Journal*, June 7, 1965, Section 2, p. 11.

110 *repeating the conventional wisdom that TV's male executives gave:* Lee Graham, "Women Don't Like to Look at Women," *New York Times Magazine*, May 24, 1964, p. 48.

111 *After a year and a half on the air:* "Voice of Video," *Daily Press Sun*, Newport News-Hampton, Virginia, April 10, 1966, p. TV6. The column was written by James Mellon. *Berkshire* (Mass.) *Eagle*, April 2, 1966, TV Week, p. 4.

111 *she hired a manager:* Interview with Ray Katz in 1989, quoted in Oppenheimer, *Barbara Walters*, 170. "Raymond Katz, 83, a Producer for TV, Film and the Theater," *New York Times*, March 28, 2000, p. 21.

111 *It was "a more clearcut indication":* Interview with Bill Monroe in 1988, quoted in Oppenheimer, *Barbara Walters*, 173. Bill Monroe died in 2011 at age ninety. Douglas Martin, "Bill Monroe, 'Meet the Press' Host, Dies at 90," *New York Times*, February 17, 2011.

112 *"She refused to hire a press agent":* Jack O'Brian, "Dawn Greets Barbara, a Girl of 'Today,'" *New York Journal-American*, October 11–17, 1964, p. 10.

112 *In her biography:* Walters, *Audition*, 147–48.

112 *The answer appeared:* "Guess Star: Can You Identify This Personality?," New York *Sunday News*, July 18, 1965.

112 *Her close-up was on the cover:* "The 'Today' Show's New Outlook," *TV Magazine*, July 18, 1965.

112 *She made a guest appearance:* Walters, *Audition*, 148.

112 *The biggest splash:* "Early to Rise, Wealthy and Wise," *Life*, February 18, 1966.

113 *The bosses at NBC told Barbara to turn off her personal publicity machine:* Oppenheimer, *Barbara Walters*, 172.

113 *An Associated Press profile:* Cynthia Lowry, "Barbara Walters Fills 'Today Girl' Spot on TV," *Wisconsin State Journal*, June 7, 1965. The story was also published in *The Miami Herald* and elsewhere. Cynthia Lowry, "A Little Woman Goes a Long Way," *Miami Herald*, June 6, 1965, p. 12.

113 *Barbara asked what she should call her:* Walters, *Audition*, 142. This account

in Barbara Walters's memoir conflicts with a passage in *The Fabulous Bouvier Sisters: The Tragic and Glamorous Lives of Jackie and Lee*. In it, Walters is quoted as saying Lee Radziwill told her, "Forgive me, but would you please make no reference to my sister and not refer to me as 'Princess'?" She reportedly said, "If you've no objection, I'd prefer to be addressed simply as 'Lee Radziwill' for the purposes of this interview." Sam Kashner and Nancy Schoenberger, *The Fabulous Bouvier Sisters: The Tragic and Glamorous Lives of Jackie and Lee* (New York: HarperCollins, 2018).

113 *A decade later, Lee Radziwill knew who she was:* Judy Klemesrud, "For Lee Radziwill, Budding Careers and New Life in New York," *New York Times*, September 1, 1974, p. 42. At the time, Radziwill was promoting *Conversations with Lee Radziwill*, a TV program featuring six interviews she had done with prominent people, but the program wasn't renewed. She died in 2019 at the age of eighty-five. Robert D. McFadden, "Lee Radziwill, Ex-Princess and Sister of Jacqueline Kennedy Onassis, Dies at 85," *New York Times*, February 16, 2019.

114 *By Barbara's count, she often did two to four interviews a program:* Walters, *Audition*, 152.

114 *Her interview with author Truman Capote:* Interview with Philip Seymour Hoffman, *The Leonard Lopate Show*, WNYC, February 5, 2014.

114 *She had the first, surprisingly pensive interview with Grace Kelly:* Stephen Battaglio, *From Yesterday to TODAY: Six Decades of America's Favorite Morning Show* (Philadelphia: Running Press, 2011), 74–77.

114 *He sent her a handwritten letter:* Letter from Richard Nixon to Barbara Walters on White House stationery, dated June 12, 1972. It was addressed to "Barbara Walters (Mrs. Lee Guber)" at her home address.

114 *He did his part to help:* Battaglio, *From Yesterday to TODAY*, 76.

114 *The story made global headlines:* "Queen Left in Lurch," *Montreal Gazette*, November 11, 1969, p. 4.

114 *"Philip Again":* Norman Cook, "Philip Again: Palace Denies American TV Suggestion of Queen's Abdication," *Liverpool Daily Post*, November 11, 1969, p. 1.

115 *The kerfuffle caused no hard feelings:* Ian Ball, "Prince Writes to Reporter," *Daily Telegraph*, November 29, 1969.

115 *The prince also sent a friendly note to Nixon:* Letter from Prince Philip to

Richard Nixon, dated November 7, 1969. It was handwritten while in Greenland and signed, "Yours sincerely."

115 *The secretary of state:* June Weird, "Barbara Walters' Non-Stop World," *Rochester* (New York) *Democrat and Chronicle*, June 22, 1969, p. H1.

115 *"As a regular viewer of the Today Show":* Letter from Dean Rusk to Barbara Walters, dated August 28, 1967, quoted in Walters, *Audition*, 174.

116 *She had asked that particular question:* Philip Nobile, "Barbara Walters for Women's Lib, but Not Violently," Gannett News Service, *Elmira* (New York) *Sunday Telegram*, March 12, 1972, p. 9A. In the 1971 interview, she had cushioned the question with a roundabout windup: "Mr. Secretary, forgive me for putting it this way but some people wonder when they read the Pentagon Papers that they think, how could our secretary of State have been— oh dear, forgive me, Mr. Secretary—how could he have been so stupid?"

116 *He didn't take offense:* Interview with Dean Rusk on February 19, 1989, quoted in Oppenheimer, *Barbara Walters*, 191–92. Rusk died of congestive heart failure in 1994, at age eighty-five.

116 *in the 1969 interview, she had also pressed him on Vietnam:* Interview with Dean Rusk by Barbara Walters, Dean Rusk Personal Papers, Richard B. Russell Library for Political Research and Studies, University of Georgia, Athens, Georgia.

116 *When the interview was over and the cameras were off:* Weird, "Barbara Walters' Non-Stop World," p. H1.

116 *"Rusk Denies Opposing De-Escalation":* *Washington Post*, March 24, 1969, p. A2.

116 *LBJ's office in Austin called:* Leonard Lyons, "The Lyons Den," *Minneapolis Star*, April 3, 1969, p. 6B.

116 *"I can't believe that if a man":* Weird, "Barbara Walters' Non-Stop World," p. H1.

116 *The news Rusk made did appear on the* NBC Nightly News: "Rusk/Vietnam /Offensive," *NBC Evening News* for March 24, 1969, Vanderbilt University News Archive.

117 *"I always knew I was hard working":* Weird, "Barbara Walters' Non-Stop World," p. H1.

117 *"It's as if she has to keep going":* Chris Chase, "First Lady of Talk," *Life*, July 14, 1972, p. 59.

117 *"Boy, the power is over"*: Don Carleton interview with Barbara Walters, Television Academy Foundation, May 23, 2000.

Chapter 18: "It's a Girl!"

118 *In 1968, Lee Guber and Barbara participated*: In her memoir, Barbara Walters didn't acknowledge Roy Cohn's role in arranging the adoption, but one of her closest friends, speaking on condition of anonymity, told me Cohn knew the other couple well and had made key arrangements. Also in Oppenheimer, *Barbara Walters*, 185.

118 *"She's ours!"*: Walters, *Audition*, 164. In her memoir, Barbara Walters said she swore the reporter to secrecy "for fear our baby's biological mother would learn we were the parents." But the interview appeared in the newspaper ten days later.

118 *"Congratulate me, I just became a mother"*: Carol Kramer, "Television Reporter Thrilled by News She's a Mother," *Chicago Tribune*, June 24, 1968, Section 2, p. 23.

119 *For years, Barbara would call her sister "Jackie"*: Author interviews with Bridget O'Brian and Kate O'Brian.

119 *"Jackie was never with an unfamiliar babysitter"*: Walters, *Audition*, 377.

119 *"Between the two of them"*: Walters, *Audition*, 170.

119 *"I took her home on a Friday"*: Elisabeth Bumiller, "So Famous, Such Clout, She Could Interview Herself," *New York Times*, April 21, 1996, Section 2, p. 1.

120 *"It would be like bringing in a puppy"*: "A Daughter's New Horizon," NBC's *Dateline*, October 18, 2002.

120 *when the* Today *show went off the air*: Susan Berman, "Mother and Daughter: The Very Private World of Barbara Walters," *Parents*, July 1979, p. 57.

120 *She kept a baby book*: Walters, *Audition*, 166.

120 *As Jacqueline's first birthday approached*: Lois Caplan, "Women's World," *St. Louis Jewish Light*, April 23, 1969, p. 8.

120 *"We spent every weekend I was home together"*: Walters, *Audition*, 170.

120 *Lee would grumble that his wife declared*: Author interview with a member of their social circle, speaking on condition of anonymity.

120 *"I have often said that if you don't work"*: Bumiller, "So Famous, Such Clout, She Could Interview Herself."

121 *"Sure, she'll say to me she wishes I didn't have a job"*: Berman, "Mother and Daughter: The Very Private World of Barbara Walters."

121 *"Getting a child into private school in New York"*: Walters, *Audition*, 379.

121 *For Jackie's seventh birthday:* Author interview with Barbara and Richard Lustig, who had a son in Jackie's class at Dalton.

121 *When a paparazzo snapped them:* Photo by Lawrence Schwartzwald, *Daily Mail*, December 18, 2013.

121 *"If Barbara is couture"*: "A Daughter's New Horizon," NBC's *Dateline*.

Chapter 19: A Melody Played in a Penny Arcade

122 *The Women's News Service:* Norma Sue Woodstone, "Often Wives More Famous: Husband's Role Quite Complex and Could Be Devastating," Women's News Service, *Arizona Republic*, May 18, 1969, p. M3.

123 *During the first days: Newark Evening News*, May 9, 1965. Lee Guber called Barbara Walters "the world's champion sleeper" for her ability to easily fall asleep, wake up early for the *Today* show, and then sleep in late on the weekends. Lloyd Steward, "Easy Sleeper Awake on TV," *Fort Worth Star-Telegram*, November 13, 1970, p. B1.

123 *"Our schedules began to resemble"*: Walters, *Audition*, 210–11.

123 *Lee's first Broadway show:* Lee Guber, *Catch Me if You Can*, *Playbill*, opened March 9, 1965. Note: Lee Guber's final Broadway show, staged a decade after his divorce from Barbara Walters, was the biggest financial flop of all. In August 1986, *Rags* closed after four performances, though it would be nominated for a Tony award as best musical. Lee Guber, *Rags*, *Playbill*, 1986.

123 *She had taped the commentary:* Sheilah Graham, *Pittsburgh Press*, January 18, 1967, p. 72.

123 *"Lee's involvement in the theater"*: Walters, *Audition*, 213.

124 *Lou and Dena and Jackie moved back to Miami Beach:* Walters, *Audition*, 181.

124 *She used her savings:* Walters, *Audition*, 181–82.

124 *"We're going over budget"*: Leo Seligsohn, "A New Beachhead for Guber and Gross," *Newsday*, June 29, 1978, p. 71.

124 *"It looks to me like we're going to lose a lot of money"*: "Clouds Over Jones Beach," *Newsday*, September 12, 1978, p. 35A.

124 *"There are not many husbands who would tolerate"*: Interview with Judith Crist, quoted in Oppenheimer, *Barbara Walters*, 184.

125 *She was always traveling:* Interview with Ben Crossrow in 1988, quoted in Oppenheimer, *Barbara Walters*, 209.

125 *Lee told friends:* Oppenheimer, *Barbara Walters*, 211.

125 *Sally told me she didn't realize:* Author interview with Sally Quinn.

125 *"It's a melody played in a penny arcade"*: Sally Quinn, "Barbara Walters: Woman of 'Today,'" *Washington Post*, January 30, 1972, p. E1. The song "It's Only a Paper Moon" was written for a 1932 Broadway play called *The Great Magoo*, then popularized with versions recorded by Nat King Cole, Ella Fitzgerald, and others.

125 *In June, their separation was still a secret:* Barbara Walters, "Barbara Walters Lists Her 10 Most Fascinating Men," *Wilmington Morning News*, June 27, 1972.

125 *"We had problems we couldn't solve"*: Earl Wilson, *New York Post*, July 19, 1972, quoted in Oppenheimer, *Barbara Walters*, 211.

126 *"The Barbara Walters-Lee Guber bustup"*: Earl Wilson, "Daughters 'Melt' Jack Leonard," *Indianapolis Star*, July 24, 1972, p. 21.

126 *New York Daily* News *columnist Suzy:* Suzy, "Barbara, Lee Split; Divorce Ahead?," *Miami Herald*, July 20, 1972, p. 4C.

126 *Barbara called it the best of times:* Walters, *Audition*, 209. Note: Their marriage wasn't formally dissolved until 1976, when Barbara was granted an uncontested divorce in New York State Supreme Court.

Chapter 20: McGee's Law

127 *When Hugh Downs retired:* Stephen Battaglio, *From Yesterday to TODAY: Six Decades of America's Favorite Morning Show* (Philadelphia: Running Press, 2011), 89.

127 *"I have the strong feeling"*: Paul Farhi, "New Face of TV News First Seen in the '70s," *Washington Post*, July 23, 2006. The quote from Reuven Frank was attributed to *Newsweek* in 1971.

127 *"It never occurred to me"*: Arthur Unger, "Barbara Walters, TV's Chatty Prober: 'For Me, Liberation Might Well . . .'" *Christian Science Monitor*, August 6, 1973, p. 12.

128 *"He was not at ease"*: Battaglio, *From Yesterday to TODAY*, 97.

128 *"There are days when I come in to the studio"*: Philip Nobile, "Barbara Walters for Women's Lib, but Not Violently," Gannett News Service, *Elmira* (New York) *Sunday Telegram*, March 12, 1972, p. 9A.

128 *When Wald told him Barbara would be covering*: Walters, *Audition*, 216.

129 *She told a reporter*: James Conaway, "How to Talk with Barbara Walters About Practically Anything," *New York Times Magazine*, September 10, 1972, p. 40.

130 *The plot, such as it was: Deep Throat* starred an actress with the stage name Linda Lovelace, who later wrote that she was coerced and sexually assaulted during the production. It was part of what became known as "the golden age of porn," with movies that featured fuller plot lines and higher production values than sexually explicit films had in the past.

130 *Wald recalled:* Author interview with Richard Wald.

131 *"If I just came into the studio every morning"*: Conaway, "How to Talk with Barbara Walters About Practically Anything."

131 *"[T]hat's when I got the reputation"*: Walters, *Audition*, 206.

131 *The White House press corps:* Bernard Gwertzman, "Nixon's Aide Says Peace-Plan Foes Help the Enemy," *New York Times*, February 8, 1972, p. 1.

132 *"What things, what kinds of criticism"*: Gwertzman, "Nixon's Aide Says Peace-Plan Foes Help the Enemy."

132 *Those critics included South Dakota senator George McGovern:* When Barbara Walters asked if South Dakota senator George McGovern was doing that—that is, consciously aiding and abetting the enemy—H. R. Haldeman said, "I am expressing a personal feeling that I think applies where it applies." Gwertzman, "Nixon's Aide Says Peace-Plan Foes Help the Enemy."

132 *His comments "set off a fusillade"*: Don Oberdorfer, "Democrats Answer Nixon Aide Charge That Critics 'Consciously' Aid Enemy," Louisville *Courier-Journal*, February 8, 1972.

133 *She found Nixon "charming"*: The Howard Stern Show, Dec. 10, 2014.

133 *Barbara found the romance astonishing:* Walters, *Audition*, 237.

133 *"[E]veryone in journalism knew it"*: Sally Quinn, *We're Going to Make You a Star* (New York: Dell, 1975), 256–57.

133 *But McGee flatly denied he was sick:* Battaglio, *From Yesterday to TODAY*,

97. Executives asked Jim Hartz, an anchor at NBC's local station who was close to Frank McGee, to find out about his health. "I swear to you, there's nothing wrong with me," McGee told him.

134 *Lee Stevens of the William Morris Agency:* Battaglio, *From Yesterday to TODAY,* 103.

134 *Seven months later, McGee died:* Farnsworth Fowle, "Frank McGee of N.B.C. Dead; Newsman and 'Today' Host, 52," *New York Times,* April 18, 1974, p. 44.

134 *From a hospital bed:* Peter Punt, "How Jim Hartz Won the Great TV Host Hunt," *New York Times,* September 22, 1974, p. 121.

134 *Mamye was by his side:* Walters, *Audition,* 246–47. *Jet* magazine wrote about the episode: "Black NBC Production Assistant Fired," *Jet,* July 18, 1974.

134 *their plans to be married had been stalled:* "Black NBC Production Assistant Fired," *Jet,* p. 20.

134 *She filed a complaint charging NBC with racial discrimination:* Walters, *Audition,* 247.

134 *"Frank dead?":* Walters, *Audition,* 246.

134 *"I wasn't billed as a co-host":* Dusty Saunders, "Barbara Walters: Despite Critics, a Genuine Pioneer," Scripps Howard News Service, *Cincinnati Post,* January 27, 1992, p. 4B.

135 *"Barbara Walters will be cohost":* Walters, *Audition,* 247.

135 *Sally Quinn already:* Albin Krebs, "C.B.S. Picks Woman as Half of Its Team for 'Morning News,'" *New York Times,* June 22, 1973. Sally Quinn's first show was on August 6, 1973; her final show was on February 1, 1974.

135 *The announcement wasn't accompanied by a bigger office:* Walters, *Audition,* 270.

135 *Meaney was close to Barbara Walters:* Interview with Donald Meaney in 1988, quoted in Oppenheimer, *Barbara Walters,* 194.

135 *the first pair of women to anchor:* Eun Kyung Kim, "Hoda Kotb Joins Savannah Guthrie as Co-Anchor of TODAY," Today.com, January 2, 2018.

135 *The list of prospects:* Les Brown, "NBC Will Replace McGee by July 31," *New York Times,* July 19, 1974, p. 70.

136 *Brokaw also found the idea of doing ads "repulsive":* Gary Deeb, "Brokaw Nixes Huckster Role," *San Francisco Examiner,* July 17, 1974, p. 15.

136 *"Jim doesn't mind sharing the stage with me":* Punt, "How Jim Hartz Won the Great TV Host Hunt."

Chapter 21: When Love Is Not Enough

138 *At the time, interracial relationships were still considered scandalous by some:* When the Supreme Court legalized interracial marriage with the *Loving v. Virginia* decision in 1967, sixteen states still had anti-miscegenation laws on their books.

138 *They were surreptitiously photographed sitting side by side:* The photograph by T. Stephen Eggleston was posted in December 2012 on his blog, *T. Stephen Eggleston Presents My EggClectic Interests*, tseggleston.com.

138 *"I was excited":* Walters, *Audition*, 255–57.

138 *"God knows what she thought of me":* Walters, *Audition*, 256.

138 *In September, White House photographer David Hume Kennerly:* "Barbara Walters and Senator Edward Brooke: The Secret Was Already Out," *New York*, May 2, 2008.

139 *"They have been luncheon partners":* Maxine Cheshire, "VIP: Brooke, Walters Deny Romance," *Boston Globe*, September 21, 1975, p. C1.

139 *"Still denying any 'romance'":* Maxine Cheshire, "VIP: Susan Ford Wants Career Now," *Boston Globe,* November 4, 1975, p. 17.

139 *The situation was becoming untenable:* Walters, *Audition*, 255.

139 *Pete Peterson, a good friend:* Walters, *Audition*, 258.

139 *"Roy Cohn told me":* Author interview with an associate of Barbara Walters, speaking on condition of anonymity.

140 *Her reputation was "solid and aboveboard":* Walters, *Audition*, 258.

140 *Brooke would never publicly acknowledge his relationship:* Barbara Walters isn't mentioned in Edward W. Brooke's autobiography, titled *Bridging the Divide: My Life*, published in 2007 by Rutgers University Press.

140 *After wavering over whether to include it in hers:* Walters, *Audition*, 254.

Chapter 22: Careful What You Wish For

141 *After thirteen years at* Today: George Gallup, "Mrs. Betty Ford Gets Most Votes as Woman Most Admired in U.S.; Rose Kennedy Second," *St. Louis Post Dispatch*, January 13, 1977, p. 12A.

141 *"As the anchor, you are the automatic head":* Barbara Matusow, *The Evening Stars* (New York: Ballantine, 1984), 201–2.

142 *She wanted "to move into":* Interview with Frederick Pierce in 1988, quoted in Oppenheimer, *Barbara Walters,* 247.

142 *That was more than any other anchor had ever been paid:* Douglas Brinkley, *Cronkite* (New York: Harper, 2012), 523.

142 *one griped she had gotten "too big for her britches":* Interview with David Adams, vice chairman of NBC, quoted in Oppenheimer, *Barbara Walters,* 256.

142 *In his memoir, an exasperated Roone Arledge:* Roone Arledge, *Roone: A Memoir,* (New York: HarperCollins, 2003), 209. The Treaty of Ghent, signed in 1814, ended the War of 1812 between the United States and Great Britain.

142 *"They hated her":* Author interview with Richard Wald.

143 *She was making $700,000 a year:* Walters, *Audition,* 283.

143 *"The prevailing thought was that delivering the news":* Walters, *Audition,* 281.

143 *"She gave me hell about that":* Author interview with Richard Wald.

143 *"I liked, trusted, and respected him":* Walters, *Audition,* 284.

144 *"I don't know who won the game":* Walters, *Audition,* 281.

144 *Roone Arledge was making a name for ABC Sports:* Leonard Sloane, "ABC on Its Way Out of the Cellar, *New York Times,* November 9, 1975, p. F1.

144 *She called ABC "the schlock news network":* Walters, *Audition,* 285.

144 *In 1975, the nightly news on CBS had:* Kay Gardella, "New Look for ABC News by the Fall," New York *Daily News,* April 27, 1975, p. 2.

144 *Fred Pierce:* Interview with Fred Pierce, quoted in Oppenheimer, *Barbara Walters,* 248.

145 *"People are interested in many things":* Ron Powers, *The Newscasters: News Business as Show Business* (New York: St. Martin's Press, 1978), 92.

145 *"In truth it was a bargain for ABC":* Walters, *Audition,* 286.

145 *One more thing:* Walters, *Audition,* 193–94.

145 *"If you're going to work this hard":* Author interview with Jennifer Maguire Isham.

145 *He had been a reporter for* The Minneapolis Times*:* Douglass K. Daniel, *Harry Reasoner: A Life in the News* (Austin: University of Texas Press, 2007), 25.

145 *"To tell you the truth, I don't exactly like working":* Harry Waters, "The New Look of TV News," *Newsweek,* October 11, 1976, p. 76.

145 *"He didn't want to be paired with anybody":* Interview with Bob Siegenthaler, quoted in Daniel, *Harry Reasoner*, 158.

146 *NBC president Herbert Schlosser:* Walters, *Audition*, 284.

146 *"Barbara Walters Sheds Mate No. 2":* Associated Press, "Barbara Walters Sheds Mate No. 2," *Los Angeles Times*, March 23, 1976, p. 2. Barbara Walters and Lee Guber said in court papers that they had lived apart since May 1974. The divorce was granted on March 22, 1976.

146 *One gossip columnist said "the television prima donna":* George Daacon, "Names in the News," *Vancouver Sun*, March 23, 1976, p. 38.

147 *"I escorted Barbara to lots of parties":* Alan Greenspan, *Age of Turbulence: Adventures in a New World* (New York: Penguin, 2008), 80–81.

147 *That led to some confusion at her apartment:* Walters, *Audition*, 260–61.

147 *It was Greenspan:* Walters, *Audition*, 287–89.

147 The New York Times *read:* Les Brown, "ABC News Offers Barbara Walters $1 Million a Year," *New York Times*, April 21, 1976, p. 1.

148 *"I was with her on Nixon's China trip":* "History's Moment in Media: Barbara Walters Made Headlines on the Evening News," MediaVillage.com, April 16, 2018.

148 *"It appeared yesterday that Miss Walters's departure from NBC":* Robert D. McFadden, "Barbara Walters Accepts ABC's Office," *New York Times*, April 23, 1976.

148 *Barbara fired back:* Val Adams, "'Today,' Losing Barbara, Searches for Tomorrow," New York *Daily News*, April 24, 1976.

149 *"The line between the news business and show business has been erased forever":* Charles Seib, "Walters: Newsperson or TV-Age Communicator?" *Washington Post*, April 28, 1976, p. B1.

149 *In an interview that aired: ABC Evening News*, October 5, 1976. Note: Some accounts say Anwar Sadat's comment about Barbara Walters's salary aired on the first night of the new broadcast, on October 4, 1976. But his recorded interview appeared in two parts, and this exchange was shown on the second night.

149 *"Some of you may have seen speculation about this":* Harry Reasoner on the *ABC Evening News*, April 22, 1976.

150 *"It's an incredible compliment about her career":* Author interview with Brian Stelter.

150 *When Radner died of ovarian cancer:* Barbara Walters, "Ms. Walters Reflects," *Vanity Fair,* June 2008.

Chapter 23: Failure

151 *Agriculture Secretary Earl Butz had resigned:* John Dean, "Rituals of the Herd," *Rolling Stone,* October 7, 1976. The offensive joke: "I'll tell you what the coloreds want. It's three things: first, a tight pussy; second, loose shoes; and third, a warm place to shit. That's all!" The magazine *New Times* was the first to identify Earl Butz as the speaker. Richard Goldstein, "Earl L. Butz, Secretary Felled by Racial Remark, Is Dead at 98," *New York Times,* February 4, 2008.

151 *Her picture was splashed on the covers of that week's editions:* Jerry Parker, "The Biggest Story Was Walters," *Newsday,* October 5, 1976, p. 3A.

152 *ABC's evening news show ran a perennial third place in the network ratings:* Associated Press, "Harry and Barbara Show Ups ABC News Rating," (Missoula, Montana) *Missoulian,* October 6, 1976, p. 3. In New York, the A.C. Nielsen Co. ratings showed ABC with 31 percent of the viewing audience, CBS with 16 percent, and NBC with 14 percent.

152 *He had told* Playboy *magazine:* Robert Scheer, "The *Playboy* Interview: Jimmy Carter," *Playboy,* November 1, 1976, pp. 63–88. The interview was distributed to reporters on September 21, 1976.

153 *The Israeli leader was so furious about the broken commitment:* Walters, *Audition,* 302. Golda Meir died on December 8, 1978, at the age of eighty.

153 *At the end of the broadcast: ABC Evening News,* October 4, 1976.

153 *"None dare call it show biz":* "Bah-bar-ah's Bow," *Time,* October 18, 1976, p. 67.

153 *"She is changing our conception of news":* Roger Rosenblatt, "One More Piece on Barbara Walters," *New Republic,* October 23, 1976, p. 31.

153 *The* Los Angeles Times *published a front-page, multipart series:* Robert Scheer, "Crisis in TV News: Show-Biz Invasion," *Los Angeles Times,* May 29, 1977, p. 1.

154 *"Miss Walters has not faltered or fumbled embarrassingly":* John J. O'Connor, "TV: Miss Walters as Co-anchor," *New York Times,* October 6, 1976, p. 65.

154 *Newsday said she had gotten off to "a good start":* Marvin Kitman, "She Reads Well, Too," *Newsday,* October 5, 1976, p. 3A.

154 Time *magazine called her debut:* "Bah-bar-ah's Bow," *Time.*

154 *Siegenthaler's suggestion that they try:* Interview with Bob Siegenthaler, quoted in Douglass K. Daniel, *Harry Reasoner: A Life in the News* (Austin: University of Texas Press, 2007), 168.

154 *He seemed "as comfortable on camera with Walters":* Rosenblatt, "One More Piece on Barbara Walters."

154 *Hundreds of women wrote personal letters:* Walters, *Audition,* 306.

154 *Anita Colby, the supermodel and socialite:* Interview with Anita Colby, quoted in Oppenheimer, *Barbara Walters,* 268–69.

155 *Actor John Wayne, whom she had never met:* Walters, *Audition,* 309.

155 *"It was cats and dogs":* Author interview with Lynn Sherr.

155 *"she would come in":* Author interview with Ellen Rossen Westin. In 1992, Rossen married Av Westin, who for a time was executive producer of the *ABC Evening News.* "Weddings: Ellen Rossen, Av Westin, *New York Times,* October 25, 1992, p. 13.

156 *"He just hazed her":* Author interview with Bob Iger.

156 *The only person Barbara felt free to confide in:* "Exit interview," *New York Times,* 2004.

156 *Westin told me:* Author interview with Av Westin.

156 *Russell Baker offered his services:* Russell Baker, "Sunday Observer: Counseling Anchorpersons," *New York Times,* March 27, 1977, p. 197.

157 *Art Buchwald of* The Washington Post *imagined:* Art Buchwald, "Babs, You're One in a Million, Hawwy Weasoner, I Wuv You Too," *Washington Post,* March 1, 1977, p. B1.

157 *On* The Tonight Show, *Johnny Carson chatted: Barbara Walters: Her Story,* ABC News, 2014.

157 *"The $1-million on-air marriage of Harry Reasoner and Barbara Walters":* Frank Swertlow, "ABC May Split Reasoner, Miss Walters," *Kansas City Star,* February 4, 1977.

157 *"The Showdown at ABC News":* Jeff Greenfield, "The Showdown at ABC News," *New York Times,* February 13, 1977, p. 9.

157 *"Welcome back," David Brinkley said:* Walters, *Audition,* 304.

157 *During the last three months of 1976:* Greenfield, "The Showdown at ABC News."

158 *"We feel that the new co-anchor format":* Barbara Matusow, *The Evening Stars* (New York: Ballantine, 1984), 221.

158 *Forty million Americans tuned in:* Kay Gardella, "New Look for ABC News by the Fall," New York *Daily News,* April 27, 1975, p. 2.

158 *"Everything I had worked for":* Walters, *Audition,* 308.

158 *Decades later, when she was named one of Time magazine's:* "The 100 Most Influential People in the World," *Time,* May 10, 2010.

159 *"I didn't know how she was going to live through it": Audition: Barbara Walters' Journey,* ABC News Special, May 7, 2008.

159 *"I was drowning":* Bill Carter, "The Tender Trap," *New York Times Magazine,* August 23, 1992, p. 23.

159 *Her mother, who had always doubted her husband's big ambitions:* Walters, *Audition,* 308.

159 *By then, Lou Walters was living at the Miami Jewish Home and Hospital for the Aged:* "With Barbara," *Miami Herald,* November 6, 1985, p. 3D. Barbara Walters, accompanied by her mother, spoke at a fundraiser for the home that raised almost $15.5 million.

159 *"He was very frail":* Walters, *Audition,* 308.

Chapter 24: Fidel

161 *"Cielito Lindo":* The lyrics in English are, "Ay, ay, ay, ay / Sing, and don't cry / Because singing makes rejoice / Sweet pretty one, our hearts."

161 *Yasir Arafat had inscribed his photo:* Bill Carter, "The Tender Trap," *New York Times Magazine,* August 23, 1992, p. 23.

162 *"A turning point in my career":* Walters, *Audition,* 329.

162 *Barbara had met Castro during a trip to Cuba in 1975:* "Barbara Walters to Make Cuba Trip," *Austin American-Statesman,* May 1, 1975, p. 61.

162 *"The Cubans decided to do a full-court press":* Author interview with Peter Kornbluh. Kornbluh is the coauthor with William M. LeoGrande of *Back Channel to Cuba: The Hidden History of Negotiations Between Washington and Havana* (Chapel Hill: University of North Carolina Press, 2015).

162 *"The mysterious Cuban leader hadn't given a television interview in sixteen years":* Walters, *Audition,* 324–25.

162 *That would be news to Dan Rather:* "Castro, Cuba and the U.S.A.," *CBS Reports,* October 22, 1974.

163 *three years older than Barbara:* Peter Kornbluh, "'My Dearest Fidel': An ABC

Journalist's Secret Liaison with Fidel Castro," *Politico Magazine*, May/June 2018. Lisa Howard, depressed and despondent after a miscarriage, committed suicide on July 4, 1965, at age thirty-nine.

164 *He was candid about his public policy but not about his personal life:* Fidel Castro, who faced repeated threats of assassination, including by the CIA, carefully kept his wife, children, and grandchildren secret in the interests of their safety. Author interview with Peter Kornbluh, director of the Cuba and Chile Documentation Projects for the National Security Archive.

164 *After the cameras were off:* Walters, *Audition*, 327.

164 *When* Fidel Castro Speaks *aired on ABC in June:* "Cuba Shows ABC Castro Interview," *New York Times*, June 25, 1977, p. 5.

164 *They showed the questions Castro parried:* Barbara Walters, "An Interview with Fidel Castro," *Foreign Policy*, September 15, 1977.

164 *the* New York Times *reviewer praised the skills:* John J. O'Connor, "TV: Visit with Castro," *New York Times*, June 9, 1977, p. 74.

165 *"I love to flirt and be flirted with":* Barbara Walters, *How to Talk with Practically Anybody About Practically Anything* (New York: Doubleday, 1970), 126.

165 *After she arranged the guest list for a dinner party:* Sally Quinn, "Fidel's First Dinner Party," *Washington Post*, October 15, 1979.

165 *The unmentioned evidence for that view:* Kornbluh, "'My Dearest Fidel': An ABC Journalist's Secret Liaison with Fidel Castro."

165 *"We did not have a romance":* "A Conversation with Barbara Walters," Harvard University, Kennedy School Institute of Politics, October 7, 2014. Barbara Walters was interviewed by David Gergen.

165 *"There was chemistry":* Author interview with David Westin.

166 *"I felt he liked me":* Walters, *Audition*, 353.

166 *Andrea Mitchell, NBC's chief foreign affairs correspondent:* Andrea Mitchell, *Talking Back . . . to Presidents, Dictators, and Assorted Scoundrels* (New York: Penguin, 2005), 294.

166 *"I remember saying to him":* Emily Cronin, "When Walters Met Castro," *Harper's Bazaar*, January 21, 2014.

166 *Westin made his case at an impromptu meeting with the Cuban dictator:* David Westin, *Exit Interview* (New York: Sarah Crichton Books, 2012), 76–77. In an interview with the author, Westin said Fidel Castro had asked him, "How long have you been president of ABC News?" For four years, he replied. Castro said, "You will do well. Okay, fine. It's exclusive."

167 *They all learned from the New York tabloids:* Michael Starr, "Barbara-NBC Fight for Fidel," *New York Post*, October 4, 2002.

167 *Castro tried to make amends:* Author interview with Andrea Mitchell.

167 *Barbara had her exclusive:* Barbara Walters said the second interview didn't match the first one. "It wasn't as important an interview, or as exciting an interview," she told ABC's *Nightline* on November 26, 2016, in an interview with Byron Pitts when Fidel Castro had died.

Chapter 25: Comeback

168 *Cronkite had developed a friendly relationship:* Walter Cronkite, *A Reporter's Life* (New York: Alfred A. Knopf, 1996), 312–13.

169 The New York Times *splashed the story:* Bernard Gwertzman, "Sadat Seeks Israeli Invitation to Make Address in Parliament; Begin Agrees, Wants U.S. to Help," *New York Times*, November 15, 1977, p. 1. The transcript of the interviews ran on p. 2.

169 *The new president of ABC News, Roone Arledge, had gotten a heads-up:* Arledge, *Roone: A Memoir*, 183–85. "Peter, ever the contrarian, proved difficult to convince," Arledge wrote. When Jennings did the interview without a crew, "the result was like the proverbial tree falling in a forest with no one around."

170 *"Peter held this against me for years":* Walters, *Audition*, 337.

170 *Barbara flew to Tel Aviv on Friday:* Walters, *Audition*, 337.

170 *Roone was working his contacts:* Arledge, *Roone: A Memoir*, 186.

171 *"She hopped out of it":* "Walter Cronkite: Witness to History," *American Masters*, PBS, July 2006.

171 *When the two men connected in that groundbreaking satellite interview:* Cronkite, *A Reporter's Life*, 313–14.

171 *The official plane flew from Cairo to Ismailia:* Walters, *Audition*, 339.

172 *The network was broadcasting the arrival live:* Gerald Eskenazi, "Michigan Beats Ohio State, 14–6, and Gains Berth in Rose Bowl," *New York Times*, November 20, 1977, p. 8.

172 *Barbara already had arranged for an interview later that day:* Walters, *Audition*, 340.

173 *"Mr. President, don't you think she's the prettiest reporter you've ever seen?":* Bob Williams, "How Barbara Beat Walter to It," *New York Post*, November 21, 1977, p. 3.

174 *Four years later, he would be assassinated:* William E. Farrell, "Sadat Assassinated at Army Parade as Men Amid Ranks Fire into Stands; Vice President Affirms 'All Treaties,'" *New York Times*, October 7, 1981, p.1.

174 *At 5:50 p.m. Eastern Time Sunday:* Charles B. Seib of *The Washington Post*, "Now This Is What's Called a Media Event," *Philadelphia Inquirer*, November 27, 1977, p. 4K.

174 *"Well, did Barbara get anything I didn't?":* Williams, "How Barbara Beat Walter to It."

174 *Lou Walters, the father with whom she had such a tangled relationship:* Louis Calta, "Lou Walters, Nightclub Impresario and Founder of Latin Quarter, Dies," *New York Times*, August 16, 1977, p. 36.

174 *"I was heartsick but not surprised":* Walters, *Audition*, 330.

175 *She didn't hold a memorial service in New York:* Walters, *Audition*, 330.

175 *"Lou Walters, Nightclub Impresario and Founder of Latin Quarter, Dies":* Calta, "Lou Walters, Nightclub Impresario and Founder of Latin Quarter, Dies."

175 *United Press International described him:* "Lou Walters, Latin Quarter Founder, Dies at Age of 81," *Fort Lauderdale News*, August 16, 1977.

175 *The obituary in* Variety *gave:* Joe Cohen, "Lou Walters, Top Cafe Showman of Latin Quarter Era, Dies at 81," *Variety*, August 17, 1977, pp. 2, 62.

175 *But with him gone, the situation with Dena and Jackie kept deteriorating:* Walters, *Audition*, 364–66.

175 *The beloved star of* I Love Lucy *talked about her celebrated marriage: Interview of a Lifetime: Lucille Ball,* The Barbara Walters Special, ABC, December 6, 1977.

176 *"Barbara at that time was like a wounded bird":* Author interview with Ted Koppel.

176 *The Arafat interview was marked by tragedy:* Peter B. Flint, "2 ABC Producers Die in Air Crash," *New York Times*, September 24, 1977, p. 19. In her memoir, Barbara misspells Buckman's last name as "Buchman."

176 *The interviews "put me back on the map":* Walters, *Audition*, 342.

176 *Chancellor didn't get a joint interview with Begin and Sadat until Monday:* John Carmody, "Chancellor to Hoist Anchor," *Washington Post*, December 3, 1977, p. E1.

177 *Barbara called her conversation with Begin and Sadat:* Arthur Unger, of the

Christian Science Monitor, "For Television's Barbara Walters, a Private Life's Still Important," *Lansing State Journal*, November 8, 1978, p. C3.

177 *It proved to herself, and everyone else:* Mary Ellin Barrett, "Keeping Up with Barbara Walters," *Cosmopolitan*, June 1982, p. 213.

177 *"The best interviewer in the business":* Arledge, *Roone: A Memoir*, 175.

177 *They had kept in "quiet touch":* Arledge, *Roone: A Memoir*, 177.

177 *her failure as an anchor had opened the door for his rise:* Marc Gunther, *The House That Roone Built: The Inside Story of ABC News* (Boston: Little, Brown, 1994), 57.

177 *"He has had his shot":* Frank Swertlow, "Will ABC Make Room at the Top for Roone?" *Chicago Daily News*, February 18, 1977, p. 17.

177 *"Part of my job was to monitor the two of them":* Author interview with Av Westin.

178 *Roone set out to cast in new roles:* Gunther, *The House That Roone Built*, 43.

178 *Watching the evening news co-anchored by Barbara and Harry:* Arledge, *Roone: A Memoir*, 175.

178 *Over the years, any number of her bosses would be intimidated:* Author interview with Richard Wald.

178 *Roone wasn't deterred by a devastating assessment of her from Frank Magid Associates:* Barbara Matusow, *The Evening Stars: The Making of the Network News Anchor* (New York: Ballantine, 1984), 225.

178 *In September 1975, Roone had launched:* Gunther, *The House That Roone Built*, 23. Note: In October 1975, NBC began its late-night *Saturday Night* to better reviews and a longer life on the air. After the ABC show was canceled, NBC added the word "Live" to its show.

179 *"It was something that he wanted":* Interview with Bill Sheehan, quoted in Oppenheimer, *Barbara Walters*, 275.

179 *"Then Roone Arledge decided to let Harry go back to* 60 Minutes*":* Virginia Heffernan, "Barbara Walters: The Exit Interview," *New York Times*, September 5, 2004.

179 *Roone believed in star power:* Author interview with Bob Iger.

180 *Indeed, she professed to be delighted:* Arledge, *Roone: A Memoir*, 191. Barbara Walters told Roone Arledge, "This is what I've been wanting to do from the day I was hired. Right from the start, I asked them *not* to put me on the air just to read."

180 *"We did all of that, really, to save Barbara"*: Gunther, *The House That Roone Built*, 69.

180 *Harry derided it as "the Arledge shell game"*: Harry Reasoner, *Before the Colors Fade* (New York: Alfred A. Knopf, 1981), 188.

180 *TV critic Marvin Kitman noticed*: Marvin Kitman, "The Barbara Walters Disappearing Act," *Newsday*, October 23, 1977, Part II, p. 2.

180 *"By this time she was digging her way back"*: Author interview with Sam Donaldson.

181 *"I thought it was a little bit of overkill"*: Author interview with Dale Leibach.

181 *While fifty journalists had arrived*: Recollections of the precise number of journalists differ. Jerry Rafshoon thought the number was fifty; Dale Leibach remembered it as forty.

Chapter 26: The Man She Married (But Only Once)

182 *For a time, she dated John Warner*: John Warner served as U.S. Navy secretary from 1972 to 1974, during the Nixon administration. He married Elizabeth Taylor in 1976; they divorced in 1982. He was elected to the U.S. Senate in 1978, later serving as chair of the Armed Services Committee.

182 *Over the years, she sometimes attended events with Henry Kissinger*: Author interview with Henry Kissinger.

182 *When she was between marriages*: Author interview with Chris Wallace.

183 *Leo-Arthur Kelmenson was neighbors with Barbara*: Walters, *Audition*, 367. According to Oppenheimer, *Barbara Walters*, 321, Roy Cohn told friends he was responsible for introducing Barbara Walters to Merv Adelson; he had worked for one of his Las Vegas ventures.

183 *When her father worked in Las Vegas*: Bryan Burrough, "Remembrance of Wings Past," *Vanity Fair*, March 2013, p. 254.

183 *Back then, those men*: Walters, *Audition*, 367.

184 *But he also wanted her to know he was battling allegations*: Lowell Bergman and Jeff Gerth, "The Hundred-Million-Dollar Resort with Criminal Clientele: La Costa," *Penthouse*, March 1975, p. 47.

184 *Adelson filed a libel suit*: Richard West, "Jury Rules Penthouse Did Not Libel La Costa Owners," *Los Angeles Times*, May 14, 1982, p. 1.

184 *"Well, that's bull":* Burrough, "Remembrance of Wings Past."

184 *After dinner, she relayed Adelson's earnest admission:* Author interview with Phyllis McGrady.

185 *a fortune estimated at $300 million:* Elaine Woo, "Merv Adelson dies at 85; TV Mogul and Philanthropist," *Los Angeles Times*, September 10, 2015.

185 *The twenty-seven-acre spread was called the Lazy A:* Gael Greene, "Western Spirit at the Lazy A Ranch," *Architectural Digest*, December 1994, p. 148.

185 *the two were spotted at a Hollywood reception:* Robin Adams Sloan, "Gossip," Glen Falls (New York) *Post Star*, September 15, 1984, p. 14.

185 *In November, the syndicated columnist:* Robin Adams Sloan, "Margot and Mate at Odds," *Indianapolis News*, November 12, 1984, p. 17.

186 *A year after they met:* Walters, *Audition*, 369.

186 *He gave her a white diamond engagement ring:* "Those East-West Power Brokers Barbara Walters and Merv Adelson Wed After an 11-Month Engagement," *People*, May 26, 1986.

186 *"Our life is going to be so bicoastal":* "Barbara Walters to Marry," *New York Times*, June 14, 1985, p. C30.

186 *"I anguished about it":* Walters, *Audition*, 368.

186 *Barbara went to Florida for the surgery but left to give a long-scheduled speech in Milwaukee:* Walters, *Audition*, 370.

186 *In November, the two sides reached a settlement:* Katrina Brooker, "Crash Landing," *Fortune*, November 10, 2003, p. 128.

187 *She conferred with Ann Landers:* Bob Morris, "Foot-in-Mouth Disease," *New York Times*, August 12, 2007.

187 *"I tried to convince myself that Merv was primarily a businessman":* Walters, *Audition*, 372.

187 *Liz Smith, the gossip columnist close to Barbara:* Liz Smith, "Collins Enjoys Wages of 'Sins,'" Decatur (Illinois) *Herald and Review*, February 16, 1986, p. C2.

188 *"Jackie said to her":* Interview with Wendy Goldberg, quoted in Oppenheimer, *Barbara Walters*, 324.

188 *"Her feelings for Merv meant a great deal to me":* Walters, *Audition*, 373.

188 *"I became Mrs. Merv Adelson":* Walters, *Audition*, 373. Barbara Walters said later she had never "touched pot or any kind of pill" except for the Valium she took to get through her wedding. Walters, *Audition*, 380.

188 *She hadn't bought a wedding dress:* George Christy, "Wedding Bells Ring

for Barbara Walters," *Five Cities* (Arroyo Grande, California) *Times-Press-Recorder*, June 27, 1986, p. 21.

188 *She would later call her failure to order a wedding dress:* Arnold Scaasi, *Women I Have Dressed (and Undressed)* (New York: Scribner, 2004), 37.

189 *The collection of about eighty guests:* "Barbara Walters Marries TV Executive Merv Adelson," Associated Press, May 11, 1986.

189 *"It was all extremely touching and lovely":* Walters, *Audition*, 373.

189 *"This is the way it will always be":* "Those East-West Power Brokers Barbara Walters and Merv Adelson Wed After An 11-Month Engagement," *People*, May 26, 1986.

189 *A photo from the party:* Walters, *Audition*, photo insert.

190 *One of the early inaccurate references:* Curtis Sittenfeld, "View from the Top," *Vanity Fair*, May 8, 2014.

190 *At that time, Merv Adelson was still married to his second wife:* "Carl Reiner Tennis Pro/Am Celebrity Tournament," *Los Angeles Times*, August 1, 1982, p. 7.

190 *When Barbara died in 2022:* Irin Carmon, "Let's Have a Real Conversation About Barbara Walters," *New York*, March 13–26, 2023, p. 32. The magazine incorrectly described Merv Adelson as "Walters's third husband, whom she married twice." Also: "Barbara Walters, Legendary News Anchor, Has Died at 93," by Todd Leopold, Emma Tucker, and Jamiel Lynch, CNN, December 31, 2022. It said, "Walters was married . . . twice to entertainment mogul Merv Adelson."

190 *NPR said she was married five times to four different men:* David Folkenflik, "Trailblazing Journalist Barbara Walters Has Died at 93," *Weekend Edition Saturday*, NPR, December 31, 2022.

190 The New York Times *got it right:* Bruce Weber, "Merv Adelson, Las Vegas Developer-Turned-Daring TV Producer, Dies at 85," *New York Times*, September 10, 2015.

190 *A story in 2023:* Small, Zachary, "Celebrity Treasures Bolster the Auction Business," *New York Times*, September 30, 2023, p. C2.

Chapter 27: The Runaway Daughter

191 *"She got into the cab":* Author interview with Anita Siegenthaler.

192 *She and a friend were caught off campus:* Walters, *Audition*, 381.

192 *A twenty-something assistant who worked for Lee Guber's theatrical business:* Author interview with Amanda Butterbaugh.

193 *For four frantic days:* Walters, *Audition,* 383. Jane Pauley, in an interview with Barbara Walters and Jacqueline in 2002, said the episode lasted longer. "For an entire month Barbara didn't know where she was or what to do about it," Pauley said. She also said that the incident occurred in 1984; it happened in 1985. Jane Pauley, "A Daughter's New Horizon," *Dateline,* NBC News, October 18, 2002.

193 *"I felt like such an outcast":* Pauley, "A Daughter's New Horizon."

193 *"It was really rough going":* Author interview with Kate O'Brian.

193 *she would start by telling new acquaintances:* "Born in My Heart: A Love Story," ABC News, April 20, 2001.

193 *"Particularly when you're young":* Author interview with Chris Wallace.

194 *"'There are two ways that mommies who want babies have them'":* Susan Berman, "Mother and Daughter: The Very Private World of Barbara Walters," *Parents,* July 1979, p. 57.

194 *"She's a very different child from me":* Gene Shalit, "Barbara Walters," *Ladies' Home Journal,* June 1981, p. 26.

194 *"I'm not particularly worried about Jacqueline":* Shalit, "Barbara Walters."

195 *Within a year, Jackie was drinking booze:* Pauley, "A Daughter's New Horizon," *Dateline.*

195 *"You are in fantasyland":* Audition: Barbara Walters' Journey, ABC News Special, May 7, 2008.

195 *Then she heard that her daughter had been hanging out:* Walters, *Audition,* 380. Barbara Walters called them "the Eighty-fourth Street Gang."

195 *"Older boys from what was left of nearby Irish Yorkville":* Celia McGee, "Cop Is a force as a Writer," New York *Daily News,* April 13, 2004, p. 37. Edward Conlon, who discussed the 84th Street Gang, had attended Regis High School on East 84th Street, then became a police officer and an author.

195 *Her mother worried about the course Jackie was on:* Author interview with a close associate of Barbara Walters, speaking on condition of anonymity.

195 *"I should have known":* Pauley, "A Daughter's New Horizon."

196 *When Jackie was sent to boarding school in Maine:* Ron Reagan, "Barbara Walters: She's Candid Off Camera," *Ladies' Home Journal,* June 1984, p. 144.

196 *"I had a huge fear I was nothing inside":* Susan Dominus, "Barbara as a Mom," *Glamour*, April 30, 2008.

196 *ABC producer Jessica Stedman Guff:* Author interview with Jessica Stedman Guff.

197 *"I never felt like I fit into her world":* Pauley, "A Daughter's New Horizon."

197 *"I was just running": Audition: Barbara Walters' Journey*, ABC News Special, May 7, 2008.

197 *Jackie and her friend had hitchhiked to New Mexico:* Martin Clancy and Christina Caron, "Walters' Personal Revelations," ABC News, May 7, 2008.

197 *"Don't leave me in this horrible place":* Walters, *Audition*, 383.

197 *In the summer of 1986:* Walters, *Audition*, 443–44.

198 *When she was at a photographer's studio in New York in 1982:* Author interview with Michael Raab.

198 *At the height of his influence:* "Who Came to Dinner?" *New York Times*, December 5, 1973, p. 46. Six State Supreme Court justices attended the celebration, as did Mayor-elect Abraham Beame. President Nixon sent a congratulatory letter. The party raised money for two charities, the Cardinal Spellman Foundation and the American Jewish League Against Communism. Steven R. Weisman, "Several Hundred Friends Salute Roy Cohn, a Lawyer for 25 Years," *New York Times*, November 30, 1973, p. 73.

198 *Only his most loyal friends testified:* Margot Hornblower, "Roy Cohn Is Disbarred by New York Court," *Washington Post*, June 24, 1986.

199 *Barbara bragged about Jackie's job:* Barbara Walters, speaking at the Museum of Broadcasting television festival, held at the Los Angeles County Museum following a retrospective of her career, March 19, 1988. Oppenheimer, *Barbara Walters*, 313. "TV & Video," *Los Angeles Times*, March 21, 1988, Part VI, p. 2. "The Museum of Broadcasting's 5th Annual Television Festival in Los Angeles," full-page ad in the *Los Angeles Times*, February 19, 1988, p. 29.

199 *The station's public affairs director, Joella Werlin:* Author interview with Joella Werlin.

199 *"So did I feel guilt?":* Walters, *Audition*, 170.

199 *At the gala at the Museum of Broadcasting:* Barbara Walters, speaking at the Museum of Broadcasting television festival, held at the Los Angeles County Museum following a retrospective of her career, March 19, 1988. Oppen-

heimer, *Barbara Walters*, 313. "TV & Video," *Los Angeles Times*, March 21, 1988, Part VI, p. 2. "The Museum of Broadcasting's 5th Annual Television Festival in Los Angeles," full-page ad in the *Los Angeles Times*, February 19, 1988, p. 29.

Chapter 28: The Honeymoon and the Arms Dealer

203 *Reagan was excited by the information:* Ronald Reagan, *The Reagan Diaries* (New York: HarperCollins, 2007), 459.

203 *"Iran Arms Dealer Used Barbara Walters":* Edward T. Pound and Andy Pasztor, "Iran Arms Dealer Used Barbara Walters to Secretly Pass on a Message to Reagan," *Wall Street Journal*, March 16, 1987.

203 The New York Times *followed:* Gerald M. Boyd, "Barbara Walters Gave Reagan Papers on Iran," *New York Times*, March 17, 1987, p. 9.

203 *In the* New York Post: Walters, *Audition*, 451.

203 *A UPI columnist dubbed it "Barbara Walters-gate":* Mark Schwed, "Barbara Walters-gate," UPI, March 20, 1987.

203 *In short order, Khashoggi ran into financial problems:* William Norwich, "Yacht's the Ticket," New York *Daily News*, August 4, 1988.

204 *Together, they bought the entire sixth floor:* Betty Liu Ebron, "Apple Sauce: Wa-Wa's Waiting for a Buyer," New York *Daily News*, October 30, 1988, p. 6.

204 *Then it would be listed for sale for $19.75 million:* Compass listing, 944 Fifth Avenue, Upper East Side, Manhattan, NY 10021. Posted April 20, 2023.

204 *Merv decided to buy a new home in Bel Air, too:* Marietta Tree, "Barbara Walters and Merv Adelson," *Architectural Digest*, October 1988, p. 223.

204 *The guest list was eclectic New York royalty:* Suzy Says, "'Big Apple' and 'Big Orange' Throw Party in N.Y.," *Palm Beach Daily News*, October 1, 1986, p. 2.

205 *Keel then sang a love song:* Walters, *Audition*, 373.

205 The Wall Street Journal *had just published:* Jonathan Kwitny, "Seeds of Success: Two Lorimar Officials Have Had Ties to Men of Underworld Repute," *Wall Street Journal*, September 15, 1986, p. 1.

205 *Lorimar eventually withdrew the offer to buy the TV stations:* Paul Richter, "Who Shot Lorimar?: After Film and Video Losses, Studio Mulls Merger, Sees Recovery Ahead," *Los Angeles Times*, April 10, 1988.

205 *"Merv Adelson and Molasky are known in Las Vegas"*: Ed Reid and Ovid Demaris, *The Green Felt Jungle* (New York: Trident Press, 1963), 102.

206 *"I would like to thank* The Wall Street Journal *for underwriting tonight's party"*: Walters, *Audition*, 374.

Chapter 29: Loss

207 *Barbara was back in Miami: The Barbara Walters Special* with the Don Johnson interview aired on December 8, 1987. *Sweet Hearts Dance*, released in 1988, may be most memorable for the cameo role played by the then-mayor of Burlington, Vermont, a quirky political independent named Bernie Sanders.

207 *The segment's producer:* Author interview with Phyllis McGrady.

208 *A few months later, when Barbara was in California:* Walters, *Audition*, 374.

208 *Dena died in June 1988:* Walters, *Audition*, 371–72.

208 *"I realized that, after all those years of worry and responsibility"*: Walters, *Audition*, 375.

209 *In a book:* Jeanne Safer, *The Normal One: Life with a Difficult or Damaged Sibling* (New York: Free Press, 2002), 69–82.

209 *At a dinner party:* Author interview with Jeanne Safer.

209 *"What a burden"*: Author interview with Jeanne Safer.

209 *Barbara was at Arthur Ashe Stadium:* The interview generated news coverage. Kevin Mulligan, "Life Without Doc in House," *Philadelphia Daily News*, July 30, 1999, p. 158.

210 *A group of special-needs children on a field trip:* Author interview with Katie Nelson Thomson.

210 *"I think Barbara recognized"*: Author interview with Anne Sweeney.

Chapter 30: Diane

211 *On the last full day of President Richard Nixon's tour of China:* Also notable in the photo is the apparent absence of any person of color, either in the press corps or the White House staff. The picture included three female journalists and four female staffers from the White House press office. Among the other journalists on the trip were Frank Cormier of the Associated Press,

Jerry terHorst of *The Detroit News*, Max Frankel of *The New York Times*, Eric Sevareid of CBS, Theodore White of Public Broadcasting, Hugh Sidey of *Life* magazine, James Michener of *Reader's Digest*, and syndicated columnists Joseph Kraft and William Buckley.

212 *Three other NBC correspondents were on the trip:* They were John Chancellor, Herb Kaplow, and John Rich.

212 *The third female journalist:* Douglas Martin, "Fay Gillis Wells, 94, Aviator and Journalist," *New York Times*, December 9, 2002. Fay Gillis Wells was a pioneering female pilot and foreign correspondent who reported from the Soviet Union and elsewhere with her husband, Linton Wells. In 1941, President Franklin Roosevelt asked the couple to investigate possible locations in Africa for a Jewish homeland; they recommended Angola.

212 *"There's Nixon," Barbara said two decades later:* Author interview with Bill Carter. The profile he wrote was titled "The Tender Trap," in *The New York Times Magazine* on August 23, 1992, p. 23. Note: Diane Sawyer was an assistant to White House press secretary Ron Ziegler, not an assistant press secretary, a higher-ranking position.

213 *A chapter of his memoir is titled "Landing Diane":* Roone Arledge, *Roone: A Memoir* (New York: HarperCollins, 2003), 329–45.

213 *Barbara saw it as a betrayal:* Phyllis McGrady, a top producer at ABC, told me in an interview, "Barbara thought it was a betrayal that Roone hid this from her until it was going to happen and then sort of said, 'Oh, by the way, we're hiring Diane Sawyer.'" Another senior executive at the network told me, "It was almost like she'd been jilted for a younger, taller blonde."

213 *"Roone Arledge, who was my savior":* The Charlie Rose Show, August 1, 2008.

213 *A few days before the announcement:* Arledge, *Roone: A Memoir*, 338.

214 *"The fact is that the people who run the network news divisions":* Edward Klein, "Winning Diane: How ABC's Roone Arledge Snatched Her Away from CBS," *New York*, March 13, 1989, p. 36.

215 *"Barbara was wonderful":* Author interview with an ABC executive who worked with both Barbara Walters and Diane Sawyer, speaking on condition of anonymity.

215 *"You know, the* All About Eve *thing":* All About Eve, released in 1951, stars Bette Davis as Margo Channing, a Broadway star who at age forty is anxious about her future. Anne Baxter portrayed Eve Harrington, a fan who maneu-

vers herself into Margo's life and undercuts her personally and professionally, eventually becoming a Broadway star herself.

215 *"When I arrived, I'm sure it was confusing to her"*: Author interview with Diane Sawyer.

215 *But to her surprise and dismay, Diane discovered ABC had no system*: At CBS's *60 Minutes*, the executive producer would designate what correspondent would take the lead on a prospective story, a system known as the "green sheet." Author interview with Diane Sawyer.

216 *"Television is a tough game"*: Walters, *Audition*, 331.

216 *Barbara confided in friends her fear*: Separate interviews by the author with three friends of Barbara Walters with whom she confided those fears.

216 *When she was at the* Today *show, she had disappointed some*: Sheila Weller, *The News Sorority: Diane Sawyer, Katie Couric, Christiane Amanpour—and the (Ongoing, Imperfect, Complicated) Triumph of Women in TV News* (New York: Penguin, 2014), 57–58.

216 *Eventually the network reached a settlement*: Marlene Sanders and Marcia Rock, *Waiting for Prime Time: The Women of Television News* (Champaign: University of Illinois Press, 1988), p. 137.

216 *More than a decade later, when Barbara had moved to ABC*: Carole Simpson, *NewsLady* (Bloomington, Indiana: AuthorHouse, 2010), 105–16.

217 *Then she distributed the documents they had prepared*: Weller, *The News Sorority*, 156–57.

217 *Over the next few years, some progress was made*: Simpson, *NewsLady*, 117–22.

218 *Thomas Root was at the center of a headline-grabbing mystery:* In the interview on *Primetime*, he denied having attempted suicide. He was back in the news three years later, when he was convicted of counterfeiting, forgery, and fraud. He was sentenced to thirty-three months in prison. Stephen C. Fehr, "Mystery Pilot Gets 33 Months in Fraud Case," *Washington Post*, January 18, 1992.

218 Primetime *booker Maia Samuel persuaded Root*: Gunther, *The House That Roone Built*, 290–91.

218 *"It was a complicated internal ABC situation"*: Author interview with Victor Neufeld.

218 *Her producers on the show*: Author interview with Diane Sawyer.

219 *"None of us could get over the fact"*: Author interview with Ira Rosen.

219 *Soon afterward, Barbara tried to upend another interview:* Gunther, *The House That Roone Built*, 327.

219 *When Barbara scheduled her own Hepburn interview a year later:* Alan Mirabella, "'Primetime Live' vs. '20/20,'" *EW*, November 1, 1991. "The shows are very different," ABC spokeswoman Sherrie Rollins said. "They share a healthy competition."

219 *"There were no rules":* Ramin Setoodeh, *Ladies Who Punch: The Explosive Inside Story of The View* (New York: Thomas Dunne Books, 2019), 18–19.

219 *"Roone loved pitting people against each other":* Author interview with Phyllis McGrady.

219 *"How is thievery an honorable position":* Author interview with Ira Rosen. The interview with John Hinckley Jr. never took place because of problems getting permission to bring a camera to the interview at St. Elizabeth's Hospital in Washington, D.C.

220 *"My childhood was the world":* Nadine Brozan, "Chronicle," *New York Times*, May 7, 1994.

220 *"You made me ruthless":* Lloyd Grove, "Kiss of the Anchorwomen," *Vanity Fair*, August 1994.

220 *embraced Diane afterward:* Author interview with Diane Sawyer.

224 *(For the record, Diane told me):* Author interview with Diane Sawyer.

224 *"All this dismayed me":* Memo from Barbara Walters to Roone Arledge, dated April 16, 1996, Roone Arledge Papers, Rare Book and Manuscript Library, Columbia University in the City of New York.

224 *Four years earlier, during the previous round of contract negotiations:* Walters, *Audition*, 398.

225 *"The American people have now had an adequate opportunity":* President Bill Clinton on ABC's *20/20*. The interview was recorded at the White House on August 23, 1996, and broadcast on September 20, 1996.

225 *"He never sparkled with me":* Walters, *Audition*, 416.

225 *There was a mantra in the hallways of ABC:* Three veterans of ABC, separately and without prompting by the author, volunteered this saying in interviews with them.

225 *"I was standing with Diane at the elevator":* Ira Rosen, *Ticking Clock: Behind the Scenes at* 60 Minutes (New York: St. Martin's Griffin, 2021), 152.

226 *A year and a half later, that laying-down-the-law session:* Jim Rutenberg, "Media: Working to Unite Stars and Factions at ABC News," *New York Times*, February 11, 2002, p. C1.

226 *"The greatest TV diva duel":* Michelangelo Signorile, "Rosie O'Donnell's Endless Outing," *San Francisco Examiner*, March 8, 2002, p. A5.

226 *"This had nothing to do":* David Bauder, "ABC News Stars Deny Interview Caused Rift," Associated Press, February 21, 2002, p. 20.

227 *They sat together in an ABC conference room:* Author interview with Jeffrey Schneider.

227 *"I'm going to tell everybody":* Bauder, "ABC News Stars Deny Interview Caused Rift."

227 *"It was a constant battle royale":* Author interview with Connie Chung.

227 *Barbara argued that Jennings and Ted Koppel:* Grove, "Kiss of the Anchorwomen."

227 *"There were times when we competed":* Author interview with Ted Koppel.

228 *"Roone's beloved was Diane Sawyer":* Author interview with Ted Koppel.

228 *Roone was in Washington:* Author interview with a source who was there, speaking on condition of anonymity.

228 *"Newsmagazines in general":* Virginia Heffernan, "Barbara Walters: The Exit Interview," *New York Times*, September 5, 2004.

229 *For her last piece on 20/20:* Walters, *Audition*, 572.

229 *"More frogs":* Walters, *Audition*, 561.

229 *"For years, it seemed that there had been":* Author interview with Ben Sherwood.

Chapter 31: You Can't Have It All

231 *"She was at a point in her life":* Author interview with Maurie Perl. Joan Rivers, the comedian and a friend who had her own struggles with men, said at the time, "I know she wanted it to work, but I've always said it's either marriage or a career," adding sardonically, "I call my career 'Harry.'" Jeannie Williams, "Rivers Sad for Friend Walters," *USA Today*, September 13, 1990, p. 2D.

231 *Connie Chung found herself seated next to Merv:* Irin Carmon, "Let's Have a Real Conversation About Barbara Walters," *New York*, March 13–26, 2023, p. 32.

232 *She warned Barbara that her husband's picture:* Bryan Burrough, "Remembrance of Wings Past," *Vanity Fair*, March 2013, p. 254.

232 *A close colleague told me:* Author interview with a close colleague of Barbara Walters, speaking on condition of anonymity.

232 *"She never really forgave me":* Burrough, "Remembrance of Wings Past."

232 *"It is with great sadness":* Liz Smith, "Barbara Walters & Hubby Separating," New York *Daily News*, September 11, 1990.

233 *"You can have a great marriage":* Al Cohn, "Walters' Advice on Career, Marriage: Women Can't Have It All," *Newsday*, September 20, 1989, p. 8.

233 *Merv was in financial trouble:* Katrina Brooker, "Crash Landing," *Fortune*, November 10, 2003, p. 128.

233 *He filed for personal bankruptcy in 2003:* Brooker, "Crash Landing."

233 *Once the titan of Lorimar:* Michael Schneider, "Lightforce Ignites," *Daily Variety*, May 25, 2004, p. 2.

233 *"She says, 'Jessica, you have to put Merv on the show'":* Author interview with Jessica Stedman Guff.

234 *Near the end of his life:* Burrough, "Remembrance of Wings Past."

234 *His fourth wife would haul him:* David McCormack, "Barbara Walters Bankrupt Ex-Husband, Now 83, in Court for Unpaid Child Support," *Daily Mail*, April 16, 2013.

234 *After Barbara died:* "The Estate of American Icon Barbara Walters at Bonhams," Bonhams auction house, September 29, 2023.

Chapter 32: The Yin and the Yang

235 *"Barbara often would ask":* Author interview with Deborah Roberts.

236 *"She inspired me":* Author interview with Norah O'Donnell.

236 *"For me, to see someone like that made me imagine the possibilities":* Author interview with Katie Couric.

236 *She credited her:* Curtis Sittenfeld, "View from the Top," *Vanity Fair*, May 2014.

236 *"She earned the right to be a diva":* Irin Carmon, "Let's Talk Barbara Walters: Seventeen Leading Broadcasters on Her Legacy and Making Their Way in the World She Made," *The Cut*, March 13, 2023.

237 *"She mom'ed the correspondents whom she liked":* Author interview with Connie Chung.

237 *In 1970, an unemployed writer named Pat Mitchell:* Author interview with Pat Mitchell.

239 *"ABC's ACE reporter Lynn Sherr":* Liz Smith, "'Art' Gives U.S. Superstars the

Brush," *New York Post*, November 21, 1997, p. 14. *Hors de combat* is French for "out of combat" or "out of action."

240 *She stepped in to help when Nancy Shevell McCartney:* Author interview with Nancy Shevell McCartney.

240 *The original group included:* Author interview with Maurie Perl.

241 *"She could carry a grudge":* Author interview with Bill Carter, who covered Barbara Walters when he was the TV reporter for *The New York Times*.

241 *In a cover story in* People *magazine:* "Nipped, Tucked and Talking," *People*, February 7, 2002.

242 *In fact, while Barbara had cosmetic surgery earlier in her career:* Author interview with Lori Klein.

242 *Mary Alice, who happened to be watching the show that morning:* Author interview with Mary Alice Williams. She no longer had a copy of the email she sent; she relayed its contents from memory.

242 *Susan Mercandetti, who had been a colleague at ABC:* Author interview with Susan Mercandetti.

242 *Cynthia McFadden arrived at one of Barbara's famous dinner parties:* Author interview with Cynthia McFadden.

242 *The first time Deborah Roberts had a story on 20/20:* Author interview with Deborah Roberts.

Chapter 33 The Barbara Walters Interview

244 *"Nobody calls it the 'Peter Jennings interview'":* Elisabeth Bumiller, "So Famous, Such Clout, She Could Interview Herself," *New York Times*, April 21, 1996, Section 2, p. 1.

244 *When one of her interviews was over:* Author interview with Chris Wallace.

245 *"Almost single-handedly, Barbara Walters turned TV":* James Wolcott, "Barbara Knows Best," *Vanity Fair*, September 1, 2001.

245 *"She is a reporter":* Author interview with Richard Wald.

245 *"Barbara didn't deal with management or channels":* Author interview with Robin Sproul.

246 *"The Shah blurs into Anwar el-Sadat and then turns into Mr. T":* John Corry, "The Barbara Walters Prism," *New York Times*, September 9, 1984, p. 35.

246 *Finally, in 1992, he agreed to talk with her:* Interview of Mark David Chapman by Barbara Walters, *20/20*, ABC News, December 4, 1992.

247 *"We were seated in essentially the mezzanine":* Author interview with Ellen Rossen Westin. Note: Westin wasn't sure what item of clothing Barbara Walters described in the letter; it might have been a red scarf or something else easy to spot.

247 *she got on the air: Issues and Answers*, ABC News, September 30, 1979.

247 *"I do so much homework": Barbara Walters: The Art of the Interview*, ABC News, May 25, 2016.

248 *Larry King bragged that he didn't prepare:* Jeff Lunden, "Veteran Broadcaster Larry King Dies at 87," *Weekend Edition Saturday*, NPR, January 23, 2021.

248 *"I never write down a question, ever":* Author interview with Ted Koppel.

248 *"A hooker, a teaser and a conclusion":* James Conaway, "How to Talk with Barbara Walters About Practically Anything," *New York Times Magazine*, September 10, 1972, p. 40.

248 *Rick Klein, an ABC political director who helped her prepare for some interviews:* Author interview with Rick Klein.

249 *"It was like bang, bang, bang":* Author interview with Rob Wallace.

249 *"She had a question in there":* Author interview with Rick Klein.

249 *Michael J. Satin, a white-collar defense lawyer in Washington:* Michael J. Satin, "What Barbara Walters Can Teach Us About Direct Examination," *American Bar Association Journal*, Winter 2017.

250 *Early on,* Newsweek *described her questions:* Elizabeth Peer, "Barbara Walters—Star of the Morning," *Newsweek*, May 6, 1974, p. 56.

251 *Barbara asked former first lady Mamie Eisenhower:* Interview of Mamie Eisenhower by Barbara Walters on *20/20*, ABC News, November 8, 1979.

252 *"She interviewed everyone at that moment":* Author interview with Betsy Shuller.

252 *"I would ask questions about their childhood":* ABC special with Bill Geddie.

253 *She hadn't been warned:* Author interview with Maurie Perl.

253 *In 1976, first lady Betty Ford seemed inebriated:* Walters, *Audition*, 403–4. A decade later, in 1987, Barbara Walters interviewed Betty Ford about her struggle with addiction.

253 *Eventually Barbara conceded she had made a mistake:* Walters, *Audition*, 405.

254 *"It gets harder and harder to interview the twenty-one-year-old star"*: Barbara Walters, "Barbara Walters Tells All," *Ladies' Home Journal*, April 1998, p. 115.

254 *"It is as if Mr. Carter had just become Louis XIV"*: Associated Press, "Barbara Walters Criticized for Her Carter Interview," *Toledo* (Ohio) *Blade*, December 22, 1976, p. P6.

254 *"How dare I say something so corny"*: Walters, *Audition*, 315.

255 *Years later, as an adult*: A video with Brooke Shields, *Vogue*, October 2021.

255 *"And I thought, 'This isn't right'"*: Interview with Brooke Shields, *The Drew Barrymore Show*, November 22, 2022.

255 *"When she dropped the question"*: Jason Sheeler, "Ricky Martin Doesn't Want to Hide Who He Is Anymore: 'I Am a Man with No Secrets,'" *People*, June 2, 2021.

255 *"When I think back on it now"*: Issie Lapowsky, "Barbara Walters: My Questioning of Ricky Martin's Sexuality Was 'Inappropriate'": New York *Daily News*, May 9, 2010.

Chapter 34: Bette Davis and the Dalai Lama

257 *"She was a populist"*: Author interview with Jeff Zucker.

257 *"During my twenty-five years at 20/20"*: Walters, *Audition*, 454.

257 *The range of her interests was reflected in the chapter titles of her memoir*: Walters, *Audition*.

258 *"I don't think Barbara . . . was deeply introspective"*: Author interview with a close friend, speaking on condition of anonymity.

258 *She was promoting her autobiography*: Bette Davis's autobiography, written with Michael Herskowitz, was titled *This 'N That* and was published in 1987 by Simon & Schuster. B. D. Hyman's memoir, *My Mother's Keeper*, was published in 1985 by William Morrow.

259 *"Did you get mellow, mellower, as you got older?"*: The Barbara Walters Summer Special, ABC, March 30, 1987.

260 *Barbara interviewed the spiritual leader of Tibetan Buddhism*: "Heaven: Where Is It? And How Do We Get There?" *The Barbara Walters Summer Special*, ABC News, December 20, 2005.

260 *"I'm certainly not a Buddhist"*: Walters, *Audition*, 514.

260 *"It was a few days later; we were heading home"*: Author interview with Rob Wallace.

260 *"I felt very, very different"*: Walters, *Audition*, 514–15.

Chapter 35: *The View*

261 *"We should do a daytime show"*: Author interview with Bill Geddie.

261 Now Caryl & Marilyn: Real Friends *was going into reruns:* The short-lived talk show featured Marilyn Kentz and Caryl Kristensen, a comedy pair who called themselves "The Mommies."

262 *"We had failed in that daytime, that time period again and again and again"*: Author interview with David Westin.

262 *Barbara had occasionally appeared on it:* Walters, *Audition*, 541.

262 *The show's featured headlines should be ripped from the tabloid:* Interview with Pat Fili-Krushel, quoted in Setoodeh, *Ladies Who Punch*, 18.

262 *"Roone felt it was potentially dangerous"*: Author interview with Bill Geddie.

263 *"And I said, 'You know what? That's a great idea'"*: Author interview with David Westin. Roone Arledge would never acknowledge he was wrong. In his 424-page memoir, published when *The View* was heading into a successful sixth season, Arledge discusses his dealings with Barbara Walters at length but never mentions *The View* or his opposition to it. Arledge, *Roone: A Memoir* (New York: HarperCollins, 2003).

263 *She held up a copy of the* New York Post: "39 Dead in Cult Suicide," *New York Post*, March 27, 1997.

263 *"We've all seen it"*: Barbara Walters: Her Story, ABC News, May 21, 2014.

264 *When Barbara called the mass suicide a senseless tragedy:* Setoodeh, *Ladies Who Punch*, 25.

264 *"Barbara and I looked at each other"*: Author interview with Bill Geddie.

264 *"This is a very difficult note for me to write"*: Author interview with Mary Alice Williams, who showed me the thank-you note.

264 *"I wasn't sure if it would be a success"*: Author interview with Joy Behar.

265 *"We hired her because she wasn't intimidated"*: Author interview with Jessica Stedman Guff.

265 *Eventually, even the august* New York Times *would call it:* Amanda Fitz-Simons, "How 'The View' Became the Most Important Political TV Show

in America," *New York Times Magazine*, May 22, 2019. The co-hosts shown on the cover were Joy Behar, Whoopi Goldberg, Sunny Hostin, Abby Huntsman, and Meghan McCain, talking to guest Jill Biden, whose husband Joe Biden was running for president.

265 *Geddie recalled a conversation:* Author interview with Bill Geddie.

265 *"She saw the writing on the wall":* Author interview with Joy Behar.

266 *Diane had lobbied for the change:* Arledge, *Roone: A Memoir*, 403.

266 *"We hadn't taken lemons":* Walters, *Audition*, 564.

266 *she told* The New York Times: Jim Rutenberg, "Move Against Barbara Walters Touches a Nerve," *New York Times*, May 21, 2001, p. C1.

266 *"She loved to be on the air":* Author interview with Alexandra Cohen.

266 *"I think there was a time when I was considered too serious":* Ramin Setoodeh, "Barbara's Long Good-bye," *Variety*, April 8, 2014, p. 30.

266 *But on* The View, *"I could be funny":* Barbara Walters: Her Story, ABC News, 2014.

267 The View *was being shot in Las Vegas:* Setoodeh, *Ladies Who Punch*, 8. The date was February 16, 2004.

267 *Four years later,* The View *was back:* "Lance Burton Does an Illusion with Barbara Walters on 'The View,'" LanceBurton.com, posted June 26, 2008.

268 *Barbara developed a routine:* Setoodeh, *Ladies Who Punch*, 35.

268 *"A few more steps to your right":* Walters, *Audition*, 544.

268 *"I was always saying, 'Make sparks'":* Author interview with Bill Geddie. When he left the show, he took the sign with him. It was displayed amid favorite photos in his office at his California home.

268 *"I sometimes said, 'Enough with the penises'":* Walters, *Audition*, 545.

268 *"A genius bit of television":* James Wolcott, "Barbara Knows Best," *Vanity Fair*, September 1, 2001.

268 *"We didn't create a new format":* Setoodeh, *Ladies Who Punch*, 3.

269 *"The idea that those women":* Caryn James, "Feet on the Ground, Heads Without Bubbles," *New York Times*, August 21, 1997, p. C11.

Chapter 36: Monica

270 *Her sit-down that day with Bill Gates:* Paul Andrews, "Bill Gates Sings for Barbara Walters—Software Magnate to Show Softer Side—and a New Talent—on National TV," *Seattle Times*, January 29, 1998.

270 *"The biggest 'get' of my career":* Walters, *Audition*, 520.

271 *"Her lawyer was on TV more than I was":* Walters, *Audition*, 525.

271 *He would be immortalized in media:* On February 1, 1998, Ginsburg appeared on ABC's *This Week*, CBS's *Face the Nation*, CNN's *State of the Union*, Fox News Sunday, and NBC's *Meet the Press*.

271 *Finally, her longtime producer, Katie Nelson Thomson:* Author interview with Katie Nelson Thomson.

272 *At the time, Clinton allies had begun portraying Monica Lewinsky:* Julian Borger, "Clinton Aide Called Monica a Stalker," *The Guardian*, February 8, 1999. British reporter Christopher Hitchens signed an affidavit saying Sidney Blumenthal, then a senior aide in the Clinton White House, had told him Lewinsky was "a stalker" and the president was "the victim of a predatory and unstable sexually demanding young woman."

272 *Hillary Clinton seemed to initially believe:* Dan Merica, "Documents Reveal Hillary Clinton's Private Reaction to Her Husband's Cheating Scandal with Monica Lewinsky," CNN, February 10, 2014. Hillary Clinton's description of Monica Lewinsky was in contemporaneous notes written by a close friend, Diane Blair.

272 *She was in legal peril as well:* Monica Lewinsky signed a sworn affidavit on January 7, 1998, in a civil case brought by Paula Jones against Bill Clinton. "I have never had a sexual relationship with the President," she testified. The affidavit was submitted to lawyers for Paula Jones on January 16, 1998. *Clinton v. Jones*, 520 U.S. 681.

273 *Monica called her father:* Andrew Morton, *Monica's Story* (New York: St. Martin's Press, 1999), 218.

274 *Diane Sawyer volunteered to introduce Bernard Lewinsky:* Author interview with an ABC source who was told this by William Ginsburg at the time.

274 *"Most of my colleagues":* Walters, *Audition*, 526.

274 *He managed to leave the misimpression:* Jim Yardley, "1,000 Unlikely Elbow-Rubbers Meet at a Time Gala," *New York Times*, March 4, 1998, p. B1.

275 *"Humor has always been very important to me":* Setoodeh, *Ladies Who Punch*, 64. Author Ramin Setoodeh interviewed Monica Lewinsky for his book.

276 *Finally, in September, Starr released a nearly five-hundred-page report:* Walters, *Audition*, 529.

276 *"[W]hen you finally decide to do an interview":* Letters seeking interviews with Monica Lewinsky provided by a knowledgable source on condition of anonymity.

277 *Monica's team said Judy Smith, a public relations consultant*: Author interview with Katie Nelson Thomson.

277 *She would later be the inspiration*: Malcolm Venable, "Judy Smith Talks the Legacy of 'Scandal' and Informing Olivia Pope," *Shondaland*, April 15, 2022.

277 *"I never say we have the interview"*: Author interview with Katie Nelson Thomson.

277 *One was Australian-born media baron Rupert Murdoch*: Jenny Hontz, "News Corp. Offers $3 Mil to Lewinsky," *Variety*, October 8, 1998. Josh Young, "How Oprah Dumped Monica," *George*, March 1999, p. 68. A knowledgeable source speaking on condition of anonymity confirmed the Fox offer.

278 *On April 4, two months after her tearful testimony*: James Barron with Edward Wong, "Public Lives," *New York Times*, July 30, 1998.

278 *"I understand why you want this money"*: Author interview with David Westin.

278 *In the end, Monica was interviewed by*: Howard Kurtz, "Carlson: Lewinsky's Quiet Helper," *Washington Post*, February 12, 1999, p. C1.

279 Hello! *magazine, sort of the European version of* People: Walters, *Audition*, 534. Monica Lewinsky also signed a contract and made a TV commercial for Jenny Craig, Inc., a weight-loss company.

279 *But it was still "a little atypical, a little unusual"*: Author interview with a senior ABC executive, speaking on condition of anonymity.

279 *But an interview with her*: Walters, *Audition*, 532.

279 *"Believe me, I know how difficult this decision is for you"*: Letter from Barbara Walters to Monica Lewinsky, November 3, 1998.

280 *"I believe every word of it"*: Handwritten note from Barbara Walters to Richard Carlson, November 4, 1998.

280 *When the interview was announced in November*: Doreen Carvajal and Lawrie Mifflin, "Diana's Biographer and ABC's Walters Get Lewinsky Deals," *New York Times*, November 17, 1998, p. 1A.

281 *When the arrangement*: Jane Mayer, "Bad News," *The New Yorker*, August 14, 2000.

281 *"an unorthodox step"*: Paul Farhi, "ABC Paid to Secure Lewinsky Interview," *Washington Post*, August 9, 2000.

281 *"Did ABC Pay to Get Monica?"*: Jessica Graham, "Did ABC Pay to Get Monica?" *New York Post*, August 7, 2000.

281 *Westin defended the $25,000 payment:* In a final twist, ABC failed to pay Theodore Olson's bill for more than a year, eventually paying after Richard Carlson intervened. Richard Wald said the bill got "lost in the shuffle" during a change in financial executives at the network. Paul Farhi, "ABC Paid to Secure Lewinsky Interview," *Washington Post*, August 9, 2000.

281 *Carlson was able to make his case directly to Starr:* According to a knowledgeable source on condition of anonymity.

281 *four days after the Senate acquitted Clinton:* Walters, *Audition*, 536.

281 *The interview was back on track:* Lawrie Mifflin, with Stuart Elliott, "Lewinsky Proves to Be Popular with Both Viewers and Sponsors," *New York Times*, March 5, 1999, p. A14.

282 *A memo titled "Key Messages/BW Interview":* Memo titled "Key Messages/ BW Interview" and dated October 22, 1999, provided by a knowledgeable source on condition of anonymity.

282 *She finally agreed:* According to a knowledgeable source on condition of anonymity.

283 *"She takes her work very seriously":* Curtis Sittenfield, "View from the Top," *Vanity Fair*, May 8, 2012.

284 *In their negotiations before the interview:* Morton, *Monica's Story*.

285 *"It was terrifying for me":* Setoodeh, *Ladies Who Punch*, 64.

285 *She was still "somewhat shell-shocked":* Sittenfield, "View from the Top."

285 *Her glossy lipstick caused a brief sensation:* Joanne Trestrail, "Those Lips, Those Eyes," *Chicago Tribune*, March 16, 1999. To inquiries, the makeup firm responded: "On the program '20/20' Wednesday, March 3, 1999, Monica Lewinsky was wearing all Club Monaco Cosmetics. She was wearing Sheer Lip Colour in 'Glaze' ($13 U.S.) with Lip Pencil 'Bare' ($10 U.S.). Her eyes were done with Black Mascara and 'Topaz and Bronze' Eye Colour. She wore 'Hint Hint' Cheek Colour, Liquid Foundation Makeup and Pressed Powder."

285 *"I remember very kindly she acquiesced to my request":* Setoodeh, *Ladies Who Punch*, 64–65.

286 *"How am I doing, guys?":* Author interviews with two people who were on the set.

286 *Monica said at one point:* Eric Mink and Helen Kennedy, "My Affair with the President," New York *Daily News*, March 2, 1999, p. 4.

287 *The day before the interview aired:* Mink and Kennedy, "My Affair with the President," pp. 4–7.

287 *ABC insiders suspected some disgruntled employee:* Elizabeth Jensen, "Not the Usual '20/20' Interview," *Los Angeles Times*, March 3, 1999. ABC and the National Association of Broadcast Employees and Technicians had been battling for months over a new contract, and the week before the Monica Lewinsky interview aired the network declared negotiations at an impasse and implemented the new contract over the union's objections.

287 *A week earlier,* The Washington Post *had plastered on its front page:* Howard Kurtz, "Lewinsky Apologizes to Nation for Ordeal," *Washington Post*, February 25, 1999, p. A1.

287 *Without identifying his source:* Author interview with Howard Kurtz.

287 *At the party were both ABC colleagues:* Author interview with Chris Vlasto.

288 *The Nielsen rating of 33.4 for* Monica: In Her Own Words *smashed the record:* The previous record was Diane Sawyer's interview with Michael Jackson and Lisa Marie Presley in 1995, averaging 37.5 million viewers. Oprah Winfrey's interview with Michael Jackson in February 1993 had a bigger audience, averaging 62.3 million viewers. But it was produced for ABC by the entertainment division, not the news division. Lisa De Moraes, "Monica Lewinsky Beats the Competition," *Washington Post*, March 5, 1999, p. C1.

288 *The show attracted an average of 48.5 million viewers:* Mifflin, with Elliott, "Lewinsky Proves to Be Popular with Both Viewers and Sponsors."

288 *In a* USA Today/*CNN*/*Gallup Poll afterward:* "Poll: Public Remains Unsympathetic to Lewinsky," CNN.com, March 5, 1999.

Chapter 37: Trump

289 *The first time she interviewed Trump:* Barbara Walters, *20/20*, December 11, 1987. The *20/20* interview was recounted in *Front Row at the Trump Show* by Jonathan Karl (New York: Dutton, 2020), 2–5.

290 *"Jacuzzi journalism," scoffed the TV reviewer for* Newsday: David Friedman, "Walters' Hot Airing of Donald Trump," *Newsday*, December 11, 1987, Part II, p. 11.

290 *Barbara sent Trump a sympathetic letter:* Letter from Barbara Walters to

Donald Trump, dated June 14, 1990, included in Donald Trump, *Letters to Trump* (Winning Team Publishing, 2023).

291 *She would take a tough tack:* Barbara Walters Interviews Donald Trump, *20/20*, ABC News, August 17, 1990.

291 *"I'm gonna get that woman":* Selina Scott, "Donald Trump Used His Power Games on Me," *The Times* (of London), May 13, 2023.

291 *When* The View *was launched seven years later:* New York Times Magazine, June 22, 2019.

291 *"He was on all the time":* Author interview with Joy Behar.

292 *After he was elected president in 2016:* Author interviews conducted on condition of anonymity.

292 *"You needed a guest":* Author interview with Bill Geddie. *The View* skit in which Barbara Walters played a short-order cook was on February 9, 2004. "Today's TV Talk Shows," *Los Angeles Times*, February 9, 2004, p. E22.

292 *Trump had called a news conference:* Rick Maiman, Associated Press, "Trump: Miss USA to Keep Crown," *Boston Globe*, December 20, 2006. Note: Tara Conner turned twenty-one the day before the news conference.

292 *(She would later credit Trump for her decade of sobriety):* Tara Conner, "Donald Trump Made Me Great Again: Former Miss USA," *USA Today*, March 1, 2017. In the op-ed, she said she had been abusing alcohol and illicit drugs since she was fourteen years old.

293 *Rosie, watching on TV at home, steamed:* Rosie O'Donnell, *Celebrity Detox* (New York: Grand Central Publishing, 2007), 143–44.

293 *He would disparage her:* In the first presidential debate, on September 26, 2016, Donald Trump acknowledged he said "very tough things" to Rosie O'Donnell, "and I think everybody would agree that she deserves it, and nobody feels sorry for her."

294 *He wrote an open "Dear Rosie" letter:* Amy Bonawitz, "Trump: Barbara Lied to Both of Us," CBS News, January 9, 2007.

294 *By now Trump was denouncing O'Donnell:* Stephen M. Silverman, "Donald Trump Continues to Blast Rosie O'Donnell," *People*, December 22, 2006.

294 *"I was hurt now":* O'Donnell, *Celebrity Detox*, 155, 161.

295 *The ferocious argument that followed was detailed in the* New York Post: "Rosie Blows Up at 'Liar' Babs," *New York Post*, January 9, 2007, p. 10.

295 *"I definitely yelled":* Setoodeh, *Ladies Who Punch*, 168.

295 *The show went on that day, and two days later:* Jacques Steinberg, "Rosie O'Donnell to Leave 'The View' in June," *New York Times*, April 25, 2007.

295 *He issued a statement calling Barbara a liar:* Marcus Baram, "Trump Calls Barbara 'Sad Figurehead' After Her 'Pathetic Man' Comment," ABC News, January 10, 2007.

295 *Geddie already had told Barbara:* Author interview with Bill Geddie.

295 *Rosie would go off the air in May:* "Rosie's Gone from 'The View,'" CBS/AP, CBSNews.com, May 25, 2007.

295 *"Barbara Walters, arguably the most poised person on this planet":* O'Donnell, *Celebrity Detox*, 194.

295 *In her book, Rosie wrote:* O'Donnell, *Celebrity Detox*, 85–86.

Chapter 38: One More Time

297 *She was "driven to interview":* Time, *Firsts: Women Who Are Changing the World: Interviews, Photographs, Breakthroughs* (New York: Liberty Street/Time Inc. Books, 2017), 170.

297 *In 1997, when Hugh Downs refused to interview sportscaster Marv Albert:* Emily Langer, "Hugh Downs, Omnipresent Television Broadcaster, Dies at 99," *New York Times*, July 2, 2020. Marv Albert pleaded guilty to misdemeanor assault and battery charges in a case involving allegations of sexual assault. One year later, the judge vacated the plea and dismissed the misdemeanor charge, saying Albert had met the conditions for dismissal that the court set at the time of sentencing. Patricia Davis, "Marv Albert's Record Cleared in Biting Case," *Washington Post*, October 9, 1998.

298 *"Dictators and generals, that's my speed":* Julia Reed, "Woman in the News," *Vogue*, February 1992, p. 218.

299 *"This is a very important moment in Syria":* Author interview with Ben Sherwood.

299 *He was repeatedly summoned to her office:* Author interview with Tom Nagorski.

300 *"She was both remarkably thorough and insecure":* Tom Nagorski, "Two Moments with Barbara Walters: Personal Reflections on a Groundbreaking Journalist," *The Grid*, December 31, 2022.

300 *When she and her entourage were in Amman:* Author interview with Rob Wallace.

300 *"We walked around the old city":* Author interview with Alexander Marquardt. He later became a senior national security correspondent for CNN.

300 *She outlined the language he might expect to hear:* Barak Ravid, "Bashar Assad Emails Leaked, Tips for ABC Interview Revealed," *Haaretz*, February 7, 2012.

301 *"Everyone who made snarky questions about Walters' lack of qualifications":* David Kenner, "Foreign Policy: Interpreting the Assad Interview," NPR, December 15, 2011. Kenner was an associate editor of *Foreign Policy*. "Walters pressed him on all the hot-button issues," he wrote. "Overall, it's hard to see what Assad gained from the interview. He seemed out of touch, at times incoherent, and delusional about the support that he still enjoys in Syria."

301 *She started with a softball: ABC's Barbara Walters' Interview with Syrian President Bashar al-Assad*, ABC News, December 6, 2011.

303 *Wald replied the next day:* Author interview with Richard Wald.

Chapter 39: The Fall

305 *When she was ready to leave:* Author interview with Susan Mercandetti.

307 *When Sherwood arrived in Washington:* Author interview with Ben Sherwood.

307 *Peter Brown, a debonair fixture of New York society:* Author interview with Peter Brown.

307 *The next morning, Mike Allen of* Politico *broke the news:* Mike Allen, "Barbara Walters Falls, Cuts Forehead," *Politico*, January 20, 2013.

309 *"A blend of Outward Bound and Dr. Phil":* Associated Press, "At-Risk Girls Come to Maine," *Lewiston* (Maine) *Sun Journal*, April 4, 2004.

309 *Like her mother, she had married more than once:* Jean Godden, "Burien Bride Gets Barbara Walters Here," *Seattle Times*, August 14, 1996. Even in the story in the local newspaper about her wedding, Jacqueline would get second billing to her famous mother.

309 *In 2001, she appeared for the first time on TV:* Jennifer Peterson, "Channel Hopping; Walters' Daughter Comes Out of the Shadows," *Dayton Daily News*, April 20, 2001, p. 6C.

310 *Some parents and children "have mutual acceptance from the beginning":* Susan Dominus, "Barbara as a Mom," *Glamour*, April 30, 2008.

310 *She had flown to New York from Maine:* "A Matter of Life and Death," *Barbara Walters Special*, ABC News, February 4, 2011.

310 *She spent ten days:* Barbara Walters, "Her Change of Heart," *Vanity Fair*, December 2010.

310 *She wasn't sorry when a paparazzo staking out her apartment building:* Adam Pick, "Recovery Update: Barbara Walters Is 'Feeling Great,' Walking Around New York City," HeartValveSurgery.com, June 17, 2010. The photos had previously been posted on Celebrity-Gossip.net on June 3, 2010.

311 *The New York* Daily News *ran the photograph:* "HELLO, GORGEOUS!" New York *Daily News*, June 4, 2010, p. 2.

311 *Liz Smith wrote:* Liz Smith, "Barbara Walters—Miracle of Recovery," Scripps Treasure Coast Newspapers, June 29, 2010, p. A2.

311 *There was a bit of stagecraft: The View*, ABC, July 29, 2013.

311 *some medical studies had found elderly patients especially susceptible:* "Six Tips to Reduce Confusion in Older Patients After Surgery," American Society of Anesthesiologists, March 12, 2018.

311 *concerned that she had "less clarity":* Author interview with a senior colleague close to Barbara Walters, speaking on condition of anonymity.

312 *"When the light was on":* Author interview with Deborah Roberts.

312 *"She wasn't maybe quite as quick as she was seventeen years before":* Author interview with Alexandra Cohen.

312 *When Jenny McCarthy, a co-host during the 2013–2014 season:* Setoodeh, *Ladies Who Punch*, 230–36. The movie *Mommie Dearest*, starring Faye Dunaway, was released in 1981. It was based on a memoir by Christina Crawford, the adopted daughter of Joan Crawford.

312 *Everyone remembered:* James Bennet, "Brinkley Offers Apology. Clinton Accepts," *New York Times*, November 11, 1996, p. B8.

313 *"I carried that piece of paper":* Author interview with Anne Sweeney.

313 *When she was getting ready for the festivities:* Author interview with Lori Klein.

313 *At the embassy:* Author interview with Jennifer Maguire Isham.

314 *Later they reported on* The View: Author interview with a knowledgeable source, speaking on condition of anonymity.

314 *Her return was considered so newsworthy:* David Muir, "Her Comeback," *ABC World News Tonight*, March 4, 2010.

315 *As her tenure on* The View *was about to end:* Author interview with Donna Svennevik.

315 *After her goodbye show:* Irin Carmon, "Let's Have a Real Conversation About Barbara Walters," *New York*, March 13–26, 2023, p. 32.

315 *She had moved to Florida from Maine when, in May 2013, she was charged:* Arrest report 1300012648, Collier County Sheriff's Office, Naples, Florida, May 20, 2013.

315 *The mug shot for Tony:* Associated Press, "Barbara Walters Daughter Arrested for DUI," *Christian Science Monitor*, May 22, 2013.

316 *He had an idea: What about landing Barbara Walters?:* Author interview with Jeff Zucker.

316 *"We were in a talent-grabbing mode":* Author interview with Amy Entelis.

317 *Jeffrey Schneider, the ABC spokesman:* Author interview with Jeffrey Schneider.

317 *Barbara asked Geddie:* Author interview with Bill Geddie.

Chapter 40: The End

318 *On Barbara's final day on* The View: Patrick Kevin Day, "New York Mayor Declares May 16 'Barbara Walters Day,'" *Los Angeles Times*, April 23, 2014.

318 *"Of course I'm here":* Setoodeh, *Ladies Who Punch*, 248.

319 *"The Mount Rushmore moment":* Irin Carmon, "Let's Have a Real Conversation About Barbara Walters," *New York*, March 13–26, 2023, p. 32.

319 *No one invited to appear had declined:* Author interview with Alexandra Cohen.

319 *Carole Simpson, a groundbreaking anchor herself:* Carole Simpson, a former anchor for NBC News and ABC News, in 1992 was the first woman of color to moderate a presidential debate.

319 *"It was a shock to her":* Author interview with Whoopi Goldberg.

319 *"I just want to say, this is my legacy":* The View, ABC, May 16, 2014.

320 *Just three weeks passed before ABC announced:* Andrew Springer, "The Agony of Peter Rodger, a Dad Whose Son Became a Mass Killer," *20/20*, ABC News, June 27, 2014.

320 *A few months later, she called Geddie:* "'The View' EP Bill Geddie Exiting the Daytime Talker," *The Wrap*, August 6, 2014.

320 *"I think I could do another"*: Author interview with Bill Geddie.

320 *ABC was happy to accommodate:* Lisa de Moraes, "Barbara Walters' '10 Most Fascinating People' Resurrected," *Deadline*, October 21, 2014.

320 *But the ratings tumbled:* Tim Baysinger, "Primetime Ratings: Barbara Walters 'Most Fascinating People' Special Drops from 2013," *Broadcasting+Cable*, December 15, 2014.

321 *It was Diane Sawyer who got the interview:* "Bruce Jenner: The Interview," *20/20*, ABC News, April 24, 2015.

321 *"Barbara Walters' Picks":* Matt Webb Mitovich, "Ratings: Barbara Walters' Picks Prove to Be 29% Less Fascinating," *TVLine*, December 18, 2015.

321 *After a half-century since she was hired as the "girl writer" for the* Today *show:* "The 10 Most Fascinating People of 2015" was broadcast on December 17, 2015. From November 1 to December 27, 2015, a series called *Barbara Walters Presents American Scandals* was aired by Investigation Discovery. The nine episodes were pulled from interviews she had done over the years with figures accused of crimes or involved in notorious controversies, including Robert Blake and the Menendez brothers.

322 *The size of the gift was the result of "working a very long time":* Melanie Grayce West, "A Heartfelt Gift from Barbara Walters," *Wall Street Journal*, September 30, 2014.

322 *The following February, in 2015, she donated $15 million to Sarah Lawrence:* "Distinguished Alumna Barbara Walters Donates $15 Million to Fund the Barbara Walters Campus Center," sarahlawrence.edu, February 26, 2015.

322 *But when construction on the new building:* "Sarah Lawrence College Breaks Ground on The Barbara Walters Campus Center," Sarah Lawrence College, January 18, 2018.

323 *The fall on the steps:* Author interviews with three knowledgeable sources, speaking on condition of anonymity.

323 *As it develops, it can change their personality:* "Hydrocephalus," National Institute of Neurological Disorders and Stroke, National Institutes of Health.

323 *when an aide in the Carter White House:* Author interview with Paul Costello.

323 *But in October, she was sharp and clear:* "A Conversation with Barbara Walters," Institute of Politics, Kennedy School, Harvard, October 7, 2014.

323 *there was no flash of recognition:* Author interview with Meryl Gordon.

324 *That year, Lynn Sherr met Barbara:* Author interview with Lynn Sherr.

324 *Another former colleague:* Author interview with Susan Mercandetti.

324 *"I'd go over there":* Author interview with Lori Klein.

324 *"The tragedy is that she got herself into this isolation":* Author interview with Henry Kissinger.

325 *"Everyone now interviews anyone":* Cindy Adams, "Sarah Lawrence to Honor Barbara Walters with New Building," *New York Post*, April 16, 2018.

325 *Louise Grunwald, one of her closest friends:* Author interview with Louise Grunwald.

325 *Lorinda Ash was a generation younger than Barbara:* Author interview with Lorinda Ash.

326 *For her ninetieth birthday in 2019:* Setoodeh, *Ladies Who Punch*, in the updated paperback edition.

326 *"At my funeral, you've got to be in the front row":* Author interview with Noah Shachtman.

327 *An email from Barbara Walters arrived:* Author interview with Meghan McCain.

327 *It was at one of her dinners:* Author interview with Sam Donaldson, who was seated at the table with Hamilton Jordan and Amal Ghorbal, the wife of Egyptian ambassador Ashraf Ghorbal. The incident was reported first in *The Washington Post*.

327 *"To be a friend of Barbara Walters added to your star power":* Author interview with Michael Bloomberg.

327 *She had described him as an appealing guest:* Meryl Gordon, "Citizen Mike," *New York*, April 16, 2001.

328 *He was back on* The View *a decade later:* The View, ABC, May 13, 2013.

328 *he hosted small dinners:* Gordon, "Citizen Mike."

328 *"She was on a couch, I remember":* Author interview with Michael Bloomberg.

329 *A few days after Barbara died:* Cindy Adams, "Cindy Adams Remembers Her Friend Barbara Walters," *New York Post*, January 2, 2023.

330 *"We are interrupting regular programming":* "Dead Man Talking," *20/20*, ABC News, December 30, 2022. The episode that was interrupted was a rerun of a prison interview with a former Texas veterinarian who was serving time for murdering her husband, a military veteran.

330 *Hired at ABC News a year earlier:* Author interview with Phil Lipof.

330 *"Barbara Walters would not have been pleased"*: Dylan Byers, "Morse Code," *Puck*, January 4, 2023.

330 *"Barbara Walters has always been an example of bravery"*: @POTUS, Twitter, December 31, 2022, 12:42 p.m.

331 *"The greatest of them all, by far"*: Donald Trump post on Truth Social, December 31, 2022.

331 *Daughter Jackie, who had always been so private, rebuffed:* According to two knowledgeable sources, speaking on condition of anonymity.

331 *Barbara was buried, as she had wished:* Walters, *Audition*, 371.

Epilogue: The Rulebreaker

333 *"It's no fun being nobody"*: James Conaway, "How to Talk with Barbara Walters About Practically Anything," *New York Times Magazine*, September 10, 1972.

334 *Over the decades, she appeared a dozen times:* Frank Newport and Alec Gallup, *The Gallup Poll: Public Opinion 2005* (Lanham, Maryland: Rowman & Littlefield, 2006). By 2005, the reference book says, Barbara Walters had appeared eleven times on Gallup's list of the most admired women of the year, the eighteenth highest tally. She and Oprah Winfrey, who had appeared eighteen times by then, were the only journalists among the twenty-one names listed.

334 *"Even though they've seen everything she's done"*: Author interview with Whoopi Goldberg.

334 *"Rude and peremptory"*: Liz Smith, "That O.J. Coverage," *Newsday*, June 24, 1994, A11.

334 *Barbara was privately wounded:* In an interview with the author, Bill Carter of *The New York Times* said, "I think a lot of people would be thrilled to have *Saturday Night Live* do a bit on them. You know what I mean? Wow, now you've really made it. But she had a speech impediment and that was the basis of the characterization, and I think she felt like it came off as mocking her, and she was uncomfortable with it." He added, "I think it genuinely bothered her, and the fact that people would call her 'Baba Wawa,' she didn't like it."

334 *"When I talk to the old guys in the business"*: Author interview with Bill Geddie.

334 *"While she could be dishy and funny and irreverent":* Author interview with Cynthia McFadden.

335 *She was, oddly enough, afraid of heights:* "Proust Questionnaire," *Vanity Fair.*

335 *She was nearly eighty years old and researching her memoir:* Walters, *Audition,* 60–61.

335 *Despite her coiffed hair and society pals:* Here's how Mary McNamara, the veteran culture columnist at the *Los Angeles Times,* described it: "Much of the criticism aimed at Walters over the years boiled down to the fact that she took herself quite seriously, which was, and remains, a revolutionary act in and of itself." Mary McNamara, "Critic's Notebook: For Barbara Walters, Power, Politics and Pop Culture Were Personal," *Los Angeles Times,* May 16, 2014.

336 *"Without Barbara Walters there wouldn't have been me":* Oprah Winfrey, @Oprah on Instagram, December 30, 2022.

336 *At the audition for her first TV job in the 1970s: Audition: Barbara Walters' Journey,* ABC News Special, May 7, 2008.

336 *For decades, Barbara would be a role model:* Here's one example. In 2011, Suzanne Kianpour got her first big break in journalism with a job as a producer for the BBC, assigned to the U.S. State Department. "I was like twenty-five and I had absolutely no idea what I was doing, but I had to not show that," Suzanne told me a decade later, by then an aspiring TV documentarian. "I would say to myself, 'What would Barbara Walters do?'" She scored her first scoop by deliberately copying a tactic that had helped Barbara arrange the first joint interview with the president of Egypt and the prime minister of Israel. Suzanne managed to discreetly slip her card with a note to the brother of Iranian president Hassan Rouhani, which led six weeks later to an exclusive interview with Iranian foreign minister Mohammad Javad Zarif. "My foreign editor was over the moon," she recalled. Author interview with Suzanne Kianpour.

337 *"Barbara Walters is the patron saint of TV":* Don Aucoin, "Watching Walters," *Boston Sunday Globe,* May 21, 2000, p. C1. Steven D. Stark is the author of *Glued to the Set: The 60 Television Shows and Events That Made Us Who We Are Today* (New York: Free Press, 1997).

337 *Achieving that distinction wasn't free:* "When she's called a trailblazer, you have no idea what that required," said David Sloan, who worked with her

for years as executive producer of *20/20*. "It was a constant, uphill battle of proving herself, and that was what you really didn't see. But she also knew that she was a cautionary tale. She would often say to working women, 'Don't let what happened to me happen to you. Spend more time with your children.'" David Sloan, interviewed on ABC's *Good Morning America* on December 31, 2022, the morning after Barbara Walters had died.

337 *"I don't think you can have it all"*: "Barbara Walters," *Ladies' Home Journal,* June 1981, p. 26.

337 *"It would have been nice"*: *The Charlie Rose Show*, August 1, 2008.

337 *"I think she was very happy with many, many aspects"*: Author interview with Nancy Shevell McCartney.

338 *"Happy-ish," suggested Joy Behar*: Author interview with Joy Behar.

338 *"She was essentially restless"*: Author interview with Diane Sawyer.

338 *"I didn't know her to be happy"*: Author interview with Ben Sherwood.

338 *She was shorthanding a comment*: Walters, *Audition,* 480.

338 *"What does being 'Barbara Walters' mean?"*: "Oprah Talks to Barbara Walters," *O, The Oprah Winfrey Magazine*, October 2004, p. 323.

339 *Nothing lasts forever*: Becky Burkett, "Disney's New Headquarters Building in New York Hits a Major Milestone, Celebrates with Topping-out Ceremony," disneydining.com, April 19, 2022.

339 *"I want to make something very clear"*: Lauren Effron, "ABC News Headquarters Named for Barbara Walters," ABC News, May 12, 2014.

339 *Still, she soon complained to a* Variety *reporter*: Setoodeh, *Ladies Who Punch,* 245.

Index

Page numbers beginning with 347 refer to notes.